MEDICINES OUT OF CONTROL?

Antidepressants and the Conspiracy of Goodwill

CHARLES MEDAWAR

ANITA HARDON

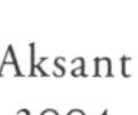

Aksant
2004

ISBN 90 5260 134 8

Cover design: Jos Hendrix
Typesetting: Hanneke Kossen
Printed and published in the Netherlands

Aksant Academic Publishers, www.aksant.nl

Contents

Preface

Much of this book is about "dependence" – but that is a word that acquires meaning entirely from context. Our "Acknowledgements" underline this: they are not only a record of heartfelt thanks, but also admissions of deep indebtedness and dependence. So who is behind this book – in particular, who funded it and on what terms?

The Joseph Rowntree Charitable Trust (JRCT) has supported the principal author's work for over 30 years – always on terms that offered liberation. JRCT's support implies no specific endorsement of this book – it signals only the Trustees' willingness to take risks in supporting projects in line with the Trust's general objectives. See: www.jrct.org.uk. The Trustees fund projects in many different areas, focusing on those that are "about removing problems through radical solutions, and not about making the problems easier to live with." In relation to corporate responsibilities, JRCT "is concerned that the business practices of all companies should respect human rights and not give rise to injustice or suffering." Trust support in this area is intended, "to achieve transparency and mutual responsibility between business, government and citizens as producers and consumers and to hold those bodies to account in the wider public interest."

Two other UK based charitable trusts gave generous financial and moral support, at critical stages of the work on this book – The Allen Lane Foundation and The 1970 Trust. Their support also goes back for many years, again on terms that have guaranteed total independence both for us and them. They offered support and then stood back, making us entirely responsible and accountable for the work done.

Such is the difference between disabling and enabling dependencies, it seems there are no conflicts of interest to declare.

This book is the product of numerous collaborations, going back many years. That makes it so much the harder to thank everyone involved, especially family and close friends. Having the freedom to write makes almost impossible demands, on the closest relationships most of all.

Directly and indirectly, and in different ways, many people played an important part in shaping this book. Many thanks, especially to Dr. Tom Allport, Margaret Ewen, Alex Garland, Dr. David Griffith, John Guest, Brian Guthrie, Dr. Hilbrand Haak, Jaap Hardon, Lisa Hayes, Catherine Hodgkin, Dr. Andrew Herxheimer, Linda Hurcombe, Caroline Medawar, Nick Perks, David Rennie, Courtney Van de Weyer and Sir Roger Walters. Inevitably, those who worked on the draft found ideas they liked, or didn't, and there were points of disagreement between them –

but they gave indispensable help in deciding what this book should and could not say.

Special thanks are due to the directors of *Social Audit* Ltd, where the principal author has been employed for over 30 years. They have contributed far more than their legal responsibilities might suggest, through commitment to the general principles underlying this book. They are: Christopher Zealley (Chairman); Andrew, Lord Phillips; Anthony Sampson, Oliver Thorold, Elaine Rassaby and Maurice Frankel.

The co-authors divided responsibilities as if between pilot and navigator. Charles Medawar is layman, a specialist on medicines policy and drug safety issues with a particular interest in corporate, governmental and professional accountability. He writes, broadcasts and lectures regularly, and runs a website (www.socialaudit.org.uk) which now attracts some 500,000 visitors a year. Anita Hardon is Professor in Anthropology of Care and Health at the University of Amsterdam. She has published widely, specialising on women's health issues and studies of medicines' use in Asia, Africa and Europe, and teaches international courses on promoting rational drug use. She currently chairs the Health Action International (Europe) Foundation board.

What has emerged from all this is a story about the promotion, regulation, prescribing and use of mood-regulating drugs, mainly antidepressants like Prozac, Seroxat and Paxil. As it unfolds a drug crisis in the making, the story develops as a picture of unhealthy dependence on corporate and professional power.

The story leads to analysis: an attempt to explain to an engaged and curious layperson the basis for thinking that, for all the triumphs and gains, pharmaceutical medicine is losing sight of health and dangerously lacking in public accountability. However, the question mark in the book title is emphatic – an invitation to make up your own mind how you find medicine and what you want it to be.

This book is in no way a guide to your medical treatment; at best it can help to explain only how and why you may be treated as you are. On the basis of your experience and what you read, you might conclude either that the control of medicines is in dire need of overhaul and rethinking, or that it is an affront even to suggest that.

Either way – or perhaps something in between – this analysis is offered for peer-review and consultation, and is meant to promote comment and debate. The authors and sponsors would welcome feedback, to help prepare the next edition of this book. This first edition is intended for only limited circulation, through 2004. A revised and popular edition of this book is planned.

Charles Medawar, Social Audit Ltd, P.O. Box 111, London NW1 8XG, UK. (charles@socialaudit. org.uk)

Anita Hardon, Health Action International (Europe), J. van Lennepkade 334-T, 1053 NJ Amsterdam, The Netherlands. (anita@haiweb.org)

1

Medicines out of control?

This book tells a story that reveals some of the workings of medicine and medicines and their impact on personal, community and global health. The story is rooted in general practice and psychiatry and revolves around the main drugs prescribed for anxiety, insomnia, depression and related mental distress.

The action runs from the mid-19th century to the foreseeable future. Over the years, the drugs in the story change and different ideas and actors hold sway. But the same patterns of behaviour emerge and the outcome is much the same. Users consistently emerge as losers – by no means universally, but always on a grand scale.

Both literally and metaphorically, all the drugs in this story cause some degree of dependence. People get hooked not only on the drugs, but also on the idea of drugs as solutions for mental distress. Subtle interplays of power and dependence nurture this process of medicalisation, as if through a "Conspiracy of Goodwill".

At the heart of medicine is this delicate but mighty interdependency, based on unfathomable mixtures of fear, inspiration, trust, hope and dreams. The basis of the Conspiracy of Goodwill is the fervent wish of all parties (health professionals, government, manufacturers and users) that drugs should be safe and effective, and never anything less. The downside is the risk of insatiable demand, unmet need, disappointed expectations and often far-fetched denial when things go wrong.

The case history

The story that unfolds in the first three chapters spans the last 150 years. Throughout this time, doctors have prescribed an uninterrupted succession of drugs for mental distress, each time believing they were not addictive and that patients had only themselves to blame if addiction set in. A pattern emerged – it continues to this day – in which one drug after another, officially proclaimed as not addictive, has later proved to be just that.

Between the 1860s and 1960s, doctors treated mental distress by prescribing alcohol and opium, then morphine, heroin and cocaine. Later came chloral, bromides, barbiturates and many similar drugs. Chapter 2 explains how each of these drugs, bar alcohol, was also used to *treat* addiction – and later found to cause it too.

The story in Chapter 3 begins around 1960, as the reality began to sink in – that "iatrogenic" dependence (caused by medical intervention) had become widespread and damaging. This realisation spurred a wholesale switch to a new class of drugs – "tranquillisers", like Valium, Librium, Ativan, Xanax and Halcion. It took over 20 years to establish that they too were addictive and another decade to address the problem. Until the 1980s, the risk of becoming addicted to a tranquilliser was officially described as remote, but the opposite again proved true.

Present day remedies for anxiety, depression and mental distress date from the 1990s. By this time, tranquillisers had been internationally "scheduled" as drugs of dependence and prescribing was restricted to the short-term; their use slowly declined. Chapter 4 tells how doctors then began to prescribe a new class of "antidepressants" instead – for longer and in larger doses than before. Prozac started this trend; it spawned other "blockbusters" – Paxil/Seroxat, Zoloft/Lustral, Celexa/Cipramil and Efexor/Effexor – all still with us today.

This time round, the risk of addiction was denied, in effect by burying the goalposts. The drugs themselves were promoted as if they were essential supplements, badly needed to help to restore levels of a key, mood-regulating, brain chemical: serotonin. At the same time, the authorities formally redefined the concept of dependence to ensure that drug prescribing couldn't possibly cause it. This meant that most doctors recognised "dependence" only in the context of uncontrolled drug use, something close to abuse. That explains why, today, dependence on antidepressants seems painfully obvious to many users, though the problem doesn't officially exist.

Crisis unfolding

Officially there is still no antidepressant "dependence" problem, but a crisis is now clearly looming. The turning point can be quite precisely dated – it came with a heavy flurry of revelations between October 2002 and the summer of 2003. If there was a pivotal moment, it was probably 25 June – when GlaxoSmithKline quietly published a small-print amendment to the prescribing instructions for Seroxat. The company had upwardly revised its 2002 estimate of the risk of withdrawal reactions – from 0.2% to 25%. The official risk of Seroxat/Paxil withdrawal problems had increased overnight from 1 in 500 to one in four.

This 125-fold increase signalled that "science" was catching up with common sense – and that sets the scene for the later chapters in this book. The case history gives way to a critical analysis of how and why the crisis arose, and its wider implications. Two related questions become central:

1. What does it reveal about the quality and direction of medical science, and the reliability of the medicines control system that – in spite of all the fuss and the precedents – it took over a decade to identify a prominent and potentially hazardous adverse drug reaction that affects one user in every four?

2. When the Internet was groaning with evidence of the problem in store, why were users' comments and complaints ignored? This is a good moment in history to be asking that question: the more this antidepressant crisis unfolds, the more it seems that narrative evidence from users can never credibly be ignored again.

The story that started to unfold as a crisis in late 2002 began in earnest in the mid-1990s: the growth of the Internet had begun to change history, as antidepressant users began to compare notes and exchange ideas. Vivid and revealing accounts of serious withdrawal and other problems began to surface, then dedicated websites began to appear, all discussing the same thing. Users were hooked once again.

Of science and common sense

During the five-year window, 1998 to 2002, the powers-that-be did all they could to deny the miserable realities that antidepressant users increasingly described. During this period, the authorities entrenched their position; they went on digging and made the hole deeper still.

Secrecy played a key part in maintaining the official denial: Chapter 5 outlines the extent and effect of it. Towards the end of this five-year window, the element of cover-up became more obvious as the weight of scientific evidence got stronger and as public protest grew. Legal actions increased the pressure, and then the media weighed in. Finally, two BBC-TV *Panorama* programmes (2002, 2003) tipped the balance, and the endgame began.

The events that unfolded thereafter – and led to consideration of a third *Panorama* programme scheduled for early 2004 – underline the value and power of user drug intelligence. These developments also challenge the relationship between "narrative evidence" and science – the orthodox view that "science" might be debased and compromised by patients' views.

The present day model of medicines control, regards "science" as the gold standard, and narrative as a base metal. But what should be driving medicine – the quest for alloyed knowledge, or something closer to shared understanding of sense and meaning? Make up your own mind on the basis of the user intelligence that emerged from 1,370 emails sent in response to the *Panorama* programme, "Secrets of Seroxat" (BBC-TV, October 2002).

Our point is that science in medicine is a means to an end – the attainment of health and well-being. Science at its best is glorious, the cleanest known method of producing knowledge. But it is far from being the only way of distinguishing between appearance and reality, and does not in itself produce solutions or outputs that are necessarily either desirable or "right". Science plays a crucial part in medicine, but democratic impulse must lead the way:

> "... science and technology can contribute to the improvement of health standards only if the people themselves become full partners of the health-care providers in safeguarding and promoting health ... people have not only the right to participate individually and collectively in the planning and implementation of health care programmes, but also a duty to do so." (WHO 1983)

The analysis that proceeds from Chapter 5 develops this theme, in trying to explain the dynamics of the antidepressant story as it unfolds into a present-day drug crisis. With medicine now on the brink of designing life itself, the same question seems more urgent than before: why is this dependence problem happening over and over again?

The answers turn out to have much less to do with molecular performance than with human motivation and organisational behaviour. What decides drug safety and effectiveness, above all, is the performance of pharmaceutical companies, government agencies and professional institutions – and the relationships between them and with users. So how did this powerful triumvirate of conspirators contribute to the health dependencies of today?

Role of the Pharmas

Central in the analysis is the role of the Pharmas, the handful of giant, mostly US-based companies that dominate international drug trade. The Pharmas' behaviour has been widely attributed to simple greed, but the underlying problem is that they have become theoretically unsustainable – no longer able to compete and grow by inventing new drugs that improve on the old. Strange at it may seem, the Pharmas are in crisis, staring down gun barrels, driven by uncertainty about their ability to survive.

Chapter 6 explains how the Pharmas became so huge that they could hope to survive only by rapidly creating mass markets for "blockbuster" and "lifestyle" drugs. The advent of Prozac and related antidepressants heralded an era in which drug innovation gave way to intensive drug marketing: this was the only way the Pharmas could secure the return on investment they needed to be able to operate on their scale. Part of the problem is to do with the Pharmas' sheer size – "institutional obesity" one might say – and by repeatedly merging, the Pharmas are getting bigger all the time.

This new and imperative emphasis on marketing involves relentless demonstrations of the triumph of benefit over risk, and the promotion of drugs for much more than they are worth. In this case, it also meant that the Pharmas tackled problems by challenging perceptions of risk and by ignoring or denying evidence of harm. In so doing, they systematically exploited the dependencies of governments and the medical establishment. There was little resistance, partly because the Pharmas were also dependent on them.

In the last quarter of the 20th century, commerce took over the reins of medicine and began to steer health towards trade. The Pharmas carefully arranged the tests and trials of their drugs; they came to dominate medical education and communication, and they sponsored more and more. From behind the scenes, the Pharmas orchestrated the widespread promotion of their products and views, through the placement and advancement of the experts and leaders they chose. In time, the imperatives of trade and the impact of commercial messages became overwhelming. "Just how tainted has medicine become?" asked a *Lancet* editorial (2002). The answer was, "heavily and damagingly so."

Commercial sponsorship both sustained and undermined the reputation and independence of political, professional and academic institutions, drug regulatory systems, even patient organisations and the World Health Organization. Through relentless lobbying, marketing, promises and threats, the Pharmas came to excel in letting others get their own way. Along the way, they began to change the face of medicine, promoting drugs directly to patients, and going to ever-greater lengths to inform people about the extent of their need.

Medicalisation and "disease awareness"

The Pharmas' determination to expand markets led to intense pressure on national governments to relax the laws that prevented them from promoting their products directly to consumers. In 1997, the US Food & Drug Administration (FDA) finally gave way, introducing new rules for "Direct-To-Consumer Advertising" (DTCA); they allowed Prozac and other medicines to be widely advertised, even on tv.

This hugely increased the demand for antidepressant and other drugs, helping to satisfy the considerable US appetite for health and pharmacological solutions. Even in the face of global health calamity, the US leads the world in "disease awareness" and concern about unmet medical need. America officially reveres 170 official "Health Observances", including 74 "awareness months" and 64 "awareness weeks", each year.

Direct-To-Consumer Advertising or promotion (DTCA) helped the Pharmas both to extend and segment markets, allowing them to repeatedly relaunch their antidepressants for an expanding range of states of mind. In this way, the new antidepressants came to dominate the market for stress and anxiety: Valium out, Prozac in. By the early 21st century, prescribing levels for antidepressants in England had reached those of the tranquillisers at their peak.

Chapter 7 describes how the Pharmas applied pressure on other countries to get them to allow DTCA. The narrative explains in some detail how the UK and European governments responded to this pressure, in the face of conflict between trade and health needs. DTCA led to an explosive growth in the market, producing handsome returns on investment – but that translated as hyperinflationary growth in the drugs bill.

The battle for DTCA in Europe became most intense between 2000 and 2003. The way in which it unfolded revealed the workings of democracy at its worst and best. Much more attention was paid to patients' views – but their views were increasingly orchestrated by marketing departments, public relations agencies and Pharma-sponsored patient organisations.

Government regulation of medicines

By the 21st century, global standards for drug regulation prevailed; they mainly reflected the values of the major drug-producing nations, and notably the US. Trade and health imperatives increasingly came into conflict, as market forces, national interests and political pressures led the way.

From the early 1990s, nations began to compete among themselves in earnest, to develop partnerships with the Pharmas, to attract investment and help to share the wealth. This naturally affected the style of drug control, as did the trend to get the Pharmas to pay for it. By 2000, all major industrial nations paid for drug regulation from the fees the Pharmas paid governments for the licensing of their drugs.

This case history touches on the role of conflicts of interest, endemic secrecy and political, economic and bureaucratic pressures as factors that helped to build the dependence problem. However, the regulatory failure to see and contain the problem can be also traced to the design of the regulatory process itself – in particular to the emphasis on *pre*-marketing rather than *post*-marketing drug evaluation.

Drug regulation has traditionally focused on scrutiny of company-sponsored clinical trials that are performed before drugs come to market. There is much less emphasis on monitoring what happens when drugs are used in practice. But pre-marketing trials often have major limitations and may leave quite basic questions unanswered. Many of the drugs in this case history, for example, were first marketed at a dosage that later proved too high – a problem compounded by the tendency to define the recommended dose on the basis that "one-size-fits-all". None of the drugs in this story could have been safely prescribed in that way; indeed about half of all Prozac users may still get up to four times the dose they seem to need.

Chapter 8 contrasts the pattern of antidepressant safety regulation in the US and UK. The US FDA had the theoretical advantage of huge resources; it also had in place a system for user reporting of adverse drug reactions (ADRs). However, the FDA relies rigorously on the evidence from pre-marketing clinical trials, treating it rather like legal precedent. Because the US regulators require new and strictly "scientific" data to supplant pre-marketing evidence, ADR reports made little difference. They were regarded as "anecdotal".

By contrast, the UK regulators operate what is widely regarded as one of the best ADR reporting systems in the world, relying on it as "the cornerstone of drug safety monitoring." In this case, however, the system operated mainly to dignify the notion that no evidence of risk signals evidence of no risk. The UK drug regulators still eschew reports from patients, in the absence of "medical interpretation". Ironically, but predictably, it was the wealth of evidence from antidepressant users that finally caused the regulators to confront the reality: a substantial risk of dependence, among other damaging drug effects. In particular, the risk of drug-induced violence and self-harm had been a worry for years.

Scientific standards

Science does not and cannot operate independently of economic, political and professional imperatives. The close links between academic and clinical experts with both the Pharmas and regulators underline this, and has much to do with the quality of medical science.

The antidepressant story suggests that precious little of what passes for science amounts to honest seeking after truth – indeed the editors of the leading US and UK medical journals believe that the scientific quality is generally rather bad. In this case, as in others, the science seemed mainly directed at pointing to marginal and notional drug advantages and to papering over the cracks. The emphasis on "new and improved" and on discovery and innovation largely obscured the contribution that science might have made by revealing quite basic misunderstandings.

Chapter 9 reviews some of the techniques used in designing and interpreting clinical trials, to produce the desired results. This chapter also looks at clinical trial standards from the standpoint of patient safety. Almost all the evidence on this is secret, but one shining piece of data suggests that standards are nowhere near as high as people have been led to believe.

Good science in medicine is in short supply, but policing is mainly directed at the prosecution of isolated cases of outright fraud, rather than mainstream slipshod research. The quest for scientific integrity stops far short of encouraging individual conscience, commitment and initiative, let alone whistleblowers. Their fate gives evidence of the grip of orthodoxy in the Conspiracy of Goodwill.

The antidepressant story also reveals how a combination of scientific fundamentalism and triumphalism has obscured the importance of a range of vital human factors. The scientific community has lost sight of their importance, not only in the treatment of depression, but also in relation to its own behaviour. The influence of reward and punishment systems and pressures to conform and comply, evidently have a profound effect on the conduct of medical science and on perceptions of benefit and risk.

Iatrogenesis

Among other examples of medicalisation, this case history asks how far the damage done by medicines goes, beyond the direct harm of intervention. What does the antidepressant story reflect of what Ivan Illich called "social" and "cultural", iatrogenesis – implying loss of personal autonomy, reduced confidence in health and diminished opportunity for making sense of illness and disease?

Adverse drug reactions exemplify direct "iatrogenesis" – harm from medical intervention. However, the first, faltering, credible estimates of the overall impact of ADRs on health only began to appear at the turn of the 21st century. Meanwhile, the indirect effects – the impact of medicalisation on the health of people and community – have barely been explored. Irrational belief in the goodness of medicines is contained through the Conspiracy of Goodwill.

Chapter 10 brings the story back to the unfolding of the antidepressant crisis. Much of this chapter details the findings of a unique analysis of the operation of the UK adverse drug reaction reporting system – based on a survey of over 1,500 (anonymised) ADR reports sent to the regulators by health professionals. These reports matched the *Panorama* sample of reports from users: both focused on the two main worries with the new antidepressants, and Seroxat (paroxetine) in particular. Along with the risk of withdrawal symptoms, there had for years been strong, nagging concerns about drug-induced violence and suicidal behaviour.

This analysis revealed this ADR reporting system to be "chaotic and misconceived", ensnared by process and jargon, and starved of the resources and imagination needed to make it work. The combination of low levels and standards of reporting, flawed data processing, uncritical interpretation and lack of follow-up had a devastating effect on perceptions and understandings of benefit and risk. In spite of conducting several formal reviews, the regulators had systematically failed to follow-up even reports of suspected drug-induced suicide.

Beyond lack of scrutiny, closer inspection of the data revealed systematic burial of evidence of risk, notably by crunching numbers and mincing words. One striking feature of the antidepressant story – but it applies widely – was the difference between the words of patients who speak their minds, and the approved terminologies that left meanings far behind.

The 1990s saw "depression" formally redefined as a serotonin-deficiency disease and the scourge of millions – a convenient and seductive, but deeply simplistic view. The term, drug "dependence" was redefined, to propose that loss of personal autonomy could never arise in a therapeutic setting, but only within a few blocks of "Skid Row". The ubiquitous term, "discontinuation symptoms" – *newspeak* for withdrawal symptoms – implied that antidepressants carried no risk of dependence. Wishful thinking proposed "discontinuation symptoms" as evidence of the effectiveness of vital remedies, important for reducing overwhelming risks. Then suicides became routinely described as "non-accidental overdose"; and the broad-spectrum term, "emotional lability", was employed – as if to fail to distinguish between a drug-induced attempted suicide and an outburst of tears.

User reports of adverse reactions attempted to describe some human reality. Collectively, they were often more informative than the reports the regulators relied on.

Towards resolution

Chapter 11 anticipates the outcome and the limitations of a major UK government review of the risks of antidepressants. This was originally intended to last only a couple of months, but then the review committee found they had opened a can of worms. The review that was finally set up in the summer of 2003 is due to report in early 2004.

At the time of writing, there is even talk of the unthinkable – perhaps major prosecutions to come – but the terms of reference of the review seem to guarantee that its major output will be in the form of more prudent small-print warnings to promote safer drug use. It is already clear that the review will miss the wider point – the need for new management in medicines' control, for a coherent policy on drug safety and for standards of public accountability that will sweep this dismal past away.

The antidepressant story is specifically about drugs that work on the mind, but it illustrates what seems to be happening with medicines of many kinds. All drugs go through the same mill. The same companies make them, and teach the same doctors what and how to prescribe. All medicines are tested, recommended, marketed and regulated in much the same way – and the same standards of science prevail.

To that extent, this story underlines some linkage between the two major crises in health: under- and over-consumption of drugs. Health inequalities and lack of access to essential drugs dominate the world order. At the same time, the US market exemplifies what is fast becoming a global trend: increasingly people are persuaded that health is the product of assiduous risk aversion, acute disease awareness and routine drug consumption.

What happens when everyone is constantly alerted to this threat or that affliction, and urged to screen body and mind for every sign of disease? Does it really promote personal responsibility, health awareness, empowerment and choice? Or does it help to make people feel ill and create burdens that no national health service can withstand?

Market-driven medicine seems now to have surpassed the point of diminishing health returns. If health is the desired outcome, can it really make sense to invest in drug innovation and consumption on the Pharmas' terms? This story suggests no end of better alternatives – none more radical than the notion that medicine produces most health when conducted within a framework of honest science and decent human and democratic values.

The reality seems to be that community is the bedrock of individual health. Drug response, personal health and the ability to negotiate the trials of life all reflect your uniqueness as an individual. On the other hand, what you experience of the quality of medicine and medicines is overwhelmingly decided by factors beyond your control. In the end, personal health is largely predicted by the health and well-being of others, above all by their example, attitudes and behaviour. No one escapes if other people feel ill or are impoverished, desperate, miserable or insecure.

2

Sedative hell

Between the 1860s and 1960s, doctors treated mental distress by prescribing alcohol and opium, then morphine, heroin and cocaine. Later came chloral, bromides, barbiturates and many similar drugs. Bar alcohol, each of these drugs was also used to treat addiction – and later found to cause it too.

Alcohol had its heyday in medicine around the 1850s, mainly under the influence of Professor R.B. Todd of Kings College Hospital, London. Todd was determined to prove the superiority of his theory of "alcohol stimulation" over the prevailing and contradictory theory that the body should be "depleted", through blood-letting and other kinds of purge. The *Lancet* (1865) reported that the good professor even "found reason to give twenty or thirty ounces of brandy a day to young patients."

Alcohol stimulation therapy became something of a craze, in spite of the efforts of the National Temperance League to promote more sober prescribing – and in defiance of a growing body of medical opinion that consumption had gone too far. "There is not a tittle of evidence that it can 'antagonise' any one disease," said one *Lancet* editorial in 1865. But five years later, the same journal complained that alcohol was still prescribed, "with lavish profusion in those numerous nervous afflictions to which weakly persons (more especially women) are prone."[1]

Naturally, many people got hooked and incapacitated on alcohol, but prescribers assumed that they had brought this failure on themselves. That was partly because doctors perceived the problem as "intoxication" – they thought drug-seeking behaviour gave evidence of lack of breeding or willpower, or some other character defect. Doctors found it hard to acknowledge they might have contributed to the problems they described; they tended to blame patients, especially those with the temerity to blame them:

---

1 For a more detailed, fully referenced account of the events described in this chapter, see Medawar 1992. Different drugs are now used, but "more especially women" are so treated to this day. About two-thirds of all prescriptions for tranquillisers and antidepressants are for women.

> "We now diagnose with confidence the existence of concealed drinking habits in thousands of cases which would have passed undetected not many years since. One of the most remarkable features of these secret drinkers is their inordinate propensity to tell lies, and their favourite falsehood, when they are detected, is to lay the blame of their evil habit on some apocryphal medical prescription of stimulants. Those observers, however, who have carefully studied the genesis of alcoholic excesses are aware that the habit springs, in the immense majority of cases, from the temptation supplied by states of bodily or mental dejection and misery, and very often from a peculiar weakness of the nervous system which is inherited." (Anstie 1865)

At that time, doctors did not think of drug dependence or addiction as a problem. That happened later, following the first "scientific" demonstrations of the existence of withdrawal symptoms, towards the end of the 19th century. The evidence came from the asylums; it was obtained by abruptly withdrawing entrenched users from their drugs and then systematically recording what happened.

None of this was well understood at the time doctors started treating alcoholism with opium. Well into the 20th century, doctors needed reminding that the use of "opium and other narcotics may ... lead to a craving for these which is quite as serious as the original condition" (Cushny 1928). Chemical differences between alcohol and opiates means there is no "cross-dependence" between them. So alcoholics treated with opium stayed dependent on alcohol and became dependent on opium as well: two crutches for the legless patient instead of one.

Nevertheless, alcohol in moderation was regarded as a serious medicine at least until World War II, and it could be prescribed on the National Health Service in Britain until 1984. Cushny's famous *Textbook on Pharmacology and Therapeutics* (1928) recommended alcohol above alternatives for very much the same conditions that tranquillisers would treat in their day:

> "The action which lends alcohol its value in therapeutics is not its stimulant but its narcotic value, which allays the anxiety and distress of the patient, promotes rest and sleep, and thus aids toward healing, or at the worst renders illness more tolerable. Small quantities of other narcotics might be substituted for alcohol, but none of them perhaps excels it in producing that spirit of hopefulness and restful confidence that contributes so much to recovery."

Alcohol is now rarely prescribed, though commonly found in many "tonics" and is still the most widely used remedy for mild-to-moderate mental distress. Alcohol abuse is today a major and growing cause of many health problems and much personal and social distress – but the health benefits of alcohol in moderation will no doubt be broadcast for years to come. When the *New England Journal of Medicine* (9 January 2003) reported on "Roles of Drinking Pattern and Type of Alcohol Consumed in Coronary Heart Disease in Men", it was translated the same day as, "Study: frequent drinking can help heart" (*ABC News*), or "Frequent tipple cuts heart risk" (*BBC News*).[2]

Alcohol illustrates a basic principle for all drugs ever prescribed for mental distress. Risk and benefit relate critically to drug dosage and duration of use, and widespread use signals a risk of dependence.

From opium to morphine

It was natural doctors should try opium to treat alcohol addiction. Opium was a staple calming remedy: for most of the 19th century, it could still be bought at the grocers along with the ginger beer. Druggists or apothecaries sold it as "laudanum", (opium dissolved in alcohol), and it was the main ingredient in many patent medicines, as well. Because opium was widely available, most habitual users sustained their habit well enough to avoid the symptoms of withdrawal, so evidence of dependence/addiction was missing.

Though doctors barely perceived drug dependence as a problem, the concept was hardly a secret. Thomas De Quincey (1821) came to the point in *Confessions of an English Opium Eater* – though hardly to apologise for his habit. Apart from his obvious reverence for "just, subtle and mighty opium ... fascinating and divinem," De Quincey let it be known that he had started taking it for medical reasons: "infirmity and misery do not, of necessity, imply guilt." He also claimed to have nearly succeeded, where many others had failed: "I have struggled against this fascinating enthralment with a religious zeal, and have, at length, accomplished what I never yet heard attributed to any other man – have untwisted, almost to its final links, the accursed chain – which fettered me."

The secret was not that opium had addictive qualities; it was more to do with the number and rank of those hooked. De Quincey claimed that they included many pillars of society, but was discrete enough to mention no names:

> "But who are they? Reader, I am sorry to say, a very numerous class indeed. Of this I became convinced some years ago, by computing at that time, the number of those in one small class of English society (the class of men distinguished for talents, or of eminent station), who were known to me, directly or indirectly, as opium eaters; such for instance as the eloquent and benevolent —, the late dean of —; Lord —; Mr —, the philosopher; a late under-secretary of state (who described to me the sensation which first drove him to the use of opium, in the very same

2 Mukamal et al. 2003. See also http://abcnews.go.com/sections/living/ 9 January 2003; http://news.bbc.co.uk/1/hi/health/2638399.stm 9 January 2003.

words as the dean of ..., viz., 'that he felt as though rats were gnawing and abrading the coats of his stomach'; Mr ...; and many and others hardly less known, whom it would be tedious to mention ..."

De Quincey kept company with the great and good, but was out on a limb in discussing his opium habit. Most kept such matters private, as the writer, Sir Walter Scott, succeeded in doing for well over 100 years. Scott's own habit was revealed only by accident, through the discovery of a druggist's ledger in an attic in Scotland in the early 1960s. The record showed that between 1823 and 1825 Scott and his wife had been sold 22 quarts (25 litres) of laudanum and 18 dozen opium lozenges and pills. This was quite a productive time in his life too: Scott visited France in 1826 to collect material for his *Life of Napoleon*, which was published in nine volumes the following year.

Working class opium users had less need for discretion. De Quincey described the demand as already "immense" in London, and spreading far beyond. In Manchester, opium eating had become established among cotton workers, "so much so, that on a Saturday afternoon the counters of the druggists were strewed with pills of one, two or three grains in preparation for the known demand of the evening. The immediate occasion of this practice was the lowness of wages, which at that time would not allow them to indulge in ale or spirits."

In spite of the high consumption, doctors were not much worried about the opium habit. The main health concern was to do with the effects of the drug when regularly used to soothe infants – they appeared "shrank up like little old men" or "wizened like little monkeys" and about deaths by overdose. Some deaths were accidental, others not. There was good reason to conceal the difference: suicide remained a criminal offence in Britain until 1961.

Unwittingly, De Quincey had witnessed some of the earliest pressures to restrict the supply of opium – ostensibly for safety reasons, but also to establish a monopoly of supply. Several "respectable druggists" had told him that they got into "daily troubles and disputes," when trying to distinguish between opium eaters with a habit and those who wanted it "with a view to suicide." Unlike your average grocer, professionals were coming to recognise the difference between someone likely to remain a customer and someone who wasn't.

By the mid-19th century, doctors began to treat mental distress with morphine in place of opium. As morphine was a refined, more potent form of opium, they might have expected comparable problems – by analogy between, say, the effects of a pint of ale or a glass of gin. However, doctors came to believe that morphine was safer: it began to replace opium and alcohol and was used to treat addictions to both.

The popularity of morphine, and belief in its superiority over opium, grew with the invention of the hypodermic syringe in 1854. Doctors believed that an injection caused less irritation in the gut, because the drug bypassed the stomach and directly entered the bloodstream. The early medical literature on subcutaneous injection of morphine "was unreservedly euphoric about its uses" – as of course many users were too. In 1868, one expert who advocated the use of hypodermic morphine for neuralgia (nerve pain) declared: "as to the question of danger, let me say, positively, that there is absolutely none" (Anstie 1868).

At first, only doctors used the hypodermic syringe; later they taught patients how to inject themselves. In time, both drug and syringes passed into the hands of patients and their relatives and servants, and the habit spread as more and more people learned how to get morphine under their skin. Before long, the hypodermic habit had become almost fashionable. The author of a popular 1887 report on *Morphinomania* noted that some society women possessed "a regular arsenal of little injecting instruments" and also dressed for the part.

> "Ladies even, belonging to the most elegant classes of society, go so far as to show their good taste in the jewels which they order to conceal a little syringe and artistically made bottles, which are destined to hold the solution which enchants them. At the theatre, in society, they slip away for a moment, or even watch for a favourable opportunity of pretending to play with these trinkets, while giving themselves an injection of morphia in some part of the body which is exposed, or even hidden from view." (Sharkey 1887)

By the 1880s, there was some concern about this, even some alarm, and it slowly crystallised as pressure for laws that would restrict the sale of such drugs only to doctors. This was a slow process: there was official resistance, not least because of the British government's own interests in the opium trade between India and China. This generated for the Exchequer about £2million[3] a year, enough to pay for nearly half of the total cost of the civil service and crown.

Later, Queen Victoria's government set up the Royal Commission on Opium, but to little effect. In spite of many submissions from concerned doctors – and a damning minority report and critique by Joseph Rowntree[4] – the Royal Commission concluded in 1895 that the moderate use of opium was "not attended by any injurious consequences." After two years of research both in Britain and India, the commissioners (bar one) found that opium was used intelligently as medicine and in moderation as a stimulant. They did not object to the colonial trade in opium, noting that, "to deprive the natives of the drug would cause great suffering."

3 Significant fluctuations in the relative value of different currencies over the years makes it unrealistic to give dual values (£/US$) in the text. At the end of 2003, US$1 = £0.58 or € 0.83; £1 = US$1.72 or € 1.42; and € 1 = US$1.21 or £0.70.

4 Substantial support and funding from the Joseph Rowntree Charitable Trust, for over 30 years, made possible the writing of this book.

Freud, denial and cocaine

Cocaine was first isolated in 1860 and used mainly in the US as a tonic – later to evolve as the real and original thing. By the late 1870s, coca preparations were promoted to "young persons afflicted with timidity in society" and as "a powerful nervous excitant." Perhaps because it was much diluted and widely available, little evidence of addiction was seen.

Before long, cocaine was introduced into European medicine, initially as a treatment for morphine addiction. The effective launch date was 1884, when Sigmund Freud published his monograph, *On Coca.* Freud himself used cocaine at this time, both to study and enjoy its effects: "I take very small doses of it regularly against depression ... and with the most brilliant success." He was oblivious to any risk of addiction and pressed the drug on patients, family, colleagues and friends. His official biographer later concluded that, "looked at from the vantage point of our present knowledge, he was rapidly becoming a public menace" (Jones 1953).

The young Freud specifically recommended cocaine as a cure for addiction, and through this "discovery" he hoped to provide for his future and make his name. He staked the drug's benefits partly on observations reported in two notably obscure US medical journals, and partly on the manufacturers' claims. But his main authority for endorsing cocaine was personal experience: in his paper, Freud claimed that he personally had treated a case of morphine addiction with remarkable success. Freud was referring here to his attempts to treat his close friend, Dr. Fleishl. In fact, the treatment and then the friendship entirely failed.

Freud's seminal paper was in time discredited, though not in the author's mind. One prominent doctor accused him of introducing, after alcohol and opium, "the third scourge of humanity," but Freud clung tenaciously to his theories. In a later paper (1887), he did concede that some people might get addicted to cocaine, but only if previously addicted to morphine.

Later still, Freud argued that what might seem to be an addiction was attributable not to the drug but to the injection – a point he underlined for the benefit of his colleagues with some fanciful observations about cerebral blood flow. Some may have believed this, but not Freud. Deep down, he thought the problem lay with the syringe: "patients who have an unwonted dread of it leave no doubt about its symbolic meaning to the unconscious mind." Two years earlier, Freud had specifically recommended injections of cocaine, but this was forgotten. His biographer later concluded that this earlier paper and Freud's recollection of the whole episode, "seems to have been completely suppressed."

Notwithstanding this Freudian skid, the apparent delights of cocaine soon persuaded doctors to restrict others and restrain themselves. By 1887, Dr. Watson had plucked up courage to remonstrate with Sherlock Holmes:

> "I suddenly felt that I could hold out no longer. 'Which is it to-day,' I asked, 'morphine or cocaine?'
> He raised his eyes languidly from the old black-letter volume which he had opened.
> 'It is cocaine,' he said, 'a seven-per-cent solution. Would you care to try it?'
> 'No, indeed,' I answered brusquely. 'My constitution has not got over the Afghan campaign yet. I cannot afford to throw any extra strain upon it.'
> He smiled at my vehemence. 'Perhaps you are right, Watson,' he said. 'I suppose that its influence is physically a bad one. I find it, however, so transcendently stimulating and clarifying to the mind that its secondary action is a matter of small moment.'
> 'But consider!' I said earnestly. 'Count the cost! Your brain may, as you say, be roused and excited, but it is a pathological and morbid process which involves increased tissue-change and may at least leave a permanent weakness. You know, too, what a black reaction comes upon you. Surely the game is hardly worth the candle. Why should you, for a mere passing pleasure, risk the loss of those great powers with which you have been endowed? Remember that I speak not only as one comrade to another but as a medical man to one for whose constitution he is to some extent answerable'." (Conan Doyle 1887)

Freud was one of the greatest of the many experts to have insisted over the years that the decisive element in drug addiction was the personality of the user, not the nature and effects of the drug. Throughout his lifetime, he insisted that any addiction to cocaine "was not, as was commonly believed, the direct result of imbibing a noxious drug, but to some peculiarity in the patient" (Jones 1953). Freud's views underline how patients may become scapegoats and guinea pigs, when reputations and fortunes are on the line.

Even the greatest minds may be quite blind about themselves. Freud was fatally addicted to tobacco and made repeated, unsuccessful efforts to stop smoking ("a torture ... beyond human power to bear") over a period of 45 years. In the last 16 years of his life, he had 33 operations for cancer of his mouth and jaw; he acknowledged the cause but, until his death in 1939, he smoked "an endless series of cigars" (Brecher 1973).

The key factor in the understanding of addiction, when it finally came, was that it called for medical intervention – something more sophisticated than flagellation and purge. The recognition of a withdrawal syndrome, and that doctors could do something about it, began to temper the view that addicts were "practically as moral imbeciles, often addicted also to other forms of depravity" (Movat 1892). This was harsh and unfair: by the turn of the 20th century, an estimated one doctor in ten was addicted to an opiate or cocaine (Berridge 1978).

Just before Queen Victoria died, doctors were presented with a new drug – diamorphine. It had been developed by the German-based Bayer company, in 1898, and was sold under the brand name, Heroin. Originally promoted as a "non-addicting cough suppressant" for infants, before long it was used to treat all the addictions gone before. Well into the 20th century, doctors still needed reminding that such treatments did not work:

> "The morphine habit has often been combated by the substitution of other drugs, such as heroin or cocaine, but the result generally has been that a new and even more dangerous habit has been substituted for, or often merely grafted on, the original. Numerous drugs have been proposed for the cure of morphinomania, but none of them seems to have the slightest effect." (Cushny 1928)

By this time, alcohol was under Prohibition in the US (1920-1933) and "narcotics" were controlled by international law. By then, there was a large illegal trade in opiates, with organised commerce somewhat involved. In 1927, the Chairman of the British delegation to the Opium Advisory Committee of the League of Nations had "no doubt whatever that Hoffman La Roche and Company was not a firm to which a licence to deal with drugs should be given." Thirty years later, the same company would discover Librium and Valium, the first of the benzodiazepine tranquillisers. Roche would become a star.

Non-narcotic solutions

By the turn of the 20th century, the infant pharmaceutical industry was beginning to sort itself out. Leading companies increasingly sought and made contact with doctors. They needed doctors to prescribe and endorse the new and more potent compounds they were beginning to make, and doctors were pleased to have new treatments to try and use. Product claims were still extravagant – but perhaps they didn't appear so bad, because the old brashness was giving way to a more deferential tone. The purveyors of patent medicines had traditionally emphasised that their products offered far more than any doctor could. Now the embryonic pharmaceutical companies began to propose to doctors and gently tell them what to do.

As alcohol, opiates and cocaine began to lose favour, doctors were steered towards other drugs. The first major alternative was chloral hydrate, a sedative-hypnotic (calming/sleeping drug) in its own right, also prescribed to treat addiction. Doctors increasingly favoured chloral, finding it less dangerous than opium in overdose and less popular for suicide.

Introduced in 1869, chloral was welcomed as "a new wonder drug" and "a sensational medicine". Even by today's standards, demand was huge: within two years, around 50 million doses were used in England alone. Habitual chloral eating was soon widespread, but there was little concern because few fatalities were recorded, and habitual use was generally inconspicuous. Chloral didn't produce euphoria like morphine or cocaine, and it had an unpleasant taste: it could lead to addiction but was never considered a major drug of abuse.

In fact, chloral was quite toxic – fatal at about five times the dose that doctors then prescribed – or ten times the dosage normally used today. In the late 19th century, doctors were much more inclined to prescribe high doses for their patients, especially those who failed to get well. When doctors used really high doses, they described their treatments as "heroic". Far from denoting empathy with patients, the term implied that doctors were the heroes because of their confidence in the drastic treatments they used.

Chloral is still sometimes prescribed today, and its survival over the years underlines how safe drugs may be if used sparingly, and how risky if not. The difference mainly comes down to dosage, and how well it is adjusted – given wide variations in individual drug response. This is still a major challenge to doctors, though the theory was founded years ago. In 1886, *Chemist & Druggist* reported that some individuals were more affected by a low dose of chloral than others who had five times more. The same applies with all kinds of drugs for mental distress – though dosing regimens hardly reflect it, to this day.[5] In theory, users should start at a low dose, working up to the dose that produces the best response. In practice, this doesn't much happen, though things have certainly improved.

In the past, doctors gave higher doses and then tended to deliver firm opinions, one way or another, on the value of the drug – and, by extension, of themselves. Hence the observation by the pioneer psychiatrist, Henry Maudsley (1895), that his colleagues held such polarised views. Maudsley favoured something in between:

> "Unhappily, experience speaks with directly contradictory voices: one physician of an asylum, after a full trial of the hydrate of chloral, endorses the description of it as 'crystallised hell', another considers it the most useful drug we have in the treatment of insanity ... Such are the contradictory voices of experience. One requires to know the character of the experimenter in order to decide which voice to trust; albeit one may feel pretty sure in a question of the action of a medical drug, that he who is least heroic in his use of it, and least confident in his opinion of its powers, will be most likely, in virtue of his mental temperament, to have observed accurately and to have inferred soundly."

Maudsley was one of the first doctors to advocate a holistic approach: "the wise physician will treat his patient, not an abstract melancholic entity." He also raised shrewd questions about the real benefit of treatment which involved "putting the nerve cells

5 The imperative to serve mass markets and to simplify treatment dictate "recommended" doses that approximate to the norm; they are often still much too high (Cohen 2001; Cross et al. 2002). See Chapter 8.

of the patient's brain into chemical restraint, so to speak," wondering if this might promote and prolong mental illness rather than cure it. Was it possible, he asked, that a drug like chloral could sedate as intended, while harming the patient all along?

> "And yet so little of this is considered that one frequently hears the long continued use of some sedative lauded with naive exultation, and without a word being said, or apparently without a thought being given, as to whether patients recovered better, or recovered at all, by taking it ...
>
> A single dose, or an occasional dose from time to time, at the commencement or in the course of a mental disorder, as a palliative, may certainly be useful, but its habitual use is pernicious ... When that which may be used fitly as a temporary help – whether it be stimulant or narcotic – is resorted to as an abiding stay, the result cannot fail to be disastrous."

Underlying Maudsley's concerns was another idea far ahead of its time: that the sleep induced by drugs like chloral might not work like the real thing. The prevailing wisdom was that chloral promoted "natural" sleep – in the sense that the sedated patient could be roused. "But it is not considered ... that natural sleep and narcotic-enforced sleep may be two different conditions ... the chloral-produced state looks like sleep, and all the rest has been assumed."

For all these insights, Maudsley was less enlightened in some views. His thoughts about masturbation, for example, were generally in keeping with the times. His references to "the miserable sinner whose mind suffers by reason of self abuse" and to this "vicious habit", "utter moral perversion" etc. underline the closeness and confusion there still was between guilt, illness and sin.

> "Physicians, the new guardians of morality, simply substituted new names for ancient evils: madness became mental illness; drunkenness became alcoholism; and the sin of Onan became masturbation. The old sins to be confronted and overcome were, by the late nineteenth century, diseases to be cured." (Parssinen & Kerner 1980)

Ordeal by bromides

The grip of such preoccupations was underlined by the introduction of Kellogg's Cornflakes in 1898, specifically as a remedy for "self pollution" or "self-abuse". Masturbation was not only a sin; in the 19th century many doctors believed it led to insanity. They thought it caused epilepsy – itself regarded as a hallmark of madness, if not the work of the devil – and this partly explains how the bromides came to be used.

Potassium bromide was first recommended in 1857 by a man whose very name inspired thoughts of a cure. Sir Charles Lowcock had used it to treat epilepsy, finding that it had a strong anti-aphrodisiac effect. Indeed the bromides did suppress the symptoms of epilepsy (but not by dulling desire) and before long they were established as a valuable class of drugs.

Bromides came to be prescribed for many illnesses and for almost every unapproved state of mind, including addiction of all kinds. They were also given to children, even as drugs like Ritalin are used today. A correspondent to the *Lancet* in 1917 suggested that: "A physician need have no hesitation in keeping an excitable or nervous child on a trifling dose of bromide throughout the greater part of his school-days." Another expert suggested, "the bromides are called for whenever there is excitement" – yet also for depression – "a disease in which cerebral nutrition is quite surely lowered and perverted" (Seguin 1877).

Bromides also played their part in the defence of the realm. Some years after World War II, a prominent British psychiatrist, Dr William Sargant, described how bromide and other sedatives had been used to encourage soldiers to face battle. They were used both to restore shattered nerves, and as prophylactics. They dulled the mind:

> "Millions of pounds in pensions were, for instance, saved in World War II simply because it was at last realised that immediate and heavy 'front line' sedation was generally more effective in the prevention of chronic neuroses, and of so-called 'malingering' reactions, than all the threats of shooting for cowardice and the verbal exhortations and moral punishments used instead as treatments from time immemorial." (Sargant 1958)

Bromide toxicity is not unknown today, and there were safety concerns many years ago. At first it was feared that bromides might cause permanent impotence, perhaps having "the power to absorb the testicle or other glandular structures", but the prevailing view was that these were among the most valuable medicines there were. Later, the potential dangers of overdose and addiction were mentioned more: a *Lancet* editorial (1889) emphasised that "every experienced practitioner ... must have noticed that the bromides are not as harmless as they were first thought to be."

The problem of bromide intoxication (bromism) was first identified around 1850, and published case reports listed most of the symptoms of toxicity known today. Then it was recognised that bromides were only slowly excreted – a critical finding, because it meant that drugs accumulated in the body, in effect building up the dose. However, it took some years for the implications to sink in: meanwhile, patients were routinely prescribed doses of bromides that built up to toxic levels, so the longer bromides were used, the more damage they tended to do.

Why was the problem not seen? An important reason was that the main symptoms of bromide toxicity included "increased restlessness with disorientation followed by paranoid trends, hallucinations, and apprehension" – all of which indicated the need for drug treatment. This set up a vicious cycle: those who behaved abnormally because of bromides were treated with more bromides. Comparable problems exist to this day.

The breakthrough came in 1927, when a simple test was developed to measure concentration of bromides in the blood; these could then be compared with levels known to be toxic. Some hospitals used tests to distinguish between bromism and mental illness – but they were exceptions to the rule. The use of bromides continued on a grand scale: by 1930, they were included in four out of ten general practice prescriptions in Britain. Looking back, some 20 years after the event, Dr. William Sargant described how patients he had seen in some institutions were kept in states of chronic bromide intoxication, day after day.

> "My first locum appointment in a mental hospital, in 1934, showed me rows of patients sitting silently along benches with drooping heads and salivating mouths. You could generally tell the heavily drugged patients during a ward round because you could pat them on the backs of their heads while they were sitting in rows. This was because their relaxed heads fell so far forward on their chests. All these tranquillised patients were then using bromides in truly enormous doses." (Sargant 1958)

It takes time for understanding and for medical practice to change. Dr. William Sargant and others had vigorously campaigned to restrict the use of bromides since the 1930s, but bromism still accounted for an estimated 10% of all admissions to UK psychiatric institutions in the 1950s, and reports of toxicity could still be found in the world literature as the 20th century drew to a close.

Something of the same has proved true for most drugs of tranquillity. Either through continuous use, or during withdrawal, these drugs tend to produce symptoms that mimic mental illness – including the very conditions for which they have been prescribed. Bromides, barbiturates, tranquillisers and antidepressants have all been used in their day to treat the very symptoms of illness that they themselves have caused.

Enter the barbiturates

The first barbiturate, Veronal, was developed by Bayer in Germany and came to Britain in 1903. It was advertised as "absolutely safe and without toxic effects", but the first reports of fatal overdose soon appeared and the numbers grew. There were also warnings about the barbiturate habit – though the risks seemed much lower than with drugs like morphine, still the gold standard of addiction in those days. By the end of the 1920s, "chronic barbiturate poisoning" was common, though addiction was hardly recognised at all.

After Veronal came many more. During the 1930s, prescriptions for barbiturates tripled as the use of bromides declined; by mid-century thousands of barbiturates had been synthesised and hundreds were used. There was little to choose between them, though doctors were readily persuaded otherwise. All barbiturates sedate (at lower doses) or induce sleep (higher) or intoxicate (higher still), sometimes fatally. Choice of drug made much less difference than doctors were led to believe: in the US, some 50 different barbiturates were available by 1940. For therapeutic purposes, five would have been fine:

> "New barbiturates are constantly being introduced, usually under confusing trade names, and claims are often made that a particular compound is superior regarding potency, margin of safety or duration of action. At times it appears that the only goal in producing new barbiturates has been to obtain their exclusive sale by the manufacturer." (Goodman & Gilman 1941)

The barbiturates were among the first "me-too" drugs, chemically and otherwise so similar to existing compounds as to offer no real therapeutic gain. Numerous "me-too" drugs are used today though, in polite circles, they are now called "innovative chemical extensions." All the major pharmaceutical companies depend on them: they have no option, because real breakthroughs are hard to come by and correspondingly rare.

As the barbiturates were used more and more, so medical opinion began to divide. By the mid-1930s there were two camps: one unreservedly critical of barbiturates, the other emphatically not. The top man on the high ground was Sir William Willcox, head of St. Mary's Hospital Medical School in London. His views on barbiturates were years ahead of their time. In 1927, he warned that barbiturates should be given "only on prescription, to be retained by the pharmacist, and the total number of doses ordered should not exceed six." Cushny's *Textbook* (1928) said much the same.

By 1934, Willcox had become convinced the barbiturates occupied "the foremost place among drugs of addiction," but the medical profession largely ignored him. The declining reputation of the bromides led to increased demand for barbiturates and patient demand was strong. There was also concerted opposition to Willcox, led by a psychiatrist, R.D. Gillespie; he not only held strong opinions but also had misleading statistics to support them. He had never once seen a case of barbiturate addiction, he said, arguing that withdrawal was "not accompanied by the distressing subjective results and objective manifestations that accompany withdrawal of alcohol or morphine."

Gillespie also reported that he had scoured the world literature, finding reports of only 157 fatalities from barbiturates before 1932. He emphasised that barbiturates accounted for only one in every 400 suicides, a proportion "remarkably small". This same line of argument – the presumption that no evidence of risk equals evidence of no risk – is still often used today.

The barbiturates were increasingly prescribed during Willcox's lifetime, and long after his death, in 1941. In the US, barbiturates are still sometimes used; in Britain their use is now reserved for "severe intractable insomnia", a euphemism for unshakable addiction. As the hypnotic (sleep-promoting) effects of barbiturates wear off after a few weeks, the main justification for prescribing them for longer would be to prevent a crisis for the patient if the drug were withdrawn. And so it was for years.

Why did it take so long? Part of the answer is over-reliance on lack of evidence, the belief that no news is good news. There was natural resistance to look for or report problems, because positive results had a negative effect on commercial and professional reputations. And all the denials seemed convincing too. There was so much prescribing that reported problems seemed relatively rare – and doctors and patients often mistook withdrawal symptoms for relapse as well.

There were indeed no obvious signs that therapeutic barbiturate addiction was much of a problem. Even in the mid-1970s, the organisers of a high-profile campaign to reduce barbiturate prescribing declared that addiction was an essentially invisible problem: "most practitioners never or only rarely see an easily recognisable case of gross barbiturate abuse and it is difficult to realise what a national problem this has become" (Bennett 1976).

There was one other reason why some doctors said problems were rare while others refuted that. They were talking about different things – "addiction" and "habituation" – and much in between. The term "addiction" took its meaning from experience with the opiates – meaning intoxicated and hooked – whereas "habituation" just meant hooked. This confusion went back some way:

> "Addiction to the barbiturates, in the strict sense of the word, probably does not occur. Habituation, in contrast, is not infrequent and certain patients may experience craving and psychic disturbances after the barbiturate is withdrawn. This phenomenon is, however, rather characteristic of the sedative-hypnotic group of drugs." (Goodman & Gilman 1941)

The observation that relatively few patients were badly affected reinforced the view that problems were more to do with user than drug. Most barbiturate users just went on taking the prescribed dose, so the physical manifestations of addiction weren't seen. The problem could be defined only if and when drugs were withdrawn, so the true picture was never clear.

Addiction false and true

It took until 1950 to establish beyond doubt that the barbiturates were "true" drugs of addiction, thus correcting "the erroneous impression, which has been widely held in both the United States and England, that abstinence symptoms did not follow the abrupt withdrawal of barbiturates from chronically intoxicated persons." This was the conclusion of Dr. Harris Isbell and associates at the US Public Heath Service Hospital in Lexington, Kentucky.

"Working under strict if bizarre experimental conditions, Isbell's team gave five "volunteers" maximal and increasing doses of barbiturates, keeping them effectively dead drunk for several months. Then they withdrew the drug abruptly. They concluded that, "in fact, addiction to barbiturates is far more serious than is morphine addiction."

> "In the first 12 to 16 hours after abrupt discontinuation of medication, the patients appear to improve. Their thinking and mental status becomes clearer and most of the neurological signs of intoxication disappear. As the signs of intoxication decline, the patients become apprehensive and so weak that they can hardly stand ... Anxiety, tremor and weakness continue to increase (until) usually about the thirtieth hour, one or more grand mal convulsions which are indistinguishable from those occurring in idiopathic epilepsy, occur ... Generally, patients have no more than three major convulsions but numerous minor episodes, which are characterized by clonic twitching without loss of consciousness, or by writhing athenoid movements of the extremities, which may occur before, between, or after the major convulsions ... Whether or not convulsions occur, barbiturate addicts are likely to become delirious, usually between the third and seventh days of abstinence. The onset of the psychosis is often heralded by insomnia of 24 to 48 hours duration after which the patients begin to experience hallucinations and delusions..." (Isbell et al. 1950)

The Isbell study broke new ground but only slowly began to change old ways. No one disputed its main conclusion, but the study was otherwise so perversely interpreted that the point was entirely missed. The experts agreed that the barbiturates were true drugs of addiction – but only after long exposure to huge doses. The extreme conditions of the study even reinforced the view that barbiturates would be safe in therapeutic use. Four years after Isbell published, the *Lancet* (1954) reported: "Thus 'addiction' occurs only with habitual ingestion of 'far above therapeutic doses', and ... mainly psychologically abnormal people are likely to increase the doses so far." At least until the 1960s, it was widely believed "that barbiturate addiction is rare except in fundamentally very disturbed individuals."

What doctors needed to know was whether there was some threshold of dosage and/or duration of treatment above which withdrawal symptoms could be expected to reinforce drug-taking. One of the first people to throw light on this was a "neuropsychiatrist" at the Henry Ford Hospital in Detroit. Dr. E.J. Alexander applied treatment that involved putting patients on barbiturates to keep them asleep for about 16 hours a day, for a week or so, and then abruptly stopping the drugs. He was positively trying to bring on withdrawal symptoms, believing they had some beneficial effect.

In 1951, Alexander published a prominent review, showing that, even after a week on high therapeutic doses, his patients had withdrawal symptoms, including marked irritability and insomnia, tremor, hallucinations and sometimes convulsions. He concluded that dependence would often result from the dosages used in ordinary clinical practice. He also made the critical point that family doctors might be prescribing barbiturates in effect to ward off symptoms of drug withdrawal. Later in the 1950s, others reported the same. Notable was Dr. Richard Hunter, a psychiatrist at Guy's Hospital in London. He warned that barbiturate dependence could develop after only a few weeks – and then ...

> "... not only do the patient's symptoms for which barbiturates were in the first place prescribed, return in full force when a dose wears off, which might but for drug-taking have subsided without treatment – but they are reinforced by the symptoms of barbiturate abstinence ... From then, the drug is no longer taken for the original symptoms, but simply to ward off increasingly distressing abstinence symptoms. The cause of this exacerbation may not be recognised by doctor or patient – both may think his original illness has got worse. This may lead to yet further increase in barbiturate dosage with the result that not only do abstinence symptoms become severer, but the symptoms of barbiturate intoxication are added as well ... Thus a mild psychiatric disturbance, in all likelihood amenable to one or two sympathetic interviews, becomes converted into a serious and perhaps protracted illness." (Hunter 1957)

Dr. William Sargant came to share these views. In 1958, long after his campaign against the bromides, Sargant began to reflect how "fashion and authority in drug prescribing may certainly change in the most startling way." Sargant was by this time musing that he might have gone too far in proposing the routine use of barbiturates. He thought that this might have been, "in rebellion at some of the absurdities of my St. Mary's teaching on sedatives."

Sargant was referring here to his student days, under Sir William Willcox, when "the giving of any barbiturates was considered a major therapeutic crime." One generation later, the physician who had earlier been shocked by the sight of patients drugged with bromides was now seeing some of the worst effects of barbiturate intoxication. The saddest cases Sargant described were patients who had undergone brain surgery because their doctors didn't realise that barbiturates had made them so ill:

> "... in 1944 I made the statement that these barbiturates, in moderate doses, did not cause addiction in the true sense of that word, nor severe symptoms on withdrawal. But I think that this statement has now to be modified. For I, with others, have come to realise that patients with chronic tension states may continue to remain tense and anxious for many years, because they are, in fact, suffering more from a self-induced or doctor-induced chronic barbiturate tension state than from a persisting anxiety neurosis per se. I am now seeing patients who have had one,

two or even three leucotomies performed for a chronic persisting tension and who have then turned out to be, probably, cases of chronic barbiturate addiction." (Sargant 1958)

Even so, barbiturate consumption continued to rise well into the next decade. In 1964, questions were asked in Parliament, but the Minister of Health was unmoved. "I have no evidence that harmful effects or dependence occur at all frequently in relation to the number of prescriptions."

By then, the waters of understanding had been further muddied by the introduction of many other new drugs, not chemically classified as barbiturates but otherwise quite like them. From the mid-1950s, there was a stream of breakthroughs – each one pronounced safe and later found not to be. The star of the barbiturate side-show was meprobamate (Miltown, Equanil), but there were many others too.[6] One was Mandrax (methaqualone + diphenhydramine) – which received the warmest of recommendations from Dr. William Sargant in 1973. It was withdrawn from the market soon after, following numerous reports of overdose, dependence and abuse from the 1960s on.

The 1960s also marked the start of a wave of illicit drug abuse. In Britain, the Department of Health at first claimed there were only 200-300 barbiturate addicts, suggesting that the so-called drug problem was a media fiction. Meanwhile, in the US, the Food & Drug Administration (FDA) had estimated the extent of the problem by comparing the amounts of drugs manufactured with the amounts legitimately prescribed. By 1965, the FDA suspected "that approximately half the 9,000,000,000 barbiturate and amphetamine capsules and tablets manufactured annually in this country are diverted to illegal use" (*NEJM* 1965).

In Britain, the curtain finally fell in 1979, by which time even more patients had been persuaded to depend on newer drugs instead. Years after the horse had bolted, the UK Committee on Review of Medicines concluded that barbiturates were not lastingly effective and had "a high addiction potential" in normal therapeutic use. In the US, the Institute of Medicine (IOM) also concluded that tolerance developed with these drugs, and that they were effective only in the short-term. The IOM kindly described this not as addiction, but as "nightly reliance on drugs for sleep."

---

6 Other widely used barbiturate-like drugs included methyprylon (Noludar), ethchlorvynol (Placidyl, Serensil) and glutethimide (Doriden).

3
Tranquillisers

~ *With the 1960s and 1970s, came a wholesale switch to a new class of drugs – "tranquillisers" like Valium, Librium, Ativan, Xanax and Halcion. It took over 20 years to establish that they too were addictive, and another decade to do much about it. Until the 1980s, the risk of becoming addicted to a tranquilliser was officially described as remote, but the opposite again proved true.* ~

Chlordiazepoxide was first synthesised in 1955 but then nothing happened. The inventor was a research chemist at the Swiss firm, Hoffman La Roche. He had been tinkering creatively, but then got distracted, so the two small bottles of white powder lay around in his lab for two more years. Eventually, as a precaution before throwing it out, he arranged for an evaluation of the new compound in animal studies, and the results were outstanding. Two years later, chlordiazepoxide was on the market as Librium – the first of a large family of related drugs, the benzodiazepines. After Librium came Valium, Ativan, Dalmane, Halcion, Xanax and many more.[1]

With an eye to marketing, Roche did further tests with Librium on animals, including "vicious, agitated monkeys, dingo dogs and other wild animals" in captivity in the San Diego and Boston zoos. The climax involved a filmed demonstration of a tranquillised lion alongside a lamb. Then Roche asked over 800 US doctors to try the new drug on their patients. Their published reports all praised it; many conveyed real excitement about its effects:

> "The effect of Librium on the symptoms of excessive withdrawal and tension (excessive control) is remarkable, and may be illustrated by the description by one patient, a teacher: 'I think it is miraculous. I was feeling outgoing. The effect was so liberating I felt very excited and very outgoing ... I would walk into the class completely unprepared and end up well'." (Toll 1960)

Although it had to compete in a market now flowing with different sedatives and hypnotics, Librium quickly caught on: "few drugs have had so enthusiastic a reception in both lay and medical press." This was both because and in spite of the failure

---

1 For a more detailed, fully referenced account of the events described in this chapter, see Medawar 1992.

of Roche and its investigators "to observe any of the established disciplines of the controlled clinical trial" (*Medical Letter* 1960). The investigators hadn't compared it with other drugs or placebo (an inert pill, disguised as the real thing) and none of the early trials was controlled or conducted "blind". The selected investigators and their patients believed they were testing an exciting new drug, and they soon proved it to be so.

Roche welcomed this, but might have felt wary too, because a drug that made miserable patients feel so good might prove a drug of addiction. So company reviews conveyed none of this excitement. In the US, Roche soberly attributed what it called good "patient acceptance" to the superiority of Librium over alternatives. Similarly, Dr. John Marks of Roche UK used bland terms such as "beneficial effect" or "favourable response". Neither review mentioned that Librium sometimes made patients feel euphoric. Roche wouldn't have wanted to alert either drug abusers or the regulators to the evidence of pleasurable effects.

Valium (diazepam) appeared in 1963 and Roche promoted it, along with Librium, as if there was a real difference between these new "tranquillisers" and the older "sedatives". There wasn't: both produce some calming effect, relieve anxiety and tension, and at higher doses promote sleep. But Roche kept quiet about this as well: they could hardly admit that these remarkable new non-sedating sedatives were sleeping pills too. Instead, Roche told doctors how to minimise unwanted side effects such as drowsiness – either by reducing the dose, or by waiting a few days until the effects wore off. The drowsiness faded as patients developed tolerance to the drug.

This marketing strategy left the way open for the next "benzo", Mogadon (nitrazepam), which Roche UK launched as a sleeping pill in 1965. It was really just another Librium – but was promoted hard with quite different instructions for use. Following precedent, there was little reliable evidence to go on – reports of trials had "appeared in relatively inaccessible journals and are mainly of poor quality" – but Mogadon soon became the most prescribed sleeping pill in the UK.

This marketing strategy worked so well that Dr. William Sargant admitted at a symposium, seven years later, that he had always thought there were major differences between diazepam and nitrazepam. Now he knew they were much the same, but used at different doses, and taken either by day or at night.

> "I have only just learned that 'Valium' and 'Mogadon' are similar. Here is a supposed expert being led up the garden path by this situation. I hope that this conference will in some way make a strong resolution that in the future drugs with similar action and effects are grouped together. Because of advertising, doctors are going from one drug to another quite unscientifically." (Sargant 1972)

Although the benzos were very similar to each other, there was one decisive difference between them and the barbiturates. The benzos were relatively safe in overdose, while barbiturates were implicated in suicides and accidents more than any other drug. In Britain, by 1970, there were over 20,000 emergency hospital admissions for barbiturate poisoning, including some 2,000 deaths. Roche worked on this, warning doctors to switch patients from barbiturates to Mogadon, to avoid having a death on their hands. "Mogadon: far safer, far better", the company claimed. In one famous advertisement, the headline by the tombstone said, "some people take barbiturates until the day they die."

A prime mover in the campaign against the barbiturates was an Ipswich general practitioner (GP), Dr. Frank Wells – later to become Medical Director of the Association of the British Pharmaceutical Industry (ABPI). In a 1973 paper, Wells described how he and his colleagues had switched every patient in their practice from barbiturate sleeping pills to Mogadon: about half had been taking them for over five years, the longest for 26 years.

But this was only the start: "At the end of the first three months, all that had happened was the substitution of a cheap, effective, hazardous, and toxic hypnotic, by an expensive, effective, safer alternative." The real purpose was to support and encourage patients to reduce their consumption or stop. One year later, about half the patients had stopped and about a quarter were on a lower dosage. It was an important initiative, but with critical limitations too.

Wells and his colleagues had taken for granted that Mogadon was not a drug of dependence, and had interpreted their results accordingly: "One of the objects in doing this exercise was to substitute a known habit-forming drug by one which was known not to produce dependence." So what this exercise really amounted to was drug withdrawal, achieved though the inadvertent use of double-blind techniques. It showed that doctors could greatly reduce the consumption of sleeping pills in practice – but also that about one patient in four was unable to quit, not even with strong encouragement and support.

Benzos versus barbiturates

Long before Wells and his colleagues reported, the World Health Organization's (WHO) Expert Committee on Drug Dependence (1950) had drawn attention to the implications of cross-dependence: "... any substance which will sustain an established addiction – i.e. will adequately replace the drug which has produced the addiction – must be considered as also capable of producing an addiction." In other words, if a patient on a barbiturate could be switched to a benzo, without withdrawal symptoms, it was because their dependence had been transferred. It was like beer instead of gin.

Moreover, Dr. Leo Hollister and colleagues at the Veterans Administration Hospital in Palo Alto, California, had tested Librium in a 1961 study that pretty much duplicated Isbell's work on barbiturate withdrawal. In the Hollister study, 11 psychiatric in-patients were treated with "monumental doses" of Librium for two to six months, before the drug was surreptitiously and abruptly withdrawn. Ten of the 11 patients had severe withdrawal reactions and two had seizures – pretty much a replay of barbiturate withdrawal. The main difference was that Librium was cleared from the body more slowly, so the withdrawal symptoms were more attenuated and took longer to appear.[2]

Later, Hollister studied Valium. The protocol (1963) was similar to his earlier study with Librium, but patients got only twice the recommended maximum dose and were treated only for six weeks before the Valium was withdrawn. Even with this reduced exposure, six of the 13 patients had withdrawal symptoms, including one with convulsions. Both Hollister studies were widely reported and their findings generally ignored. Again it was assumed that dependence on benzos resulted only from prolonged treatment at excessive dosages, and otherwise affected only the "addiction prone".

One investigator who identified such patients was Dr. H. Angus Bowes, Director of the Institute of Neurology and Psychological Medicine in Grand Forks, North Dakota (population 39,008 in 1970). Roche had recruited Bowes to test both Librium and Valium and he reported enthusiastically on both (1965), in spite of his observation that one or two patients had staggered along to see him. "Five of my five hundred patients have become overtly dependent on Valium and presented themselves for examination with slurred speech, ataxia, a dry mouth and dilated pupils. They were all addictive personalities..." Bowes did not discuss the possibility that other residents of Grand Forks might have been staggering around their own homes. Patients had to flaunt the evidence for dependence to be seen.

Then, as now, there was still much confusion about meanings and definitions, though the WHO Expert Committee on Drug Dependence had tried hard to sort things out. In 1964, the committee recommended that the terms "habituation" and "addiction" be abandoned. Instead, the term "dependence" should be used – referring to the type of dependence involved. WHO defined in detail what it meant by "dependence of the barbiturate type" – and concluded that Librium produced just that. This was on the basis of Hollister's work, also because of "cross dependence" between benzodiazepines, alcohol and barbiturates. The committee chairman – who was also a consultant to Roche in the US – "said he felt Librium and Valium

---

2 Patient rights, as they are understood today, were barely developed at this time. Reform began with the Nuremberg Code (1949), prompted by revulsion over the behaviour of doctors in Nazi concentration camps. The Code said many of the right things, but did not deter many experiments that left patients reeling. The turning point came with the Declaration of Helsinki in 1964. This defined clinical investigation and treatment in terms of benefit to the patient: "clinical research on a human being cannot be undertaken without his free consent, after he has been fully informed".

should be classified with the barbiturates and had told Roche this," but diazepam wasn't scheduled, all the same.

Because WHO's mandate in this area related specifically to controlling international drug traffic, the Committee hardly focused on problems that arose in therapeutic use. Its report emphasised the dangers of high dosages, suggesting the measure of the problem was severity of withdrawal symptoms – but the greater problem was that most people didn't withdraw. They went on taking their drugs for years: in Britain, every tenth night of sleep was drug induced at this time. Conspicuous abuse by a small minority was considered more of a problem than entrenched use by millions. Neither could function without their drugs, but most kept it under control.

Meanwhile, the US government had been concerned enough about the diversion of drugs to illicit markets to schedule both barbiturates and amphetamines, under a law that required manufacturers to keep records to show what quantities of drugs they made and where they were distributed. This meant those drugs were less prescribed. Soon after, there were hearings on Librium and Valium, leading to a recommendation in April 1967 to schedule them too. The long story of how Roche kept the US government at bay for years has been well documented elsewhere; legal process triumphed over good sense:

> "On March 28, 1973, the Third US District Court of Appeals in Philadelphia issued a forty-four page decision on the Librium and Valium case. In it, the court noted the evidence that Valium and Librium produce euphoria, tolerance, withdrawal and paradoxical rage, that they are diverted illegally and have a substantial potential for significant abuse, was ample. But the Court said, at the very beginning of the FDA hearing in 1966, FDA Counsel James Phelps did not submit to Roche Laboratories the report of the FDA Advisory Committee which included mention of Librium and Valium.[3] The report did not contain information which would have materially changed the case, but the appeals court said the denial of the report to Roche Labs was a denial of due process, and it therefore reversed the hearing examiner's ruling against Librium and Valium. So, after hearings, lobbying battles and court proceedings lasting about eight years, Librium and Valium succeeded in escaping regulation. 'We won everything but the case,' a government lawyer remarked on the appeals court decision." (Pekkanen 1973)

3 James Phelps later passed through "the revolving door". In 1980, he set up a practice that later became "one of the most extensive food and drug practices in the United States". This was one of many law firms where the attorneys, formerly regulators, began to work for companies instead.

Measuring tranquilliser effectiveness

Before too long, there were noises off, not only about the risks of benzos, but also about their effectiveness. There was a vast amount of "evidence", but the dearth of sound data meant that, "about all one can safely and tritely conclude is that all of these drugs affect performance under some conditions" (McNair 1973). Hollister's continuing research (1972) even caused him to wonder if these drugs worked at all: "Considering the widespread and continuing use of these drugs, it may seem impertinent to question their efficacy. Yet a number of well-designed controlled studies have failed to elicit consistent differences between drug and placebo therapy of anxiety."

Measuring the effects of drugs on anxiety is problematic, especially in long-term studies. Anxiety comes in numerous guises and different people see and feel it in different ways. Levels of anxiety fluctuate and "severity" is hard to define when so much depends on the patient's own assessment and on the doctor's style of interpretation. The reliability of research remains low to this day.

However, when subjects are tucked in and wired up in a bedroom-like sleep laboratory, it is easy enough to measure how long it takes to fall asleep, how long sleep lasts and more. The basic routine in a sleep study involves three different stages. Before taking the test drug, subjects spend a few nights in the laboratory to settle in: this allows researchers to make baseline measurements, so before-and-after comparisons can be made. Then there is a period "on-drug" and then the period during and after withdrawal.

Serious sleep studies began in the 1960s. Dr. Ian Oswald and colleagues at the Royal Edinburgh Hospital were among the first to use measurements from electroencephalograms (EEGs): volunteers were wired up all night so the EEG could record electrical messages from different parts of the brain. The EEG not only registered major activity in the brain; it could also detect little murmurs and signs of dreams or nightmares too. It was a turning point in drug evaluation: "Recent research using EEG techniques has shown that hypnotics do not induce natural sleep, and have made plain how ignorant we formerly were about their effect on sleep; and how much more ignorant we shall appear when new techniques become available in future" (Oswald 1968).

Oswald showed that, when someone stopped taking sleeping pills, some "backlash effect" made the insomnia worse than before the drug was started. This rebound developed quickly and again prompted the question: did patients go on taking these drugs mainly to avoid the effects of withdrawal, and were they mistaking this for "relapse"? Oswald suspected that what had always previously been dismissed as a psychological dependence might actually be very physical – even if it was not obvious and could barely be measured at all:

> "We see so many patients, whom we would not call barbiturate addicts, who just take a couple of sleeping pills each night, and who are extremely resistant to any suggestion that they should give them up. We learn from them that these pills were started, often in hospital, 5 or 10 years ago and have never been stopped. 'I've tried to stop them, doctor, but I just can't sleep properly without them.' And so it goes on year after year, and 10 per cent of all NHS general practitioner prescriptions are for sleeping pills. Five hundred million sleeping pills a year in England & Wales – excluding hospital and private prescribing ... Is it solely a psychological dependence, has the patient merely learned that swallowing the pills opens a quick avenue to oblivion? Or has her physiology been changed, so that the drug is now woven inextricably into her brain chemistry so that, if the drug were suddenly lacking, a violent chemical perturbation would arise?"

Oswald's studies broke new ground. They showed that sleeping pills gradually ceased to work, and also began to explain how dependence on drugs like Mogadon could be created and sustained. Similar studies were done in the US, notably by Dr. Anthony Kales; he began to investigate why so many patients continued to sleep badly in spite of taking sleeping pills. Kales (1974) further defined the rebound phenomenon and also found that sleeping pills became increasingly less effective after continuous use. Usually within two weeks, tolerance to the effects of sleeping pills had developed to such an extent that duration of on-drug sleep was no greater than it had been pre-drug.

But there were exceptions to this rule: two Roche products, Mogadon (nitrazepam) and Dalmane (flurazepam). Both drugs had become popular for the very reason that later explained their decline. The Kales team had found that Dalmane went on working for at least a month. This was because it was cleared from the body very slowly – which also meant it tended to accumulate, especially in elderly people.

As the body ages, it becomes less efficient, so drugs are broken down and excreted more slowly. With repeated dosing, levels of sleeping pills tend to build up and up until toxic levels are reached. That led to hangover effects the following day and increased the risk of accidents and falls. It also produced toxicity that mimicked states of senility and illness that were easily misdiagnosed. This happened both with Dalmane in the US, and with Mogadon in the UK.

The problem was exemplified in a letter to the *British Medical Journal* about a 75-year-old woman, referred to hospital after a suspected stroke. She had been in an old people's home for six years, and had previously been "ambulant, continent and oriented" – but then there was a complete change. Her case evoked the image of drooping heads on the bromide wards seen by Dr. Sargant, 40 years before:

> "Nitrazepam is popular because of its rapid effect and is widely used in residential homes and elsewhere, where it is convenient or necessary for old people to be "

> 'switched off' with the lights ... Despite statements to the contrary made in advertising literature, nitrazepam (Mogadon) seems a particularly unsuitable hypnotic for old people. Members of this department have come to recognise a characteristic syndrome of disability caused by nitrazepam, of which the following case is typical: (This woman) had become dysarthric (slurred inarticulate speech etc) confused and disorientated and, if left undisturbed, would sit staring blankly into space. She tended to fall to the left and to stumble when attempting to walk. Specific questioning elicited the information that she looked better and seemed mentally more alert when in bed than when sitting out and that she had been taking one tablet (5 mg) of nitrazepam nightly for at least a year. We advised stopping the nitrazepam and on review three days later she was said to be 'completely her own self' and had gone out on a charabanc trip. After four months she remains well." (Evans & Jarvis 1972)

Reports like this eventually led to formal reappraisals on both sides of the Atlantic. In the US, the Institute of Medicine (IOM 1979) published an extensive review; it again criticised the overwhelming lack of hard evidence and was scathing about the studies that had been done. The IOM had reviewed about 150 efficacy studies, almost all sponsored by companies. It found: "The results of most of these are extremely difficult to interpret. There has been a failure to set high standards of interpretability, replicability, and general validity in the published studies." The IOM also concluded that benzodiazepines and barbiturates were "probably equally effective in short-term use" and otherwise suggested that benzos were not as different from the barbiturates as generally believed. Their relative safety in overdose was a real advantage, but there were still reasons for concern.

In the same year, 1979, prescriptions for benzos in the UK peaked at 30 million/year. There was much evidence to suggest that dependence on sleeping pills was largely an iatrogenic disease – "a condition created and maintained by doctors" – but the problem was deeply ingrained. No doubt some doctors, at least in their hearts, shared the despondent views of this Suffolk GP:

> "In 20 years of practice, I am unaware of ever having helped a patient by prescribing a hypnotic, but I have written many such prescriptions and continue to do so. By prescribing hypnotics, I have caused much misery and harm and prevented many people, including myself, from taking a more positive attitude to a common symptom. I have no doubt caused dependency and habituation on a wide scale ... Experience has taught me, very slowly, much that my clinical teachers did not. I can think of no subject worse taught to medical students or to hospital residents than that of the management of sleeplessness ... I was taught by example how easy and laudable it was to start such drugs. No-one ever discussed the difficulties of stopping them. It is understandable that such ignorance continues to be wide-

> spread. Only a general practitioner watching his patients over a long period of time can possibly be aware of the mischief caused by hypnotics. By the time he becomes fully aware of the natural history of hypnotic users many years of habituation will have ossified a pattern of prescribing. To change this will cost both the patients and doctor a superhuman effort." (Stevens 1973)

Probably most doctors agonised less. During the 1970s, about three-quarters of all psychotropic medicines were supplied on "repeat prescription". Usually this meant the receptionist signed the prescription form; patients wouldn't see the doctor for months on end, sometimes not for years.

Methodology of denial

By the mid-1970s, an estimated 10-20% of "ambulatory adults" in the US and other Western nations were regularly using benzos. There was some concern but it was isolated, if not squashed. Publication of the occasional report of suspected dependence typically attracted a bullish response from the manufacturers – asserting that the problem was relapse, not withdrawal. This was the typical company line: "The quoted withdrawal signs are evidence of the anxiety accompanying the patient's depressive illness, allowed to burst forth once the (drug) was discontinued..." (Harry 1972).

The climate was such that the British pharmaceutical industry's research arm felt able to propose that the prescribing laws for benzodiazepines should be relaxed or removed (OHE 1975). The loudest voices claimed that, considering the extent of mental illness, prescribing levels were "rather on the conservative side and there may indeed be underuse" (Marks 1978). Probably most doctors were actually incapable of diagnosing dependence on benzos, at this time.

The direct evidence for this is slight but sweet; it comes from the heart of a review by two US psychiatrists (Maletzky & Klotter 1976). They conducted an exercise in which a panel of 14 doctors was asked to read the case notes of 50 patients, some showing clear signs of drug dependence, others not. The symptoms were described in some detail, though the drug in question was not identified. When they had read the notes on each case, the doctors were asked to rate the severity of the addiction there seemed to be. This is what they found:

None	*Slight*	*Moderate*	*Great*	*Severe*
19	11	11	6	3

Then panel members were told that the drug in question was Valium and asked to reassess the severity of addiction in each case. At this point, the doctors opened their eyes but closed their minds. Received wisdom ruled:

None	*Slight*	*Moderate*	*Great*	*Severe*
36	9	5	0	0

Nevertheless, Roche was concerned and in 1976 the company convened a "Round Table" of nine US experts, under the chairmanship of Dr. Leo Hollister. The proceedings were later published as a brochure and used to promote Valium. The Round Table consensus was that physical dependence was rarely a problem in therapeutic use: "I have never seen a case of benzodiazepine dependence", said one selected expert; it was "an astonishingly unusual event," said another (Greenblatt 1976). "Valium cannot produce anything resembling addiction," said yet another; "it is only with extraordinarily high doses over a long period of time that we see tolerance and withdrawal effects" (Cohen 1976). The participants decided that, "abuse of diazepam has been grossly over-reported." The media were blamed for patients getting scared.

But where did Hollister stand? Earlier on, he had produced damning evidence on Librium and Valium, yet now he was presiding over consensus denial. Hollister explained that, after his earlier studies, he had been expecting "a flood of reports of withdrawal reactions" but it never came. "The probable reason is that patients abort these reactions early on because they think their original symptoms are returning, and they get back on the drug. So we never see the full-blown picture." This pretty much confirmed that there was a widespread dependence problem, but Hollister never pressed the point, and no one encouraged him to do so.

Back in Britain, Dr. John Marks had also set out to prove a negative, using a full-frontal NERO defence: "no evidence of risk equals evidence of no risk." Marks had been Managing Director of Roche UK but had by this time left the company for academic life. With help from Roche, he had compiled what he claimed was a full list of 118 published medical reports (1961-1977), which gave "at least minimal information" about benzodiazepine dependence. Claiming to make "every effort to be critical but unbiased," Marks then analysed each report. He began by rejecting 18 papers because, "inspection of the original publication has shown there is no evidence of dependence."

He excluded, for example, a 1975 report of "several patients" having withdrawal symptoms after routine treatment with benzos. Marks rejected it because, "the text quoted number of cases as 'several'." He also dismissed a report by Dr. Anthony Clift (1972), who had shown that long-term consumption of hypnotics could be greatly reduced simply by encouraging patients to use them cautiously. Clift had found no difference between dependence on barbiturates and benzodiazepines, but

Dr. Marks decided this was invalid, "as there is no clear evidence presented of dependence."

Among the remaining reports, Marks found 401 cases in which patients had also abused alcohol or other drugs, and 57 cases where they had not. On this basis, Marks coyly asked whether it was appropriate to blame the drug at all: "The concept of a dependence-producing 'capacity' or 'potential' which resides in a drug itself has been questioned by some authorities in respect of drugs other than narcotics. These authorities suggest it is more relevant to speak of 'dependence prone individuals' who abuse a variety of substances and can develop dependence on any or all of them." It was, said Marks, "widely agreed" that any risk with benzodiazepines was very much lower than with barbiturates. He then estimated a minuscule order of risk, by relating the numbers of *reported* cases of dependence to the total numbers of prescriptions for benzos over the years.

> "The dependence risk with benzodiazepines is very low and is estimated to be approximately one case per 5 million patient months 'at risk' for all recorded cases and probably less than one case per 50 million months in therapeutic use." (Marks 1978)

This analysis was absurd because it discounted everything that was unnoticed, uninvestigated and unreported. Later it became clear that fewer than one case in several thousand had ever been reported but Marks' conclusions were widely publicised and well received at the time.

Two years on, the UK regulators (then the Committee on the Review of Medicines) endorsed these conclusions, again assuming that no evidence of risk equals evidence of no risk (the NERO defence). The Committee arrived at its estimate by relating the 28 adverse drug reaction reports ("Yellow Cards") they had received from doctors, to the total numbers of prescriptions issued. This "Systematic Review of the Benzodiazepines" concluded: "The number dependent on benzodiazepines in the UK from 1960 to 1977 has been estimated to be 28 persons. This is equivalent to a dependence rate of 5 – 10 cases per million patient months" (CRM 1980).

The trouble with Ativan

And so the market grew. By the early 1980s, there were 17 different (but essentially similar) benzos on the UK market. Marketing sustained the illusion of uniqueness; another factor was variability of response. Age, gender, genetic and other factors meant different people reacted in different ways. If you gave two people the same dose of a benzo, one could end up with a concentration of the drug in the body 20-times higher than the other. But the significance of this was (and is) largely unknown.

The main thing that distinguished all these benzos was their "half-life", a measure of how long, on average, it took for the drug to clear the body.[4] Most of the Roche benzos had long half-lives. Their sales began to decline in the 1980s, because of worries about drug accumulation. These were prompted, not least, by the competition – notably the US company, John Wyeth. They had three intermediate half-life products on the market. Oxazepam was promoted as "preferred for the elderly" (Serax in the US, Serenid-D in the UK). Then there was temazepam – still the most popular sleeping pill in the UK – and lorazepam (Ativan) "for anxiety".

It was Ativan that eventually gave the game away. The problem was first revealed to a Belgian hospital psychiatrist, Dr. René de Buck; however, he ducked the evidence, delaying progress for a decade. De Buck was one of the first to test Ativan, before it came on the market in 1972. At Wyeth's prompting he gave high doses of Ativan to 30 anxious patients, for one month. On their own initiative, two patients stopped taking the test drug and both had convulsions – but De Buck's brief account of what happened was buried deep in the published report. In the all-important summary (abstract) of his paper, de Buck concluded: "lorazepam is a very safe drug." Wyeth naturally agreed. No further investigation was done; no warnings were given.

Why did Ativan finally reveal what had been a closely-guarded open secret for 20 years? One reason was the shorter half-life: withdrawal symptoms came on sooner and harder than with the longer-acting benzos, so there was less mistaking what they were. Another reason was the high dose. With regulatory approval, Wyeth recommended double dosages in some countries – exactly the same dose of lorazepam for Americans with "severe anxiety" as for Brits whose anxiety was "mild". The British regulators failed to notice this for over a decade.

The realisation of dependence on Ativan was slow to come. Eight years passed before the buried bits in de Buck's report were noticed (Dr. Marks missed them too) and by then other clinicians were starting to report the same. One of the first was a British psychiatrist, Dr. Peter Tyrer, but it happened only by chance. Tyrer had written to *The Lancet* (1979) to report a case of withdrawal convulsions from an antidepressant, but he mentioned in passing that the patient had stopped taking Ativan as well. That prompted a letter from a Canadian hospital team: they had seen two cases of withdrawal convulsions from Ativan in the previous year. Maybe the antidepressant wasn't responsible, but Ativan was?

Tyrer's response points again to the role of received wisdoms. He replied that this hadn't occurred to him and his colleagues, because they knew of no published

---

4 The mid-point measure is used, mainly because many drugs aren't cleared from the body at a constant rate, and the drug "half-life" is an average figure, because of variations in individual response.

reports of seizures following withdrawal from lorazepam and, "there is no indication that physical dependence on lorazepam or other benzos can take place over such a short time." But soon after, Tyrer changed his mind: he'd just seen another patient having withdrawal convulsions after stopping lorazepam on its own.

Tyrer went on to do the first systematic studies of benzodiazepine withdrawal, along with a team at the Maudsley Hospital in London, under Professor Malcolm Lader. In 1981, they established the existence of what they called, "normal dose dependence" – pretty much what had always happened with sedatives and tranquillisers of all kinds. From this point, there was no going back – but there was not much going forward either.

Finally in 1983, Wyeth sent out a "Dear Doctor" letter to all UK prescribers. Ostensibly a safety measure, it repeated advice about the need for gradual withdrawal after high-dose, long-term treatment with Ativan, to avoid what the company called, occasional "psychological" reactions. Wyeth also advised that 20 years' experience had shown the dependence risk to be one case per 50 million patient months. The regulators (CRM 1980) were in no position to disagree.

Meanwhile, Dr. John Marks (1983) had abandoned that estimate. He had decided there was a greater risk of dependence than he originally thought, especially with shorter-acting benzos, and with Ativan above all. Meanwhile, Wyeth, Roche and the other manufacturers did what they could to obstruct the introduction of the modest new warnings the UK regulators suggested, as well as the scheduling of benzos proposed by the WHO.

Xanax and Halcion

Two other benzodiazepines came on the market late in the day – both products of the US-based Upjohn Company (now part of the Pfizer empire). They were Xanax (alprazolam) for anxiety and Halcion (triazolam) for insomnia.

Xanax was the last benzo to be introduced in Britain, in 1983, but it was never much used. Having struggled to get the whole industry to agree to circulate even modest warnings about dependence risk, the government had finally decided to introduce a Limited List. From 1985, this restricted the number of benzos that could be prescribed on the National Health Service (NHS) at public expense.

Xanax was a casualty in the UK, but it is still hugely popular in North America. In 2002, alprazolam was still the 11th most prescribed drug in the US.[5] The dependence risk is still only faintly acknowledged in the small print warning of the Xanax label:

---

5 The most prescribed drug in the US (2002) was another drug of dependence, a synthetic opiate painkiller, hydrocodone.

"Some patients may prove resistant to all discontinuation regimens", i.e. once on, never off.

Of all the benzos, Halcion had the most troubled history of all. The trouble began in 1979 when a Dutch psychiatrist, Dr. Cees van der Kroef, reported that Halcion might cause acute psychotic reactions, paranoia and confused thinking. The national press and media picked up the story and caused such a stir that Halcion was almost immediately taken off the market in The Netherlands. It stayed off for the next ten years and was reinstated only at a much lower dose. As with Ativan, the original dose had been far too high. Meanwhile, Halcion had become the best selling hypnotic in the US, and in the world.

Concern about the behavioural effects of Halcion came to a head in 1989 when Professor Ian Oswald (from the sleep research unit in Edinburgh) wrote to the *Lancet* to say he thought that van der Kroef was right, and that Halcion should no longer be sold. Oswald proposed that agitation, amnesia and psychotic reactions constituted a syndrome, linked to rebound anxiety. Back in 1982, Oswald had found that the clash between the short half-life (two to five hours) and the 24-hour interval between doses taken each night meant that some users got agitated in the day – "between-dose withdrawal".

Oswald accused Upjohn of failing to investigate the drug properly, and of organising studies that would necessarily fail to establish the seriousness of this rebound anxiety. Then, in 1991, Dr. Kales' sleep research team in Pennsylvania published a new report that established that high therapeutic doses of Halcion consistently produced next-day memory impairment – "apparently far more so than either temazepam or placebo." Dr. Kales and others joined Oswald in suggesting that Halcion should be withdrawn from the market.

In August 1991, the temperature rose again, as Upjohn made a large out-of-court settlement in the US of a claim that Halcion had led a patient to murder her mother. This was one of several cases in which a US criminal court had dismissed or reduced murder charges, on the grounds the defendants had been under the influence of the drug. Upjohn began to face increasing numbers of civil actions both in the US and UK.

The re-investigation of Halcion led to the disclosure, for the first time, of crucial data about psychiatric adverse effects that investigators had recorded in an early study, but which Upjohn failed to disclose. The disclosure was dramatically orchestrated by *Panorama* (BBC-TV 1991). In September 1991 Upjohn sent the missing data to the UK and other authorities, apologising for a "transcription error". Halcion has been off the market in the UK, The Netherlands and several other countries, since then (Abraham & Sheppard 1999).

Triazolam remains available in the US, Canada and elsewhere, but subject to many warnings and restrictions on use. Above all, it is recommended only for short-term use – seven to ten days. In Canada, the mean duration of use in the mid-1990s was estimated at 1.7 years.

Slouching towards understanding

Common sense began to triumph over authority, leadership and expert opinion, but only through public protest. Sparks of understanding had begun to fly by the end of the 1970s, with US Congressional hearings about benzodiazepine prescribing and dependence, but they had made little impact on drug regulation. In Britain, the dawning came later but made more of a mark.

The UK turning point was 1985, when the BBC-TV programme, *That's Life* teamed up with MIND, (the UK's National Association of Mental Health), to survey the distressing evidence from thousands of benzo users. This and other media coverage helped to dispel the image of the "dependence prone". Class didn't come into it: anyone could get hooked, just as De Quincey had found. The enduring nature of the benzodiazepine problem was underlined by a later *Panorama* programme on the subject, (BBC-TV 2001). The role of the media and *Panorama* crops up in this story again and again.

By the mid-1980s, the official count of 28 cases of dependence was looking very thin: credible estimates were suggesting that 500,000 people might be dependent on benzos, maybe more. As the problem unfolded, there was increasing concern that long-term use of benzos also carried risks of cognitive and mental impairment, amnesia and "emotional blunting". These were the main focus in the legal action that began in the UK in 1988, initially with several hundred people claiming compensation for dependence on Ativan. It seems puzzling there was no legal action in the US, where litigation is part of the way of life. Perhaps it was because of the greater emphasis on the triumph of individual free will: the stigma of dependence made it that much harder to link problems to prescribing of the drug.

The legal action in Britain finally stirred the drug regulators. In 1988, the Committee on Safety of Medicines (CSM) finally acknowledged the risk of dependence in a low-key statement advising short-term use and gradual withdrawal. The CSM denied there was anything special about Ativan (lorazepam): "No epidemiological evidence is available to suggest that one benzodiazepine is more responsible for the development of dependency or withdrawal symptoms than another."

But the year before, Dr. Heather Ashton from Newcastle University had sent the CSM evidence to the contrary, based largely on clinical experience with over 500 dependent patients, one-third of them on lorazepam. Ashton told the CSM that the recommended dose of lorazepam was too high, and that the lack of low-dose tablets frustrated gradual withdrawal. In 1989, Wyeth brought in a half-strength tablet and the recommended dosage was halved. It was all very discretely done: neither doctors nor patients were alerted, just a change in the small print, no more.

By 1992, over 12,000 claimants had joined the legal action, most complaining about Ativan, though diazepam and other benzos were also involved. These claims were mainly funded under the UK Legal Aid scheme for people with low incomes –

but finally the government pulled the plug. With exhaustive help from the manufacturers, the case had dragged on and on, reaching the point where legal costs threatened to exceed the amounts claimed in compensation. One or two cases are still running even today, but the vast majority simply faded away.

Long after the horse had bolted, the Royal College of Psychiatrists and the American Psychiatric Association (APA) issued knowing reports, resisting any suggestion of blame. The APA task force not only acknowledged the dependence problem, but also made a special plea that the word "dependence" be used to distinguish between what happened in therapeutic use from problems of "addiction" and "abuse":

> "Historically, long-term, high-dose, physiological dependence has been called addiction, a term that implies recreational use. In recent years, however, it has become apparent that physiological adaptation develops and discontinuance symptoms can appear after regular daily therapeutic dose administration ... in some cases after a few days or weeks of administration. Since therapeutic prescribing is clearly not recreational abuse, the term dependence is preferred to addiction, and the abstinence syndrome is called a discontinuance syndrome." (APA 1990)

Within a few years, the APA would completely abandon that definition – not just moving the goalposts, but de-camping to another ballpark. By the mid-1990s, antidepressants like Prozac had become established in place of the benzodiazepines, and "dependence" would be a problem no more.

4
Drugs to defeat depression[1]

Present day remedies for anxiety, depression and mental distress date from the 1990s. By this time, tranquilliser use had declined and dependence was officially seen as a problem. Doctors then began to prescribe a new class of "antidepressants" instead, and for longer and in larger doses than before. Prozac started this trend; it spawned a raft of "blockbusters" – Paxil/Seroxat, Zoloft/Lustral, Cipramil/Celexa and Efexor/Effexor – all still with us today.

Until the 1960s, drugs played a lesser part in the treatment of what was then known as "depression". A *Lancet* annotation (1955) acknowledged that, "most psychiatrists would regard them as ancillary to other modes of treatment", but went on to acknowledge the value of amphetamine-barbiturate combinations. The idea was synergy: amphetamines lifted mood and the barbiturate kept the lift within bounds. Through general practice prescribing, and growing diversion for illicit use, both drugs were increasingly consumed. Meanwhile, older habits died hard; this correspondent chided the *Lancet* for failing to mention the remedy he preferred:

> "Sir, – Your annotation... does not mention opium. I think this is still a valuable drug in the treatment of minor depressive syndromes, many of them with anxiety, which are so commonly seen in psychiatric outpatient practice ... I have been prescribing (it) for many years. I have never seen a patient become addicted to it (it is extremely unpleasant to take) and only once has a patient attempted to use it for ostensible suicidal purposes ..." (Skottowe 1955)

The story of modern antidepressants also begins in 1955 – with iproniazid, a drug for tuberculosis. By chance, it was found to produce "excessive good spirits", making some patients "feel 'too well'" with the result that they failed to observe ordinary precautions, overexerted themselves, or discontinued treatment prematurely" (Kline 1964).

---

1 For a more detailed, fully referenced account of the pre-1997 events described in this chapter, see Medawar 1997.

Iproniazid had this effect because it inhibited an enzyme (monoamine oxidase), which inactivated noradrenaline and other neurotransmitters – substances that transmit impulses (from nerve fibres to nerve cells) in the brain. This led to the development of more potent inhibitors than iproniazid, and also promoted new thinking about the biochemical basis of depression and the actions of antidepressant drugs. The original thinking was that depression was due to a deficiency of brain noradrenaline, and that manic symptoms came from excess.

Four MAOIs (Monoamine Oxidase Inhibitors) were on the market by the end of the 1950s. They were originally described as "psychic energisers" but rank as the earliest drugs still licensed for used as "antidepressants". Imipramine arrived a year or two later: this was the first of many "tricyclic" antidepressants. Originally promoted as "psychostimulants", they were developed through research on antihistamines (anti-allergy drugs).

The "tricyclics" are still very widely used, though their popularity began to decline in the 1990s, with the introduction of a new class of antidepressant, the Selective Serotonin Reuptake Inhibitors (SSRIs). The SSRIs, exemplified by Prozac (fluoxetine), became hugely popular: in Britain, by the start of the 21st century, antidepressant consumption levels were approaching those of the benzodiazepines at their peak.

First steps in treating depression

The scientific medical literature of the 1960s suggests that the original antidepressants were given a hesitant welcome – partly because of uncertainty about what "depression" was. Until these drugs were discovered, the extent of depression was unknown, and there were no good estimates of market size. Even so, it was a relief to have any drug that could relieve what depression was then perceived to be, because the alternatives were grim.

The standard treatment for severe depression was electro-convulsive therapy (ECT). Until the mid-20th century it was given without a muscle relaxant: later, benzodiazepines were used to prevent the fractures and bone dislocations that were frequent "complications". The uncontrolled convulsions caused sudden, massive muscular contractions: one in five men (one in 20 women) could expect fractures of the middle back vertebrae after ECT treatment. The standard textbooks took for granted that the benefits outweighed these risks: "Such fractures may cause considerable pain and discomfort, but they are usually not disabling and do not, in the opinion of workers in the field, constitute a contraindication to further shock therapy" (Drill 1958).

In those days, doctors recognised two main kinds of depression: in the classic, "endogenous" depression, the mentally and physically overwhelmed patient felt only tortured thoughts, with head sunk in hands. The word, endogenous, signalled a cause that came from within and naturally led to talk of chemical imbalances and wayward molecules. By contrast, "exogenous" depression indicated some morbid response to the trials of life. Either way, "depression" was regarded as a serious handicap and carried some stigma; it was "not fashionable to be depressed" (Kline 1964).

Early assessments of the new antidepressants again revealed a gulf between the proposed benefits of drugs and their performance in controlled trials. The hard evidence was thin: it did suggest that the MAOIs and tricyclics improved on placebo, but the difference was small, and not "as one might have anticipated after reading published reports of uncontrolled trials" (Cole 1964).

Later, the US National Institutes of Health (NIH) found much the same. The NIH team analysed 490 studies reported in 71 leading medical journals from 1955 to 1966: "the methodology of drug research is of more significance to the outcome of a clinical trial than is the drug being studied ... In well-designed studies, the differences between the effectiveness of antidepressant drugs and placebo are not impressive" (Smith et al. 1969).

During the 1970s and 1980s there were many attempts to develop new drugs, but more effective antidepressants did not emerge. Even so, the illusion of clinical effectiveness was maintained, partly because of the miraculous effects these drugs sometimes seemed to have. The historian, Edward Shorter (1997) has noted, "how resurrectionlike the recovery from depression can be, a recovery that each new generation of antidepressant drugs believes that it alone has achieved; witness the resurrectionist rhetoric accompanying the introduction of the drug Prozac." Each miracle fuels hope for many more.

But did improvements come from treatment or something else? Doctors could never be sure, partly because depression was cyclical – descending, then lifting on its own – and also because of placebo effects, the non-drug factors that led to recovery. No-one knew much about them, only that placebo effects were pervasive, subtle and sometimes magically strong.

> "I am sure many colleagues have shared with me the following embarrassing experience. I prescribe a tricyclic drug for an outpatient with a typical or 'classical' endogenous depression. The patient returns to see me three or four weeks later. She is very much better. When I remind her of the importance of continuing drug therapy despite the improvement, she smiles and says 'Oh doctor, the tablets did not agree with me, so I stopped taking them after the first two or three days'." (Merry 1972)

The great difference between then and now is that depression used to be thought of as a self-limiting state of mind. After two decades of experience with the original antidepressants, the great medical textbooks and the experts emphasised that most cases of depression would cure themselves. The prevailing wisdom was that depression usually needed no drug treatment – a heresy today.

> "... depression is, on the whole, one of the psychiatric conditions with the best prognosis for eventual recovery with or without treatment. Most depressions are self-limited and the spontaneous or placebo-induced improvement rate is often high." (Cole 1964)

> "perhaps 80% or more of depressed patients will eventually recover without treatment." (Byck 1975)

> "affective disorders have a very high rate of spontaneous remission, provided sufficient time passes." (Baldessarini 1980)

Medical opinion has since radically changed: today's drugs are barely more effective than the older drugs, yet drug intervention is now seen as imperative. Certainly in the US, and increasingly elsewhere, the "failure" to prescribe would be thought negligent, perhaps legally indefensible. The impulse to prescribe is reinforced by a climate of fear; the nature and strength of it can be felt in the fearsome size of the estimates made of the dangers of depression.[2]

Belief in the importance of drug treatment for depression became inflamed during the 1990s – the age of Prozac and the many similar drugs that dominate the market today. Brave new talk about the biological basis of depression helped to set the scene. The welcome rumour was that depression was actually a deficiency state – and that normal mood could be restored by boosting levels, not of noradrenaline, but another key neurotransmitter, serotonin. The message was that depressed people needed antidepressants just as some diabetics needed insulin – and the drugs they needed were Selective Serotonin Reuptake Inhibitors (SSRIs).

There were and are many reasons for doubting that levels of brain serotonin were the key to depression (Healy 1998); one was simply that SSRIs were demonstrably no more effective than other antidepressants that had no effect on the serotonin system at all. Another reason was that SSRIs increase levels of brain serotonin from the outset, but antidepressant effects take about two weeks to "kick in". If serotonin were a simple key, why would antidepressants not work in about one case in three and often prove hardly more effective than a placebo?

Serotonin deficiency theories were nevertheless widely promoted and sincerely believed. The widespread acceptance of these ideas had little to do with the facts, but

---

2 One widely quoted statistic is that "15% of people with depression end up killing themselves" – Dr. Rodrigo Muñoz, past president of the American Psychiatric Association (Noonan & Cowley 2002). See also Wolpert (1999): "around 10 to 15 per cent of depressed patients will eventually die by suicide" – which implies about one suicide case per week for the average GP. These figures are upwards of 300-times the true figure. The 15% estimate came from limited hospital studies of severe, intractable depression and would not apply to the great majority of people who might these days be regarded as depressed.

they were easy on the mind. The Pharmas primed and pumped out this message and it was widely received as welcome news. The notion that depression resulted from some simple lack or imbalance of brain serotonin was both persuasive and misleading, a fine example of the Conspiracy of Goodwill.

The notion of "chemical imbalance", with serotonin to prove it, was something of a placebo for everyone. It made psychiatry seem more credible, scientific and potent; it helped doctors to persuade patients to accept treatment, and it helped the Pharmas to sell their SSRIs. The "serotonin hypothesis" made depression seem more "normal" by reducing the "stigma" of mental illness. Talk of "disease" and the notion of chemical deficiency relieved patients of blame and responsibility and of the feeling they might be failures who had brought misery on themselves. Above all, the idea that SSRIs worked by correcting a serotonin deficiency underwrote the notion of drug effectiveness, and all but scotched the possibility of dependence as well. It suggested that people were not "dependent" on these drugs but really did need them.

Growing the antidepressant market

The first SSRI (zimeldine) was introduced in 1980, but was taken off the market soon after, when found to cause rare but serious neurological reactions. Next came fluvoxamine (Faverin/Luvox); it made no great impact, then or since. But then came fluoxetine (Prozac) and that began a huge expansion of the market for depression – just as the benzos went into a serious decline. Prozac became the focus of overwhelming volumes of air time and web space, scores of books, millions of words in print. Prozac would dominate the antidepressant market throughout the 1990s, in spite of fierce competition – at first from paroxetine and sertraline, later from venlafaxine and citalopram. When Prozac finally came off patent in 2001, paroxetine (Paxil, Seroxat) took the lead. See Table:

Year of UK launch	*Drug name*	*Brand names*	*Manufacturer*
1987	fluvoxamine	Faverin, Luvox	Duphar, later Solvay
1989	fluoxetine	Prozac	Eli Lilly & Co
1990	sertraline	Lustral, Zoloft	Pfizer
1991	paroxetine	Seroxat, Paxil, Aropax	SmithKline Beecham, later GlaxoSmithKline
1995	venlafaxine	Efexor, Effexor	Wyeth
1995	citalopram	Cipramil, Celexa	Lundbeck, Forest
1995	nefazodone	Dutonin, Serzone	Bristol Myers Squibb

Patents and brand names mean everything to the Pharmas. In order to stimulate the development of new drugs, global laws protect patents, giving the inventors exclusive marketing rights for up to about 20 years. While products are on patent, companies can charge what they will. Thereafter, generic drug manufacturers can sell unbranded versions of the identical drug, usually at a fraction of the originator's price.[3] Around 2000, for example, a month's supply of an unbranded tricyclic would have cost about US$2.50; a branded version of the same drug, or any of the SSRIS, would have cost around 30-times more.

At prices like these, what was the basis of demand? Much of it came down to promotion that went far further and wider than any real difference between the drugs – which, as in the past, came down mainly to safety in overdose. Quite early on, recognition of a potentially dangerous interaction between MAOIs and certain foods (e.g. cheese, yeast extracts) had helped to promote the tricyclics; they in turn lost some ground to the "quadricyclics", newer drugs promoted as safer in overdose. Then came Prozac and the other SSRIS: they were claimed to be more palatable at higher doses and safer in overdose too.

The manufacturer of Prozac was the US-based Eli Lilly & Co. It left the hype to its agents, but played this safety advantage low-key: there was no campaigning about people taking alternatives to Prozac until the day they die. The tone was set by Dr. Stuart Montgomery, giving the chairman's summary at a 1994 Lilly-sponsored symposium. Montgomery concluded that, for both legal and practical reasons, "it is difficult to justify the first-line use of toxic antidepressants when safer alternatives are available." In fact, the therapeutic gain was small, and had no discernable effect on reduction in suicide. It is true that SSRIS are less toxic than tricyclics – but "the overall incidence of death by suicide does not appear to have been reduced as patients have resorted to other means of suicide" (Reynolds 1996).

Safety in overdose was not what made Prozac and the others the major blockbusters they came to be. What really caused the SSRIS to take off was heavy demand in response to saturation publicity in lay media. How much of it was sponsored, prompted, catalysed or bought is not clear and never will be. However, the hallmarks were a wealth of anecdotal evidence about marvellous drug effects, the transformation and enhancement of lifestyle, and the devastating effects of depression and just plain coping with life.

Two best-selling books by independent authors set the tone. One was *Prozac Nation*, a vivid, painful and self-conscious account by a young American woman, lurching from one life crisis to another, who found much comfort in Prozac along

3 The cost of drug ingredients represents only a small fraction of the retail price. The ingredients reportedly represented 3.5% of the retail price of Paxil; 0.9% of the cost of Zoloft and 0.05% of the cost of Prozac (importeddrugs.com, September 2003).

the way (Wurtzel 1996). Presumably unconsciously, she gave vivid descriptions of strong placebo effects at work, including faith in her doctor and in the pure magic of serotonin:

> "Then there's Prozac. It's so new at this point that Dr. Sterling still refers to it as fluoxetine. Prozac, like Zoloft, Paxil and other drugs of its type which were not yet available as I lay in Stillman in 1988, acts only on serotonin. It is very pure in its chemical objectives. Its drug family will come to be known as selective serotonin reuptake inhibitors (SSRIs), and it can act very powerfully and directly within its narrow domain. Since fluoxetine's aims are less scattershot than that of its predecessors, it tends to have fewer side effects."

The other book, *Listening to Prozac*, had by then made its mark. The author was Dr. Peter Kramer (1993), a somewhat beamed-up East Coast psychiatrist whose proffered credentials suggested keen identification with the world of *Startrek* and Captain Kirk: "My quest has led me deep into territories whose results inform my clinical work but whose culture and customs are foreign: cellular physiology, pharmacology, history of medicine, animal ethology, descriptive psychiatry ..." His book boasted scholarship, but pure soap kept it at the top of the bestseller list for months. His book promoted the idea of fluoxetine as a sensitive chemical instrument, perhaps the key to personality transformation, happiness and profound fulfilment in life.

Kramer's book optimistically explained some of the very little known about the chemical niceties of mood regulation, but the nub of it was this: "since you only live once, why not do it as a blonde? Why not as a peppy blonde?" Where the science faltered, Kramer turned to patients to explain: "'Three dates a weekend', Tess told me. 'I must be wearing a sign on my forehead!' Within weeks of starting Prozac, Tess settled into a satisfying dating routine with men."

Eli Lilly aloofly emphasised its distance from all this, chiding over-enthusiasts and choosing sober words to emphasise that Prozac was an important drug for a dire state of mind. Lilly wanted to be seen as having nothing to do with all the hype. Indeed Kramer spelled it out: his contact with Lilly had been very limited and the company was in no way responsible for his conclusions.

Other reports from the field might have had Lilly running scared, albeit all the way to the bank. The most alarming identified a US West Coast clinical psychologist who had apparently put all of his 700 patients on Prozac (Toynbee 1995). Alas, he never published the results.

Where Prozac led, rival drugs followed, as did phenomenal public demand. Eli Lilly and the other SSRI Pharmas helped the market to grow. They teamed up with the psychiatric establishment and selected experts. Each helped the other to expand reputations and the market for depression, and between them, they helped the increasing numbers diagnosed as "depressed".

From the early 1990s, professional initiatives came in waves to encourage both patients and doctors to recognise and treat depression more aggressively, and to use higher doses of antidepressants over longer periods of time. Teams of sponsored and chosen experts rewrote and transformed the treatment guidelines for depression. At the same time, they formally redefined the condition known as "depression" in ways that opened up the market as never before.

The foremost definitions of depression were developed by panels of experts convened by the American Psychiatric Association (APA), an organisation close to the Pharmas and financially deeply dependent on them. The APA's *Diagnostic and Statistical Manual* was originally compiled in 1952 as a tool for the national census of mental disability, but it developed into a diagnostic bible.

The fourth edition, known as DSM-IV, became internationally recognised as the prime guide to recognising depression and, implicitly, when and how to treat it. Over the years, the APA produced a threefold increase in "diagnostic entities", variants of depressive illness: there were 106 different kinds of depression in DSM-I, and over 350 in DSM-IV (1994).

This relentless expansion of definition meant that, "depression in the vocabulary of post 1960s American psychiatry has become tantamount to dysphoria, meaning unhappiness, in combination with loss of appetite and difficulty sleeping" (Shorter 1997). In authenticating more and more diagnoses, the DSM process helped to promote a dramatic increase in drug use (the dominant treatment mode) for conditions that became wider and wider in scope. The details of the transition are mostly a mystery, but the nub of it came to be openly acknowledged in the marketing trade press:

> "Watching the Diagnostic and Statistical Manual of Mental Disorders (DSM) balloon in size over the decades to its current phonebook size would have us believe that the world is a more unstable place today than ever. In reality, the increasing number of identified emotional conditions has resulted from breaking the problems into their component parts to better assess treatment options. Not surprisingly, many of these newly coined conditions were brought to light through direct funding by pharmaceutical companies, in research, in publicity or both." (Parry 2003)

The way in which depression was defined also helped market expansion by promoting checklist diagnosis. This was done, "by counting symptoms, preferably those that are easily observable, and those that are easily agreed upon by direct questioning of the patient" (Van Praag 1996). The nub of it was conveyed by a full-page Prozac advertisement (1993) that summarised the nine major symptoms of New Depression. Only three ticks were needed for a plausible diagnosis; then Prozac could be for you:

First line ... for all nine symptoms of depression

❑ Depressed mood	❑ Sleep disturbances	❑ slowness/restlessness
❑ Loss of interest	❑ Weight/appetite change	❑ guilt/feelings of worthlessness
❑ Fatigue	❑ Lack of concentration	❑ thoughts of death

Prozac, fluoxetine hydrochloride

In time – especially through Direct-To-Consumer Advertising (DTCA) – the diagnostic criteria became softer still. This was the message on Wyeth's Effexor website (2003):

The Change You Deserve

- Are these symptoms of depression interfering with your life?
- Not involved with family and friends the way you used to be?
- Low on energy?
- Not motivated to do the things you once looked forward to doing?
- Not feeling as good as you used to?

If you're experiencing symptoms of depression and you're not where you want to be, talk to your doctor about your treatment options.

The credibility of the SSRIs was built not so much on their effectiveness, as on professional and public belief in the need for treatment. The 1990s marked the beginning of an era of intense concern and publicity about the serious nature of depression: it was widespread, closely linked to suicide; severely distressing and badly under-treated. The time had come to fight "the stigma" of depression and to encourage sufferers to get the help they deserved.

The professional and lay media drove these messages home, persuading whole nations to examine their state of mind. Generating publicity was the key objective in countless public relations programs, and there were always pegs and hooks to hang these stories on. Ritual opportunities were provided, for example, by many US National Health Observances. Officially recognised occasions included: Childhood Depression Awareness Day, National Anxiety Disorders Screening Day, Mental Health Month, National Suicide Awareness Week, National Trauma Awareness Month, Mental Illness Awareness Week and National Depression Screening Day.

Alongside this intense promotion came ringing professional endorsements and urgent statements of concern: a much publicised US Consensus Statement on the Under-treatment of Depression reported that, "the vast majority of those treated with antidepressant medication are not prescribed an adequate dose for a long enough time"; the extent of under-diagnosis meant that, "only about one in ten of those suffering from depression received adequate treatment" (NDMDA 1997).

Meanwhile, in Britain, the SSRI Pharmas joined in the sponsorship of a major "Defeat Depression" campaign.[4] It was orchestrated by the Royal College of Psychiatrists with the Royal College of General Practitioners rather in tow. The thrust of the campaign (1992-1997) was to explain depression and encourage people to recognise it; to persuade sufferers to come forward for treatment; and to emphasise there should be no stigma attached to such a commonplace but distressing illness and a major social problem as well.

The Defeat Depression campaign focused on what the organisers believed were widely-held misconceptions. One was the general failure to recognise depression for the complex and hidden disease it might be: the campaign was a response to "the tragedy that, despite the availability of effective treatments, 70 per cent of sufferers go untreated." Another focus of the campaign concerned the public's failure to recognise the importance of drug treatment, and the value of the new SSRIs.

Do antidepressants work?

Apart from safety in overdose, the main advantage claimed for the SSRIs was that users liked them more than tricyclics and alternatives, when prescribed at the full recommended doses. That was made to seem very important because few doctors actually did prescribe tricyclics at the full recommended dose. Doctors were well aware that many patients disliked these older drugs, because of the strong and unpleasant side effects – so they traditionally prescribed them at well below the recommended dose. If they hadn't, many patients would have refused.

Repeated surveys in the 1970s and 1980s showed that about nine out of ten GPs prescribed tricyclic antidepressants below the recommended dose. The experts and specialists had routinely complained about this, but to little effect – and so it came to be that, for over 25 years, depression was routinely treated with "sub-therapeutic" doses of tricyclics. "Sub-therapeutic" doses were, literally, doses at which there was no measurable difference between the effects of antidepressants and dummy pills.

---

4 "The campaign's total income amounted to £449,800 of which only £129,530 (28.8%) came from pharmaceutical companies. It is true that most, but not all, of the companies who contributed were manufacturers of SSRI antidepressants ... As to the College's policy with regard to accepting financial assistance from commercial organisations, we are prepared to accept funds from any reputable organisation provided there are no strings attached ..." Letter from R.E. Kendell, President of the Royal College of Psychiatrists, to *Social Audit* (28 November 1997).

That is how it was for the best part of three decades: although depression was typically treated with potent drugs (with sometimes bad side effects), their actual effectiveness in treating depression was equivalent to that of a strong placebo. Many clinicians and patients would have rather assumed that recovery was linked to some specific drug effect, but there was no scientific proof. Even so, from the early 1990s, a new spirit of intervention caught on. Under the influence of heavy marketing, depression suddenly became a widespread "disease", though readily "conquered" thanks to the SSRIs.

The selling point, that more patients could tolerate the full dose with SSRIs, still didn't make the SSRIs any more effective in treating depression than the tricyclics and other drugs had been. This is clear because tricyclics are still widely used, not only as antidepressants in their own right – but also as the main yardstick (comparator drugs) for testing the efficacy of SSRIs and newer antidepressants. Extraordinarily, all the evidence shows that all antidepressants, old and new, have one key thing in common. In terms of effectiveness, there is no measurable difference[5] between them.

However challenging this might have seemed to "biological psychiatry", the evidence from controlled clinical trials was overwhelming and never in dispute. Over the years, scores of different antidepressants have been tried and spoken for, but the evidence consistently showed that their effect on depression was indistinguishable. The old and new were all officially "effective" – that is to say, stronger than placebo. In practice, that meant something like an average 60% response to active drug, compared to about 40% on placebo.

Prozac and the other SSRIs were not exceptions to this rule, and there was no good evidence that their effectiveness had anything much to do with their distinguishing chemical characteristics. Yes, antidepressants can and do "work" – but they seem to have little specific effect on depression. One might suit someone better, or not – but across the board, they all proved much the same.

Given the essential similarities between dozens of different drugs, promotional efforts naturally focused on the prevalence and severity of depression. Doctors were alerted to its many and subtle manifestations. They were told to look out for conditions labelled as "masked", "smiling" and "hidden" depression, and it was never clear where "anxiety" stopped and "depression" began. It had long been accepted that "anxiety" was a major part of "depression" but there is still controversy about

---

5 There are unquestionably differences that show up from user to user, and differences in drug profiles (as with benzodiazepines, barbiturates etc) – but no antidepressant drug manufacturer has ever proved to the satisfaction of the drug regulators the existence of any global superiority of one drug over another in treating depression. If such differences existed, they would of course be prominently advertised. They are not. This suggests a remarkable lack of specificity in drugs used to treat depression.

which was what. Some believe they are variants of a single disorder; others suppose they are distinct but overlapping entities. Either way, pretty much everyone agrees that most patients with depression can be diagnosed as anxious too.

The overlap between anxiety and depression is prominent in an important diagnostic tool, the Hamilton Rating Scale for Depression (Hamilton 1967). This "HAM-D" scale was originally designed just as a checklist for clinical practice, but is still the most widely used measure of depression, in drug trials.[6] Because the HAM-D scale includes many questions about "anxiety", an effective anti-anxiety drug may substantially affect the score for "depression" too. The distinction between depression and anxiety was also blurred by the new, dominant theories about the biological basis of depression, and the role of serotonin (5-HT), because serotonin is closely linked to anxiety too.[7]

To this extent, marketing and labelling began to count more and more (Healy 1990, 1991), and there was some "repositioning" of anxiety through the promotion of depression. During the early 1990s, anxiety went on the back-burner and depression became the dominant "disease". People who had been anxious, tended to be diagnosed as depressed; later most of the SSRIs were used for anxiety too.

The consumption of antidepressants over the years shows the transformation that came with the SSRIs. There was initial growth in the 1960s as the first antidepressants caught on; thereafter, consumption remained stable for the next 20 years. Then came the SSRIs and an explosive surge in use. Meanwhile, the effectiveness of the drugs had never really changed:

Number of NHS prescriptions for antidepressants (millions) in England and Wales

1961	1971	1981	1991	2001
1.4	7.1	7.9	8.9	25

Testing the efficacy of SSRIs

Do antidepressants work? The definitive answer is the legal one. A company can market a medicinal drug only with a licence, which is granted only when drug efficacy (i.e. superiority over placebo) has been proved. Most countries require this and

6 It goes without saying that clinical testing for levels of brain serotonin is not an option.

7 "... a great number of new compounds, with relatively specific actions on the 5-HT system ... have begun to appear on the market. Are they anxiolytic or antidepressant or both? The overview, above, of the behavioural effects mediated through 5-HT receptors suggests that 5-HT has more to do with anxiety than depression. This however, is an issue that is likely to be confounded greatly by the efforts of drug companies to market their products" (Healy 1991).

have agencies to enforce the law. The Food & Drug Administration (FDA) rules in the US.

Licensing ultimately depends on the results of clinical drug trials. They are regarded as the gold standard of medical scientific evidence, the closest approximation of a true and fair view. However, they are only approximations, and even the strictest regulators let much go by. For example, in spite of the overlap between "anxiety" and "depression", the FDA approved fluoxetine (Prozac) on the strength of efficacy trials in which people took anti-anxiety drugs at the same time.

The FDA (1988) relied on four pivotal studies designated as "adequate and well-controlled trials which provided evidence of efficacy" of fluoxetine, by comparison with placebo. In three of these four trials, one-quarter of the enrolled patients (135/540) took benzodiazepines (or chloral) as well as fluoxetine. If these 135 patients are excluded from the analysis in these three trials, fluoxetine does not show statistically significant efficacy over placebo. The one study that did prohibit the use of other such medicines was also the only one of the four to find no statistically significant difference between fluoxetine and placebo (Breggin 1994).

Another procedure that skewed results involved selecting patients to take part in trials, only after a preliminary screening to eliminate those who responded to placebo. This is standard practice today. The procedure involves taking a baseline measure on the Hamilton scale (HAM-D), then putting everyone on placebo for a week. Anyone whose HAM-D rating drops to below, say, 80% of the original value is then excluded from the trial. This makes a trial more sensitive as a way of finding out how the drug performs in test subjects who don't respond to placebo. However, as a measure of what happens in practice, it makes the test drug look much better; it also grossly underestimates the strength of placebo effects:

> "A few years ago, we tried an experimental design in one of our studies which we hoped would eliminate 'placebo reactors' and increase our sensitivity in distinguishing between drugs. All depressed patients who entered the hospital and were candidates for the study were first placed on a week of placebo treatment. At the end of the week, the psychiatrist was then asked to make a decision as to whether the patient should be admitted to the study ... We lost 50% of our potential sample, as that number of patients had shown a degree of spontaneous improvement which would have confounded the effects of future treatment. The tendency of depressed patients to improve spontaneously certainly creates difficulties in the clinical evaluation of drugs." (Hollister 1972)

The expectations of patients and investigators – both hoping that new drugs will improve on the old – complicate matters even more. Hence the requirement for "blindness" in drug trials – normally the "double-blind" procedure when neither investigators nor patients know whether they are giving or taking the test drug or a placebo. The regulators require evidence from properly blinded studies; however antidepressant side effects are distinctive and well known, often a give-away to all parties concerned. The regulators presumed blindness over the years, in spite of the evidence it was never there:

> "Most antidepressant drugs cause side effects which are recognisable by experienced investigators in a significant proportion of patients. Patients who come into the consulting room for assessment, perhaps for the sixth time and rather bored with the whole thing, but with their mouths so dry that one can hear their tongues scraping and clicking about in their mouths, are likely to be taking, say, amitryptyline, rather than the placebo." (Leyburn 1967)

If it was hard to improve on standards of blindness, it would have been quite feasible to measure the degree of unblinding – and therefore the validity of the study. However, in the absence of any regulatory requirement, this was (and is) rarely done:

> "... asking clinicians and subjects to identify the treatment condition can serve as a model for assessing blindness in larger scale studies with positive results. This strategy is simple to perform, cost-effective, and may enhance our ability to evaluate the internal validity of any outcome study." However, "a Medline review did not reveal any published report specifically relating to unblinding with SSRIs." (Piasecki et al. 2002)

These and other factors confounded test results, and helped to create the impression that the new SSRIs really were different and special. Only later in the 1990s did the mundane reality begin to show. By then, there were enough controlled studies for meta-analyses (the pooled results of several comparable trials) to show there were in fact few significant differences between the old and new. The SSRIs were not really more effective, nor obviously more acceptable to most patients: in general practice, over half of all patients stopped taking SSRIs within two to three months of starting them (Inman et al. 1993).

In time, doubts grew about the real superiority of SSRIs over placebo. Meta-analyses of controlled trials also suggested that placebo effects accounted for about three-quarters of the benefit attributed to active drugs (Kirsch & Sapirstein 1998). An analysis of the efficacy data submitted to the FDA between 1987 and 1999, for the six most popular US antidepressants found that "approximately 80% of the response to medication was duplicated in placebo control groups." In short, the advantages of antidepressants over placebo were usually statistically significant – sufficient to secure a marketing licence – but their clinical advantage proved small (Kirsch et al. 2003).

The difference between drug and "active placebo" was still less impressive. Using an "active placebo" meant lacing an otherwise inert drug with, for example, just enough atropine to mimic the drying up effects of a tricyclic antidepressant. Though this improved the standard of blinding, few such studies were done – but those that were consistently failed to demonstrate the superiority of the test drug over placebo (Moncrieff et al. 1998).

The complexities that arose in testing for SSRI efficacy underline the problems involved in measuring more subtle adverse effects, especially those that affected relatively few people. Thus, the allegations that SSRIs could induce violence and suicidal behaviour first surfaced in the early 1990s (Teicher et al. 1993) but remained non-proven through the next decade. Such evidence was hard to measure when few people were affected, especially when most evidence was missing or withheld (Healy 2003).

The risk of dependence

When the MAOIs and the tricyclics first arrived, there was some concern about their dependence potential, as the labels "psychostimulant" and "psychic energiser" might imply. "In view of the euphoria sometimes produced (by amitryptyline) there may be a small risk of addiction in susceptible individuals" (Fullerton & Boardman 1959). However, such concerns diminished before too long. Confidence grew in the idea that the new drugs had some specific action on depression, and there was little danger of drug-seeking behaviour. "Addiction to increasing the dose is not acquired, since raising the dose produces unpleasant side-effects" (Sargant 1961).

Even so, right from the outset, there was reason to believe that antidepressant withdrawal could be a problem – with the added risk that withdrawal symptoms were not easily recognised for what they were:

> "The withdrawal syndrome complicates the evaluation of patients after drug discontinuation since both patients and physicians often interpret the onset of symptoms as an upsurge of 'anxiety' related to incipient relapse, and resume treatment with the gratifying subsidence of the 'anxiety'. This may cause both patients and physicians to overvalue the importance of the medication to the patient's stability." (Kramer et al. 1961)

Later, Professor Ian Oswald (1971) did sleep studies, measuring the withdrawal effects with the tricyclic antidepressant, imipramine. He characterised it as "a drug of dependence not abuse." Oswald found, "withdrawal abnormalities after imipramine, maximal after about four days and lasting a month ..."

The first major published review of antidepressant withdrawal (Dilsaver & Greden 1984) reported "considerable variation in the symptomatology developing when antidepressant dosage is decreased or these drugs are discontinued." Four main manifestations of withdrawal were described: gastrointestinal and general bodily distress with or without anxiety and agitation; sleep disturbances; tremor and movement disorders and paradoxical activation or mania. The review concluded that, "the incidence of significant symptomatology following antidepressant withdrawal is surprisingly high." Later the independent *Drug & Therapeutics Bulletin* (1986) circulated a review to all doctors in the UK, saying much the same:

> "The withdrawal of antidepressants can produce changes in mood, appetite and sleep that are apt to be incorrectly misinterpreted as indicating a depressive relapse ... The probability of depressive relapse is low in the days and weeks after the discontinuation of antidepressants, and the cumulative probability of relapse increases as a function of time when the patient is medication free ... In contrast, the frequency of antidepressant withdrawal symptoms is high in the first 2 to 14 days following the last dose."

Finally, in 1990, the first formal warnings about antidepressant withdrawal appeared in the main UK prescribing guide, the *British National Formulary.* These warnings did not, and still do not, mention the root cause of all the iatrogenic dependence gone before: doctors and patients are liable to miss withdrawal symptoms, because they mimic the symptoms of the underlying complaint.

And the confusion was self-reinforcing. Few doctors suspected withdrawal reactions; therefore many fewer ever reported it – and so no warnings emerged. The invisibility of the problem was underlined by the count of adverse drug reaction (ADR) reports that UK doctors sent in. By the mid-1990s the Medicines Control Agency/ Committee on Safety of Medicines (MCA/CSM) had been sent only a few dozen "Yellow Cards" for suspected withdrawal/dependence problems with tricyclics, out of the perhaps 200-million-odd prescriptions issued since 1963.

When the dependence problem did finally begin to surface, it was not because of Prozac, but in spite of it. Prozac (fluoxetine) hid the problem, just as the long-acting benzos had done. Fluoxetine and its breakdown products (metabolites) have an unusually long half-life, measured not in hours but days. This made withdrawal symptoms much less obvious and acute, much harder to recognise or describe.

The two most troublesome drugs proved to be paroxetine and venlafaxine (cf lorazepam and triazolam). Both had short half-lives, but paroxetine was much the more conspicuous, partly because of its giant market share.

However, the withdrawal problem with paroxetine was revealed not in the *pre*-marking clinical trials, but only through *post*-marketing surveillance. The pre-marketing trials had discounted the possibility of withdrawal symptoms; as a result, both the manufacturers and regulators greatly overestimated the long-term effectiveness of SSRIs. This can be seen from one of the key trials that "proved" the long-term effectiveness of paroxetine. It was conducted jointly by Dr. Geoff Dunbar from SmithKline Beecham (SKB), and by Dr. Stuart Montgomery, the SSRI expert on the UK Committee on Safety of Medicines (1987-1992). Montgomery was based at St. Mary's Hospital, London. His links with the pharmaceutical industry left his predecessors, Drs. Wilcox and Sargant, far behind.

In the Montgomery & Dunbar trial, half of a select group of 135 satisfied and established paroxetine users was suddenly switched to placebo. The trial design took no account of the evidence that withdrawal symptoms were prominent, nor that they mimicked the symptoms of depression, producing marked increases on the HAM-D scale. As the design discounted the possibility of withdrawal symptoms, naturally the trial showed that many people more had "relapsed" in the group switched to placebo. Montgomery and Dunbar inferred lasting drug effectiveness by counting all cases of withdrawal as a relapse into depression.

History was repeating itself yet again. The UK regulators not only accepted Montgomery and Dunbar's evidence that paroxetine was lastingly effective, but also actively defended their interpretation (Rawlins 1998). In the meantime, it was never clear how many users couldn't or wouldn't stop, if indeed they wanted to do so. The blurred distinction between can't/won't was underlined in reports along the following lines:

> "Although Prozac is not addicting or habituating, people often remain on the medication for extended periods. This should not be surprising, since many are suffering from chronic conditions. After being on, off, then back on Prozac, one woman patient told me, 'If you ever take me off this drug, I'll break your kneecaps!'" (Manolis 1995)

The author of *Listening to Prozac* reported much the same: "it is not addictive", he pronounced: "patients do not crave Prozac, and there is no known withdrawal syndrome":

> "We lowered the dose of medicine and two weeks later Julia called to say that the bottom had fallen out: 'I'm a witch again.' She felt lousy – pessimistic, angry, demanding ... and then she used the very words Tess had used: 'I don't feel myself' ... Julia resumed taking the higher dose of Prozac. Within two weeks, she felt somewhat better; after five weeks, she was 'almost there again', with many more good days than bad. She said work had been torture on the lower dose of medicine." (Kramer 1993)

With Prozac, the reality was hidden by the attenuation of withdrawal, but why was the risk of dependence barely discussed? One reason was fear: raising doubts was always likely to unleash a heavy response – especially the accusation of scaring off patients from taking life-saving drugs. That is what happened, in response to a review of Kramer's book, published in *Nature.*

The reviewer (Medawar 1994) had lightly suggested that the book was pretentious hype ("soap not science"), but then seriously proposed that the risks of dependence with antidepressants might compare with benzodiazepine tranquillisers. The precedents and parallels seemed striking: "it would be folly not to undertake searching enquiries into how Prozac is used and misused and to what effect." A few weeks later, *Nature* published three angry letters, all saying much the same. As if to promote thoughts of a global consensus, the letters came from different continents: one was from a former editor of the *British Journal of Psychiatry*, another came from an Australian doctor; the third presented a US patient's perspective. The message was unanimous: the review was ill-motivated, biased and uninformed; heretics risked blood on their hands. These letters showed remarkable homogeneity of construction and consistency of tone, nicely illustrating how critical comment was received.[8]

As the 1990s progressed, it became more obvious that paroxetine withdrawal was a problem. The first inkling of this was in 1993. By then, the UK Committee on Safety of Medicines (CSM) and Medicines Control Agency (MCA) had received a flurry of Yellow Cards reporting withdrawal reactions – only 78 reports for paroxetine, but this was more than for all the benzos combined. The CSM/MCA issued a one-paragraph statement, in a newsletter read by an estimated 14% of doctors, reminding doctors of the need for gradual withdrawal – but again not mentioning the possibility of mistaking withdrawal and "relapse". This was understandable because the regulators still confused the two.

---

8 "It would be regrettable if serious depressive illness, often involving the risk of suicide, remained untreated through people being misinformed about the well-established properties of antidepressants" (Letter 1); "In denying the effects of a new and easily tolerable antidepressant ..." (Letter 2); "I doubt whether he would deny insulin to a patient condemned to diabetes, but would he deny antidepressants to people suffering from another genetically linked disease, chronic depression? (Letter 3)

"It is impossible to deal here with his entire shoal of red herrings, but ..." (1); "The real axe he has to grind is an anti-psychiatry and anti-doctor one ..." (2); "His tone ... gives the impression that he considers prescription of psychoactive drugs to be the lazy doctor's approach, and ingestion of the drug a moral failing ..." (3)

"During the past 35 years, there has been no evidence that any antidepressants ... cause "addiction" or "dependence" (1); "What then does he have to say about the fact that even the tap water can be addictive (psychogenic polydipsia)?" (2); He should: "pause to consider ... before trotting out his next denunciation" (3)

"I have for several years been in frequent (often daily) contact with someone who takes Prozac under the close supervision of a psychiatrist. This person, whose family history is rife with depression, has achieved remarkable stability after a grim period of contemplating suicide. There seem to be no adverse effects" (3); "Although antidepressants may have a few mild 'rebound' symptoms on discontinuation, this cannot be equated with dependence" (2); "Diabetics are 'dependent' on insulin and people with high blood pressure are dependent on hypotensives, in the sense that they will become ill again if they stop taking the drugs. Many sufferers from depression are in the same position" (1)

The analogy between diabetes and depression – as if to emphasise the biological basis of depression – became commonplace in the 1990s. The manufacturers of Prozac, Eli Lilly & Co, have been the world's leading supplier of insulins since the 1920s.

In 1996, the CSM/MCA reported a follow-up investigation. It was perhaps more searching than the 1980 "systematic review" of the benzodiazepines, but relied again on the NERO defence – no evidence of risk equals evidence of no risk. Once more, the regulators had counted up the Yellow Cards and found how few there were in relation to the millions of doses prescribed:

> "It appears that the reports represent genuine withdrawal reactions, but the low frequency of reporting per thousand prescriptions, together with the published comparative studies suggest that, overall, symptoms due to stopping an SSRI are rare. The absolute risk of a withdrawal reaction with any of the SSRIs may be so low that differences are undetectable except through spontaneous reporting where drug exposure is high ... There was no evidence of a physical drug dependency syndrome ... The withdrawal symptoms observed do not appear to be severe ... this study suggests that they are relatively mild."[9] (Price et al. 1996)

By 2000, the CSM/MCA had received over 1,000 Yellow Cards reporting paroxetine withdrawal problems – a relatively huge number but still a tiny fraction of the true amount. By this time, many case reports and several studies had been published. They suggested an intensity and frequency of SSRI withdrawal problems to be compared with the benzodiazepines.

The literature also included reports of newborn babies having withdrawal reactions after maternal use of SSRIs in pregnancy. These reports might have raised suspicions, because they suggested the very physical nature of the bond between body and drug. With a newborn, the question of "psychological dependence" or "dependence-prone personality" didn't arise. No systemic study of neonatal SSRI withdrawal has been published to this day.

Changing the meaning of "dependence"

Right from the start of their Defeat Depression campaign, the Royal Colleges of Psychiatrists and General Practitioners addressed the "mistaken belief" that antidepressants caused dependence, emphasising that SSRIs should NOT be compared with benzodiazepine tranquillisers. The Campaign's first press release was headlined, "Antidepressants not addictive ..."; the organisers were concerned "that people may fail to take the medicine in the mistaken belief that it can cause dependence" (RCP/RCGP 1992).

9 In fact, the doctors reporting to the CSM had rated 8 out of 10 cases not as "mild", but "moderate" or "severe".

Six years after the review in *Drug & Therapeutics Bulletin*, the RCGP even claimed to have searched the literature, finding "no evidence of antidepressant rebound or withdrawal" (McBride 1992). The President of the Royal College of Psychiatrists went further, echoing the findings of Montgomery and Dunbar: "Obviously a person who is still suffering from depressive illness from whom the drug is then withdrawn would suffer a return of depressive symptoms that could have very serious consequences. This, however, is an indication of their efficacy not of dependence" (Sims 1992).

On this basis, the Defeat Depression Campaign emphasised the need for radically different standards of treatment. Fears of dependence were denounced as misconceived, the result of misunderstanding. In future, there should be more prescribing for depression, and serious consideration should be given to continuing treatment indefinitely.

In conjunction with the Defeat Depression Campaign, the Royal College of Psychiatrists backed a related "Consensus Statement". It was about the recognition and management of depression by GPs. The statement began with a pointed reference to the tendency to prescribe tricyclics at low and less effective doses. There was no direct reference to SSRIs, but "many newer compounds are less toxic in overdose and have fewer side effects."

The Consensus Statement then recommended extending the treatment period. Previously, the advice was to give antidepressants "for several weeks"; this changed to a recommendation to treat patients for at least several months, "to prevent relapse". The statement warned that depression was recurrent and potentially dangerous. It proposed that candidates for long-term therapy included "patients who lack social support, and patients with continuing social difficulties (such as unemployment or dysharmony in interpersonal relationships)." Doctors were urged to counsel their patients to get them on board: "The patient clearly should be given as much information as possible in deciding whether to continue. Advice should include the facts that antidepressants are not habit-forming or addictive and that a minimum of four months treatment is advised for classic depression to prevent relapse. This will enable the patient better to make an informed choice about continuation with treatment" (Paykel & Priest 1992).

The Consensus Statement went on to suggest that, even in less serious cases, drugs could prevent depression "for up to three years". The evidence for this was slight: the US drug label said the efficacy of Prozac, "was established in 5- and 6-week trials with depressed outpatients ... the antidepressant action of Prozac in hospitalised depressed patients has not been adequately studied ... The effectiveness of Prozac in long-term use, that is, for more than five to six weeks, has not been systematically evaluated in controlled trials ..."

Throughout the next decade, the Royal College of Psychiatrists reassured patients that there was no dependence problem – and because the experts believed this, they naturally assumed antidepressants to be much more effective than they really were. This was the Royal College's message to patients until mid-2002:

> "I've heard about tranquillisers – are antidepressants addictive? No. There is no evidence that antidepressant drugs cause dependence syndromes. People do not increase the dose during long-term treatment and there is no evidence of 'tolerance' to antidepressant effects. "Craving" does not occur, and the drugs do not have 'street value'. Some people experience short-lived problems such as stomach upset, dizziness or vivid dreams at night, shortly after stopping antidepressants, but these probably do not represent true 'withdrawal' symptoms, and can be prevented by cautious reductions in dose at the end of the treatment period." (RCPsych 1992-2002)

The whole tone of the Royal Colleges' campaign was determined by a momentous but surreptitious shift in the official meaning of "dependence" at around this time. The last glimmer of shared understanding between the experts and users was to be found in the 1990 report of the American Psychiatric Association's "Task Force on Benzodiazepines". This had emphasised that the term "dependence" should be used to distinguish between what happened with tranquillisers in a therapeutic setting, as opposed to "addiction" and "abuse".

That definition of "dependence" was consistent with the central idea in DSM-III – that withdrawal symptoms, on their own, and in the absence of any evidence of abuse, satisfied the definition of "dependence". But by the time DSM-IV (1994) was published, that definition no longer applied. The new definition of dependence specified that the presence of withdrawal symptoms – in the absence of at least two other distinctive features of a drug problem – was not "dependence" at all.[10] At a

---

10 "A maladaptive pattern of substance use, leading to clinically significant impairment or distress, as manifested by three (or more) of the following, occurring at any time in the same 12-month period: (1) *tolerance*, as defined by either of the following: (a) a need for markedly increased amounts of the substance to achieve Intoxication or desired effect (b) markedly diminished effect with continued use of the same amount of the substance. (2) *withdrawal*, as manifested by either of the following: (a) the characteristic withdrawal syndrome for the substance ... (b) the same (or a closely related) substance is taken to relieve or avoid withdrawal symptoms. (3) the substance is often taken in larger amounts or over a longer period than was intended. (4) there is a persistent desire or unsuccessful efforts to cut down or control substance use. (5) a great deal of time is spent in activities necessary to obtain the substance (e.g., visiting multiple doctors or driving long distances), use the substance (e.g., chain-smoking), or recover from its effects. (6) important social, occupational, or recreational activities are given up or reduced because of substance use." (7) the substance use is continued despite knowledge of having a persistent or recurrent physical or psychological problem that is likely to have been caused or exacerbated by the substance (e.g., current cocaine use despite recognition of cocaine-induced depression, or continued drinking despite recognition that an ulcer was made worse by alcohol consumption)" (APA, DSM-IV 1994).

stroke, even "therapeutic dependence" on benzodiazepines officially ceased to exist. Once again, the problem revolved around the true meaning of "dependence" but, this time, the new definition both radically changed the meaning and defied common sense. To compound the problem, the authorities then failed to explain, or even to acknowledge, that this enormous shift of meaning had taken place.

The Pharmas zealously promoted the new definition, but the medical establishment welcomed it too – because it characterised "dependence" as something that no competent doctor would ever cause. As if by law, and at a stroke, "dependence" had again come to mean something like frank drug abuse. In line with tradition, dependence problems were pinned on users once again.

Internationally, the risk of New Dependence was considered so small, that the regulators never requested the SSRI Pharmas to test their drugs. In the UK, doctors and patients weren't told this, but the US label was more forthright: "Prozac has not been systematically studied, in animals or humans, for its potential for abuse, tolerance or physical dependence ..." The same was true for paroxetine, sertraline, venlafaxine, citalopram and the others too.

Pennies begin to drop

It had happened often in the past and no doubt will in future – evidence of a drug problem begins to emerge only when the product is targeted by the manufacturer of a rival drug. It was Eli Lilly & Co that began to drop hints about the problem, in an attempt to cut the competition down to size.

In the early-1990s, paroxetine (Paxil, Seroxat) and sertraline (Zoloft, Lustral) had begun to erode Prozac's dominant market share. Lilly decided to try to correct this by drawing attention to their shortcomings – and here, Lilly was careful not to talk about "withdrawal symptoms", referring to "discontinuation symptoms" instead. Lilly more or less invented this term as a description of SSRI withdrawal, but it was natural that its competitors should embrace it. It implied that any discomfort felt when stopping a drug simply gave evidence of its profound effects on depression.

Lilly was taking a gamble on the long half-life of fluoxetine. The company was counting on the fact that, because Prozac was only slowly cleared from the body, withdrawal problems were much less conspicuous, and much less often reported than with the two competing drugs. It was a risky ploy – a bit like the manufacturers of diazepam pointing the finger at lorazepam – and it had to be delicately done.

Around Christmas 1996, Lilly organised a "closed symposium" in Phoenix, Arizona, inviting seven experts to form a "Discontinuation Consensus Panel". From this one-day meeting, the panel of seven managed to produce two "Consensus Statements" – "A Hypothetical Definition" and "Possible Biological Mechanisms" of SSRI withdrawal. Eight papers were later published in a Lilly-sponsored journal supplement: all emphasised the superiority of fluoxetine over the other SSRIs. People didn't need to taper down the dose when stopping Prozac, said the experts: because the drug cleared the body so slowly, the tapering effect was built in.

The centrepiece of the Lilly attack on Prozac's rivals was a sponsored study, led by Dr. Jerrold F. Rosenbaum from the Massachusetts General Hospital, one of the participants at the closed symposium. The results were first presented at a 1997 Lilly-sponsored conference, held on Amelia Island ("Florida's Timeless Treasure" etc). Again, the trial was properly controlled, but its very design guaranteed that Prozac would come out on top (Rosenbaum et al. 1998).

The general idea was that established users of fluoxetine, paroxetine or sertraline would have their medications secretly (double-blind) withdrawn for about a week, before going back on drug. What happened then was entirely predictable: after a break of two or three days, the level of fluoxetine in the (average) body remained high, while the people who had been on paroxetine or sertraline were more or less drug free. It was like seeing which held water longest – buckets with holes in the bottom, or buckets with pinholes.

Along with this cunning design, the authors developed detailed checklists to record the severity of withdrawal symptoms. Although the short duration of the trial gave little indication of what happened when people stopped fluoxetine – it produced excellent data about withdrawal from the other two drugs. The results indicated that the UK regulators, among others, had underestimated the risk of SSRI withdrawal problems by far.

The Rosenbaum study showed that most patients on paroxetine and sertraline experienced withdrawal effects, and that about one-third had "substantial increases" in depression. The authors charitably described this as a "breakthrough of depressive symptoms" or "a relapse in depression", but on the strength of evidence that suggested anything but. The rapid onset clearly pointed to withdrawal symptoms producing depression – rather than anything to do with the unmasking of some depression that had been lurking there all the time. *The Drug & Therapeutics Bulletin* (DTB 1986) had warned of this a decade before.[11]

Why, from this point, did common sense not prevail? The short answer is that, for all the evidence of withdrawal symptoms and the limited efficacy of antidepressants, by then the die was cast. It was and is generally believed that not taking antidepressants increased the risk of relapse. Even the DTB (1998) had concluded that the evidence for this was "very strong", citing three weak papers to support its claim.[12]

11 "The probability of depressive relapse is low in the days and weeks after the discontinuation of antidepressants ... In contrast the frequency of antidepressant withdrawal symptoms is high in the first 2 to 14 days following the last dose."

And that left open the awesome possibility of sensitisation. Might exposure to antidepressants make patients more sensitive to subsequent episodes of depression? This possibility has still not been properly investigated, but there seems good reason to do so (Fava 2003). Sensitisation was a worrying thought, especially when mooted by one of the top company-sponsored researchers in the field:

> "Some circumstantial evidence suggests that antidepressants are sensitising and increase the risk of recurrence, but without maintenance treatment, patients are going to have a recurring course of illness with devastating consequences. I believe that a decision to start maintenance treatment represents a commitment to long-term therapy, because stopping the medication will lead to recurrence." (Keller 1994)

As the 20th century drew to a close, one further factor began to count. The growth of the Internet meant that, for the first time, patients were able to compare notes and to describe their experiences with medication. They reported severe withdrawal problems in droves, even as the manufacturer of paroxetine redoubled their insistence that there was "no scientific evidence" that Paxil/Seroxat/Aropax was habit forming, or caused dependence or addiction. Until mid-2003, the officially approved UK patient information leaflet said this:

> "These tablets are not addictive. Everyone has a substance caused serotonin in their brain. Low levels of serotonin are thought to be a cause of depression, and other related conditions. This medicine works by bringing the levels of serotonin in your brain back to normal."

Increasing numbers of patients found such advice incredible – and so it also seemed from the numbers of Yellow Card reports that doctors sent in. Of all the reports of withdrawal problems on the whole UK database of adverse drug reactions, paroxetine topped the list by a wide margin, and five of the top six drugs were SSRIs or drugs like them. Venlafaxine came second, then fluoxetine (4th), sertraline (5th) and citalopram (6th). They were all well ahead of lorazepam (8th). By the start of the new millennium, the SSRIs had left the benzodiazepines far behind.

---

12 The *DTB* relied on a review by Belsher & Costello, (1988) that mainly drew attention to basic research problems and to the need for caution in drawing any conclusions: "Rates of relapse reported by different investigators exhibit considerable variability due to methodological factors ...", etc. The authors of this review didn't mention the possibility that withdrawal effects might be misinterpreted as relapse – though they had noted a consistent trend towards "relapse" soon after discontinuation: "The longer patients stay well, the less likely they are to relapse in future ..." Nor did the cited papers by Angst (1992) and Thase & Sullivan (1995) mention the possible confounding effects of withdrawal symptoms. The latter referred only to the need for gradual withdrawal with older antidepressants – but "It is not clear if similar tapering strategies are needed for SSRIs and other newer medications".

5
From secrecy to common sense

Between 1998 and 2002, the powers that be did all they could to deny the miserable realities that antidepressant users described. The authorities entrenched their position; they went on digging and made the hole deeper still. Secrecy played a fundamental part in this – but user reports on the Internet and in the media increasingly exposed the nonsense of official denial.

The evidence summarised in the last chapter was written up in a 20,000-word paper, "The Antidepressant Web" and published in the *International Journal of Risk and Safety in Medicine* (Medawar 1997). Early in 1998, the whole paper was posted on a new website, the aim being to set out the evidence for review and to get answers to the questions it raised.

This website, *ADWEB*, was run by *Social Audit Ltd.* a tiny policy-analysis unit, originally set up in 1971 as a transatlantic offshoot of Ralph Nader's public interest network. *Social Audit's* remit was not so much to explore the safety of specific medicines, as to try to relate the apparent risks and benefits to organisational policies and behaviour. Was dependence in some sense a by-product of power? How did the experts and authorities on drug safety and health policy explain and justify their position? Why did they think the risks were so low?

From 1997, a steady stream of enquiries went out to all corners of the UK drug safety system and *ADWEB* developed as a sprawling mass of new evidence and correspondence. The hundreds of pointed letters *Social Audit* sent out were posted to *ADWEB*, linked to facsimile copies of the replies, including the institutional letterhead with all the coloured emblems and logos too. The decision to publish the authorities' replies facsimile was provocative but deliberate: it was to faithfully reproduce what they wrote, to try to open things up and to mirror all the hidden meanings and carefully chosen words. How did the guardians of "the public interest" interpret and discharge the responsibilities they assumed?

The main focus in *ADWEB* was on the Medicines Control Agency (MCA). Publicly, the MCA had responded to publication of "The Antidepressant Web" by dismissing the analysis as "an opinion" that was "not supported by the evidence", but "inappropriate" and "flawed".[1] Behind the scenes, however, the MCA promised they would "thoroughly investigate".

This assurance came from the director of the MCA, Dr. Keith Jones. Outwardly an amiable man, his professed commitment to openness seemed both incredible and quite sincere. Jones said that the Agency would be "consulting widely with relevant bodies on this matter, to gain their perspective on the view you have presented." So began a correspondence with the regulators that would last for years, uphill all the way.

The correspondence began with a request that Dr. Jones explain what advice the MCA was seeking and from whom. Weeks later, Jones replied: "We are seeking the views of a wide range of expert advisers and other relevant bodies"...but to say more than this, "would harm the frankness and candour of advice and opinions given."

As the MCA refused a meeting, *Social Audit* then appealed through the Agency's formal complaints procedure. Four months later, one of Dr. Jones' deputies ruled: "I find no reason not to release this information." It took six months therefore, just to establish that "consulting widely" meant the MCA was asking the drug manufacturers what they thought and turning to other drug regulatory agencies in the EU. It took another six months, and two further complaints, to establish that their entire submissions were both secret. They were protected as, "commercial and other information supplied in confidence," and "information received in confidence from foreign governments."

This early exchange set the tone. The secrecy and the sensitivities ran so deep that *ADWEB* was bound to develop in time as something of a protest, more of a campaign. No doubt the authorities felt aggrieved by *Social Audit's* persistent questions, especially when their bland obfuscations provoked many more. Innocent enquiries frequently led to surreal entanglements, and often to formal complaints.

By the time Jones left, in October 2002, several hundred letters had passed between *Social Audit* and the MCA. The correspondence often bordered on the Kafkaesque, but there was some respite too. One long strand of website correspondence likened the non-meeting of minds to the famous Dead Parrot sketch.[2] Another mused unilaterally about the need for a new manual, to help classify institutional pathologies in the manner of a DSM-IV: "major secrecy disorder" and much more.

---

1 "... current evidence does not show that SSRIs are associated with dependence" – UK Department of Health press statement, 2 December 1997. See http://www.socialaudit.org.uk/4320MCA.htm#Statement.

2 This was a classic from Monty Python's Flying Circus. Google will produce over 2,000 citations to "dead parrot sketch", including several linked to full transcripts.

Time and again, *Social Audit* offered one bit of cheek and then turned the other. In one particular case, after months of delay, the MCA finally produced the requested document, painstakingly gutted for sense and meaning. Over twenty passages had been erased, and in each of the blanked-out spaces someone had written in careful longhand: "Withheld under Exemption 13 of the Code of Practice on Access to Government Information." To safeguard against repetitive strain injury and stifling boredom in the Agency, *Social Audit* ordered to be made a large rubber stamp, with the same key message on it, in bold red. A brief correspondence ensued:

> Dear Mr Alder,
> I have pleasure in enclosing the rubber stamp I promised to send you in my letter of 30 January. It is self-inking – but of course it will not last for ever, and will leave a much better impression if very sparingly used ...

> Dear Mr Medawar,
> Thank you for the rubber stamp which you enclosed with your letter of 10 February. I have taken advice and I am pleased to say that its financial (as opposed to operational) value is such that I do not need to declare it as a gift or inducement ...

But these lighter moments were fleeting and, over the years, the relationship became strained. The long correspondence led to many formal complaints, all at least partly upheld. They included three referrals to the Parliamentary Ombudsman, to establish rights of access to basic information. Information withheld extended to details of the possible conflicts of interest recorded in the minutes of meetings of the Committee on Safety of Medicine (CSM).

Over the years, *Social Audit* made contact with all kinds of agencies and organisations, not only the MCA/CSM. Many others seemed to have contributed in some way to the mess that was unfolding, whether by default or design. Barbed letters winged their way to ministers, parliamentarians, government departments, royal colleges, medical journals, universities, ethics committees and professional societies, and to international agencies like the European Commission and the World Health Organization (WHO). They generally proved to be brick walls.

Not much of this barrage was directed at companies. It was enough to know that they and their agents kept a close watch on the website, and that they would pounce if *Social Audit* got it wrong. But no company ever made contact, in anger or otherwise. Meanwhile, the number of *ADWEB* visitors just grew: the log recorded over a million hits per year by the end of 2002.

Official secrecy

The tendency to secrecy becomes a major theme in the analysis ahead. Secrecy is part of the fabric of medicine and basic to the Conspiracy of Goodwill. It has preserved the mystery that helps medicines seem to work; it gives space for hope and therefore also provides countless opportunities for promoting it.

However, the emptiness of the official response to *Social Audit* signalled a different order of secrecy. It seemed to have little to do with protecting users, nor to sustaining important rights like personal privacy or the companies' ownership of their creative know-how. The problem that unfolded had more to do with the kind of secrecy that promoted abuse of power and undermined public trust:

> "... when a health scare like BSE[3] occurs, the people want to know the facts, people want to know what the scientific advice is in full, and they need to be sure that the public interest always comes first. They want to know if there was any relaxation of regulations which resulted in public safety being compromised ... The only way to begin to restore peoples' trust is therefore to be completely open about what the risks are ..." (Blair 1996)

These democratic sentiments seemed to go nowhere: under British law, pharmaceutical companies still enjoy an almost absolute right to secrecy in all communications with the regulators. Soon after taking office in 1997, the Blair government did produce a White Paper that said all the right things, but it led almost nowhere. A pitiful UK "Freedom of Information" Act – no match for the US Freedom of Information Act, 1996 – was eventually produced, for implementation in 2005 (cfoi.org.uk). Nothing much changed in the meantime: the only spur to disclosure was a voluntary Code of Practice on Access to Government Information (Cabinet Office 1997), reluctantly introduced by the Conservative government in 1994.

The MCA/CSM correspondence with *Social Audit* revealed a system not only pickled in secrecy, but also skilled and devious in denying that this was so. The correspondence did not often impart much information, but it did usefully illustrate the quality of denial. Often enough, the point was not that the Agency had strong evidence, but that they didn't: the secrecy often seemed to signal paucity of understanding, more than the depth of knowledge that the secret-keepers would claim.

The MCA/CSM vigorously upheld the secrecy laws. In the whole correspondence with *Social Audit*, they only once came close to admitting that perhaps the secrecy went too far. This when trying to explain how the law prevented them even from revealing the names of companies (and products) censured for misleading advertising.

3 BSE = Bovine Spongiform Encephalitis – "mad cow disease".

Here, at the turn of the Millennium, was this brave new world of disease awareness, direct-to-consumer advertising (DTCA), patient information and consumer rights. And there were the MCA/CSM struggling not to be seen to regret that they were unable to disclose any evidence of their effectiveness in advertising control. This particular thread of correspondence lasted just under four years:

30 JANUARY 2000 *Social Audit* requested information "about the number of occasions on which the MCA has made representations about advertising to licence holders, also the identity of manufacturer/product in each case, and the nature of complaint."

28 JULY 2000 The MCA stalls. They point to all kinds of problems, including the pressures of work involved before holidays. They emphasise the effort they make and its considerable worth. *Social Audit* might be asking too much: "Information about the type of breaches identified are not centralised within the MCA and can only be identified from individual paper files. I have not been able to discuss the scope of this work and the time it would take with the relevant staff within the MCA due to annual leave (and will not be able to do so until the end of August). I shall of course pursue that as soon as possible but I must flag up now that this work might incur a charge or – should the diversion of resources be considered to be too great – the MCA might decide that it cannot meet your request."

11 OCTOBER 2000 By this time, the MCA had stalled for longer than it would have taken to review a new drug licence application. Then they refused: "As a result of those discussions, including taking account of advice from my legal advisors, I consider that the information you requested concerning the identity of the manufacturer/product, and the nature of the complaint should be withheld ..."[4] However, in the same breath, the MCA warmly invited *Social Audit* to back off – dropping a broad hint that they'd got the point and would do something. They wordily announced a review: "The Agency recognises that the regulation of advertisements for medicinal products is an area of legitimate public concern, and we are grateful for your interest. We are currently reviewing our policy on what information we can make public concerning our regulatory activity on advertisements, whilst remaining within the Code."

29 november 2002 Two years later, *Social Audit* again asked the MCA to disclose the names of companies/products involved in misleading advertising. Failing that,

4 "... under Exemption 4(c) of the Code of Practice on Access to Government Information". Exemption 4(c) relates to legal proceedings and exempts "Information relating to legal proceedings or the proceedings of any tribunal, public enquiry or other formal investigation which have been completed or terminated, or relating to investigations which have or might have resulted in proceedings".

what happened to the review that began two years before? Had any such review taken place, and what was the result?

4 MARCH 2003 The MCA eventually replied, still relying on the legal opinion it had two years earlier: "Our legal advice has been that the Agency is constrained from making identifiable information available on individual advertising cases, without the permission of the companies involved." There was no evidence of any review: "Consideration of these issues has so far been internal to the Agency." The US Food and Drug Administration (FDA) had for years published its Warning Letters to companies whose promotions overstepped the mark. Meanwhile, the MCA droned on. "We are not satisfied that the current position on the disclosure of information about advertising casework is in the best interests of public health and are continuing to explore the possible options for increased disclosure of details of cases investigated. This has taken much more time than originally anticipated."

1 DECEMBER 2003 Just as this book went to press, the Agency announced that it would from then on (not retrospectively) publish summary information relating to its investigations into advertising complaints.

This level of secrecy somewhat distinguished the MCA from its counterpart agency, the European Medicines Evaluation Agency (EMEA). The EMEA was founded in 1995. It professed a strong commitment to openness: EMEA was quite sensitive to the need to be seen to be "transparent", an express European goal. Searching the EMEA website yielded numerous citations, linking the word "transparency" to all kinds of initiatives, presentations, workshops, "infodays", technical reports, working parties, consultations, press statements and publications. On the face of it, EMEA was well ahead of the MCA/CSM, if behind the FDA.

EMEA made one unique and important contribution to transparency, but without intending to do so. It quantified for the first (and perhaps only) time the extent of the secrecy in drug regulation there actually was. Because EMEA had been set up in the computer age, and was run as a fervent bureaucracy, the Agency knew exactly how many documents (of 60 different types) it had, including the security classification of each one. Determined both to seem transparent and to protect commercial confidentiality, the EMEA had devised a security classification system that gave everything but nothing away. The system distinguished between five different levels of transparency/secrecy – with every document not only classified, but also listed in a Master Catalogue, a complete index of documents, that was accessible on the Internet until March 2002.

The EMEA classification system ranged from "public documents" to "confidential". The former meant the full document was available, including its title. Importantly, the EMEA classification system distinguished between "Real Title" (which described what the document was about), and "Model Title" (which didn't).

This distinction gave rise to four stations of secrecy. Transparency of the second kind was designated "Text restricted" – meaning the Real Title of the document was disclosed, but not its content (unless/until the restriction was lifted). The next classification was, "Text confidential"; this meant the real title was published, but the text never would be. Then came, "Restricted" – both the document title and contents were secret, unless/until declassified. (There was no evidence this happened). Finally, "Confidential" meant that that no part of the document would ever see the light of day.

In February 2002, *Social Audit* did a quick sample analysis (about 7%) of the 22,000 documents listed on the EMEA Master Catalogue – and then made the mistake of publicly questioning the authorities about the results. This analysis suggested that eight out of ten documents were considered so secret that neither title nor content could ever be disclosed:

Public documents	4%
Text restricted	4%
Text confidential	11%
Restricted	3%
Confidential	78%

Later, *Social Audit* tried to repeat the exercise, to check trends and look for evidence of any de-restriction, but in vain. The Master Catalogue had been removed from the EMEA website in March 2002 and put under review: "we apologise for any inconvenience this may cause while we carry out this exercise..." One year later, the Master Catalogue was still "under review' and, by autumn 2003, it had altogether disappeared.

EMEA revealed one other crucial thing about the law of secrecy in drug regulation – that the key concept of "commercial confidentiality" goes undefined. This is a fatal obstacle to public accountability: if there are no criteria for classifying documents, there is simply no way of knowing or challenging what is properly classified and what not.[5]

Lack of information, compounded by this lack of definition, permits a breadth of interpretation that makes it impossible to know where private and public interests begin and end.

---

5 The European Commission explained that security classifications were "decided on a case by case basis". Moreover, "there are neither standing operating procedures nor other documents relating (to) the interpretation and/or implementation of the above-mentioned Regulation. For this reason, we cannot provide (you) with the requested information" (Brunet, February 2002). Without some clear definition, how could European Commission and EMEA staff know whether a document was classifiable, or not? How could they achieve any consistency in classification, and how could a presumption of transparency ever be guaranteed?

Growth of the Internet

The Internet introduced completely new opportunities for gathering, presenting and communicating evidence of all kinds – with many still to be exploited and explored. It meant a huge acceleration in the speed of communication and made cosmic quantities of information available at the same time. One way and another, the Internet made a profound difference to the history of the Selective Serotonin Reuptake Inhibitors (SSRIs).

ADWEB was set up early in 1998, in the early days of the first explosive growth of the Internet. By this time, messages about SSRIs had begun to appear in odd chat rooms, but it was too early to imagine that this trickle would become a flood. *ADWEB* was designed accordingly: it was not patient friendly. It was conceived as an evidence-based argument, mainly directed at a small community of policy-makers, academics and health professionals.

The logs recorded that *ADWEB* reached this audience far beyond expectations but although the website made its mark, still it failed to elicit any significant onsite feedback from the community of "health providers". Though never intended as such, *ADWEB* evolved instead as one of the main websites where distressed SSRI users let off steam.

This discussion all took place on a linked, but quite separate, part of *ADWEB*, where email chat was spontaneous and unedited. In time, several thousand reports appeared from SSRI users. The main themes were: even with gradual dose tapering, SSRI withdrawal could be frightening and seemingly impossible; drug companies seemed to be behaving abominably and too many doctors were ill informed. Most of all, users reported their fears that they were seriously ill or going mad – until they found out about withdrawal symptoms and learned that many other people had them too. The main focus was on paroxetine (Paxil/Seroxat, etc), but fluoxetine (Prozac), sertraline (Zoloft/Lustral), venlafaxine (Effexor/Efexor) and citalopram (Celexa/Cipralex/Cipramil) were all prominent too.

The immediate reaction of many who found these websites was relief and amazement that so many other people had logged on. Many described the kind of anguish that De Quincey had known:

> "Oh my God, I cannot believe how many others are/have experienced the hellish withdrawal effects of coming off Paxil!?! I have been going through a personal hell the past 5 days as I have discontinued my Paxil addiction ... I feel like I am going insane and have no one to turn to for help. No one can understand the horrendous effects of coming off Paxil unless they themselves have experienced it. Over the past 5 years of taking 10-30 mg of Paxil, I have failed 3 times at coming off it. I am not going back this time, despite having every withdrawal symptom described by others. My life is hell right now and I am gathering every ounce of strength I can

muster to get through this on my own. Work is impossible – I just sit at my desk. I can barely walk, never mind partake in my usual physical activities!! I am alone and need help, yet there is none."

From around 2000, user reports along these lines began to appear much more frequently, not only on *ADWEB*, but on a growing number of other, dedicated websites. There were perhaps two main reasons these user reports did not have the immediate effect one might have expected. One was that they were not generally designed as adverse drug reaction reports: the emphasis in many messages was on making contact with other users and lending or seeking advice and/or support.

The other reason was that the regulators had no system in place for evaluating such evidence, nor did they see any need for one. They would have been influenced by thoughts of the complexities of processing and managing such data. The MCA/CSM "Yellow Card" adverse drug reaction reporting scheme had evolved as essentially a number-based system, that depended on pigeon-holing, "preferred terms" and symptom counts. The regulators probably felt defeated by wordy user reports, unable to fit such round pegs into their own carefully-crafted square holes.

However, the growth of the Internet began to change history. By the end of 2002, user reports of adverse drug reactions (ADRs) could never credibly be discounted again.

Panorama on paroxetine

If there was a turning point – it may be too early to say – it was marked by the TV programme, *Panorama*, broadcast in October 2002. *Panorama* is the BBC's flagship current affairs programme, the longest-running public affairs TV programme in the world. Over four million people watched "Secrets of Seroxat", a programme that described the mental turmoil that SSRIs sometimes caused and the problems on withdrawal. The programme attracted a record response, including some 65,000 telephone calls, 124,000 website hits, and 1,374 emails.

This huge response prompted *Panorama* to do a follow-up programme, and that led to *Social Audit* helping to analyse the 1,374 emails sent in. The results were then compared with one "thread" of 862 emails from the *ADWEB* site, sent in before the *Panorama* broadcast. The emails to *Panorama* and *ADWEB* were both about paroxetine withdrawal, but *Panorama* had also focused on the possibility of some linkage between thoughts and acts of violence and/or self-harm.

Concerns about violence and suicidality had first surfaced with fluoxetine (Teicher et al. 1993); later they involved paroxetine, sertraline and other SSRIs. The evidence had mounted, but the issue remained unresolved after repeated and continuing official reviews. Part of the problem was how to detect a rare adverse drug reaction (ADR), and to be sure it was not linked to depression itself.

Here, there was huge scope for doubt and for wishful thinking. If bad reactions were so rare, the problem seemed more to do with the (idiosyncratic) drug user, not the drug. With so many reports of great benefits, how could these drugs do such harm? If someone tried to commit suicide soon after taking an antidepressant, surely it was because they were depressed? Why point to the drug, especially when it was well known that antidepressants could take weeks to "kick in"?

These presumptions were reinforced because the scientific evidence was inevitably thin. Rare ADRs would hardly show in the average clinical trial: a study involving 50 carefully selected patients on the test drug could hardly be expected to reveal a risk of maybe one in a thousand. But what of the evidence from widespread clinical use? The problem too was that the intelligence depended on what clinicians reported and perceived – and the lack of any system for evaluating direct evidence from patients. The MCA/CSM refused reports from patients; they assumed they lacked value, being "unscientific" and "anecdotal". Indeed, the collections of emails from *Panorama* and *Social Audit* both proved to be highly skewed.

There was no way of knowing how representative or unrepresentative these emails were, nor of what. Most failed to report even basic data, like dosage, duration of treatment or diagnosis (though no-one had ever requested, or explained the value of such details). It was therefore easy to find fault with any *individual* email – and yet their collective weight seemed profound.

The *Panorama* emails included 13 reports of suicide. Doctors had reported 21 such cases on Yellow Cards sent to the MCA/CSM between 1992 and 2002. The programme makers found that none of their cases had been reported on Yellow Cards, though even the briefest of accounts seemed to demand investigation:

> "My son Robert committed suicide (in) March this year after being on Seroxat only 7 weeks ... He became a lot worse whilst on this medication ..."

> "My husband shot himself after 4 days on Seroxat never having been suicidal in his life ..."

> "prior to his death, his behaviour became bizarre after telling me he was stopping the medication suddenly because he had problems with his libido ..."

Both the *Panorama* sample and Yellow Card counts (1992-2002) included comparable numbers of reports of attempted suicide (47 versus 49), but not of *thoughts* of violence or self-harm (92 versus 2).

> "After 3 days on paroxetine, he sat up all night forcing himself to keep still because he wanted to kill everyone in the house ..."

> "In the space of one week, he underwent a complete personality change, going from someone who was kind, gentle, caring and strong, to a suicidal wreck who couldn't think straight, became aggressive, insulting to his friends and totally believed he was someone else."

"He became anxious to the point of screaming with the rapidity of thoughts going through his head. (He) would never have contemplated suicide before, he was of placid nature and was horrified when he heard of other people trying to commit suicide."

The emphasis on numerical analysis of Yellow Card reports meant there was no way of detecting whether thoughts and acts of violence or self-harm were worst when starting the drug, or later on. Collectively, the *Panorama* reports suggested that ill effects were linked more to changes in drug concentrations, not to dosage levels. Users reported problems not only when starting paroxetine, but also after a dose increase and during withdrawal.

"I was put on it and within a week could not stand up, shook uncontrollably, could not swallow solid food, suffered panic attacks. Within a week I was admitted to hospital after collapsing in the GP's surgery. The dose was immediately doubled and a fortnight later I made my 1st (of many) suicide attempts."

"One weekend we went away, I forgot my tablets. I became irrational, violent, and asked my husband to commit suicide with me."

"I like many others tried to come (off) the drug cold turkey. After 4 days I was suffering jerking movements, feeling suicidal and constantly arguing with my wife."

Ten *Panorama* emails described immediate and serious drug reactions. On Yellow Cards, comparable narrative would be disaggregated – classified by symptoms or parts of the body most affected, if reported at all.

"I was prescribed Seroxat after my father died. I took just one tablet. Within hours I was taken so ill an ambulance was called and I was rushed to hospital. I really thought I was dying, the symptoms were horrendous, shocks, sickness, numbness in hands, legs & feet to name a few, eventually leading to acute hyperventilation, unusual for a woman of 32 with no history of this before, I was told. The hospital clearly stated that this was a reaction to the drug. It took me a week to fully recover from just one tablet and I could hardly move my limbs for the first four days."

"I took Seroxat 2 years ago because I have a breathing condition called 'chronic hyperventilation syndrome' which is exacerbated by stress and anxiety. I have never been depressed or had suicidal feelings. However I was prescribed Seroxat to reduce stress & anxiety. A day or two after taking the pills I (went) into a severe state of mental turmoil. I felt really suicidal. It was so severe that all I did was stay in bed for two or three days. Fortunately I recognised Seroxat and stopped taking it immediately."

> "My mother was on Seroxat for anxiety. She did not read the small print as regards side effects and after taking her first tablet she suffered from a panic attack which she had never experienced before. She phoned her GP and she was admitted to hospital there and then. Whilst in hospital, they continued to treat her with Seroxat insisting that it would take several weeks to kick in. My mother was not the same person and it was hell for her and the family. She attempted suicide which was totally out of character, at the age of 72 and always health conscious. We still cannot understand what happened. In the end she took herself off as she realized something was drastically wrong."

Nine reports suggested possible sensitisation, again revealing a possible risk that numerical analyses could not show. Here, users described how withdrawal was uneventful in the first course of treatment, but troublesome later on.

> "Seroxat is in my view a very good drug and has helped me to get back to my usual self. Six months after starting them, I came off 'cold turkey' with no side effects whatsoever but the panic attacks returned and so I was put back on them about five months later. Since then I have tried to come off them and haven't been able to due to the common side effect: head shocks. I've tried to wean myself off but still get this horrible sensation."

> "I have taken Seroxat on two different occasions in my life. The first time I stopped taking them the side effects were minimal, and I was quite happy to be prescribed them the second time ... This time was totally different. I was very ill for about a week when I started to take them (nauseous, faint, totally unable to care for myself – I was hardly able to get out of bed). After about 6-9 months ... I began to get a strange whooshing feeling in my head. The GP told me it would not be the tablets – although wasn't keen to find out what it could be! I decided I would gradually reduce the tablets in order to come off them, but found it extremely hard."

Twenty-three *Panorama* emails described bad reactions after a dose increase. These emails suggested that when patients went back to their doctors saying they felt worse, this was interpreted as the failure of an "effective" drug to control underlying symptoms, rather than a sign of adverse effects. It seemed a moot point: was a reduction of dosage called for instead?

> "After a couple of months on Seroxat I had complained of feeling worse instead of better, and my dose was increased! That month was horrendous. I didn't know what planet I was on, and every night my bed was drenched from sweat. After complaining I felt even worse, my dosage was drastically reduced to what it had originally been, which of course led to more side effects..."

> "My symptoms got worse on the drug and I was constantly sleeping, spaced out and self-harmed regularly. When I told the doctors I was getting worse my dosage was increased to 30mg instead of 20mg and things got worse from then on."

Attempts at withdrawal

In both the *Panorama* and *ADWEB* samples, there were many reports of "electric shock" sensations in the head, with linked visual problems and "whooshing" sensations; these were among the most common, distressing, disabling and distinctive features of withdrawal. This was how users described what the authorities called "dizziness" or "paraesthesia" – the hallmarks of paroxetine withdrawal. People often said they found it quite difficult to describe these symptoms, just as some doctors found it hard to understand.

> "Twenty four hours after the last dose I begin to feel extremely strange reactions in my brain, which have proved extremely hard to describe to the GP. A slew of weird sensations in my brain gather pace as time wears on. It feels like little electric misfirings going off in there resulting in a feeling of disorientation. It's almost like the brain is having its version of goose pimples! It took me ages to figure out that this feeling was the result of not taking the pill. It was and is hard to get across to the doc that these strange feelings are not because of taking the pill but the lack of it."

> "I too am experiencing the 'electric head'. What an appropriate name. My Dr. told me that it was simply my anxiety returning. I explained that my eyes felt jumpy when I looked from side to side, but he still attributed it to returning anxiety. It's good to see others having the same symptoms, so I know I'm not imagining things!"

Even among the 234 *Panorama* emails classified as "positive" about paroxetine, four out of ten people also reported problems on withdrawal:

> "Seroxat was the drug that saved me from a potentially life threatening mental disease. I was at suicide's door because of my depression, but it did help me get better, however, weaning myself off this was really bad, the head shocks would sometimes be that bad I would vomit."

> "I do accept that there is a problem with stopping Seroxat and the leaflet should emphasise this more forcefully. However this should be part of a much calmer and rational debate. I have been on Seroxat for nearly three years and I think I can say it has probably saved my life."

> "Seroxat CAN be an absolute lifesaver – it was for me at first (but) it is the only drug I have been prescribed that has had SEVERE enough withdrawal symptoms that I have had to keep going back on it because I feel so ill."

Some users decided to stop treatment by themselves; others came to recognise withdrawal symptoms after a missed dose or two, often after not renewing a prescription. One woman had been on paroxetine for one month when she accidentally ran out of tablets:

> "Within 36 hours I was having dizzy spells and was physically sick. But what scared me the most was that on Tuesday when visiting the doctors I ON PURPOSE walked in front of a moving car. Thank goodness the driver stopped and I was OK."

> "I forgot to take mine for two days about a month ago. I then disappeared and tried to kill myself. When I did return home I was just like a scared baby and would not let anyone near me for days. This could have been avoided if I was told."

In line with some reports in the medical literature, users frequently wrote that doctors either denied the existence of withdrawal symptoms and/or interpreted them as something else. Both the *Panorama* and *ADWEB* samples showed that this had sometimes prompted self-referral for hospital emergency treatment, sometimes leading to complex investigations. These included EEG, blood tests, endoscopy and various scans and/or symptomatic treatment for other conditions. Misdiagnosis of apparent withdrawal symptoms had led to interventions for viral infections, influenza, arthritis, inner ear infections, "trapped nerve", stroke, vertigo, allergy to other drugs, brain tumour, meningitis and serious mental illness.

Both the *Panorama* and *ADWEB* samples also suggested factors that might have contributed to substantial under-reporting of Yellow Cards, especially about withdrawal. Many users had never associated adverse effects with taking or stopping paroxetine. Upwards of 10% of the *ADWEB* emails from first-time visitors conveyed this: users overwhelmingly reported that knowing the reason brought relief, though it could be distressing too:

> "Only discovered this site last night, have read nearly every post. Feeling ghastly, but so relieved that I am not alone."

> "My teenage daughter was on Seroxat last year – my blood ran cold when I watched the programme – whilst on it she was having hallucinations, nightmares, was suicidal and self-harming."

> "My doctor told me there is no particular way to come off them and he told me to come off of them at my own discretion. I was going on holiday in two weeks time to celebrate finishing my exams, so decided to try and come off them in time so

> that I could drink. Unfortunately in the second week I felt this slight twinge in my head when I moved from side to side. This only happened once or twice in an evening so I didn't worry about it. Nothing really happened again for about 4 days when I started getting the feeling more frequently. It's like an electric zap gets fired off in my brain which makes everything feel very unstable. To start off with this was okay – however yesterday I was having to lean against a wall to steady myself and today I can barely stand up. I decided that I would look into it and see if anyone else had experienced these symptoms and, hey presto, there you all are."

Up to this point, late 2002, the British regulators ignored drug experience reports from users. The US FDA was one of the few agencies that did accept reports from patients – but what happened to them was entirely unclear.[6] The regulatory tendency was to rely on reports from health professionals. On principle, the MCA/CSM, the EMEA and most regulators discounted rich evidence of a kind that doctors could not provide, and which systems based on number-crunching would never reveal.

Yellow Cards filter the patient's account and are written in doctors' words, usually a condensed translation into medical shorthand of what the patient tried to say. This opens up all kinds of opportunities for misunderstanding or misinterpretation; it also leads to omission of detail, especially the non-medical consequences of unwanted drug effects. The mails in this survey pointed to far-reaching problems, mainly to do with relationships and employment, also driving.

Collectively, the *Panorama* and *ADWEB* user reports revealed basic failures of communication (including warnings) and prescribing strategy. Advice in prescribing guidelines, for example, had traditionally focused only on the need to start drug treatment; patients emphasised the need to stop. Their main reasons were: changed circumstances (notably trying to become pregnant; end of a period of acute stress – e.g. examinations, job loss, fractured relationships); unwanted drug effects (notably weight gain, loss of libido, depersonalisation; concern about effects of the drug on behaviour); and fear of dependence. Via *ADWEB*, some Americans reported financial/health insurance problems too. Users also identified factors that promoted under-recognition and/or under-reporting of problems: lack of time and opportunity for patients to speak, reluctance to report intimate details (e.g. mental stability, loss of libido); perceptions of the help they had or didn't have from their doctors; and their understanding (or not) of instructions for use or warnings given.

The gulf between user experience and official understanding, through 2002, was reflected in the UK Patient Information Leaflet for Seroxat: "These tablets are not addictive" ... "remember that you cannot become addicted to Seroxat" ... the with-

---

6 The FDA had never done any specific analysis on the impact of consumer reporting. Goetsch R., (FDA), personal communication, 19 September 2002.

drawal symptoms some people have when stopping paroxetine "are not common and (they) are not a sign of addiction."

Meanwhile, in late 2002, the US FDA intervened in a California court case to defend GSK's right to describe paroxetine as "non habit forming", in advertisements in the print media and on TV. GSK later dropped this claim, in spite of the FDA's endorsement (but Pfizer let it run).[7]

The meaning of "discontinuation"

The powers that be came to believe in the tales they told. Having hyped serotonin and after helping to rewrite the definitions and guidelines, the SSRI Pharmas had apparently become convinced that a "discontinuation syndrome" was quite different from a "withdrawal syndrome", and they went to great lengths to promote this idea.

The word "discontinuation", as a euphemism for withdrawal, had entered the medical literature pretty much from the time of Eli Lilly's Christmas-in-Arizona "consensus panel" meeting, in late 1996. In the previous three years, Lilly had seen Paxil eroding Prozac's market share, and Lilly had decided to fight back. The point of the campaign was to draw attention to the withdrawal symptoms seen with Paxil, even after a missed dose or two.

Lilly needed to be sure that the problem would not be perceived as "dependence" as that would have implicated Prozac as a member of the same class of drugs. Lilly, as it were, needed to throw Paxil overboard but without rocking the boat. So they threw out a lifeline: by promoting the word, "discontinuation", Lilly kept the boat afloat. SmithKline Beecham (SKB) and the other SSRI Pharmas grabbed at the word and developed the concept. A detailed 1998 internal SKB briefing (revealed in 2003) advised employees that, "Terminology such as 'withdrawal symptoms' should be avoided as it implies dependence." The briefing emphasised that "discontinuation events are not a major clinical issue" and staff were advised: "Highlight the benign nature of discontinuation symptoms, rather than quibble about their incidence."

Publicly, SKB had always denied that paroxetine withdrawal was a problem but, behind the scenes, the company was telling its people that Prozac caused such problems too: "With fluoxetine, however, such symptoms may occur several weeks later and last several months." SKB also argued that the problem wasn't the drug, but the way it was used: "The severity of symptoms does not appear to be related to either

7 The US patient information leaflet for Zoloft (sertraline) asked: "Is Zoloft habit forming? No. In medical studies, it has been shown that Zoloft is not addictive and not habit forming" (October 2003).

dose or treatment duration, but to abrupt discontinuation." The company concluded that the issue, "has been almost entirely driven by marketeering and is often based on misinterpreted or carefully selected data."

Over the years, and at the insistence of the Pharmas, this notion of "discontinuation" gained ground. It readily survived the merger, in 2000, that produced GlaxoSmithKline. GSK briefed its press and media staff to tell enquirers, "Discontinuation symptoms are completely different to addiction or dependence ..." [8]

In the same breath, GSK media people were told to say that the UK and European regulators had investigated thoroughly, and had "concluded that SSRIs do not cause dependency/addiction." ... "Seroxat is clearly shown as being neither addictive nor causing dependence." In fact, the European regulators had concluded that, "the lack of evidence for dependence does not prove the absence of a problem and any evidence, which will emerge or will be produced, should continue to be evaluated" (EMEA, April 2000).

To their credit, the European regulators had abandoned the NERO defence – no evidence of risk equals evidence of no risk – but then they seemed to go off the rails. They produced a policy paper that mused about the need to conduct batteries of studies on animals in order to confirm or deny the ample human experience of withdrawal and dependence problems (EMEA, December 2000). Nearly ten years downstream of paroxetine, the regulators had begun to think about requesting (but not requiring) both pre-clinical (animal) and clinical studies to establish what thousands of users already knew. This proposal to sacrifice some animals might best be understood as some gesture of faith or atonement, offerings to the Gods of Hope and Delay. There was simply no point in focusing on animal studies, when physical dependence and withdrawal problems were already clear from the experience of newborn infants, after exposure to SSRIs during pregnancy. Neonatal withdrawal problems had everything to do with the properties of the drug and nothing to do with relapse into depression. What better model of the risk of dependence could there be?

However, the European drug regulators did resist pressure to adopt the term "discontinuation". At a 1998 CSM meeting, one (unidentified) member proposed that this term be formally adopted, but most members disagreed. Two years later, the European regulators decided the same: "The term 'withdrawal reactions' should be used, not 'discontinuation reactions', as has been proposed by some marketing authorisation holders."

---

8 GlaxoSmithKline: "Reactive Key Messages and Issues Document" (19 December 2001).

FDA preoccupation with "abuse"

By contrast, the US authorities assumed the Pharmas' position. In its deposition/affidavit to the California court, in late 2002, the FDA advised: "SSRIs, as well as other kinds of drugs, have been known to cause withdrawal symptoms known as 'a discontinuation syndrome'. There is a critical difference between this phenomenon and the drug-seeking behaviour associated with habit-forming drugs." The decisive point for the FDA was lack of evidence of "drug seeking behaviour or drug abuse" – but one of its top medical scientists (Temple 2002) also proposed that symptoms on stopping antidepressants should be compared with the sometimes serious discontinuation symptoms found when stopping certain heart drugs.

The reasoning behind this comparison was entirely unexplained and, from a consumer-health perspective, might have seemed unintelligible. Why didn't the FDA compare the SSRIs with the benzodiazepines? That seemed all the more perplexing when it was clear that the claim, "non habit forming" was widely misunderstood, and when the regulators had been exposed to unprecedented levels of ADR reports and consumer complaints. The FDA only explained that they had previously reviewed the Paxil advertisements that made the "not habit forming" claim. They had approved them, subject to the addition of one further piece of advice: "Don't stop taking Paxil before talking to your doctor" (McCallum et al. 2002).

The comparison with heart drugs also seemed pharmacologically awry: it was as if the FDA believed that the antidepressant effects of SSRIs arose by virtue of their selective effect on levels of brain serotonin. Unlike the specified heart drugs, the SSRIs and other antidepressants were highly unspecific and unpredictable in action, and the symptomatology of the withdrawal syndrome sharply distinguished them from the heart drugs.

The significance of the invitation to make efficacy comparisons between SSRIs and heart drugs was very much to do with the seniority of the author – the Acting Director of the FDA's Office of Drug Evaluation, who was also Director of the Office of Medical Policy. The authorship invited the court to suppose that the linkage between SSRIs and drugs for heart problems was scientifically validated – though the only thing his statement actually said, legally, was that drugs other than SSRIs could cause bad reactions on discontinuation, and they weren't drugs of abuse either.[9]

Even so, the FDA reference to withdrawal from heart drugs raises a question that seems almost a conundrum: how can a drug that is often hard to distinguish from

9 "There are a number of drugs with unequivocal discontinuation syndromes that the FDA and others would not consider to be habit forming. For example, beta-blockers, used to treat high blood pressure, have a serious and even dangerous discontinuation syndrome. Clonidine, also used to treat blood pressure, does as well, as do nitroglyerin and its relatives. None of these drugs is associated with drug-seeking behaviour or abuse" (Temple 2002).

placebo, nevertheless exert such a powerful grip on some users? The key points to bear in mind are first, that placebo effects may be very strong (often to be compared with the effects of active drugs) and, secondly, that the resemblance between SSRIs and placebo in treating depression in no way indicates lack of potency of the SSRIs in other ways. Whether and to what extent the effectiveness of antidepressants in treating depression actually depends on their capacity to cause dependence remains wholly unexplored.

In praise of transparency

Throughout this period, 1998-2002, there was apparently only one person in one agency who clearly saw the point. He was a pharmacist, Dr. Tokuo Yoshida, Secretary of the WHO Expert Committee on Drug Dependence. Not long after publication of *The Antidepressant Web*, he had written this:

> "There is obviously some confusion about the concept of dependence ... The simplest definition of drug dependence given by WHO is 'a need for repeated doses of the drug to feel good or to avoid feeling bad' (who, Lexicon of alcohol and drug terms 1994). When the patient needs to take repeated doses of the drug to avoid bad feelings caused by withdrawal reactions, the person is dependent on the drug. Those who have difficulty coming off the drug even with the help of tapered discontinuation should be regarded as dependent, unless a relapse into depression is the reason for their inability to stop the antidepressant medication."
>
> "In general, all unpleasant withdrawal reactions have a certain potential to induce dependence and this risk may vary from person to person. Dependence will not occur if the withdrawal symptoms are so mild that all patients can easily tolerate them. With increasing severity, the likelihood of withdrawal reactions leading to dependence also increases ..." (WHO 1998)

Such was the lack of organisational support for Yoshida that it took another five years to get these issues discussed by the full WHO Committee. Their report (2003) was necessarily tentative, but endorsed pretty much the same point; the Committee also noted that three SSRIs (fluoxetine, paroxetine and sertraline) "are among the top 30 highest-ranking drugs for which drug dependence has ever been reported." Privately, Yoshida concluded, "I am really amazed how such a simple terminology question can confuse so many highly educated and intelligent people so deeply." The confusion was still unresolved when, alas, Yoshida retired from the WHO, in early 2003.

There is another postscript to this log of 1998–2002. Soon after the analysis of the *Panorama* emails, an old friend of *Social Audit*, Dr. Andrew Herxheimer, asked the

MCA/CSM if they would provide us with some of the anonymised and processed Yellow Card reports for paroxetine. What had doctors reported about the problems of withdrawal, dependence and suicidal ideation with paroxetine? The idea was to compare the value of patients' and professionals' reports of suspected ADRs. However, expectations of disclosure were low: no drug regulatory agency had ever disclosed such data before.

Over the years, the British regulators had been intensely secretive about ADR data – refusing even to reveal the *numbers* of Yellow Cards sent in for particular drugs. The official view was that the figures were "easily open to misinterpretation"; disclosure "would increase the danger to the public" and might cause "unjustified public alarm" (Sackville 1993). Until the mid-1990s, this policy was reinforced with (almost hilariously) oppressive restrictions on professional and academic use.[10]

Herxheimer's request was therefore extremely sensitive – all the more so because the analysis of the *Panorama* emails had been written up in the *International Journal of Risk & Safety in Medicine* (Medawar, Herxheimer, Bell & Jofre 2003), with publication to coincide with the second *Panorama* programme, *Emails from the Edge.*

It was the richness of the evidence from users, plus a chance discovery, that had prompted Herxheimer's request to the MCA/CSM. The discovery was in a corner of the MCA/CSM website, where the regulators advertised the services they offered for sale to companies.[11] One was a pricey electronic subscription service, providing companies with so-called ASSPs (Anonymised Single Patient Prints), the chapter and verse of each Yellow Card report, as processed by scientific staff at the MCA. If the MCA/CSM provided this information to companies, some general right of access was implied – at least, Herxheimer's request would have been hard to refuse.

However, the MCA rose to the occasion: for whatever reason, they provided the evidence promptly and for free. The spreadsheets that the MCA/CSM sent were astonishing. The data was rich, potentially of great value, but also so poorly organised and presented as to invite misinterpretation. Had these data been effectively and imaginatively used, the risk with SSRIs might well have been contained, years before the uproar came.

---

10 For years, the MCA/CSM released data to academics and professionals only on these terms: "Neither the print itself nor any information extracted or derived from it should be published IN ANY WAY without the consent of the CSM/MCA ... If you wish to use the data in a seminar or lecture, a copy of the overheads together with details of the reasons for the talk and participants should be forwarded to the director, Post-Licensing Division, MCA ..." After a barrage of correspondence from *Social Audit*, this requirement was dropped in 1996. This restriction on academic freedom appeared to have gone unchallenged for over 30 years.

11 This section of the Agency's website was later removed – nowhere to be found by the end of 2003.

6
Explaining the Pharmas

Drug safety and effectiveness depend, above all, not on molecular performance, but on the behaviour of pharmaceutical companies, government agencies and professional institutions – and the relationships between them and with users. The Pharmas now lead this triumvirate, even while fighting against the odds for their own survival. The Pharmas press their influence everywhere, often creating global conflict between trade and health needs.

The ultimate justification for the Pharmas' existence is to discover and develop new drugs. The reason for their high prices and profits is to fund research and development (R&D) and to compensate them for the risks. We pay extra for new drugs now by way of investing in new drugs for the future.

Society encourages innovation by awarding patent protection for new drugs. This gives companies monopoly rights to sell new products at whatever price they can command until the patent expires, usually around 10 years from the time marketing begins. This distinguishes the "research-based" Pharmas from the producers of generic (out-of-patent, unbranded) drugs.

Patent protection and brand names are basic to the Pharmas' survival because of the high price premiums involved. The *average* price of a branded product is around three to four times more than the generic equivalent – but much higher margins are sometimes seen. With major brands, huge investments are at stake: almost from the moment Prozac came off patent in 2001, Eli Lilly lost upwards of US$1 billion per year.

Three golden ages of innovation have brought us thus far. The first dates from the start of this case history, with the isolation and synthesis of many plant-based chemicals (notably morphine, codeine and quinine). Next came a range of products derived from coal tar chemistry, like aspirin and barbiturates, along with great advances in microbiology and immunology. The last great wave of innovation was around the mid-20th century, with the development of antibiotics among many other discoveries that transformed drug therapy and saved many lives (Redwood 1987, 1997).

However, by about 1970, progress in drug innovation had begun to slow down. The promise of gene therapy seemed great, but by the end of the century, remained unfulfilled. The complexities were and are immense: "It is still possible to imagine successful gene therapy for a single gene disease. It is almost inconceivable for a multiple gene disease, and certainly not within the lifetime of any of today's giant pharmaceutical companies" (Horrobin 2000).

For all the progress and promises for the future, innovation was in decline. The fact is that the key compounds from which most of the drugs in our case history were derived had all been synthesised before the 20th century began.

What was there to show for all the drugs developed for mental distress in the last quarter of the 20th century? Not a lot, in the minds of pioneers in the field. Their views[1] were systematically recorded by Dr. David Healy (1996, 1998, 2000), a practising psychiatrist and historian of psychopharmacology. The reality pretty much came to this:

> "... if you really want to reduce the thing to basics, the discoveries which opened the path for the development of modern psychiatry are the discoveries of the effects of chlorpromazine, lithium, imipramine, and meprobamate ... With all fairness to the vast array of drugs which followed, the best any of these drugs has done is to substitute one side effect for another, while creating by their rapidly growing number a tremendous turmoil for physicians, and by their steadily increasing cost a serious financial burden for patients." (Ban 1996)

An important reason for this slow progress is simply that drug innovation is a complex and expensive business, fraught with risk. At the best of times, drug development takes years and outcomes are never guaranteed – and everything takes place in a context of uncertainty about the shape of markets in future.

The development of Prozac (fluoxetine) shows how deep the uncertainties go. Fluoxetine was the outcome of concept-based research, an idea well worth exploring – but the process was nothing like as focused or romantic as Eli Lilly would have one believe. True conspirators of goodwill might imagine drug discovery as some highly focused process, driving towards health solutions at impossible cost. The reality is that discovering molecules is relatively easy and cheap; the expensive and risky bits

---

1 "In my opinion, if you look at the history of psychopharmacology, since, say, 1964 – thirty years now – nothing radically new has been introduced. Perhaps the only original idea was the discovery by Japanese colleagues that a drug such as carbamazepine, used as an anti-epileptic, could be protective in manic-depressive disease" (Pichot 1996).

"We had the monoamine oxidase inhibitors and in 1959 we have the first tricyclic antidepressant. There has been no important progress after 1959. Some differences in the mechanism of action but equivalence in potency. Maybe smaller differences in side effects which have not been exploited in clinical practice. Clozapine may represent a progress in the treatment of the psychoses but that's all" (Garattini 1996).

"Not much has changed in practice. We know how to do it faster and a little better but the modus of doing it has not changed" ... As regards treatment, I think we probably have enough on the shelves to serve us for some time if we learn how to use it" (Lehmann 1996).

are more to do with progressively screening, sifting and testing many thousands of new compounds to find out what they do and to gauge their market worth.

Fluoxetine (Prozac) was never conceived as a treatment for depression: long after it was first synthesised, in 1972, Lilly was still wondering what to sell it for. They knew it acted on brain serotonin, but had not found it especially effective for depression. And so Lilly organised meetings to get advice from leading clinical investigators. At one of these meetings, a pioneer in the field, Dr. Alex Coppen, enthused about the possibilities of serotonin for depression. He later recalled: "I always remember the Vice-President of Research saying, 'I thank Dr. Coppen for his contribution, but I can tell you we won't be developing fluoxetine as an antidepressant'" (Coppen 1996).

At the time this would have seemed a reasonable decision, because tranquillisers then ruled and the depression market seemed dull. There was no reason to assume that boosting levels of brain serotonin was the key to controlling depression. Indeed, Lilly was simultaneously developing drugs related to fluoxetine that worked in a "balanced" way – on both the serotonin and noradrenaline neurotransmitter systems. The fate of these drugs is another indicator of the uncertainties of innovation.

Though atomoxetine and duloxetine both had some antidepressant effect, they eventually came to market in the early 21st century, mainly as treatments for ADHD (attention deficit hyperactivity disorder), and depression and urinary incontinence, respectively. As serotonin is widely distributed in the body, such drugs have all kinds of effects. Lilly developed another Selective Serotonin Reuptake Inhibitor (SSRI), dapoxetine, which they later sold on as a possible treatment for premature ejaculation. Antidepressants are notorious for inhibiting sexual response and desire.

Meanwhile the costs of R&D had soared: a ten-fold increase between 1980 and 2000. The Pharmas claimed that, including all the failures, it cost US$800 million to develop each new drug (Tufts 2001) and later estimates suggested a figure twice as high (Bain 2003). However, the figures were in dispute, not least because much basic data were never disclosed. Using the best available data, the US Health Research Group (2001) found that, "the actual after-tax cash outlay – or what drug companies really spend on R&D ... is approximately US$110 million".[2]

By 2000, the *Wall Street Journal* could point to a clear trend: "The pharmaceutical industry is gradually shifting the core of its business away from the unpredict-

---

2 US government funding played a major part in private sector R&D expenditure. Funding from the US National Institutes of Health (NIH) or the Food and Drug Administration (FDA) had supported the discovery, development or testing of 33 of the 35 most important drugs approved in the US between 1992-1997 (Hunt 2000). Fifty-four of the 84 drugs approved by the FDA to 1997, for the treatment of cancer, had received federal funding (Arno & Davis 2002). A 1995 study from the M.I.T. Sloan School of Management found that 11 of the most significant drugs of the preceding 25 years had been discovered or developed with government funds (Gerth & Stohlberg 2000). See also: Consumers Union (2003).

able and increasingly expensive task of creating drugs and toward the steadier business of marketing them" (Harris 2000).

Expanding markets

The marketing frenzy that developed in the late 20th century might be seen as either the cause or the effect of "the crisis in innovation" – and perhaps both. The turning point was around 1980, when the last great wave of innovation was drawing to a close. Vast global markets were opening up and the political climate was ripe, with Reagan and Thatcher at the helm. The following example illustrates the dilemma and the temptations; it also partly explains the origins of the firms that later became GlaxoSmithKline:

> Cimetidine was one of the great innovations in pharmaceutical medicine. It was the product of original, basic research led by Dr. James Black, working in the early 1970s at what was then Smith Kline & French (later to merge with Beecham). Black's basic research had established the role of histamine (H_2) in producing excess stomach acid; he then succeeded in developing an H_2-antagonist that was clinically well tolerated. The introduction of Tagamet (cimetidine) in 1976 revolutionised the treatment of peptic ulcer and made the company a fortune.
>
> Meanwhile, scientists at Glaxo had started to exploit this basic research in 1973, and three years later they discovered a related drug, ranitidine (Zantac). They knew that, "it really was a 'me too'. Scientifically it was thoroughly uninteresting." Tagamet and Zantac were both very effective, but through shrewd and intensive marketing – and with a rasping emphasis on some marginal and questionable clinical advantages – Zantac became one of the first Blockbuster drugs. In 1980, Glaxo looked "washed up", with profits in decline, at £66m per year. Ten years later, Zantac sales were approaching the £2 billion mark. The company had been transformed; its profits exceeded £1 billion per year (Lynn 1991).
>
> By the time of the merger that produced GlaxoSmithKline in 2000, the company's major market was the US. By then, it was spending 37% of revenues on marketing and administration, compared with 14% on R&D, and making a 28% profit overall. For every $1 billion in sales growth between 1997 and 2001, GSK invested $14 million in R&D (Angell & Relman 2002, *Datamonitor* September 2002).

The new emphasis on marketing also largely explains the growth of SmithKline Beecham's Paxil (US) and Seroxat (UK) in the 1990s. Years earlier, the company had bought paroxetine off the shelf from a small Danish company but, like Eli Lilly, they were uncertain what to sell it for. SKB had another problem too. By the time they were ready to launch paroxetine, Prozac already dominated the new market for depression, and sertraline (Zoloft, Lustral) was making inroads too. What was the future for a "me-too" like paroxetine, when Prozac was a star?

SKB decided to emphasise the unique importance of serotonin in treating depression. Eli Lilly had already laid the groundwork, hinting that depression was a deficiency disease, and SKB built on that. This was not because they had evidence that more serotonin was actually better; it was simply because paroxetine made more serotonin available than competing drugs. There was no demonstrable clinical advantage but, by going on and on about serotonin, it was easy enough to suggest there was.

It was SKB that coined the term, "Selective Serotonin Reuptake Inhibitor." The word "selective" was used pointedly to encourage the belief that paroxetine was more pure and specific in its action, and less likely to cause problems than competing antidepressants. The simple appeal of the notion that depression was caused by this biochemical deficiency prompted the other Pharmas to describe their products as SSRIs as well. No one seemed too bothered that there were equally effective antidepressants on the market (e.g. lofepramine) that had no action on the serotonin system at all.

The marketing of the SSRIs involved more than just providing copious evidence of the distinctive worth of each brand. "You don't sell the sausage, but the sizzle": disease awareness was the thing. Selling antidepressants meant underlining the risks of depression and the importance of treatment, and fighting stigma by revealing how many sufferers there were. So the Pharmas began to expand the SSRI market; their drugs were not just good for depression, but for mood disorders of all kinds.

There were compelling commercial reasons for adding to a drug's licensed "indications" – e.g. for "social anxiety disorder" or "generalised anxiety disorder". It bolstered professional credibility and expertise, legitimised drug intervention and widened the market scope. It also helped because, with every new indication, another patent could be claimed. In the US, GlaxoSmithKline won five patent extensions for Paxil between 1998 and 2001, extending the brand life by over five years and earning the company around US$1 billion per year.

By the 1990s, the Pharmas had no choice but to proceed like this. By this time the crisis in innovation was biting and worsening; it was also self-perpetuating. The sheer size of Pharmas meant they could no longer hope to survive by relying on the financial returns from investment in R&D. In time, the Pharmas' dependence on drug discovery induced more and more anxiety. It became more and more risky as a guarantee of survival, let alone a recipe for growth.

By the end of the millennium, the Pharmas were in crisis. New drug pipelines were shrinking; pressure was also growing because a whole raft of patent expiries was due before 2005. For all the promise, and the hopes that could always be raised, the boom years had come decisively to an end. The costs of R&D were rising relentlessly and fast and there was mounting pressure for "evidence-based" medicine with a corresponding emphasis by purchasers on therapeutic value for money.

How would the Pharmas respond? The solutions increasingly came to be found in the US, and to reflect American styles and needs.

US gravitational pull

Hitler ended Germany's 50-year record of world supremacy in science: "If the dismissal of Jewish scientists means the annihilation of contemporary German science, then we shall do without science for a few years." Barbarous anti-Semitism precipitated an exodus of scientific excellence, including 20 future Nobel laureates (Medawar & Pyke 2000).

In 1938, Germany held over 40% of world pharmaceutical trade and the US lagged far behind. By the early 1980s, Germany held 7% of world pharma trade and the US had over three times more. Twenty years later, the US held a half share, with the proportion expected to rise to over 60% by 2010.

For many reasons, America became the spiritual home of the Pharmas. Size alone had a lot to do with it, but the lack of price controls was decisive too. The domestic American market accounted for about 40% of all world pharmaceutical trade, so no major player could afford not to be there. At the same time, the US-based industry was investing heavily overseas. A US company was the acquirer in nine of the top ten global biotech deals in 2001.

With this concentration of power, US market values inevitably became the main driver in the globalisation of medicine. The Pharmas naturally exported American values and ways of doing things. With greater resources, better facilities, more scientists and dominant representation, US influence was bound to make its mark worldwide. The pattern of psychiatric diagnosis and prescribing is a case in point. Because all major new drugs would aim for the US market, drugs had to be tested to US standards, whatever else. Thus the American Psychiatric Association's DSM-IV became the standard global reference on the diagnosis of mental illness.

Collectively, the Pharmas aimed to create in other countries the kind of market conditions the US excelled in providing. National industry associations of course presented a local face, but their voice was unmistakably global. For example, only one of the 12 companies represented on the Board of the Australian Pharmaceutical Industry Association was Australian, the others being European (6) or American (5). Nor was there anything essentially "British" about the industry's mission in the UK: "The main functions of the ABPI are to represent the pharmaceutical industry operating in the UK in a way that assures patients access to the best available medicines by creating a favourable political and economic environment that encourages innovative research and development, and affords fair commercial returns" (ABPI 2003).

Globalisation increasingly impressed predominantly US models and methods of responding to health needs as the main markets defined them. The Pharmas carried this culture with them into other countries with quite different traditions, health priorities and abilities to cope. Conflict between trade and health imperatives would naturally result.

American healthcare was unaffordable, even in the US, and would have been destructive to any health system elsewhere. It cost twice as much per person as the average in the 15 countries of the European Union – all of which recorded a higher national life expectancy than the US. The best of American medicine was superb, but it was not equitably shared. Over 40 million Americans had no health insurance and another 40 million would be bankrupted by serious, chronic ill-health. Among them were seven million Americans whose life expectancy was "more characteristic of a poor developing country rather than a rich industrialised one" (WHO 2000).

Other countries found the US model unattractive, not only because of the high costs and inequity of distribution; another problem was the difference in health priorities and medical needs in countries rich or lean. Comprising less than 5% of the world's population, the US consumed the lion's share of global resources (Kennedy 2002) and showed many signs of it. More than any other country, the US was beset by diseases of affluence, most obviously by obesity, with diabetes and related complications. In the new millennium, overweight became the adult norm and every fourth American was obese. Only about 3% of the US population managed to maintain a normal weight, eat a nutritious diet, take adequate exercise and not smoke (CDC 2001).

Thus globalisation promoted a particular kind of innovation, far removed from the most urgent global needs. Market pressures meant that, "virtually no new drugs are being developed for diseases that predominantly affect the poor" (MSF 2001). The Pharmas served markets not communities and the difference was profound. From a commercial perspective, the value of the whole African market in 2002 was US$5.3 billion – about the same as the global market for a top Blockbuster drug (InPharm 2003).

To add to the crisis in innovation and the pressure on Pharmas, there was mounting mainstream protest in America too. The price of drugs was becoming a national scandal, especially for the expanding population of senior citizens. By 2000, close to 40% of Americans aged over 65 had no insurance coverage for prescription drugs. Americans in busloads routinely crossed the Canadian and Mexican borders to buy drugs they could not otherwise afford. This was the start of what later became an Internet-based established trade. More and more people found the cost of drugs intolerable, and their insurers and employers were up in arms.

The pressure on the Pharmas became intense and threatened their reputation. Meanwhile, GlaxoSmithKline and Eli Lilly were among the first to set up drug discount schemes for the US elderly poor, in 2002. This was over and above the US$8 billion per year of free samples the Pharmas provided for doctors at that time.

But for all the charity, the Pharmas thought that the only lasting solution would be to spread the cost of innovation among all presumed beneficiaries. Both the

Pharmas and the US government[3] believed that the real problem was that other countries just weren't paying a fair share of the cost of drug innovation. An editorial in the *Wall Street Journal* (2002) spelled it out: "the price of socialism is fewer life-easing and life-saving products."

> "Everyone likes to complain about the prices Americans pay for prescription drugs, with the political blame falling mostly on the supposedly price-gouging drug companies. But it's worth considering the role European socialism plays in the prices Americans pay for their medicines, and how the drug companies have begun to fight back."
>
> "That's right. European price controls on drugs have for years made the Continent a free rider on America's (mostly) free market in prescription drugs. Europe can't shake the habit of living off U.S.-funded research ..."
>
> "For political reasons, governments force down prices, which means that European consumers pay less but also that European countries are in effect refusing to pay their fair share of drug R&D costs. In other words, American consumers are financing the drug innovations that couldn't be developed as quickly, if at all, at European prices."

Globalisation promoted "trade liberalisation", implying reduced national regulation, but this implied two quite different things in the US and elsewhere. No other country had anything like the regulatory capacity of the US Food and Drug Administration (FDA). About two-thirds of the world's countries "still do not have laws to regulate pharmaceutical promotion or do not enforce the ones they have" (Mintzes 1998).

Globalisation brought with it the strict protection of patents and brands. From around 2000, the Pharmas enjoyed increasing international protection for "intellectual property" through agreements made in the name of the World Trade Organization (WTO), largely at the instigation of the US.

From a global perspective, investment in such innovation made little health sense. Since the late 1970s, the World Health Organization (WHO) has emphasised that almost all national health needs could be met by using a select few hundred of the best older drugs. The first branded products were included in the WHO *Essential Drugs List* in 2002. They were products for HIV and AIDS.

---

3 FDA Commissioner Mark McClellan later took up the same theme, adopting "a political, even trade issue, tone" (Bowe 2003). McClellan's draft speech argued that the US "cannot carry the lion's share of this budget for much longer", and "everyone's effort to get a free ride on new drugs will grind the global development of new drugs to a halt" (Mathews 2003).

Blockbuster imperatives

By the year 2000, there was something of a rule of thumb about the financial returns needed to sustain average industry performance. A Pharma needed to introduce, each year, roughly one new product earning around US$500 million per year, for every 1% it held of the world pharmaceutical market. To achieve *average* industry performance, a company the size of Lilly would have needed two or three such products each year; Pfizer or GlaxoSmithKline needed six or more.

None of the Pharmas came close to this mark. There had been a steady decline in numbers of New Chemical Entities (NCEs) launched each year – only about 30 per year by 2000, compared with twice that number 20 years before. The proportion of new drugs developed "in-house" also declined.

The shortfall in innovation affected even the richest and most successful firms. The head of R&D at GlaxoSmithKline, mused publicly about the possibility of just buying needed research. His opposite number in Pfizer Inc., acknowledged that, "Two drugs a year is probably not quite enough at this stage of market consolidation. It's daunting, but it's not just Pfizer that is facing this situation" (Michaels 2001).

"Market consolidation" meant companies got taken over or merged – as did Pfizer and Pharmacia in 2003. "Consolidation" was another response to the crisis in innovation; it also explains how control of the pharmaceutical sector fell to fewer firms. The combination of Pfizer + Pharmacia would give one company one-tenth of the world market – an economic power to humble most nation states. It also made Pfizer too big for predators.

The claimed efficiencies of mergers or takeovers (of the order of 2+1=4) helped to hide the pipeline problems in the short-term, but deepened the crisis overall. Once companies become too large to be able to grow organically, growing larger only made the problem worse. This in turn meant that the big Pharmas became less inclined to focus on developing drugs for smaller or poorer markets. To get returns on an outlay of US$800 million and rising, no company could afford to aim low.

Hence the Pharmas' growing dependence on Blockbuster drugs – especially antidepressants, anti-ulcer drugs, painkillers for arthritis and cholesterol reducers. Companies worth tens of billions of dollars needed to sell billions of dollars worth of drugs, and these top earners allowed more focus in the sales effort and reduced duplication of effort and resources. Blockbusters became the only way to survive. Blockbusters accounted for 6% of the US pharmaceutical market in 1991, rising to 45% by 2001. Antidepressants then comprised over 10% of all blockbusters: the top five SSRIs all sold between US$1 billion and US$3 billion a year. By then, the big Pharmas typically depended on Blockbusters for at least half their sales.

Blockbusters became the lifeblood of the Pharmas, the bedrock of the market for prescription drugs. They stood for the premium prices and volume sales that meant growth in the market and profitability.[4] In the US, Blockbusters drove up spending by over 15% each year. The average US price (2001) for one of the top 50 prescription drugs was US$72, compared with US$40 for all the rest. The top 50 accounted for nearly half of all sales; about half the growth in the US market was driven by sales of just 34 drugs – six antidepressants among them.

These Blockbusters were the products of intensive marketing, not first-rate innovation. Most were "me-too" drugs (e.g. five SSRIs) and mainly products for stress, lifestyle, "diseases of affluence" and the binds of aging.

Most new drugs offered no real therapeutic gain; they were "innovative chemical extensions" or "me-toos". About one in four innovative drugs offered advantages worth having – though fewer would be worth the premium price, if affordable at all.

> "It is widely recognised that only a very small proportion of new and modified drugs entering the market actually represent medically important advances. Some are simply 'me-too' copies of existing drugs that offer either no new therapeutic breakthroughs or marginal improvements of a very technical nature." (European Parliament 1994)

> "Only 22 percent of the drugs approved by the FDA from 1982-1999 represented important therapeutic gains." Between 1982 and 1991, the US FDA approved 258 NCEs, of which 137 (53%) were said to offer "little or no therapeutic gain", 80 (31%) offered "modest therapeutic gain", and 41 (16%) represented an "important therapeutic gain". A new, arguably less stringent classification system was then introduced. Drugs submitted for marketing were designated either for "priority" or "standard" review. From 1992 to 1999, 170 (23%) drugs were assigned for priority review (as drugs representing "significant improvement compared to marketed products ...") and 560 (77%) for standard review, as drugs that "appear to have therapeutic qualities similar to those of one or more already marketed drugs." (Public Citizen 2001)

> "Of the 2,254 drugs evaluated between 1981 and 2000, in the leading French independent journal of prescribing, 74 (3.3%) were judged a major therapeutic advance" (*La Revue Prescrire* 2001).

Intensified marketing made it possible to disguise and compensate for this quality shortfall. By 2000, most Pharmas were spending about twice as much on marketing and administration as on R&D. The US increasingly set the global tone for drug marketing, driving headlong expansion on many fronts.

4 The profitability of the Pharmas has been outstanding. From 1994 to 2001, pharmaceutical industry profitability ranged between 14% and 19%, while the median for all Fortune 500 firms ranged between 3% and 5% (Gluck 2002).

> Between 1995 and 2000, the number of marketing staff working for the US Pharmas increased by 60%, while research staff declined by 2% (Sagar & Socolar 2001). The increase was mainly due to employment of more sales representatives: "One of the best-known dogmas in the industry is that when two pharmaceutical companies go head-to-head, God smiles on the company with more medical representatives." (Cetera 1992)
>
> The number of pharmaceutical representatives doubled, and sponsored events quadrupled, between 1993-1999. More "events" were arranged, not least to reach doctors who resisted office visits: "Peer testimonials are more important now than ever because you need your loyal thought leaders to act as your sales advocates for your brand in the absence of sales time." (*RxMarketer News* 2001)
>
> Industry audits found that about half the physicians invited accepted invitations – "stating that interest in the project was the main motivator for accepting invitations (72%), with convenient location (49%) and payment of honoraria (46%) important too ..." Branded products were the topic of 77% of all events ... and more than half the attendees at restaurant and hotel meetings said they intended to begin or increase prescribing of a promoted product. (Quintiles 2001)
>
> The same source reported that this increase in marketing spend was, "largely due to sales opportunities associated with new indications for existing drugs such as Paxil (paroxetine), Prozac (fluoxetine) and Zoloft (sertraline)..."[5] The SSRIS were the most heavily marketed drugs of all. (Ellen 2001)

Alongside the marketing effort, but unmistakably part of it, the Pharmas also made it their business to promote climate change in the market environment. Their aim was to promote "free markets", with the emphasis on strong, long patent protection and lack of price controls. This involved intensive lobbying and frequent recourse to law.

> The US drug industry spent US$403 million on lobbying, between 1997-2001. By then, companies employed 623 different lobbyists, more than the total number of Senators (100) and House Representatives (435) combined (Congress Watch 2002). Pharma lobbyists included 23 former members of the US Congress and 340 "revolving door" lobbyists who previously worked for Congress or the federal government. In the year Prozac went off patent (2001), Lilly doubled the number of its

5 The industry spent US$1.5 billion in 2000 to test medicines already approved by the FDA, primarily so they could make new marketing claims to sell their products. Spending on "post-approval" drug studies tripled in the last half of the 1990s, growing faster than other clinical drug research (O'Dwyer 2002).

registered Washington lobbyists from 27 to 58. Lilly spent US$6.5 million on lobbying, more than any other Pharma. (Groppe 2002)

By the 21st century, the pharmaceutical industry had also emerged as the largest spender on US political advertising, apart from the major parties themselves (Hamburger 2002). Between 1990 and 2000, the health products industry increased political contributions to favoured candidates in US federal elections from US$3.1 million to US$26.4 million, with Eli Lilly, Pfizer and GlaxoSmithKline in the top five.[6]

At the same time, the Pharmas enhanced their reputation as heavyweight users of the law, especially to protect their patents. By 2000, they had succeeded in extending effective patent life from an average of nine years to ten years, mainly by exploiting loopholes in the 1984 Hatch-Waxman Act.

This US law was designed to promote generic drug use in line with free market values (US FTC 2002), but had proved open to abuse, described in a *New York Times* editorial (2002) as, "underhanded at best ... fraudulent at worst." The drug patent extensions claimed by some companies were adding billions of dollars each year to employee medical insurance bills. Employers joined in protest too.[7] There was ample support for law reform, but that floundered too:

> In July 2002, the US Senate passed by a 78-21 vote the McCain-Schumer bill, to stop frivolous patent extensions claims. The Bill failed when the Chairman of the House Energy and Commerce Committee, Billy Tauzin, scheduled 11th hour committee hearings, effectively blocking a vote by the whole Congress. In 2002, Tauzin ranked as the second biggest recipient of donations from the pharmaceuticals/health products sector. He received nearly US$100,000; his chief of staff left soon after to become a drug-company lobbyist. (*Atlanta Constitution Journal* 2002)

---

6 That total excluded the cost of advertising campaigns promoting industry causes, and the politicians who backed them. In the 2000 election cycle, the US Pharmas' trade association (PhRMA) spent more than US$50 million on TV ads – also spending millions of dollars on "general education grants" to support advertising campaigns run by more and less bogus "grassroots" organisations.

7 *Business for Affordable Medicine* (BAM) was set up as a high-profile public relations initiative, in 2001 – a coalition of 11 state governors, labour unions and major businesses including, General Motors, Kodak, Motorola and Wal-Mart. The Pharmas retaliated, partly by using their muscle as purchasers to put pressure on companies linked to BAM (*Washington Post* 2002). The Pharmas themselves had been on the receiving end of such practices. In the 1980s and 1990s, for example, the tobacco company, Philip Morris, reportedly put pressure on Pharmas marketing nicotine gum and patches by threatening to cut off purchases from the companies' agricultural divisions (Chang 2002).

Then, shortly before the 2002 Congressional elections, President Bush proposed a modest reform program. It was to curb only the most controversial claims for patent life extensions, but claimed savings of US$3.5 billion per year, between 2002 and 2011. That was roughly equivalent to, say, 14-times the total public sector health expenditure in Afghanistan.

The global reverberations of such trends touched everyone. Here was an industry of great social, strategic and economic importance, whose power was rapidly consolidating in the US. Naturally, the US government recognised the Pharmas as precious assets in international trade, and it protected their interests accordingly. The US State Department energetically put pressure on other countries to help them develop as Pharmas' markets. The overbearing US influence in the World Health Organization is a case in point.

However, the Pharmas were both hugely powerful and enormously vulnerable, at the same time. Vulnerability caused them to behave antisocially; their power allowed them to do so. Being both deeply dependent on their products and chronically anxious about their own foundations, the Pharmas readily got flustered, and more.

When the fate of a great institution depends on the reputation of just a handful of drug products, the prospect of a losing a Blockbuster is comparable to a life-threatening haemorrhage. From the Pharma's perspective, "if Prozac goes, Lilly could go down the tubes."[8] Prozac accounted for over one-third of Lilly's sales, at that time.

Influence at work

The influence of the Pharmas in shaping views of benefit, cost and risk is vast – but beyond credible description, short of grinding detail at interminable length. Yet imagine the corporate mind working like a chronically stressed human brain, "... not an organ of thinking but an organ of survival, like claw and fangs. It is made in such a way as to make us accept as truth that which is only advantage."[9] Pharmas are by nature intensely protective of their products and reputations; they are sensitive to criticism and well placed to defuse it. Think of the energy of tens of thousands of people deployed mainly to build the reputation of a few very precious products:

8 This was a warning from one company manager to another, to pull out all stops to save the drug. It emerged from a Lilly memorandum produced in a major court case in which fluoxetine was alleged to have induced murderous and suicidal acts (Thompson 1999).

9 Primary source untraced. It is attributed to the Nobel Prize-winning biochemist, Dr. Albert Szent Gyorgi (Torrey 1972).

Company	*Global market share (%) 2000*	*No. of blockbuster products (>$US1 billion global sales) – 2001*	*Blockbuster sales as percentage of all ethical sales – 2001*
Pfizer	7.0	8	80
GlaxoSmithKline	6.9	9	51
Merck & Co	5.0	5	63
AstraZeneca	4.4	2	48
Bristol-Myers Squibb	4.1	4	50
Novartis	3.9	2	18
Johnson & Johnson	3.8	4	56
Aventis	3.7	2	23
Wyeth	3.2	2	31
Pharmacia	3.1	2	36

With the active support of the medical establishment, the Pharmas came to enjoy powerful and increasing influence over the policies of nations, the conduct of medical science, the perspectives of the press and media, the judgement of doctors and the understandings and welfare of consumers. Their leaders mixed with heads of state. The Pharmas touched everyone, advancing a US market model of medicine as they did so. They endowed university departments and chairs, promoted those they chose; they underpinned professional education and increasingly funded their own regulation. The Pharmas became the major sponsors of countless projects, organisations and individuals; these days they systematically fund even big, "grassroots" patient organisations. Their presence is felt everywhere, for better and for worse.

There are elements of both better and worse in the following account – in which an obviously conscientious and experienced drug rep patiently explained that he knew much more about his drugs than even top specialists in the field. He was responding to a program he had seen (ABC-TV 2002), in which a small town US doctor had logged, over a four-month period, a rather shocking list of all he had been offered to change the way he prescribed.[10]

> "I have been a Pharmaceutical Representative for the past 10 years. As such, I am very proud of what I do. In fact, given the sheer number of medicines available, I believe it is impossible for providers to keep up to date without industry

10 This doctor was presented with an estimated US$10,000 worth of gifts, including a paid trip to a Florida resort, a family ski trip, dinner cruises, hockey game tickets, Omaha steaks, a day at a spa, free computer equipment and a US$2,000 cash bounty for putting four patients on the latest drug for high cholesterol, as part of a "clinical study". An estimated 61% of US doctors have accepted inducements of this kind (Kaiser 2002).

influence. I see this on a daily basis. Each day, I call on providers who are nationally and internationally recognized in their respective fields. Nevertheless, as a well-trained representative, I know far more about my particular medicines than they ever will. It is my job to provide these providers with the necessary information (i.e. where the drug should be used and where it should not be used) to appropriately prescribe these medicines. In addition, I often help providers get together on projects and/or protocols that substantially benefit patients. Having stated all this, I have seen both positive and negative pharmaceutical sales tactics ..." (Alaniz 2002)

The inference would be that doctors become more informed through contact with companies. At the same time, the system worked through intensive promotion and recycling of clinical opinions that came closest to the Pharmas' views of the value of their products. The Pharmas coached experts and groomed the chosen few.

The process of distillation of expertise was never left to chance: intensive monitoring of doctors became the norm, with particular attention paid to leading opinion. Before the age of laptops, Eli Lilly sales reps used to fill in a detailed questionnaire after attending lectures in teaching hospitals, to record in detail what each speaker said about Lilly's and competing products. It was a routine part of the job. Physician profiling in the US has since been extended to, "segmenting doctors by their lifetime value" (Elling & Fogel 2002). Depending on perspective, such techniques might seem either deeply intrusive or far advanced.

It is not possible to trace all the layers and byways of drug marketing, nor to assess with much accuracy its influence on people, institutions and culture. Too much goes on behind the scenes, or is played at arms length, sometimes under assumed names.

> The US Pharmas were the major backers of the *Alliance for Better Medicare*, which described itself as "a coalition of nearly 30 organizations representing seniors, patients, medical researchers and innovators, doctors, hospitals, small businesses and others" (Gerth & Stolberg 2000). The same companies created *Citizens for Better Medicare* (2001), to wage a US$50 million advertising campaign against laws for a government-controlled prescription drug benefit.

Marketing considerations come into play pretty much from the moment a molecule is created; indeed they have an increasing influence on the kinds of molecules that do or don't get made. The marketing effort begins long before molecules become established brands. Nowadays, major advertising agencies work side by side with scientists – "getting closer to the test tube", as they say in the trade. They also help to court opinion-formers, once a drug comes to town.

> The WPP agency that helped Forest Inc. to launch an allegedly improved version of the SSRI, citalopram,[11] (2002) invited 20 New York psychiatrists to one of the most expensive restaurants in Manhattan: "Besides dining on tournedos of beef and cabernet sauvignon, each doctor was paid $500 for attending." The WPP executive said the checks "were appropriate, because the doctors had been hired as consultants for the night to sit on Forest's advisory board." (Petersen 2002)

Much of the Pharmas' quest for power and influence is carried on indirectly. Companies operate behind the scenes, in alliance or in tandem with networks of agencies, "champions" and "friends". Directly or not, the Pharmas have a profound and growing influence all over the map – in government and regulatory activity, in academic and clinical settings, throughout the media, and in many patient organisations too.

The Pharmas' reputation for aggression, bullying and litigiousness may well be deserved, yet merely the fear of exclusion from the reward system will often provide powerful enough reasons for toeing the line. The Pharmas make abundantly clear the difference between favoured status or not and everyone knows it: they can open doors that build reputations or keep them firmly closed; make or break senior appointments and careers; provide handsome rewards or not. They can empower the right people with ease; or obstruct "enemies" at every turn. The Pharmas exert influence far, deep and wide; they specialise in letting others get their own way. This extends to product promotion as well:

> "United States professional football sensation Ricky Williams last week sparked a blaze of publicity when he revealed he had social anxiety disorder and was benefiting from both therapy and Paxil (Seroxat/paroxetine) ... 'I've always been a shy person ...', said Williams, in an interview on NBC TV. GlaxoSmithKline confirmed that the company was paying Williams, but would not say how much or for how long." (Moynihan 2002)

By the early 21st century, there was substantial evidence of unsavoury marketing practice – ranging from secret payments to big stars for "celebrity endorsements", to experts lending their names to ghost-written "scientific" papers. Ghost-writing was commonplace[12] (Mowatt et al. 2002; Yamey 2002); it was considered so unexceptional that some free-lance Pharma consultants openly advertised ghost-writing skills on their website CVs (InPharm 2003). The few writers who did object were of course legally obliged to mention no names:

---

11 For Citalopram, read Celexa/Cipramil. Escitalopram = Lexapro/Cipralex (Forest Inc.).

12 A 1998 study of 809 articles published in six different peer-reviewed medical journals, found 11% of articles had ghost authors (Flanagin et al. 1998).

"I recently had my first and last experience as a "ghostwriter" for a medical communications company. I agreed to do two reviews for a supplement to appear under the names of respected 'authors'. I was given an outline, references, and a list of drug-company-approved phrases. I was asked to sign an agreement stating that I would not disclose anything about the project. I was pressured to rework my drafts to position the product more favourably, and was shown another company-produced review as an example – it read like bad promotional writing. I asked the company to reduce my fee and rewrite the drafts themselves." (Larkin 2002)

The influence of the Pharmas and the extent of sponsorship and conflicts of interest increasingly caused deep concern. "Just how tainted has medicine become?" asked a *Lancet* editorial (2002): "Heavily and damagingly so, is the answer."

Reputations

Collectively the big Pharmas poured money into political influence and communication, and throughout the medical establishment. This happened on a scale that exposed many to the risk of becoming in some ways deeply dependent on what the Pharmas might provide – or vulnerable to what they might take away. The beneficiaries naturally became less and less inclined and/or able to be critical of what they increasingly failed to see. Independence lost its way.

Dependence was deep, from the top down. Political leaders were made well aware that, "companies have more choice than ever before when deciding where to place new investment" (Blair 2001). The UK Prime Minister's view of the Pharmas was faithful to their image of themselves:

"The UK's pharmaceutical industry has an outstanding tradition and has contributed very substantially to our economy and to the welfare of our citizens. It has provided tens of thousands of high quality jobs, substantial investment in research and development, and a massive contribution to the UK's balance of trade. UK patients and people around the world have benefited from the early introduction of new and improved medicines that would not have been discovered without work undertaken in UK laboratories ... A key feature in maintaining the UK's attractiveness will be effective partnership at the highest levels between Government and industry ... I look forward to future partnership and to the pharmaceutical industry continuing to make a significant contribution to the health and prosperity of the UK." (Blair 2001)

In this climate, few felt the pervasive influence of the Pharmas to be untoward. Most people in the thick of it had interests to declare, including most of the experts involved in drug regulation. On the UK Committee on Safety of Medicines and subcommittees (2002), over half the members listed either personal and/or professional interests, including about a quarter with direct shareholdings in regulated companies. Lists of CSM members' personal interests were varied and long. They included:

> "Fees for lectures, advice, training and other services; Honoraria; Consultancies; Shareholdings; Directorships; Advisory board membership; Grants; Sponsorship; Royalties and Prizes. Non-personal (professional) interests included: Research contracts with universities; Departmental research funding, Sponsorship of departmental staff, including research or training grants, study grants, student grants, fellowships; Sponsorship of meetings, seminars, international conference; Support for clinical trials e.g. salaries, running expenses, consultancy, equipment and drugs."

Over half of the CSM members had links with the manufacturers of the top SSRI and related drugs: Eli Lilly (fluoxetine); GlaxoSmithKline (paroxetine); Lundbeck (citalopram); Pfizer (sertraline) and Wyeth (venlafaxine). One in three members disclosed personal interests in one or more of these companies, and four out of ten had personal or professional connections with the UK's largest pharmaceutical company, the giant GlaxoSmithKline. As companies grew in size, more and more people came on board.

Alongside the world of gain for those who spoke up about the benefits of drug treatment, there was also fear – real and imagined, in the eyes of critics, "enemies" as the Pharmas perceived (and privately described) them. Still there was no shortage of criticism: in the US, it became especially loud and persistent, in protest about drug prices in America and beyond.

Worldwide the main focus was on the cost of drugs for HIV/AIDS. Millions of people were dying because prices put the drugs they needed hopelessly out of reach. Determined to protect their intellectual property rights, the Pharmas stopped other companies from providing equivalent medicines at an affordable price. Led by their international federation, the Pharmas took the South African government to court, until public protest forced them to withdraw (2001).

John Le Carré's book, *The Constant Gardener* (2000) captured this mood. It was a disturbing work of fiction, depicting murder and other excesses, committed by or in the name of a totally imaginary pharmaceutical company. The events were imagined, but Le Carré's story was also the product of carefully researched and detailed analysis.

The reviewer in *Business Week* found he "could hardly bear" to put the book down. He praised it "without reservation" as a parable about health, corporate power, development and globalisation. That was quite some compliment considering the plot:

> "The Constant Gardener revolves around a drug, a diplomat, and a murder. Dypraxa is a new cure for tuberculosis, developed by a Swiss pharmaceutical

> company that is testing it – unscrupulously, and at great human cost – among Kenyan villagers and slum-dwellers in preparation for its debut in the U.S. and other developed nations. Tessa Quayle, a diplomatic wife, attorney, and idealist, discovers the corruption and malevolence at the heart of this scheme, only to get her throat cut in the bush north of Nairobi when she threatens to expose the whole sordid mess. The novel unfolds as Tessa's husband follows her path into the darker recesses of corporate greed, Foreign Office duplicity, and medical science in the service of profit."

Beyond the storyline in *The Constant Gardener* was a depiction of the Pharmas as a part of a sick, scary world. Many readers would have inferred that companies could be grasping, manipulative, corrupting and ruthless – especially if they pondered the author's postscript. After much research and many briefings: "I came to realize that, by comparison with the reality, my story was as tame as a holiday postcard."

It felt like a defining moment and was surely linked to the public pressure that caused the Pharmas to withdraw from the South African legal action. The impact of *The Constant Gardener* was profound. It emphatically defined Pharmas as organisations that have failed us, operations to be feared. It allowed that notion to be openly discussed.[13]

For the Pharmas, it was all the more shocking and perplexing that Le Carré should insist that his metaphorical appraisal was in some sense a true and fair view. Following publication, he elaborated his concerns in a series of articles and rounds of interviews. In an interview with David Hare (2001), Le Carré explained that he had focused on the Pharmas to explain his thoughts about the mess the world was in. He deplored the abuse of corporate power and feared the impact of globalisation. He felt deeply angry about the great missed opportunities of the late 20th century, with the dissolution of Soviet power. He was scathing about Tony Blair.

The reviewer in the *Christian Science Monitor* suggested that Le Carré should keep his door locked: "Writing about the craftiness of communist spies during the cold war was daring. But writing about the venality of the pharmaceutical industry is downright reckless." No-one really believed it, but everyone knew what it meant: it was to do with silencing critics, eliminating the opposition and assassination of reputation.

---

13 This was Le Carré's 18th major work. He had always previously insisted on personal privacy, emphasising he was an artist not a sage: "Nothing that I write is authentic. It is the stuff of dreams, not reality. Yet I am treated by the media as though I wrote espionage handbooks ... to a point I am flattered that my fabulations are taken so seriously. Yet I also despise myself in the fake role of guru, since it bears no relation to who I am or what I do" (Cornwell 1996). However, with *The Constant Gardener*, the author (David Cornwell) completely redefined his position, going out of his way to elaborate the depth of his convictions.

Thus, at one and the same time, the Pharmas were linked to miracles or disasters, depending on perspective and point of view. It is understandable they should turn to aggressive use of advertising, lobbying, public relations and market research machines. Reputation is crucial to their survival.

The capacity to shape understanding and to deal decisively with embarrassing data is part of organisational survival and there is a well-developed tradecraft to go with it. With many "friends" and "champions" to help them, the Pharmas were always able to respond to talk of drug risks by orchestrating an "independent" response. Beyond that, they could come down on their critics like a ton of treacle or bricks.

Fear began with the certainty that criticism of major products was no way up the career ladder in medicine – especially not in teaching hospitals and academic centres, where Pharmas were often the main or only source of funds. Even doctors who reported suspected adverse drug reactions were not immune, and this had been privately acknowledged by the industry: "Harassment does occur. We are fooling ourselves if we believe it does not" (Jones & Mann 1987). Thus, *The Constant Gardener* touched nerves.

Can one blame companies for swamping evidence of risk and for orchestrating endless demonstrations of the benefit of their products? The reality is that the Big Pharmas behave as they do just as a cat is programmed to chase mice. If companies want to thrive in the market, they need to exploit every opportunity to demonstrate benefit, value and lack of harm. That is exactly what they do: pity they do it so well.

Pharmas and world health

In the last quarter of the 20th century, the Pharmas came to play a decisive part in the organisation of world health. Their main visible presence was through their international trade body (International Federation of Pharmaceutical Manufacturers Associations – IFPMA) but, crucially, they operated in tandem with the US and other governments and through sponsored professional bodies.

The early 1980s marked a turning point between two different world orders, one based on health imperatives (Brandt 1981), the other serving market needs. US Secretary of State, Henry Kissinger (1974) had captured the spirit of uninhibited hope, proclaiming that, "within a decade no child will go to bed hungry ..." – a bold but seemingly plausible objective in those days.

Soon after, the WHO declared, "Health for All by the Year 2000." The feasibility of this was never in doubt,[14] if the reality always was. By the end of the 20th century, there was still nearly everything to do: at its 50th anniversary annual general meeting, WHO (1998) formally adopted a new policy: "Health For All in the 21st Century."

The global conflict between health and trade imperatives proved critical in the development of the WHO, and policies for world health, especially after an important conference at Alma Ata (1978). Its resolutions proposed a fair new world, in which health needs came first and common sense prevailed. Beyond rights of enfranchisement, WHO proposed schemes for informing patients and involving them in decision-making, at treatment level and far beyond.[15] Radical proposals were in the air.[16]

The Alma Ata conference launched the WHO's "Essential Drugs" concept. The emphasis was on doing more with less and on therapeutic value for money, as matters of life or death: "The available drugs must be restricted to those proven to be therapeutically effective, to have acceptable safety and to satisfy the health needs of the population. The selected drugs are called 'essential drugs' ... of the utmost importance ... basic, indispensable and necessary for the health needs of the population" (WHO 1977).

The Essential Drug concept immediately attracted fierce opposition from trade interests. The threat was perceived as great: the WHO model list of 220 Essential Drugs implied that a relatively small number of important, off-patent drugs could meet virtually all health needs. The inference was that many drugs were superfluous, and that branded products were by no means always best. The wider point was that drug innovation could be less vital for health than it might seem to be.

So, the WHO came under intense pressure to back off, especially after the election of President Reagan in 1980. On matters like this, the Pharmas and the US State Department saw eye-to-eye, and worked hand-in-hand. If US trade interests were at stake, the government weighed in. The US attitude to the WHO applied to the whole UN system, then as now: it should not stand in the way of American interests, whatever else.

Angered by the threatened expansion of the Essential Drugs programme, and by (largely imaginary) fears of supranational regulation,[17] the US government threat-

---

14 Lack of resources did not properly explain the extent of health deprivation. In 1983, the WHO estimated that it would cost less than global expenditure on tobacco – or one-fifteenth of the global spend on arms – to provide basic healthcare worldwide (Melrose 1982).

15 "... the health education approach often remains paternalistic and commandment-like. This attitude, where it exists, perpetuates the elitist position of health-care providers who make plans, define objectives, and develop messages that aim at persuading people, thus creating a certain distance between health professionals and 'the receivers'." ... Therefore, most health education programmes have been: "basically concerned with 'telling people' what is good for them ... The underlying concept in this approach was that only a few people knew certain facts and that the majority of the population knew little or held the wrong views" (WHO 1983).

16 "Science and technology can contribute to the improvement of health standards only if the people themselves become full partners of the health-care providers in safeguarding and promoting health ... people have not only the right to participate individually and collectively in the planning and implementation of health care programmes, but also a duty to do so" (WHO 1983).

ened to withdraw from WHO and thereafter, routinely withheld its annual dues until policy concessions were obtained. This created havoc in WHO – both because the US provided one-quarter of its budget, also because the US actively sought voting rights proportional to its financial contributions. Nor was WHO exposed only to US influence: over half its budget came from the top six drug-producing countries in the world.[18]

By the late-1980s, the pressures on WHO had produced a fundamental shift in the whole personality of the organisation. The WHO was, in effect, required to focus on medical and technical matters and to leave global politics well alone. Within the WHO headquarters in Geneva, they still refer to "the major donor" in tones that confirm the US as the major influence as well.

After 25 years, the *concept* of Essential Drugs remained very much alive, and 150 countries had adopted it (Helling-Borda 2003). At the same time, the WHO was drawn increasingly into a world in which market values emerged as the dominant influence on the spirit of pharmaceutical medicine, and on perceptions of global health needs.

Pharmas and the World Health Organization

WHO's role in the later stages of our case history illustrate some of the pressures on the organisation, and something of the influence of carrot as well as stick. Alongside the intense pressure from an assertive major donor, the growing influence of carrot intensified in the mid-1980s, with the slow but inexorable trend to privatisation.

That process began when WHO member governments resolved to freeze their levied annual contributions, requiring WHO to raise funds increasingly from "extra-budgetary contributions". By the 21st century, over half the WHO budget came from funds designated for specific programmes and/or from contributions from non-governmental sources.

In this way, the WHO's Mental Heath Division came to depend on the World Psychiatric Association (WPA). However, it all happened at arms length: the WPA

---

17 The US delegate to the 1986 World Health Assembly said: "I think most delegations know that the United States was the only country to vote against the adoption of the breast milk substitutes marketing code in 1981. Before then and ever since, it has been our strong position that the World Health Organisation should not be involved in efforts to regulate or control the commercial practices of private industry, even when the products may relate to concerns about health."

18 The six major drug-producing nations in the 1980s were France, Germany, Italy, Japan, the UK and the US. Between them, they controlled about three-quarters of the world pharmaceutical trade.

provided WHO not with *financial* contributions but services in kind. The WPA itself had a tiny annual budget, though it orchestrated programmes worldwide valued at probably 100-times that amount, if not more.[19] The actual figures were not disclosed, but to work out how an organisation with a disclosed annual turnover of US$354,000 can attract over 13,000 participants to its 10th World Congress of Psychiatry in Madrid, requires little imagination.[20]

The WPA became a prime mover in the WHO's Mental Health Division. Formal agreements between the two organisations guaranteed that WPA nominees made essential inputs into WHO programmes, helping to shape the outputs too.[21] One key input from the WPA was in developing the WHO guidelines that gave rise to the abolition of "dependence" as defined in DSM-IV.[22] The closeness between the WPA and WHO/MHD was underlined by the careers of successive heads of that Division.

> As head of the WHO's Mental Health Division, Dr. Norman Sartorius (1974, 1978) was credited as first to estimate the size of the world market for antidepressants, by drawing attention to the need to help the 100 million people suffering from depression "amenable to treatment" (Ayd 1996). Sartorius left WHO to become President of the WPA.

---

19 The WPA co-ordinates international activity among 110 national psychiatric societies (e.g. the American Psychiatric Association, Royal College of Psychiatrists) "representing more than 140,000 psychiatrists worldwide." Of these, 40,000 are members of the APA; US influence is strong. The WPA is a major publisher in the field, runs regular conferences and meetings, operates several Standing Committees and includes a "scientific arm" comprising 48 different sections, whose main task is to develop ideas and standards relating to basic issues in psychiatry. These include several of commercial significance, including disease definition and diagnosis. Overall levels of sponsorship are not known, but funding for individual programmes is generally acknowledged on an *ad hoc* basis – e.g. sponsorship by Eli Lilly of a special meeting of presidents of psychiatric societies, in Singapore, "to examine the current state and prospects of psychiatry in Asia; as well as three major educational programmes – on the Diagnosis and treatment of depression, Fighting Stigma and its consequences, and Core Curriculum for the Undergraduate Teaching of Psychiatry".

20 "Very simply, the model I have in mind involves companies pumping money into the WPA and its constituent organisations, and the WPA pumping influence into WHO" (C. Medawar, *ADWEB* 11 January 1999).

21 "The appearance of the ICD-10 Classification of Mental and Behavioural Disorders has been an event of vast importance for Psychiatry... The World Psychiatric Association, the World Health Organization as well as other educational institutions and Centers have carried out presentations and seminars concerning the role of ICD-10 in different countries with great success... The files (that have been developed on the basis of experience gained in such a process) have been produced by the World Psychiatric Association and the WHO Division of Mental Health and Prevention of Substance Abuse as a courtesy to the participants of the 10th World Congress of Psychiatry". (http://www.who.int/msa/mnh/ems/icd10/icd10ekit/intro.htm)

> Dr. Costa e Silva did it the other way round. He had been President of the WPA before becoming head of the WHO Mental Health Division. He left soon after the appointment of the new WHO Director-General, in 1998, but not before her plans for downsizing his Division had apparently been turned upside down.[23]

The details are tortuous, but the main pathways seem clear: the American Psychiatric Association (APA) was the dominant influence in the World Psychiatric Association, and the Pharmas were the major resource for both.[24] Meanwhile, the Mental Health Division could put hand on heart and say, "there has been no financial con-

---

22 The 9th edition of the WHO's International Classification of Diseases (ICD-9) was the forerunner of DSM-III: both determined that withdrawal alone satisfied the definition of "dependence". ICD-10 (1992) led the way for DSM-IV (1994) in specifying that withdrawal symptoms alone did not amount to dependence, in the absence of at least two other states that were indicative of abuse. These new preconditions were proposed in ICD-10 as "diagnostic guidelines" but the American Psychiatric Association promoted them through DSM-IV as hard and fast rules. Thus the DSM-IV definition contradicted the common sense definition of dependence in the WHO's Lexicon (1995), which implied, "a need for repeated doses of the drug to feel good or avoid feeling bad."

23 When the new administration took over at WHO, the extraordinary situation arose, in which the WHO's Director-General was lobbied by an organisation in which a WHO head of division played a prominent part. A WPA statement explained: "WHO'S REORGANIZATION AND THE RE-EMERGENCE OF MENTAL HEALTH – On May 13 1998, at her inaugural speech as the new Director General of the World Health Organization, Dr. Gro Harlem Brundtland spoke of the importance of mental health and the crucial value of NGOs for the organisation. However, during the weeks that followed, news coming from Geneva suggested that a streamlined WHO would not include any distinctive mental health structure. Perceiving this as a grave threat to mental health programs everywhere (as governments usually follow WHO for the organization of their own health services), our mental health community reacted at once. An unprecedented number of letters of concern reached Dr. Brundtland's office, many of them from WPA's s leadership and various components... At press time, we have learned that mental health has not only been preserved, but has emerged strengthened ... While the WHO reorganization process has not been completed yet, it has emerged that Professor Jorge Alberto Costa e Silva, past Medical Dean and Rector of the State University of Rio de Janeiro and Past-President of WPA, will continue as the leader of WHO's Division of Mental Health." The change in emphasis was underlined in WHO's *World Health Report 2001*. The main focus was on "Mental Health: New Understanding, New Hope."

24 Some details emerge from the board minutes of the American Psychiatric Association meetings – e.g. "The Board voted to approve the proposed fee structure for 40 industry sponsored symposia starting with the 1999 Annual Meeting, which calls for increasing the current fee structure for a 3 hour session from $35,000 to $45,000". And: "The Board voted to accept the proposal of Smith Kline Beecham to enable APA to offer APA members an opportunity to create their own patient-oriented newsletter as an APA member benefit at no cost to the Association."

tribution from WPA to WHO" (Costa e Silva 1998).[25] Dr. Costa e Silva left WHO in 1999; soon after, he was elected a Distinguished Fellow of the APA.

WHO was aware of the potential for conflicts of interest, but it was a delicate[26] and uncomfortable issue, especially for the Mental Health Division – it worked closely with the WPA and relied on individual Pharmas for direct programme support. To demonstrate independence in such cases, the Division would typically ring-fence donations – e.g. Eli Lilly was one of the Mental Health Division's major direct sponsors, but its donations were earmarked for programmes such as, Suicide Prevention in the Marshall Islands.

Whatever the safeguards, the Mental Health Division itself contributed little or less to the solution of either the benzodiazepine[27] or SSRI therapeutic dependence problems. Soon after publication of *The Antidepressant Web*, the MHD set up an "informal consultation", inviting ten experts carefully chosen from around the world. Drs. Stuart Montgomery and Malcolm Lader represented the UK.

> Montgomery's earlier work on paroxetine has been mentioned: "His close relationship with the pharmaceutical industry is ... well known, and his views are generally treated with caution for that reason."[28] Lader had been one of the first to identify normal-dose dependence on benzodiazepines (Petursson & Lader 1981). However, by this time, he was consulting for SmithKline Beecham and other SSRI

25 Letter to *Social Audit*, 24 November 1998. In this letter, Dr Costa e Silva wrote that he stepped down from all WPA commitments when he took over at WHO. However, he was identified on the WPA letterhead as a member of its Council and his CV on the WHO website identified him as task force chairman for 14 international educational programmes at the WPA.

26 At organisational level, the problem was hard to confront – the feeling being that any determined attempt to address the issue might give great offence to the representatives of some countries (Aitken, D., Personal communication 2000), especially those where bribery and corruption were an established part of life. Dr. Brundtland was the first to require any declaration of personal interests by senior WHO staff in 1998, the organisation's 50th anniversary year.

27 The contrast between WHO policy on either side of the early 1980s is underlined by its position on benzodiazepines. Before that turning point, and in the face of intense opposition, the ECDD had managed to get benzodiazepines "scheduled" under international law, as drugs of dependence and abuse. However, in the mid-1990s, at the initiative of the World Psychiatric Association, the WHO published guidelines for benzodiazepines that recommended long-term treatment and estimated the actual addiction rate was about 1% of all treated cases (http://www.psykmott-ntorg.a.se/ benzoart.html). WHO was subsequently unable to substantiate this estimate. See *ADWEB:* correspondence with *Social Audit*, July to October 1998. Hoffman La Roche and other benzo manufacturers purchased many thousands of copies of the MHD/ WPA report on *Rational Use of Benzodiazepines*. However, when Roche later made the MHD a US$500,000 donation, the Expert Committee on Drug Dependence was moved out of the MHD and into another WHO Division.

28 R.E. Kendell, President, Royal College of Psychiatrists: letter to *Social Audit*, 28 November 1997.

> manufacturers, advising them about the withdrawal syndromes. On this issue, Lader was the expert spokesman for the Royal College of Psychiatrists, as well.[29]

For reasons unknown, this consultation was abandoned and the Mental Health Division played no direct part in this debate thereafter. Two other WHO units very quietly led the running on this issue, but with minimal encouragement from the Organization itself.[30] By the late 1990s, the WHO Director-General's office had to approve all proposals to generate any document with policy implications, rather than "technical" content.

By the 21st century, the future for WHO lay in the promise of Public-Private initiatives and partnerships, but always with the threat of being sidelined. That risk was underlined by the development of major, US-brokered Public-Private coalitions that by-passed the WHO.[31] A new era in the financing of global health had begun.

---

29 At the request of the President of the Royal College of Psychiatrists, Lader produced an opinion, 11 November 1997, on matters arising from *The Antidepressant Web.* Lader saw no reason to compare SSRIS with benzos; there was no dependence with SSRIS. He fully disclosed his association with SKB and other companies with SSRIS.

30 The Expert Committee on Drug Dependence (ECDD) and the Uppsala Monitoring Centre (the home of WHO monitoring of ADRS) both played low-key but important parts in this case history. Each had a measure of organisational autonomy, and also highly technical responsibilities – probably both of which enhanced their ability to act more independently within WHO.

31 The World Bank became increasingly involved in financing international health development, but the major challenge came from two funds set up independently of the UN system. In 2000, the Gates Foundation pledged US$750 million to the newly-established, Global Alliance on Vaccines and Immunization (GAVI). Soon after, the Global Fund (for people living with HIV/AIDS, malaria and tuberculosis) was set up on a Private-Private basis, with pledges of around US$2 billion, i.e. close to the total budget of WHO.

7
Medicalisation and disease awareness

∾ The pressure to create mass markets for "blockbuster" and "lifestyle" drugs – essential to the Pharmas' survival – led to the introduction in the US of Direct-To-Consumer Advertising (DTCA) of prescription drugs. DTCA proved a life-line for the Pharmas. It was a potent driver of growth in the market, producing handsome returns on investment – but it also produced hyperinflationary growth in the drugs bill. How would the UK and European governments respond to this conflict between trade and health needs? The battle in Europe defined a new role for patients' organisations, and revealed the workings of democracy at its worst and best. ∾

In the beginning, doctors wrote prescriptions in Latin and patients were told simply to take "the tablets" as prescribed. Prescription drugs were never publicly advertised, but regarded as strictly "ethical" products and promoted only to professionals. This tradition began to change, especially in the US, once big brands like Valium and Tagamet arrived.

By 1982, the head of the Food and Drug Administration (FDA) believed the US to be, "on the brink of the exponential growth phase of direct-to-consumer promotion of prescription products." There was much interest in this, not least from the media. The prospect of a vast new advertising market prompted the CBS-TV network (1984) to commission a major survey of consumer drug information needs. They found a huge market potential – but then the Opren/Oraflex crisis turned everything around.

Around 1980, Eli Lilly had introduced a new aspirin-like drug: benoxaprofen (Oraflex in the US; Opren in the UK). Wanting to make an impact in a market already full of similar drugs, Lilly had commissioned a lavish launch. The company and its agents hinted at miracles: could this be the most important development since aspirin? Might this new drug even prove to reverse the course of disease?

Inevitably, all this talk reached the general public: Lilly made sure of this by distributing press kits and audio/video tapes to radio/TV stations, and whatever else.

Prescription levels soared until the drug was withdrawn worldwide, on safety grounds, in 1983. Lilly had set the dosage too high and had skimped on the research.

They had badly underestimated and failed to report serious problems, and hardly tested the drug in the target population of older people.[1]

Within a few weeks of getting Oraflex taken off the market, the FDA called a moratorium on DTCA, to allow time for reflection. This prompted a review by a US Congressional committee (1984), and it reported a strong and rather astonishing consensus.

Professional and consumer organisations were strongly opposed to DTCA but so were the Pharmas too. The committee had consulted 27 major brand name companies. Only three favoured DTC promotion; five reportedly "waffled", and the rest were opposed. Looking back to 1984, their reasons seem remarkable; they used the same arguments against DTCA that their critics use today:

> "Advertising can inform, but it is not education; and (DTCA) should not be portrayed as a part of the education process. In fact, we have major reservations about the capacity of advertising to assist properly in that process ... the ads result in pressure on doctors to prescribe ... Additionally, we have concerns about the capacity of advertising to communicate the properties of prescription products in terms comprehensible to ordinary consumers." (Smith Kline & French)

> "The physician alone has the scientific training to make a proper diagnosis, specify the appropriate therapy, and evaluate the results ... people with chronic debilitating disease have been historically susceptible to messages concerning the efficacy of medicines and devices marketed for their illness. This consideration – plus a lack of true understanding of the course of the disease – would make them extraordinarily susceptible to product promises. This is particularly true of elderly patients." (Wyeth)

> "By their very nature, prescription drugs embody a complex set of factors with potential human effects that can best be evaluated by the physician. These factors include aspects of chemistry, physiology, unique patient characteristics, and other considerations, all of which can have a bearing on whether or not a particular medicine, at a particular dosage, is a proper therapeutic agent. Therefore, we believe that the need for the physician's supervision of any prescription drug taken by the patient is paramount and that the potential pressures of public advertising of prescription drugs on the scientific decisions of the physician are both unwise and inappropriate." (Eli Lilly)

---

1 In the early 1980s, there was still limited understanding about the influence of age on drug response: younger and older patients were often prescribed drugs at the usual adult dosage. These days, older people can expect smaller doses and pre-marketing drug testing on elderly people is more routine, but there are major gaps even so. Rochon et al. (1998) found that only 2.1% of subjects in trials of arthritis drugs (NSAIDs) were aged 65 years or more.

For the next decade, the issue went away, until the mid-1990s, when it surfaced again. By then, the Pharmas urgently needed to pump up their marketing because of the lack of innovation. Also, the Internet was beginning to bloom: that made it possible to advertise across borders, and greatly complicated advertising control. Pressure grew in the US and, in August 1997, the FDA eventually permitted DTCA of prescription drugs on radio and TV. A brand new era had begun, and the Pharmas' previous misgivings just melted away. Now the Pharmas emphasised their contribution to "disease awareness" and choice. They began to buy into patient organisations and sometimes set them up from scratch.

> The National Alliance for the Mentally Ill (NAMI) – "a grassroots organisation of individuals with brain disorders and their family members" – received US$11.72 million from 18 Pharma companies, between 1996 and mid-1999. Eli Lilly, the leading donor, gave US$2.87 million. (Silverstein 1999)

A few years earlier, the US Pharmas had opposed the Carter Administration's proposals to develop Patient Information Leaflets. Now they began to stress the importance of drug information; they talked of "expert" patients and began to fight for patients' rights:

> "A pharmaceutical company will tomorrow break new ground by encouraging the public to demand that the NHS pay to make available one of its drugs. The campaign, Action for Access, is funded by Biogen and organised by a PR company on its behalf. It will urge multiple sclerosis sufferers to demand their health authorities agree to prescribe beta-interferon on the NHS, a very expensive drug, which can help some sufferers, but not all." (Boseley 1999)

In the US, DTC promotion would have a profound influence on the growth of the market. Huge budgets promoted the major Selective Serotonin Reuptake Inhibitors (SSRIs) and other Blockbusters. Within five years, US expenditure on DTC promotion had grown from almost nothing to US$2.5 billion per year.

The timing well suited SmithKline Beecham, and made Paxil (paroxetine) one of the most promoted brands. By promoting it directly to the public, SKB was able to "reposition" Paxil more as a remedy for anxiety, and in other ways. Five years after its launch as a serotonin booster for depression, SKB won a new indication for paroxetine for what used to be "social phobia". Suddenly, "social phobia" became "social anxiety disorder" (SAD). They were the same, but different. Prevalence rates varied between 3% and 13% – depending on who thought which was what.[2]

---

2 The lower estimate came from the US National Institutes for Mental Health; the marketing people pitched high. The American Psychiatric Association (APA) said it varied a lot (Vedantam 2001).

A barrage of learned papers and presentations informed doctors about the great distress caused by this new disease. Meanwhile, the spin produced the "patient pull" – what the headlines called "shyness" and "embarrassment" were defined as the essence of SAD.

Out of the blue, SAD became America's third most common mental illness. Widespread but badly under-treated, yet easily treatable: that was the thrust of a great campaign. It was fronted by a coalition of non-profit patient and professional groups, but orchestrated by SKB's public relations agency, Cohn & Wolfe (Koerner 2002).

This agency's campaign won awards and sales surged. Paxil's product director at the time was the inspirationally named, Barry Brand. In an interview with *Advertising Age*, he explained: "Every marketer's dream is to find an unidentified or unknown market and develop it. That's what we were able to do with social anxiety disorder" (Vedantam 2001).

> Later, Paxil won FDA approval for an even broader indication, a catch-all diagnosis, sombrely identified in DSM-IV as "Generalized Anxiety Disorder". The relaxation of the DTC advertising rules permitted TV spots (targeted at 18-to-34 year-old professionals) with tag lines such as: "What if you were allergic to people?" and "Your life is waiting ..."
>
> Then came an indication for "Post Traumatic Stress Disorder". Within weeks of the 2001 terrorist attack on the World Trade Center, Paxil was there to help again: "Your worst fears," agonized one woman, seated at a kitchen table, "the what ifs ... I can't control it." "I'm always thinking something terrible is going to happen," another woman fretted. "It's like a tape in my mind" a third confessed. "It just goes over and over and over." (Hawkins 2002)

In the US, at least, DTC promotion had come to stay and, depending on perspective, that was either a good or bad thing. DTC promotion proved a potent driver of double-digit growth in the market – but that naturally translated as hyperinflationary growth in the drugs bill. The 50 medicines "most heavily advertised to consumers accounted for almost half the $20.8 billion increase in US drug spending. The remainder of the spending increase came from 9,850 prescription medicines that companies did not advertise or advertised very little" (NICHM 2001).

Direct to Europe promotion

Consumer advertising of prescription-only medicines was at this time illegal throughout Europe and in all other major markets worldwide.[3] The Pharmas needed this to change. The US market had reached bursting point: drug prices had become unpopular and unsustainable and there was intense pressure to open up markets overseas.

Within weeks of the FDA deregulation, US proposals for DTCA were on the agenda at Commissioner level in Europe (Bangemann 1997). The request to the European Commission (EC) to take "a more flexible approach" was taken quite seriously. That was partly because, in the European system, medicines' policy and regulation was controlled not by a health department, but by the European Commission's department for trade: "DG Enterprise".[4] The pressure on the EC was clear from a major agenda item on the 1998 "Mid Year Scorecard Report" of the Transatlantic Business Dialogue (TABD).[5] The message was that the Pharmas stood for the liberation of consumers, and fairness in trade:

> "IDENTIFIED PRIORITY/DEFINITION OF PROBLEM — The U.S. permits industry, subject to strict regulatory controls, to provide information about prescription medicines direct to consumers (DTC). Such communication is severely restricted in the EU. This causes an inconsistency in the regulatory treatment of industry in the transatlantic marketplace, deprives EU citizens of the right-to-know compared to their U.S. counterparts, and is out of step with technological advances whereby all citizens are able to obtain information about medicines from the Internet or other international sources but not within their own countries."

DG Enterprise responded promptly and said that talks about the possibility of lifting the ban on DTCA might be expected soon. The TABD "Charlotte Communiqué" welcomed this and requested, "that the Commission establish a working group to review DTC advertising issues." DG Enterprise did just that.

In setting up a working group, the DG Enterprise Pharmaceuticals Unit was able to sideline its health oversight committee – representatives from the health depart-

---

3 More by accident than design, New Zealand was the only other country where DTCA was allowed. Because "ethicals" had never been advertised, the practice had never been banned.

4 Drug regulation is handled by departments of health in each of the EU member states – but not in the European Commission. The reasons are historical and political. The EU was conceived as an economic union and "health" became a main agenda item only after the Treaty of Amsterdam (1999); the directorate for environment, consumer affairs and health is not strong and has a very limited role in drug regulation.

5 The TABD is a top-level forum, founded by the US and EU governments in 1995 "to forge a consensus industry agenda for government action".

ments of the EU member states. However, its new working group met only once, in 2000, and then only to endorse the Pharmaceutical Unit's proposal to circulate a questionnaire to stimulate some wider consultation. Democratic inspiration was nowhere. The outcome of this consultation was never published and the questionnaire was erased from the DG Enterprise website soon after. It was embarrassingly poor: none of the questions specifically referred to DTC promotion, and many seemed incomprehensible:

> "Do you think that it could be useful to give possibilities for the Marketing Authorisation Holder to give more information?"
>
> "Do you think it would have a public interest as far as certain classes of medicinal products are concerned?"
>
> "If yes, on which classes of medicinal products could it be possible to start?"

The consultation entirely by-passed the main health issues: what would happen in Europe if commercially inspired messages about diagnosis and treatment dominated the information diet? Would the demand overwhelm national health provision? Would DTC promotion encourage rational drug use and better understanding of the balance of benefit and risk? Might it promote drug treatments over possibly better alternatives, including non-intervention and/or less effective and cost-effective medical treatments? Might it overwhelm the supply of drug information from independent sources, and compromise the editorial independence of the press and media, and their coverage of health issues? (Davidoff 2001) What of the risks of the medicalisation of everyday life? Would DTC promotion of prescription drugs really make people feel healthier, or perhaps reduce their confidence in their own abilities (and responsibilities) to get better and stay well?

These were exactly the kinds of questions that were not being addressed in the European "debate" on DTCA. The discussion focused instead on simple win-win themes. DG Enterprise emphasised the great importance of drug innovation and the value of the pharmaceutical industry to the economy of the EU. This main theme was in complete accord with the Pharmas' own views: patients benefited from new drugs and needed them fast, and they also needed reliable information about them.

By this time, the Pharmas enjoyed support for such views from some patient organisations. The Pharmas had begun to sponsor the major players and could rely on their support. The few exceptions proved this rule:

> "When the Danish Migraine Association refused to take industry 'assistance' to write and print the magazine, organise the lectures and generally run the association, the industry, generously assisted by the research doctors, literally created a new patient organisation as a substitute for the Migraine Association in 1996." (Bulow-Olsen 2000)

Most patient groups were open, if not vulnerable, to overtures from companies and trade associations. They generally struggled for survival and big promotional campaigns empowered them; such campaigns focused on the needs of special and deserving interests and the disadvantages they faced. Groups linked to DTC promotions were therefore able to attract more members, more column inches and sound bites. For most patient organisations, sponsorship meant more exposure, prominence and sense of achievement. Many got "unrestricted" grants as well.

> In 1999, the UK-based *Patients Association* joined forces with Pharmacia and Upjohn (P&U – now part of Pfizer Inc.) in a prototype DTC television campaign aimed at "raising awareness" about urinary incontinence. The TV commercials mentioned no brand name, but urged patients to see their doctor. Those who did stood a very good chance of being prescribed the leading and most heavily promoted brand, made by P&U. The product (Detrusitol/Detrol) was relatively ineffective and P&U had also attracted repeated criticism for misleading advertising.[6] The *Patients Association* became aware of this too late: they had already supported the TV campaign and accepted a large donation from P&U. In return, the Association gave the company its "Platinum Award".

As if to complement this newfound lack of independence among patient groups, the DG Enterprise Pharmaceuticals Unit then changed its policy on consultation. The new policy was explained by the head of the Unit, Philippe Brunet (2000) in a letter to Health Action International (Europe) – the one pan-European consumer-health organisation that had researched the health implications (Mintzes 1998) and called for a proper debate. Brunet explained that DG Enterprise had turned away from the independent consumer bodies it had traditionally consulted, "since they are not able to do what we have historically looked to them to do, namely the representation of the interests of consumers as patients."

Brunet's letter went on to propose the name of Rodney Elgie, as if to signal the kind of patient representation he had in mind. Elgie stood for close partnership with the Pharmas. The extent to which they funded his work was not disclosed, but he networked and lobbied tirelessly, and was a staunch advocate of what was then being called DTC "communication":

6 P&U received five warning letters from the US FDA (1998-2000). In particular, the company was censured for headline claims that emphasised the "selectivity" of its product – suggesting that it acted specifically on the bladder, with less drying-up effects in the mouth. P&U evidence was based not on clinical trials, but on studies with cats. In the UK, the company continued to make similar claims for another two years (Social Audit 1999-2001).

> "Prozac has done more than any health professional or patient-led campaign to educate the public about the incidence of depression and the devastating consequences it may have on the sufferer ...
>
> Subject to appropriate and effective controls on advertising practices being put into place, it is now time to permit manufacturers of medicines to provide all relevant information about their products, to any patients who seek it." (Elgie 2002)

A few weeks before Brunet proposed Elgie's name, the Pharmas' strategy for promoting DTC Communication in Europe had been outlined in a trade journal, Pharmaceutical Marketing. The source was Dr. Trevor Jones, Director-General of the Association of the British Pharmaceutical Industry (ABPI). Probably he hadn't realised he would be quoted: he was speaking at a private meeting about the ABPI "Battle Plan" for promoting DTCA in Europe. Enlisting user support was central: "Patient groups offer us a big opportunity to provide them with authoritative information for them to use objectively in a way that benefits their members", he said.

Phase one of the British Pharmas' "Battle Plan" had begun in 1998 with "the Informed Patient Initiative". That had been largely completed, said Jones: "A recent publication by the ABPI, *The Expert Patient*, is part of a softening-up assault to be mounted through those interested parties and opinion leaders by stimulating public debate." Phase two of the Pharmas campaign involved "seeking alliances with patient groups" and others:

> "Now the ABPI has announced that it is launching the final stages of a campaign before it tackles the Government and the EU head on ... It is the spearhead of a carefully thought-out campaign. The ABPI battle plan is to employ ground troops in the form of patient support groups, sympathetic medical opinion and healthcare professionals – known as 'stakeholders' – which will lead the debate on the informed patient issue. This will have the effect of weakening political, ideological and professional defences ... Then the ABPI will follow through with high-level precision strikes on specific regulatory enclaves in both Whitehall and Brussels." (Jeffries 2000)

Rodney Elgie fitted this bill, but for a chequered past.[7] With help from the SSRI Pharmas, he had transformed a patient group, Depression Alliance in the UK. He then moved on to help build another industry-founded group, GAMIAN (Global Alliance of Mental Illness Advocacy Organisations); he became its President. Elgie had also been treasurer of the International Association of Patient Organisations (IAPO), founded and funded by a consortium of 30-odd Pharma companies, operating as Pharmaceutical Partners for Better Healthcare. The Pharmas' approval of Elgie was underlined by his close association with the European Federation of Pharmaceutical Associations (EFPIA). The Pharmas' preference for Elgie would set the tone in the deliberations to come.

The British way

The Pharmas had made the UK their base for advancing DTC promotion in Europe, effectively with the blessing of Prime Minister Blair. The heads of the three top UK Pharmas – AstraZeneca, GlaxoWellcome and SmithKline Beecham – had been to discuss the industry's needs with Blair, in November 1999. He immediately set up a Pharmaceutical Industry Competitiveness Task Force (PICTF) to report back to him.

This task force (PICTF) was co-chaired by Philip (Lord) Hunt, the UK Health Minister who was also directly responsible for drug regulation and stewardship of the National Health Service (NHS). The remit of the task force was to "look at the action needed to ensure the UK remains an attractive place for the R&D pharmaceutical industry to locate its business in an increasingly competitive business environment" (DOH 2001). No conflict of interest between Lord Hunt's health and trade roles was perceived.

---

7 Biographical data published alongside an article Elgie wrote for Pfizer Forum (1998) began as follows: "Rodney Elgie has been an attorney in private practice more than twenty years, rising to the position of senior partner. He became a member of Depression Alliance in 1992, and served on the Charity's Executive Committee as the honorary legal advisor. He was appointed the first full-time Executive Director of Depression Alliance in early 1995 and spearheaded the dramatic growth in both the membership of the charity and its self-help groups".

Elgie had been struck off the Roll of Solicitors for reckless and dishonest handling of clients' funds (Findings and Order of the Solicitors' Disciplinary Tribunal, Case no 5905/1990/4817, 19 Feb 1991). "The Tribunal has taken note of the testimonial letters offered in support of this respondent of which there are many and speak very highly of him. The Tribunal is not convinced that this respondent was suffering from a degree of mental incapacity throughout the whole of the time when he perpetrated the matters alleged against him and consider it not unlikely that his actions and the anxiety following his actions might well have led him into depression and mental difficulty".

Elgie left Depression Alliance in 1999. In 2000 and again in 2001, the UK Charity Commission investigated Depression Alliance because of financial and administrative irregularities. Such investigations were rare, but the details are not known. Remarks made by the new director, at the 2002 annual meeting of Depression Alliance suggest there were significant problems, but there was no suggestion that Elgie might have been responsible for them: "The fact that we are here today for this meeting is nothing short of incredible. Going into the last financial year, the Trustees could have taken the view that the risks to them personally of carrying on were unjustifiable. That they didn't demonstrates – to my mind – an exceptional commitment. That commitment inspired the small staff team to achieve what to most would have seemed impossible. It would have been tough enough to have retreated behind locked doors for six months, working on nothing but remedying the administrative problems".

There is little evidence that Elgie's background cramped his style. He was ubiquitous and prolific. GAMIAN, at the time of writing, did not disclose funding sources – but neither did three-quarters (95/125) of the patient organisation websites checked out by *Health Which?* in April 2003).

The first of several PICTF reports rather fawned to the industry – "a jewel in the industrial crown of the UK economy" – and stressed that a new spirit of cooperation had begun (Hunt & McKillop 2001). The 70-page report proposed a long list of specific measures and commitments by government to help the Pharmas to succeed. The list included an undertaking to fight the Pharmas' corner in Europe, as well.

Crucially, the PICTF also defined the "Main Competitiveness & Performance Indicators" for the industry – the main yardsticks by which to judge the Pharmas' value. At a stroke, the PICTF decided that the quality and usefulness of drug innovation should be measured only in economic terms. Though co-chaired by a health minister, the task force did not refer to the entirely uncertain and increasingly dubious relationship between drug innovation and health value. The main indicators of value that the PICTF proposed were all about the economic gains:

"– Proportion of world first patents filed for marketed new drugs divided by proportion of world R&D spend,
– UK-based companies' number of 'global top 75' new active substances, and
– % of world pharmaceutical R&D spend."

This single-minded focus on trade also meant that the task force (PICTF) missed the significance of the crisis in innovation. The task force had focused on the industry's "underperformance" in Britain and Europe, ignoring the evidence that the crisis was actually centred in the US and rapidly coming to a head. The PICTF analysis missed key points: US drug prices were going through the roof, innovation was flagging and becoming prohibitively expensive, relatively few new drugs offered worthwhile therapeutic gains, and US industry profitability was in decline (Arlington 2001). No such issues were discussed in the PICTF report. The realisation that the "crisis in innovation" affected the US as much as Europe began to sink in only three years later, by which time "solutions" to the presumed European problem had already been decided.[8]

In the moment, Lord Hunt and colleagues simply assumed the crisis was centred in Europe, and took for granted the great health dividends of the measures they proposed. They might well have wondered more about the quality of drug innovation and its real impact on health. Across the board, health standards in Europe were

---

8 The penny seemed to drop in late 2002, when the European drug licensing agency (EMEA) noticed a substantial decline in applications to market New Chemical Entities, also that "exactly the same thing had occurred in the United States". In May 2003, the European Commission put out to tender (ENTR/03/28) a research proposal to address the crisis as then perceived. The Commission wanted answers to three main questions: "Is there a world-wide crisis in innovation in the pharmaceutical sector? What are the reasons behind this crisis? What tools do we have available to kick-start innovation?" The answers would become known too late, only after completion of the Commission's major European, pharmaceutical review.

clearly highly "competitive" with those in the US. From a European health perspective, one might have concluded that phenomenal levels of investment in drug innovation produced fewer and fewer health gains.

Meanwhile, the Pharmas emphasised that what they had in mind for Europe was far removed from full-blown DTCA – which by then was causing much concern in New Zealand as well as the US. The Pharmas sensed the need to soft peddle, though privately they thought it was only a matter of time before they got their way.[9]

Philip (Lord) Hunt, doubled as co-chair of the Pharmaceutical Industry Competitiveness Task Force (PICTF), and the Health Minister responsible for the Medicines Control Agency (MCA). The MCA took up the DTC issue at once, but then did nothing of consequence for more than a year. The MCA's long correspondence with *Social Audit* later revealed both the importance of busy inaction as a tool of government and the abuse of secrecy in sustaining the illusion of valuable work. Throughout 2000, the MCA felt obliged to put up with a barrage of enquiries and complaints from *Social Audit*, rather than reveal what they weren't doing. Far from consulting on an issue of obvious public interest, the MCA went to great lengths to reveal nothing whatever of its plans – at precisely the time the European Commission was holding its public consultation. It took a ruling from the Ombudsman to establish that the MCA's disclosable annual output amounted to a three-page paper that had barely begun to explore the dividing line between more and less acceptable "disease awareness" campaigns.

As part of "a helpful package of measures" to the Pharmas, Lord Hunt also pressed DG Enterprise to set up its own task force, along the lines of the PICTF. This prompted the creation, in 2000, of the European "Group of Ten." This so-called G10 group was duly appointed but grew to thirteen. Describing themselves as "the top decision-makers on medicines from the EU," they included two EC Commissioners (co-chairs), four health ministers (UK, France, Germany, Portugal),[10] a trade minister (Sweden), three representatives from the big Pharmas (including GlaxoSmithKline), and one representative each from the generics manufacturers, the non-profit health insurers and consumers. The PICTF and the G10 initiatives were both archetypes of "Public-Private Partnership" in policy- and law-making. The PICTF had given the Pharmas an exclusive place in health policy-making, whereas the G10 process evolved as something closer to a legislative instrument, with a direct and specific input into the formulation of law.

Lord Hunt duly became a member of the G10.[11] The MCA, part of his fiefdom, then seconded one of its policy staff to provide executive support, as one of the G10

9 "... in the industry's view, the prohibition on the advertising of prescription medicines to the public is unsustainable in the longer term. Industry considers that changes to legislation will therefore be required to deliver a truly rational package and bring accurate information on their products to the market" (Hunt & McKillop 2001).

"Sherpas". These Sherpas took no credit for the G10 output: extraordinarily (or not) their names were never mentioned, but they organised and orchestrated the G10 process. These Sherpas distinctly led the way, though the lone consumer representative was handicapped. She was the only G10 member with no Sherpa assigned.[12]

The G10 Sherpas divided, in effect, as "officers" and "other ranks". The latter performed more as a traditional secretariat; the former ran the show. The dominant Sherpas – in no sense baggage carriers – were Paul Weissenberg (Director, DG Enterprise) and Brian Ager (Director of the European Federation of Pharmaceutical Manufacturers Associations). In this early example of public-private legislative partnership, Weissenberg chaired the G10 Sherpas, determined to forge consensus views.

G10 and the Pharmaceutical Review

By early 2001, DG Enterprise was looking for some way forward. Its Pharmaceuticals Unit (also under Weissenberg) had by then achieved little or no support by way of consultation: there was apparently "no appetite" among Member States for any change to the law that prohibited DTCA.[13]

10 The UK, France and Germany represented the major EU drug-producing countries. The inclusion of Portugal reflected the EU Council's adoption of "The Lisbon strategy", in March 2000, "to make the EU the world's most dynamic and competitive economy" through economic, social and environmental renewal. Significantly, the 2003 review of progress towards these objectives, emphasised the competitive success of the EU in a number of areas, including pharmaceuticals: "In the face of competition from newly industrial countries, EU industry has outperformed its main competitors. While the Union's share in world exports fell from an average of 19.3% over the 1991/95 period to 18.4% in 2002, the US share over the same period dropped from 15.1% to 12.1%, and Japan's share from 12.2% to 8.2%. Furthermore, in some major industrial sectors such as automobiles, aeronautics, mobile communications or pharmaceuticals, EU companies have achieved world leadership" (Report to the Spring European Council, 21 March 2003 on the Lisbon strategy of economic, social and environmental renewal, COM (2003) 5 final/2, Brussels, 3 April 2003).

11 Hunt resigned as a UK government minister in March 2003, in protest at the UK's involvement in the Iraq War. Deputy Prime Minister John Prescott reportedly told the BBC: "I don't know who Lord Hunt is. He is obviously a minister of government ... I'm sorry for my ignorance" (*Financial Times* 18 March 2003). By this time, only five of the original members were still serving on the G10.

12 Angela Coulter's repeated requests to have someone assigned were of no avail: she had to act as her own Sherpa, but was often unable to attend their regular meetings.

13 The Commission never revealed the response to its consultation. This reference to "lack of appetite" was mentioned only as an aside in the PICTF report.

This defined the role for the G10. It was to smooth the path for DG Enterprise, helping to steer its forthcoming proposals, not only for DTC drug promotion, but for a wide-ranging reform of EU pharmaceutical laws. The main impetus for this Pharmaceutical Review was again the concern that the Pharmas were migrating to the US. Like the UK government, DG Enterprise had relied on a detailed analysis that concluded that the US was doing "better" than Europe – but again based on the assumption that drug innovation was what really mattered, and that quality of innovation could be measured just by the economic returns (Gambardella et al. 2000).

The G10 focused only on win-win. Its main task was: "to review the extent to which current pharmaceutical, health and enterprise policies achieve the twin goals of both encouraging innovation and ensuring satisfactory delivery of public health and social imperatives." It was no part of the G10 agenda to acknowledge there might be areas of conflict between trade and health imperatives. They were trying to find "consensus" and partly achieved it by admitting minimal dissent.

The G10 process began with a call for written submissions in response to a consultation paper that emphasised the twin goals theme. At the same time, the G10 orchestrated "workshops" around Europe, tightly engineered as presentations rather than consultations, always aiming to steer clear of controversy. The G10 consultation paper proposed that:

> "the pharmaceutical industry can play a crucial role as providers of reliable, factual and balanced information about their medicines for patients that will support the appropriate and effective involvement of patients and appropriate use of their products ..."
>
> "there is a need to review national regulations which may inhibit the legitimate provision of factual information or disease education literature by industry."

The G10 paper again emphasised the need to distinguish between "advertising" and "good quality patient information." It produced a checklist of 13 elements that should be included in good quality information – which in practice would be attained in few clinical trials. Two items on the checklist underlined what advertising could never be: "refers to all relevant treatment and management options," and "includes honest information about benefits and harms."

In the nine months that passed between publication of the consultation paper and the G10 final report, virtually nothing changed. Consensus had been achieved, but really only by suggesting the need for consensus. The G10 conclusions said, yet again, that there needed to be "a practical distinction between advertising and information," suggesting this should be achieved through "a collaborative public-private partnership involving a range of interested parties." Several commercially-sponsored and officially blessed initiatives were later launched in pursuit of common ground. Some claimed to have found it and proposed "consensus" agreements (Detmer et al.

2003), but the obstacles were structural and far reaching. The challenge went further than this search for new words.

Meanwhile, DG Enterprise published a range of proposals for pharmaceutical law reform in summer 2001. They insisted that they did not intend to allow DTCA. They proposed a five-year experiment, subject to annual review, in which the Pharmas could provide consumers with approved advertising/information[14] for asthma, diabetes and AIDS – "in order to respond to the expectations expressed by patients groups." Such words were embodied in the proposed new law, and the head of DG Enterprise (also co-chair of the G10), Commissioner Liikanen, repeatedly stressed them:

> "First, we say that there must be a request from the side of patients or patient groups. I want to say that this change has been done very much due to the repetitive demands of patient groups ..."

> "Mr Liikanen said diabetes, AIDS and asthma were selected because the patient groups lobbied for it and the diseases were relatively easy to define."[15]

Six months later, at a conference organised by Health Action International (Europe) and other groups[16] resisting DTC promotion, the obvious question came up from the floor. Had the Pharmas' "ground troops" been orchestrating this demand? Which groups had been asking for such information and where was the evidence of their input? This question was put to a senior DG Enterprise spokesman, Nils Behrndt, and was also picked up by the lone consumer representative on the G10. Behrndt replied that it was the Commission's "presumption" that such demand existed. No evidence was available to support this. The industry newsletter, *SCRIP* (2002), reported as follows:

> "Mr Behrndt said that as far as he was aware, nothing had been received in writing from any patient group, and none of the delegates at the meeting was aware of expectations being expressed by their organisations, or by any other organisation for that matter. Dr Angela Coulter, chief executive of the Picker Institute and a member of the G10 Medicines Group, told the meeting that she knew of no patient groups who had asked for DTCA."

---

14 The distinction between advertising and information was further blurred by translation errors. The English-language version of the proposed EC regulations said, "It is proposed there should be public advertising of three classes of medicinal products ...", while other language versions of the same text used the term, "information to the public" (e.g. not *publicité*, but *informations*, in French). See *SCRIP* No 2712, 16 January 2002, p. 3.

15 GSK dominated the market for asthma and AIDS drugs.

16 Notably the European Public Health Alliance (EPHA).

Social Audit later requested clarification from the head of the DG Enterprise Pharmaceuticals Unit. His reply suggested that the MCA's Dr. Keith Jones had met his Gallic match: "This proposal responds to the information of certain patients ... brought to (the) Commission's attention in the past during various formal and informal discussions" (Brunet 2002).

It was always predictable that, once there was a legal foot in the door, there would be angry complaints about the injustice of depriving patients of valuable information. If patients in the three proposed disease categories (AIDS, asthma, diabetes) could benefit, why not others too? Rodney Elgie, a former lawyer, made the point that DTC promotion came down in the end to questions of civil and human rights:

> "Several Articles under the European Convention of Human Rights provide legal justification for supplying more information on medicines to patients. Article 11 states that everyone has the right to receive and impart information and ideas, without interference by public authority. Article 10 includes the right of the public to receive information: there is no suggestion that this right may only apply to scientific information. It can be legitimately argued that a ban on reasonable and responsible DTCA actually undermines the goal of improving public health, denying, as it does, patient access to important sources of knowledge concerning prescription medicines." (Elgie 2002)

Perhaps confident of victory, and counting on their ground troops to speak up for them, the Pharmas waited until shortly before a key vote by Members of the European Parliament (MEPs). Only then did the ABPI let it be known that to limit patient information to the three proposed disease categories: "would discriminate against people with other diseases" and be "grossly unfair".

The European Parliament steps in

At the time, it seemed too much to hope that the European Parliament would get to grips with the issues and sort out the DG Enterprise proposals. They were first referred to a European Parliament committee,[17] in late 2001. Two members, appointed as rapporteurs, then took soundings and prepared reports. Both were subject to intensive lobbying by the Pharmas and their ground troops, but the opposition was active too:

> This was how it seemed from the perspective of the resistance, as recorded in a chatty email from the frontline. The news was both encouraging and not. The

17 The European Parliament's Committee on Environment, Public Health and Consumer Protection.

rapporteurs "were both very friendly." Surprisingly, they seem to work in depth, to read what they receive, to be very interested in getting our documents. BUT they calmly explain that they will not be able to do much to change the project!! ... Nevertheless it might not be totally useless to continue informing (them) on the problem of information and advertising ... (Bardelay 2002)

Global developments also influenced the European debate. At about this time, the Canadian Health Minister announced that she saw no reason to allow DTCA and the Canadian Medical Association seemed to agree: Yes, Canada was exposed to cross-border advertising from the US, "but why should we make it worse?" (Haddad 2002) Australia had earlier reached the same conclusion (Galbally 2000), while New Zealand was still wrestling. The New Zealand Ministry of Health had held two enquiries on DTCA in three years, and was still under pressure to control it (Toop et al. 2003).

In Europe, meanwhile, the battle lines were fairly clearly defined. Professionals were generally opposed to DTCA – though hardly outspoken – and governments had divided along trade-versus-health lines. Countries with strong drug industries – or not – held different views.[18]

It came down to two decisive votes in the autumn of 2002 – first by the Parliamentary Committee and then by the European Parliament itself. The Committee vote was not just decisive but amazing. One by one, speakers from the main parties tabled their amendments, in each case recording the "Justification" for the votes they cast. There was almost complete unanimity: the Commission's proposals on "information" should not become law. The Committee had in effect passed a vote of No Confidence in the Commission. The official press release from the European Parliament spelled it out:

"The Environment Committee is vehemently opposed to Commission proposals to allow the pharmaceutical industry to give information on certain medicinal products. MEPS maintain the industry is incapable of providing impartial in-

18 Something of the dividing line was revealed in an important letter sent to MEPS – an unprecedented act of lobbying by nine members of the top European drug safety committee, the CPMP (Committee on Proprietary Medicinal Products). This minority, warning against DTC and other proposals, represented seven countries – but not the UK, France, Germany or Sweden, the main players on the G10. The CPMP is the oversight committee for the European Medicines Evaluation Agency; all EU member states (plus Norway) are represented on it. The signatories to this letter (25 February 2002) were Prof. Fernando de Andres-Trelles (Spain); Prof. Silvio Garattini (Italy); Dr. Lars Gramstad (Norway); Prof. Magnus Johannsson (Iceland); Dr. Fritz Lekkerkerker (Netherlands); Dr. Pasquanino Rossi (Italy); Prof. Cristina Sampaio (Portugal); Prof. Beatriz Silva Lima (Portugal); and Dr. Markku Toivonen (Finland). The signatories emphasised they did not represent either the view of the CPMP or any national authority. National governments make appointments to the CPMP, with all that implies. See: http://www.haiweb.org/campaign/DTCA/index.html

formation on its medicines and that such information should only come from independent sources."

One speaker after another denounced the DG Enterprise proposals.[19] A huge majority supported two simple amendments – the main one requesting the EC to go back to the drawing board, to consult fully and then present a report outlining a comprehensive consumer/patient information strategy. The whole European Parliament voted in October 2002. They too opposed the DG Enterprise plan, by 494 (92.5%) to 42 (7.5%).

The European Commission (DG Enterprise) gave "a qualified welcome" to the European Parliament's response. The ABPI's Dr. Trevor Jones said he was "delighted" that these highly restrictive proposals had been turned down. Perhaps there was not much else they felt they could say.

Public-private postscript

In consultation not with user groups[20] but mainly with the ABPI's "Informed Patient Task Force", the MCA later published its guidelines on "Disease Awareness." In the words of one pharma-analyst, basically these told companies to "be good, be clean, be honest, be a boy scout and don't mention your product" (Carpenter 2003).

---

19 "Information on diseases or medicines coming from industry cannot be anything but promotion, according to the WHO Ethical Criteria for Medicinal Drug Promotion ... Patients and consumers request comparative information on medicines that comes from independent sources. The proposed revision plays on smart words: information, communication, education. The proposed derogation is actually the first step forwards direct to consumer advertising of prescription medicines, nicely disguised as 'disease education'" (de Roo & Rod).

"There is a need for patients and consumers to be able to obtain accurate, understandable and reliable information on the range of treatments, including medicines. But, what appears to be moves towards Direct to Consumer Advertising should be resisted. The rationale behind the idea of a three disease trial is not entirely clear. On the one hand, those diagnosed with other diseases can reasonably argue that they are just as entitled to information. On the other hand, even a three disease trial would not give consumers and patients information on the range of therapies and could easily slip into direct to consumer advertising. Of greatest concern is the fact that the proposals would not give patients access to information about different types of treatment additional to medicinal products" (Stihler).

"We take the view that the introduction of such information measures, even on a selective and experimental basis, cannot be authorized for the following reasons: ... substantial increase in patient demand for specific, generally costly, active principles ... increased use of medication ... adverse effect on medical practice, and on doctor-patient relations ..." (Ferreira).

"Pharmaceutical companies already have the ability to explain their products on their own websites ... and it would be better to leave the existing system as it is" (Bowis).

Dr. Trevor Jones again said he was delighted: "The guidelines can only encourage companies to consider taking part on such campaigns" (ABPI 2003).

It was a stepping-stone. Because it prohibited reference to specific products, it meant the Pharmas had to use a two-pronged approach. Their advertising told people to see their doctor; meanwhile doctors were exposed to a separate campaign, linking the condition to the brand. In short, "Halitosis-Yes, Listerine-No" – as this pharma-marketing expert might have explained it:

> "This concept is by no means new. Warner-Lambert (now part of Pfizer) was looking for an opportunity to expand its market for Listerine in the 1920s. Although the product was being marketed for everything from dandruff to wound irrigation, sales were flat. Warner-Lambert found its answer by creating awareness – and anxiety – around a serious-sounding medical condition: halitosis. Whereas the harmless concept of unpleasant breath would not cause much of a stir, halitosis – through effective branding or ownership of ideas – was demonized for a range of social casualties from lack of career advancement to divorce. As the antidote, Listerine saw sales increase from $100,000 to $4 million over the next six years, and helped to make halitosis a household word." (Parry 2003)

Meanwhile, DG Enterprise was down but not out. It still had its G10 group to make the running, and it was preparing the ground for something of a legislative finale in the summer of 2003. Timed to influence an important decision by the European Council of Ministers, the G10 final report proposed, "A Stronger European-based Pharmaceutical Industry for the Benefit of the Patient – A Call for Action." The general idea was that drug innovation was most important, and that trade and health were as one. Patients counted too.

Thus, on both sides of the Atlantic, the "enfranchisement" of patients during the DTCA years followed the same general course. More attention was paid to the views and interests of patients – but mainly as represented by patient organisations concerned with chronic illness, and increasingly steered by commerce. One consequence was that basic user information needs were barely addressed. Health "illiteracy", a problem for substantial numbers of users, was never considered a priority. These patients remain disenfranchised.[21]

The focus in the European legislative process was mainly on the Pharmas' need to supply information – the main question being, where to draw the line in creating demand. The G10 solution was that patient organisations, companies and legislators

---

20 The Medicines Commission "was concerned about the very low response rate to the consultation, particularly from patient groups and recommended that these bodies be made aware when the guidelines were published". MC minutes, 7/8 November 2002 meeting, item 5.3.2: The MCA neither invited comments from *Social Audit*, nor made it aware of the finished product.

should get together and work this out. Itself a public-private partnership, the G10 proposed the development of more public-private partnerships – notably, "to produce a workable distinction between advertising and information that would allow patients actively seeking information to be able to do so, and to develop standards to ensure the quality of such information."

To this end, DG Enterprise encouraged the founding of a new pan-European patients' organisation, the European Patients Forum. It was immediately awarded a place on the EMEA/CPMP working group of patient organisations, and proposed by the G10 as "a mechanism to consider patient's (*sic*) needs in relation to information and how they can best be met."

The President of the new European Patients Forum was Rodney Elgie. European disease awareness was on its way.

---

21 "Health illiteracy, the inability of patients to read, comprehend and/or act appropriately on medical instructions, is ... an invisible but extensive problem. About 21% of adults, or 40 million to 44 million people, are functionally illiterate, reading at or below a fifth grade level ... An additional 25% of adults, another 50 million people, are only marginally literate, meaning they cannot understand, interpret and apply written material to accomplish daily tasks (Shelton 1998). "In the largest study of functional literacy in the United States ... Overall, 42% of patients ... were unable to comprehend instructions for taking medication on an empty stomach, 26% could not understand information on an appointment slip, and 60% could not understand a standard consent form (AMA 1999). Evidence from the UK was equally discouraging (Ellis et al. 2001).

8
Regulatory dependencies

The failure to contain the antidepressant crisis can be traced to the limitations of the regulatory process, in particular to the emphasis on screening pre-marketing trials, rather than post-marketing drug surveillance. This also helps to explain, among other problems, the tendency to recommend drug dosages that many find too high. The need for effective post-marketing surveillance and adverse drug reaction reporting was underlined in this case by growing conflict between regulatory 'science' and common sense.

The traditional model of medicines control was neither conceived nor developed as an enterprise for health. The main emphasis in drug regulation has always been on risk management and damage limitation. The focus is on the screening and pursuit of rogue molecules – not on the safety of doctors and users, but on 'the safety of medicines' themselves.

Medicines control was founded in the US, in the days when Germany still dominated in Pharma world trade. The system was set up in response to public protest, following a major drug disaster in 1937.[1] Leading the rest of the world by years, the US dispensed with its "feeble and obsolete" Food & Drug Acts and brought in laws with teeth.

The 1938 law required the safety screening of new drugs and helped the Food & Drug Administration (FDA) to save the US from thalidomide. Following this disaster, the "Kefauver-Harris Amendment" (1962) required manufacturers to provide evidence of efficacy, as well as lack of toxicity. Later, the US Freedom of Information Act (1966) underlined the public accountability of the FDA, to an extent undreamed of elsewhere.

Far more than in other countries, the US medicines control system was supported by great resources and conceived as a democratic endeavour. Strong Congressional

---

1 The disaster involved Elixir of Sulphanilamide, a valuable antibiotic dissolved in ethylene glycol – the highly toxic main ingredient of car antifreeze. The seminal exposé by Kallet and Schlink (1932) set the tone for the 1938 reforms; it caused a stir. Their book was reprinted five times within two weeks of publication. Both authors were closely linked to the US consumer movement, and *Consumers Union* and *The Medical Letter* have continued that tradition ever since.

oversight made it unique: the FDA was expected and required to be accessible and responsive to public expectations. Uniquely, the US approach recognised the conflict of interest inherent in all drug regulation: if a drug problem suddenly emerged, the regulators might themselves have failed.

Until the 1990s, Congressional oversight was strong and searching, and public enquiries were routinely held into the FDA's handling of drug problems. The US is the only country to have held public enquiries to investigate drug crises – but then, as trade imperatives became more pressing, these became a thing of the past. Congressional enquiries into drug problems were effectively suspended in 1992. Over the next decade, there was not one Congressional investigation, though during that time 13 prescription medicines were withdrawn for safety reasons (Sigelman 2002).

The creation of the Single European Market (1992) had made the competition for global trade that much more intense. This and the crisis in innovation meant the regulatory emphasis switched dramatically towards efficiency and market development. When FDA Commissioner Henney appeared before a Senate committee in 1999, it was mainly to emphasise that the FDA "enhances US competitiveness in global markets ... and strengthens the domestic economy as a whole by inviting increased foreign investment."

As the Pharmas became more and more part of the fabric of Washington, DC, the FDA came under increasing political pressure. Global market imperatives transformed the style of drug regulation in the 1990s. The main issue came down almost to patriotism and therefore enjoyed bipartisan support. The US Pharmas were a vital part of the national economy: now they had to compete in world markets and needed all the help they could get from Congress and the FDA.

Under the influence of the Pharmas the whole licensing process became faster and more efficient; this helped companies by reducing the erosion of drug patent life.[2] Meanwhile, alongside its regulatory work, the FDA took on more of an 'advisory' role to the 'sponsors,' the companies trying to license new drugs.[3] Worldwide, regulators began to work increasingly like consultants as the Pharmas began to pay for their own regulation. The Pharmas collectively also began to play a leading part in the development of global standards of medicines control.

Market forces increasingly came to influence the fundamentals – the meaning of 'safe' and the nature of 'effective' and the quality of drug information. The Prozac years and the advent of Direct-To-Consumer Advertising (DTCA) and promotion

---

2 "Because our reviews are more timely, nearly 18 months has been shaved off industry's drug development time, resulting in saving of nearly $2 billion per year for industry" (Henney 2000).

3 "The FDA's dual role as advisor and reviewer demanded substantial time and resources; the CDER (Center for Drug Evaluation and Research) held over 1,000 meetings with sponsors in FY2001" (OIG 2003).

marked the profoundness of this change. The climate change in the 1990s made regulators more accountable to the Pharmas. It also affected how key appointments were made.

Figureheads in US drug regulation

Dr. David Kessler was appointed FDA Commissioner in 1990 and served both the Bush senior and Clinton administrations. In office, Kessler had strongly opposed DTCA, as he admitted after he'd left: "I probably more than any individual ... stood in the way of expanding, or loosening maybe is a better term, direct-to-consumer advertising for prescription drugs ..." (Castagnoli 1998).

Kessler's departure in February 1997 opened the door to the market expansion that DTCA would bring. Six months after he left, the FDA produced the draft policy guidelines for DTCA. Kessler's departure had opened up a power vacuum: he was not replaced for two years. The failure to appoint a new FDA Commissioner may or may not have been an active political manoeuvre; it is not clear. The lack of leadership left the FDA more exposed to pressure, but Kessler's absence was perhaps not decisive. A few years later, he announced he had changed his mind on DTCA, through the best part of 180 degrees.[4]

Kessler's replacement, Dr. Jane Henney, served barely two years. The date of her departure signalled the main reason for it: she stood down the day before the Presidential inauguration of George W. Bush in January 2001. Then there was another power vacuum, 2001-2002. That led to problems reported in headlines[5] and more:

> "The Food and Drug Administration regulates almost a quarter of the nation's economy, makes life-and-death decisions about which drugs will be available to patients, employs more than 10,000 federal workers and is a key player in the national response to bioterrorism. But since the day President Bush took office, the agency has been without a commissioner – the highest-ranking federal post still vacant. And because of intense partisan politics and the sometimes competing demands of the industries that the agency regulates and the consumers it serves,

---

4 In May 2002 Kessler was keynote speaker at a big DTC conference: "DTC is here to stay and will be part of the mix because it works and has educational value for the patient population. It is now more mainstream and will be accepted just like detailing and sampling".

5 "FDA left rudderless and without a chief" (*Financial Times* 21 November 2001); "FDA power vacuum, an opportunity for big pharma?" (*Datamonitor* May 2002); "Lotronex and the FDA: a fatal erosion of integrity;" (Horton 2001) and "A muscular lobby tries to shape Nation's bioterror plan". This referred to the Pharmas strengthening White House links, following the catastrophe of 11 September 2001. For the Pharmas, this was "a great time to buy some good will" (Wayne & Peterson 2001).

> FDA watchers say it appears increasingly unlikely there will be a nominee before the fall election." (Kaufman 2002)

In March 2002, the White House eventually proposed Dr. Alastair Wood as FDA Commissioner, but then withdrew his name. The Pharmas reportedly blocked his appointment because of his views on DTCA.[6]

The Pharmas naturally denied they had opposed anyone or anything, but their position was made clear. A 'Senior Fellow' of the Manhattan Institute denounced Wood as "a bad choice for the FDA" (Goldberg 2002). Among other transgressions, Wood – "that buddy of Senator Ted Kennedy" – had required "companies to adhere to an impossible safety standard". Wood had pointed out the risks involved with intensive marketing of new drugs, whose safety profiles were still uncertain:

> "Manufacturers should behave responsibly in the promotion of new drugs for which toxicity is, by definition, currently unknown ... To encourage such responsibility, direct-to-consumer-advertising should be permitted only for drugs that have undergone a post marketing testing process that would include a sufficient number of patients to provide adequate confidence in their safety for widespread clinical use. This step could help prevent the excessively rapid uptake of new drugs at a rate that exceeds the capacity to review their safety in practice."

The White House finally appointed Dr. Mark McClellan and he took over as FDA Commissioner in November 2002. Formerly an associate professor of economics and medicine, he had been one of three members of President Bush's Economic Council and the main liaison between the FDA and the White House. The linkage between the White House and drug regulation had been signalled from the outset: the US Pharmas paid $1.7 million towards the estimated $17 million bill for the 2000 Presidential inauguration (Charatan 2001). The close relationship was underlined in other appointments too.[7]

---

6 "Bush administration interest in the candidacy of Alastair Wood MD, a highly-regarded drug expert, for FDA Commissioner post faded yesterday in the wake of the pharmaceutical industry's 11th hour campaign in opposition to Wood. That campaign relied heavily on references to Wood's writing on direct-to-consumer ads and drug safety" (*The Pink Sheet* 25 February 2002, cited by AAPS online news center, Milo Gibaldi, *Pharmaceutical Report* 1 May 2002).

7 President Bush's father had been a director of Eli Lilly; Secretary of Defense Rumsfeld had been chief executive of G.D. Searle (part of Pfizer from 2003); Bush's head of the Office of Management and Budget, Mitchell E. Daniels, Jr. had been a Lilly vice-president; Linda Skladany, previously a drug company lobbyist became a deputy commissioner at the FDA; and a former policy head for PhRMA became Assistant Secretary for Planning and Evaluation at the Department of Health and Human Services (DHHS).

One man, in particular, had helped to fill the power vacuum: he was Daniel Troy, who became FDA Chief Counsel in 2001. Troy had come from a Washington law firm, noted for its services to Big Tobacco, and for clients opposing the FDA. He was also an 'Associate Scholar' with the American Enterprise Institute for Public Policy Research: "dedicated to preserving and strengthening the foundations of freedom – limited government, private enterprise, vital cultural and political institutions, and a strong foreign policy and national defense ..."

With Troy's appointment, the FDA became more involved with 'First Amendment issues' – a coded call for deregulation by allowing the Pharmas more freedom of speech. The market increasingly underlined the great difference between the rights of human and corporate bodies, but the law did not. The question was: how far should this freedom of speech go? To what extent should a company enjoy legal protections to broadcast news of possible benefits while muting concerns about risk?

Troy's appointment made its mark. Enforcement activity was sharply reduced, and support for Pharmas became strong. The climate change was evident from unprecedented action by the FDA to protect the Pharmas from public accountability. In 2002, the FDA intervened in two lawsuits, helping Pfizer and GSK to defend Paxil (paroxetine) and Zoloft (sertraline). The new FDA actively opposed the suggestion of any problems with either dependence or suicidal ideation on Selective Serotonin Reuptake Inhibitors – SSRIs.[8]

The FDA also tried to block the increasing flow of cheaper drugs from Canada. In July 2003, the city of Springfield (Massachusetts) became the first US municipal authority to buy drugs from Canada – and at least 10 US States were trying to follow suit – a threatening sign for the Pharmas. The FDA linked its actions to the war against counterfeit drugs and the Pharmas welcomed it: "These illegal imports threaten the integrity of the US drug supply and the health and safety of American patients" (Baglole 2003).

> Meanwhile, the Pharmas lobbied hard on their own account, trying to defeat Congressional proposals (2003) to permit such importation. They went to great lengths to stir up opposition: for example, the Pharmas enlisted the support of the Traditional Values Coalition, representing 43,000 churches committed to the campaign for "sanctity of life". Their job was to try to persuade the US Congress that, to allow the importation of drugs from Canada, would make the "abortion pill" (RU-486) as easy to obtain as aspirin. (VandeHei & Eilperin 2003)

---

8 In a legal brief filed on 3 September 2002 the FDA argued that, if Pfizer had tried to include a warning that sertraline might increase the risk of suicide, it would have violated the law.

There was one other great change in the climate of US drug regulation, as the age of globalisation began. Through the 1980s, the FDA had been dominant in its field and rather aloof on the international scene. In those days, "their feeling was that if you want an international system, why not just have everybody do what the FDA does?"[9] But then the FDA and the Pharmas, in tandem, began to drive global drug regulation more in the direction of world market needs.

For better and worse, the US, European and Japanese regulators joined with the Pharmas in 1992 to establish the International Conference on Harmonisation (ICH).[10] The ICH promoted the introduction of global standards in drug regulation. The gains were mainly to do with efficiency and avoidance of unnecessary duplication; the downside related to the greater emphasis on industry self-regulation and loss of national autonomy.[11]

The Secretariat of the ICH was run by the US-dominated, Geneva-based, International Federation of Pharmaceutical Manufacturers' Associations (IFPMA). From the 1990s, the Pharmas began to play a pivotal part in supranational drug regulation: global standards have developed on this private-public partnership basis, ever since.

UK-style drug control

The thalidomide disaster led to the founding of medicines control in Europe. In the late 1950s, thalidomide had been marketed as a sleeping pill and tranquilliser, a better alternative to barbiturates and similar drugs. Thalidomide was 'safe' in overdose: it was therefore advertised as "completely safe", but it was specifically promoted for pregnant women.

Worldwide, some 10,000 severely deformed babies were born, before thalidomide was withdrawn in 1961. The UK Health Secretary in-waiting observed that Britain, among other countries, "suddenly woke up to the fact that any drug manufacturer could market any product, however inadequately tested, however danger-

9 This was the view of Fernand Sauer, founder CEO of the European Medicines Evaluation Agency (Ross 2000).

10 The International Conference on Harmonisation "on technical requirements for registration of pharmaceuticals for human use".

11 Agreed ICH texts were published as CPMP Guidelines in the EU, as draft guidance in the *Federal Register* (US), and as proposals for consultation by the Ministry of Health, Labour and Welfare in Japan. Once the ICH had agreed on a new text, its proposals were automatically published as draft Guidelines or Recommendations by the regulators in each of the three regions. Subject to further consultations, ICH proposals later became law. The interests of people living outside these main power blocks were mainly represented by the World Health Organization (WHO), which merely had "observer status" in the ICH.

ous, without having to satisfy any independent body as to its safety or efficacy" (Crossman 1963).

It took the UK authorities another decade to set up a rudimentary system of drug control. For three years after thalidomide, the Conservative government toyed with systems of self-regulation – encouraged by the UK industry association, which by then had launched its voluntary Code of Marketing Practice (ABPI 1958). The companies wanted to forestall control by law. They argued that high standards were second nature to them: "Putting aside all considerations of ethics and humanity, every company in simple self-interest would obviously wish to market only products that are both effective and safe".

The election of a Labour government in 1964 led to the appointment of a "Committee of Enquiry into the Relationship of the Pharmaceutical Industry with the National Health Service" (Sainsbury 1967). This proposed a statutory drug licensing system, to include an independent oversight body, the Medicines Commission.[1212] The Sainsbury Committee imagined that the Medicines Commission would become "in due course the accepted source of information on all matters concerning the use of medicines". Pretty much the opposite happened.

Britain adopted a style of medicines control that also focused on the pursuit of rogue molecules, but which was otherwise far removed from the FDA model. With nothing like the same resources, the UK regulators settled for a spirit of voluntarism and 'gentlemanly' behaviour, trusting the industry to play fair. Democratic inspiration and accountability played a minimal part.

Twenty-five years after the thalidomide disaster, the CSM Chairman felt able to propose that, "drug regulatory authorities should be immune from political and public pressure and above all free from the pressures of action groups" (Asscher 1986). This also conveyed the very limited impact of Parliamentary oversight, and rather suggested that the regulators felt no such pressures from the commercial sector. The regulators trusted the Pharmas: indeed they lacked the resources to do otherwise.

The closeness that developed between the regulators and companies partly explains the fundamental role of secrecy in UK medicines regulation. The 1968 Medicines Act still prohibits the regulator from disclosing, "any information obtained by or furnished to him in pursuance of this Act" – on pain of a fine or imprisonment for up to two years.[13]

After his retirement from the CSM, and on receipt of the much-coveted knighthood that went with the job, Professor Asscher admitted that the diet of secrecy had been too rich even for him. He complained that, when in office, he had felt unable "to communicate in the way that I would normally be able to do in my own medical

12 The Medicines Commission was and is the parent of the Committee on Safety of Medicines and related bodies; it exists at the interface between the professions and government.

school". He later publicly supported proposals for a modest Medicines Information Bill, which the Pharmas later killed (CFOI 1993).

Asscher's support for this Bill indicated both the modesty of its demands and the depth of the problem it addressed. His support for the campaign was qualified: Asscher had found the official secrecy a bit too oppressive, but he also urged great caution. He said he feared, for example, that if journalists ever got hold of the CSM's numerical tabulations of Yellow Card (ADR) data, there would be "a feast of drug scandals".

This delusion was rampant throughout the Medicines Control Agency (MCA)/CSM, and they went to great lengths to sustain it. Basic rights of access even to simple numerical adverse drug reaction (ADR) data were finally prised from the MCA/CSM only after a ruling from the Ombudsman on a complaint from *Social Audit* (1995).

By then, Professor Mike Rawlins had become Chairman of the CSM. The Rawlins years (1993-1998) shed more light on the grip of secrecy in UK drug regulation. Personally, Rawlins held progressive views; he favoured more transparency and said so. He thought the UK secrecy laws were excessive and unnecessary: "a small part of individual (licence) applications might (be regarded) as commercially confidential but the major proportion could, with little loss to anyone, be made publicly available" (Rawlins 1987).

Yet during his tenure, nothing changed. Rawlins had suggested, for example, that the minutes of CSM meetings could easily be published. But the MCA started to release (highly "redacted") minutes of their meetings only after Rawlins left – again after the Ombudsman had intervened (*Social Audit* 2000).

Expectations of any greater openness by his successor at the CSM, Professor Alasdair Breckenridge, would have been exceedingly optimistic. The later appointment (2003) of Breckenridge as Chairman of a restructured MCA, underlined the emptiness of the Sainsbury Committee's original recommendations. As the 1990s progressed, the CSM faded as the bureaucracy increasingly ran the show.

---

13 The Medicines Act did permit disclosure by a regulator, "made in the performance of his duty;" in practice this made no difference to the general rule. As a rule, the regulators requested permission from companies to disclose such data, and companies declined. Government ministers have also consistently declined to disclose: "*The information that we get is the company's property*" (Clarke 1983). In December 2003, the MCA announced that this prohibition would be lifted in January 2005 – to be replaced by provisions in the UK Freedom of Information Act.

Commercial sponsorship of government regulation

Both in spite and because of this tradition of secrecy, the UK medicines control system emerged as one of the strongest in the world[14] and came to play a leading part in the style of European drug regulation. Britain under Thatcher inspired the trend to Pharma-friendly regulation. The Medicines Control Agency (MCA) was set up in 1989, at arms' length from the politicians, and made wholly dependent on industry fees.[15] Other countries followed suit: by 2000, industry fees provided 70% of the income of the European Medicines Evaluation Agency (EMEA) and about half the income of the FDA's Center for Drug Evaluation.[16]

In the US, regulatory dependence on user fees led to some redefinition of priorities. The introduction of fees coincided with large cuts in public funding – but user fees could be employed only to fund the review of pre-marketing data. This meant that other drug safety programmes became seriously under-funded, especially those to do with monitoring the safety of medicines already on the market. The FDA found that, "the net effect of almost a decade of steadily increasing spending from (public) appropriations for drug review ... has resulted in steadily reduced staffing and resources for FDA core programs" (PDUFA 2000).

In time, the FDA's post-marketing testing programmes adopted an increasingly more advisory role, with a reduced emphasis on enforcement. For example, the FDA continued to require companies to conduct post-marketing trials as a condition of drug licensing – but then failed to specify any deadlines. Thus, most post-marketing trials never got off the ground and relatively few were ever completed.[17]

---

14 The effectiveness of the UK drug control system depended not so much on law enforcement and formal regulation, as on complementary factors, including strong traditions of academic excellence. One notable strength of the UK system was the *British National Formulary* – a high quality prescribing guide, funded by government but developed by through partnership between the main professional bodies for medicine and pharmacy. The *BNF* served as a model, widely used beyond the UK.

15 The spirit of the new age was reflected in one of the MCA's inaugural gestures, a foretaste of what public-private partnership might become. Freed from the constraints of government funding, and permitted to raise funds on its own account, the MCA began to charge a £250 (US$/€ 400) entry fee for attendance at its annual general meeting. This affront to democracy both raised funds and ensured overwhelming attendance by the target audience, the Pharmas: "the Agency wishes to hear and take account of the views of those to whom it provides services". This practice was later stopped and the annual general meeting just faded away.

16 When Congress authorised the FDA to start collecting "user fees" (PDUFA 1992), it was to hire an additional 600 staff to review, and speed the process of drug marketing. "The enactment of PDUFA III presents significant opportunities to address many of the findings in this report ... It calls for an increase in the user fees that CDER estimates will allow it to hire close to 300 additional employees over the next 5 years" (OIG 2003).

Commercial funding led also to increasing use of time- and money-related performance goals. Some senior FDA staff publicly lamented that "almost a sweatshop environment" had developed, along with high turnover of staff. The focus on providing service to companies also put pressure on employees whose concerns about drug safety seemed too strong (Horton 2001). The regulatory emphasis was increasingly on efficiency and compliance with due process, in preference to the expression of individual initiative or conscience.[18]

This climate did nothing to improve the already fearsome pressures to get drugs to market fast. Once the Pharmas became the main paymasters, efficiencies were certainly achieved, but not necessarily improvements. Significantly, there was no apparent progress in checking the raw data that showed what happened to *individual* patients in clinical trials. This proved a critical omission, especially with potent drugs that affected mood and mind. The vast dossiers that companies submitted to support drug licence applications typically ran to hundreds of thousands of pages, so regulators overwhelmingly relied on company summaries of clinical data – but not the data itself. That was so when the FDA embraced the user fee system in 1992. Ten years later, the Agency "still does not have a single employee responsible for auditing the accuracy and completeness of such data" (Sigelman 2002).

By the millennium, dependence on industry fees meant that even the regulators began to feel the pinch, as the innovation crisis wore on: companies were submitting fewer drugs and therefore paid less in licensing fees. Even with fee income at around the US250 million mark, the FDA had to cut back, and the same was true elsewhere:

---

17 "Some 60% of 1,339 promised post-marketing studies for drugs haven't begun, nor have 30% of 223 promised studies of biological therapies. Some of those studies have stalled for years" (*Wall Street Journal* 22 May 2003) ... "According to a recent FDA report submitted to Congress, between 1991 and 2001, FDA approved 1,090 NDAs (New Drug Applications) and sponsors agreed to conduct 2,328 post-marketing studies. That same report found that as of February 8 2002 sponsors had completed 882 of the 2,400 post-marketing commitments on file at FDA for drugs" (OIG 2003).

18 "Forty percent of FDA survey respondents who had been at the FDA at least five years indicated that the review process had worsened during their tenure of allowing for in-depth, science-based reviews. Respondents cited lack of time as the main reason. According to 58 per cent of FDA respondents, the allotted six months for a priority review is inadequate. This is considerably higher than the 25 per cent of respondents who indicated that the allotted 10 months for a standard review is adequate (page iii) ... "We also found that some reviewers have concerns about raising disagreements. In fact, 21 per cent of FDA survey respondents indicated that the work environment allowed for the expression of differing scientific opinions to a small or no extent. Similarly, an internal survey conducted by CDER of its reviewers found that one-third of respondents did not feel comfortable expressing their differing opinions. And, on our own survey, 18 per cent of respondents indicated that they have felt pressure to approve or recommend approval for a drug, despite reservations about its safety, efficacy or quality" (OIG 2003).

"Never has so much money been spent on R&D with so little result," said the director of the European Medicines Evaluation Agency (EMEA) – explaining the Agency's budget shortfall to a committee of MEPs (Lonngren 2002).

A footnote on European medicines control

The EMEA had been set up in 1995. It was based in London, following intense lobbying and horse-trading by the UK government, whose bid was supported by the Pharmas. The UK government saw EMEA as a great economic asset, underlining the point that drug regulation is very much driven by trade imperatives as well as users' needs. That was especially true of the EMEA. It was controlled by DG Enterprise, and the natural consequence of the Single European Market formed in 1992.[19]

The EMEA was also founded on the traditional model of drug regulation. The newly formed European Economic Community adopted its first directive on the control of medicines in 1965 – again with the focus overwhelmingly on drug performance in pre-marketing clinical trials. By this time, the notion of 'medical need' had all but faded from the global regulatory vocabulary. Norway was the last European country to make it a condition for licensing: if the Norwegians didn't need a drug, they didn't license it. The new Europe rejected this as a gross restraint of trade.

And what happened in the 30 years between the first European laws on drug control and the foundation of the EMEA? In summary, the European Commission negotiated agreements between Member States, whereby drug approval in one country permitted marketing in all – unless there were objections. If there were, they were resolved through an oversight committee, the Committee on Proprietary Medicinal Products. The activities of the CPMP chairman, through 1993, beggar belief.[20]

The EMEA played little or no significant part in either the genesis or resolution of the SSRI antidepressant problem. Its stance was essentially passive; it seemed to take its cues on this issue mainly from the MCA.

---

19 The Treaty of Rome (1957) founded the European Common Market. Article 2 was an agreement that, "The Community shall have as its task, by establishing a common market and progressively approximating the economic policies of Member States, to promote throughout the Community a harmonious development of economic activities, a continuous and balanced expansion, an increase in stability, an accelerated raising of the standard of living and closer relations between the States belonging to it". Historically, trade interests came first.

Dossiers and dosage

Regulatory agencies neither do research nor commission it. Their main job is to evaluate the evidence that companies provide when they apply for a product licence. The kind of evidence required is increasingly specified in internationally adopted regulations, proposed through the ICH. Companies are still not required to provide evidence of *comparative* efficacy, the information prescribers really need.

Worldwide, the regulatory emphasis is still overwhelmingly on screening the dossier – all the evidence gathered *before* a drug comes to market. 'Post-marketing surveillance' is more limited. In practice, the regulators keep an eye on the scientific literature and on ADR reports, and then take action on an *ad hoc* basis, if required.[21]

The regulatory emphasis on scrutiny of the 'dossier' – the data from *pre*-marketing clinical trials – reflected the regulatory commitment to a scientific approach. However, it tended to scientific fundamentalism: as in this case history, the regulators passively waited for things to happen and then demanded 'scientific' standards of proof before accepting that the problems were real. In the name of 'science', the regulators tended not to warn of possible risks in the absence of conclusive evidence

---

20 The Committee of Proprietary Medicinal Products (CPMP) was the key drug safety committee in Europe and comprised delegated experts from all EU countries. Until 1993, the CPMP chair was Dr. Duilio Poggiolini. He plays no direct part in this story, nor do his actions reflect on the CPMP today – but how did such a man become the chairman of such a public institution , and would this have happened without the Pharmas' support? Who knows?

Poggiolini was also head of the Italian national drug approval system, until he was brought down in an anti-corruption drive in 1993. The Italian authorities eventually charged Poggiolini with having accumulated, over about 30 years, US$180 million in bribes from companies – but prosecution never followed. Following his arrest, he and his wife were found to have 17 bank accounts between them; their safe reportedly contained a treasure trove of gifts, ranging from valuable paintings to gold coins.

The details of the case never really emerged and few now mention his name. At the time, the European Commission issued a terse statement saying it had investigated fully and found nothing wrong at European level. But they never published the results of their investigation and, ten years later, the search engines on the EC and EMEA websites had never heard of him.

Poggiolini was not alone: other members of the Italian drug approvals committee were on the take as well, even if Poggiolini was in a class of his own. His greed was such that companies could credibly claim in their own defence that they had been obliged to pay up, in order to get products approved. One of the honest souls on the approvals committee later recalled a case in which a colleague looked to extort from Pfizer, when it applied for a license for sertraline (Zoloft/Lustral): "Pfizer, for example, filed an approval application for the antidepressant, sertraline ... It had great data, an international dossier. However, — said there were problems with the data. He said, 'it doesn't convince me, I'd like to see more', even though he would not go into details, and the dossier was being held up. I think many companies experienced this" (Schofield 1993). The point is not that Poggiolini was typical, but that he rose to the top and went undiscovered for years. Corruption is that hard to pin down.

of harm. Over-reliance on the pre-marketing data in the dossier was especially marked in the US and might partly explain why the FDA was slower to get the point about SSRIs than their counterparts in the UK.

The regulators regarded the dossier as the bedrock of understanding – but this meant that, during the lifetime of a drug, they increasingly relied on aging data from often inadequate clinical trials. These trials typically comprised a rigorously optimistic assessment, based on observations of relatively few patients involved in meticulously engineered studies. The clinical investigators were very carefully selected, patients too. Patients in antidepressant trials (among others) were mostly far from representative of the people prescribed the same drugs in general practice.

> Zimmerman and colleagues (2002) compared the profiles of a typical sample of general practice patients on antidepressants with those of patients enrolled in antidepressant drug trials. They estimated that only 15% of patients seen in a routine clinical practice would be eligible for inclusion in trials.

Even the best dossiers could give only a broad indication of a drug's effects; with new drugs there was always much to learn. This applied not just to rare side effects, but also to basics, such as the 'right' dose – except that there is no 'right' dose, only a 'recommended' one. This is the dose that suits most people best, though not necessarily you.

Individual response to most drugs, especially psychoactive drugs, varies a lot. Beyond the physical factors (e.g. age, sex, weight) that point to the 'right' dose, genetic differences matter too. Years from now, the SSRI story may well reveal the fundamental influence of genetics on individual response to dose. The complexities of paroxetine metabolism are a case in point.[22]

---

21 The usual response to a problem would be to add a small-print warning to the drug "label" – known in Europe as the "Summary of Product Characteristics" (SPC) – the officially approved drug data sheet. Especially in Europe, few doctors actually read the label, but their main content filters into prescribing instructions and advice of other kinds. The key significance of the label is in defining what companies are allowed to say when making promotional claims. In the UK, the text in advertisements, for example, has to be "not inconsistent" with the terms of the label. The label also determines the all-important "indications" (what the drug could legally be promoted for) as well as the breadth of claims for drug effectiveness and safety.

22 Paroxetine is inactivated by two cytochrome P450 (CYP) enzymes. CYP 2D6 is the main pathway at low concentrations, except in "poor metabolisers" in whom this enzyme is abnormal. At higher concentrations paroxetine inhibits CYP 2D6, slowing its own inactivation, so that a dose increase leads to a disproportionate increase in plasma level; stopping the drug causes a correspondingly steep drop in plasma level, which partly explains the intensity of the withdrawal symptoms. The rate of inactivation varies greatly: the average half-life in plasma is just under 24 hours, but it ranges up to three days. About 8% of the Caucasian population are poor metabolisers who have an inefficient form of the CYP 2D6 enzyme, and they may account for many of the patients who suffer serious reactions.

The wider point is that even the 'optimum' or 'recommended' dosage of a drug may not be established for years. The examples of overdosing with Ativan, Halcion and Opren were not exceptional: studies of new drugs in both Europe and the US have suggested that about one in six products were first marketed at a dosage that later proved too high.[23]

Companies tend to recommend high dosages essentially for marketing reasons (Herxheimer 1991). They also prefer to specify a "usual" dose, even in the face of compelling evidence that one size does not fit all. The SSRI story exemplifies these tendencies, also that the regulators tend not to question them. The potential for conflict is clear: as time goes on, the Pharmas depend increasingly on developing mass markets, even as more and more is learned about the complexities of individual drug response.

Eli Lilly launched Prozac in 1988 on the basis that one-size-fits-all: the recommended dosage of fluoxetine was 20mg/day from then on. The marketing advantage in having a simple dosage regimen was great. Because there was just one tablet strength (20 mg), doctors didn't have to adjust or calculate or even remember the dosage. Patients found it easy too: just one pill a day.

The Pharmas' preference for top-of-the-range dosages was very much to do with the need to demonstrate efficacy – not only in relation to competing products but also to improve on placebo. This was especially important with antidepressants because the placebo response in depression is so marked. Moreover, when companies proposed some recommended dosage, they looked to round numbers: dose increases were done in steps of 50% or 100%, when fractions would suffice. The thinking behind this is that, if drugs were available in postage stamp strengths,[2424] doctors would rebel and patients would get confused. The net result is that upwards of one patient in three may get a dose that will be too high: "Doses are also determined by an irrational preference for round numbers. The dose excess due to such digit preference may be as much as 70% of the correct dose and on average is probably 25%" (Herxheimer 1991). On such a basis, the dosing advice for Prozac that had been established from pre-marketing studies went unchanged for years:

---

23 A study of new drugs approved in the US between 1980 and 1999 showed that about one in six products was first marketed at a dosage level later found too high: "This pattern may represent a systematic flaw in pre-marketing dosage evaluation" (Cross et al. 2002). European research has found the same (Heerdin et al. 2002). Drugs first marketed in the US were found no more likely to have dosage changes than drugs first sold in Europe.

24 Postage stamps are available in a variety of values, enough to make it convenient to lick any total amount. It costs 28p to send a first class letter within the UK, and up to 47p to sent one abroad, yet stamps are still sold in denominations of 1p, 2p, 4p, 5p, and more.

> "Studies comparing fluoxetine 20, 40, and 60 mg/day to placebo indicate that 20 mg/day is sufficient to obtain a satisfactory response in major depressive disorder in most cases. Consequently, a dose of 20 mg/day, administered in the morning, is recommended as the initial dose." (Prozac label 2003)

This recommendation hardly acknowledged the evidence of variation in individual response. It overlooked the needs of many patients – the majority, including placebo responders – who might have done better on a dose well below 20 mg/day. The regulators accepted that this exposed more patients to greater risks, believing the benefits for other patients outweighed them. The limitations of this approach can be illustrated by reference to one early study with high-dose fluoxetine (40-60 mg/day) that vividly illustrated how doses that work well for some people can have the opposite effect on others. The same study suggested that the 'therapeutic margin' of fluoxetine (the difference between a safe and toxic dose) was not high.

> "We have carried out an open study (with fluoxetine) in 12 outpatients with depression: 10 completed the trial and 2 were dropped from the study because of adverse behavioral effects. Four patients who completed the trial showed a definite improvement with ± total remission; one of these individuals (a 33-year-old female) relapsed with continued treatment beyond the 4 week trial.
>
> Four other patients showed symptom aggravation, two of whom were terminated prematurely and hospitalized. Four patients showed no change; they also showed no side effects and were all treatment resistant to all other... (drugs). Two of the four patients who improved were also drug resistant during a 3-year period before the drug trial.
>
> The four patients who showed symptom worsening all had increased anxiety, agitation, severe motor restlessness, racing thoughts, pressured speech, and assertiveness. There was a dreadful feeling of apprehension. The symptoms became unbearable in the three patients at different stages in treatment, two of whom (both females in their 50s) required hospitalization.
>
> In the four patients who showed a clinical response, a stimulant-energizing like effect was documented. Although not readily recognizable to the patient, it was clinically apparent and confirmed by the family. Assertive behavior, loquaciousness, increased energy, and general stimulant-like symptoms, rather than euphoria, were characteristic..." (Shopsin et al. 1981)

Lilly's own research studies later established that a dosage of 5 mg per day of Prozac – one-quarter of the recommended amount – was effective for half the people who took it. But because a rather higher number of people found the 20 mg/dose effective, this was the dosage the regulators approved.[25] In a broad ranging critique of this overdose problem, Cohen (2001) underlined the point with the data shown below. The figures are based on his analysis of one of the key Lilly 'dose ranging' studies (Wernicke et al. 1988). The implication is that the benefits of drug treatment for 10% of drug users is considered greater than the risks to the 50% of users who may be taking four times the dose they need.

Prozac dosage (per day)	*Response rate*
5 mg	54%
20 mg	64%
60 mg	65%

Other studies had pointed to the effectiveness of fluoxetine at dosages around 5 mg/day (Louie et al. 1993), but it took 11 years from the launch of Prozac for Lilly to introduce a 10 mg tablet that could be broken into two. The Lilly press statement (18 May 1999) claimed this would "provide physicians with the ability to customise dosages to the needs of their patients," because "some patients – particularly elderly patients – occasionally are prescribed dosages of less than 20 milligrams". However, the statement added, "The tablet version of Prozac will not be available outside the United States".

Reading between the lines, the introduction of the 10 mg Prozac tablet in the US was probably mainly to do with the increasing use of SSRIS and other psychoactive medicines in children. Though the FDA didn't license Prozac for use in children until 2003, the 1990s saw a three- to four-fold increase in antidepressant prescribing for US children anyway. "Youth psychotropic treatment utilization during the 1990s nearly reached adult utilization rates" (Zito et al. 2003).

Limitations of regulatory scrutiny

Once a drug comes on the market, the benefit-to-risk equation is almost bound to change – not always, but generally for the worse. Most drugs reveal problems in gen-

25 The Swedish and Norwegian drug authorities initially did reject Lilly's request for a licence for Prozac, on the grounds that some users responded to a 5 mg/day dosage – though it was available only in 20 mg capsules. The regulators in other countries may or may not have had concerns about this: the data aren't available. Presumably the authorities that were concerned came to relent when Prozac was made available in a syrup formulation, which would allow dosage titration. However, drug consumption statistics (England 2002) indicate that the syrup formulation accounted for under 2% of all fluoxetine prescriptions.

eral practice never suspected when the dossier is approved. Serious risks are later revealed with around half of all drugs approved.[26] In the blockbuster era, such risks increased: that was the point that had cost Dr. Alastair Wood his appointment to the FDA. How could it make sense to promote new drugs so vigorously – exposing great numbers of users – at precisely the time one knew least about the drug's effects?[27]

Such questions tended to get sidelined, as government regulation in the 1990s evolved to become both more business-like and business friendly. The process of drug licensing became more systematised and more efficient, albeit mainly in terms of compliance with reams of technical and legal specifications. At the same time, regulatory imagination and initiative seemed to diminish, not least because the Pharmas cast some shadow of fear.[28]

As the control of medicines became more responsive to the global market, so government regulation developed as a formidable first line of defence for the Pharmas. The system became less accessible and less responsive to local priorities and health needs – though on either side of the Atlantic, this happened in different ways. The American regulatory model was unique, being based on a highly legalistic framework and supported by great resources. However, these were never sufficient to meet the demand. The FDA had an unrivalled capacity to monitor and scrutinise the Pharmas, but was also under huge pressure from market trends.

> A vignette underlines this point. It involves an FDA reviewer hard at good work – but also reveals the pressure the regulators faced, having failed to stop DTCA. The reviewer was objecting to a TV commercial for Sarafem – fluoxetine packaged and

---

26 A US government study found that "of the 198 drugs approved by the FDA between 1976 and 1985 for which data were available, 102 (or 51.5 percent) had serious post-approval risks, as evidenced by labelling changes or withdrawals from the market" (GAO 1990).

A more recent analysis of the 548 new chemical entities approved from 1975-1999 found that 56 (10.2%) acquired a new black box warning (implying "special problems, particularly those that may lead to death or serious injury") or were withdrawn from the market (Lasser et al. 2002).

27 Another, related risk would be almost unresearchable but seems theoretically compelling: Blockbusters were harder to regulate. Regulatory decision-making may well have become more tentative when great fortunes were at stake, because companies would always go to the utmost lengths to defend a successful drug under threat. Moreover, when regulators did find serious risks with especially popular drugs, they and the politicians were exposed to criticism themselves.

28 In a private session, during the 2001 annual meeting of national centres for adverse drug reaction reporting (WHO-Uppsala Monitoring Centre), the subject of *The Constant Gardener* came up. This was not an agenda item, but led to a long, heated discussion about industry intimidation on regulators. The discussants passed a formal resolution to investigate, but the decision was to investigate strictly in secret. This restricted information-gathering, and the initiative quietly faded away.

licensed for severe menstrual disorders, though clearly aimed at a wider market. The FDA warning letter to Lilly was technically exact, but also seemed like a finger in a breached dyke. The introduction of DTCA inevitably promoted medicalisation, but all the FDA could do was insist that this was done by means that were not blatantly, "lacking in fair balance and misleading":

> "The graphics of the advertisement show a frustrated woman trying to pull her shopping cart out of its interlocked line-up in front of a store. The concurrent audio states 'Think it's PMS? It could be PMDD'. The imagery and audio presentation of the advertisement never completely define or accurately illustrate premenstrual dysphoric disorder (PMDD) and there is no clear distinction between premenstrual syndrome (PMS) and PMDD communicated. Consequently, the overall message broadens the indication and trivializes the seriousness of PMDD, a disorder whose hallmarks include a markedly depressed mood, anxiety or tension, affective lability, and persistent anger or irritability. For a diagnosis of PMDD, these and other symptoms must markedly interfere with work, school, usual social activities, and relationships." (FDA 2000)

Proper scrutiny of the dossier also called for meticulous attention to detail, but this was hard to do. Another example shows the subtlety and relentlessness of the pressures on regulators, as the Pharmas strived to present their products in the best possible light. In this case, another FDA reviewer had noted in his evaluation (CDER 1999) that SmithKline Beecham had been far from forthright in describing paroxetine ADRs.

> "Suicide gestures and suicide attempts were coded to the preferred term '*Emotional Lability*', which is not considered to be an adequate representation of these events."[29]

> "Female experiences of anorgasmia or delayed orgasm were coded to the preferred term '*Female Genital Disorders*' which is felt to be too vague to adequately convey the nature of these events."

Across the Atlantic, different regulatory traditions had evolved. The European process involved much less emphasis on investigation, chapter and verse, or confrontation; the UK emphasis was on trust, collaboration, closeness and conciliation. Far more than in the US, self-regulation by the industry was encouraged and much relied

---

29 "Open to change; adaptable: an emotionally labile person" – *The American Heritage® Dictionary of the English Language, Fourth Edition, Houghton Mifflin Company (2000).* Note that the term "emotional lability" continued to be used to describe suicidal behaviour: see Chapter 11.

on. High levels of secrecy encouraged this style: compliance and enforcement often seemed to amount to having a quiet word, perhaps even turning a blind eye.

Meanwhile, the UK regulators seemed well satisfied with their own performance. This was evident from a "value for money study" of the Agency by the National Audit Office (2003).[30] The gist of it was the MCA had conscientiously defined numerous targets and performance measures, all of which proved that it did an excellent job – "(almost without exception 100 per cent achieved)". At the same time, the MCA had become so steeped in accountability-by-numbers, that it missed the most important point:

> "Reported information tends to focus on targets where measurement is easiest, such as the speed of assessment of applications or the time taken to enter adverse drug reaction reports on the computer system ... There are no reported objectives or performance measures for providing effective medicines information to the public ... Reported performance measures focus almost solely on the outputs achieved (e.g. number of inspections of UK manufacturing licence holders carried out) rather than outcomes for public health." (NAO 2003)

The regulatory emphasis on both sides of the Atlantic was on the dossier as the key to understanding what effects drugs had, and how they actually worked. However, the FDA relied more heavily on evaluation of pre-marketing data in the dossier, while the MCA took more account of Yellow Card data – spontaneous reports of suspected adverse drug reactions.

The difference showed. Ten years after the launch of Paxil, the FDA-approved product label still suggested no problems with paroxetine withdrawal. Definitive estimates of the rarity of withdrawal problems were set out in tables that recorded in fine detail the results of the original clinical trials done in the 1980s. The reputation of Paxil, like that of the FDA, was enshrined in the dossier. Post-marketing drug surveillance and ADR reporting had made little difference to the safety profile. Until late 2001, the Paxil label recorded withdrawal reactions as "rare," implying an incidence of under 0.001%, and a tiny footnote barely recommended gradual withdrawal.[31] By this time, the best available evidence suggested the true incidence of reactions to abrupt withdrawal was closer to 30% – some 300-times higher than the FDA advised. The Paxil label change at the end of 2001 for the first time emphasised the need for

---

30 The NAO was "totally independent of Government;" its job was to "to scrutinise public spending on behalf of Parliament". The MCA involved minimal direct public expenditure, but stood for considerable public investment. The NAO (2003) took some account of this, as well.

31 "There have been spontaneous reports that discontinuation (particularly when abrupt) may lead to symptoms such as dizziness, sensory disturbance, agitation or anxiety, nausea and sweating; these events are generally self-limiting."

gradual withdrawal; it also acknowledged that "intolerable symptoms" might result even then.

The 2001 revision of the Paxil label produced a new set of definitive estimates of the frequency of problems on gradual withdrawal – precise (if not accurate) to the nearest 0.1%. These estimates were based on the more recent clinical trials submitted to the FDA to get Paxil approved for new indications. They identified a low incidence of "abnormal dreams," "paraesthesia" and "dizziness" as the three main hallmarks of withdrawal.

The new US label did not reflect that record numbers of patients and physicians had reported Paxil withdrawal problems. It acknowledged only that, "during Paxil marketing, there have been reports of similar events," and advised that they "may have no causal relationship to the drug". There was no indication of symptom severity, nor its impact. Regulatory science could be thus far removed from common sense.

Adverse drug reaction reporting

The UK's National Audit Office funded its reviews through fees paid by the audited agency – and so, via the MCA, the Pharmas' dues extended to payment for Parliamentary scrutiny. Far from quibbling about the audit fee, the Pharmas welcomed the NAO report and put out a press statement to say so: "its analysis is to be praised" (ABPI 2003).[32]

The scope of the NAO scrutiny was strictly limited; it seemed mainly to be an attestation of the MCA's own account of its work. The NAO was mainly critical of the MCA's failures to communicate with patients, especially through Patient Information Leaflets. Again, the ABPI heartily agreed:

> "The pharmaceutical industry also believes that patient information leaflets could be more patient-friendly, but the problem centres around tight European regulations on what information has be included and excluded, as well as how it can be presented ... the ABPI firmly believes that companies ought to have greater freedom to provide additional information to patients about medicines. At the moment, the industry's ability to do this is stifled by the law." (ABPI 2003)

---

32 This ABPI press release generally underlined the strength of the relationship between the Pharmas and the MCA. The Pharmas believed that it stood for what drug regulation should be: "The MCA is one of the best and most efficient regulatory agencies in the world, and it is a real asset to the pharmaceutical industry, the NHS and patients." The Pharmas joined the NAO, "in recognising the MCA's international standing for scientific and regulatory expertise" and also hoped it would "continue to have a prominent role as a leader in the development of European legislation".

The National Audit Office's grasp of the issues at the heart of this case-history were revealed in its model of a "simplified patient information leaflet" – with everything reduced to 15 FAQs (frequently asked questions) and simple answers. By chance, the model drug was paroxetine. The first three FAQs were as follows:

"*What does the medicine do?*
It treats mental depression by helping to maintain levels of serotonin.

Is it habit forming?
No.

How long does it take to work?
It works within one to four weeks."

Overall, the audit concluded that, safety-wise, the MCA did well. This conclusion was partly based on the relatively few drugs withdrawn on safety grounds – 12 over the previous five years.[33] However, the NAO relied on another safety indicator – the relatively low number of ADR reports sent in under the Yellow Card scheme, "the cornerstone of the Agency's work on medicines safety monitoring". The auditors optimistically reported there was "less than one adverse reaction for every 10,000 prescriptions dispensed".

No doubt with encouragement from the MCA, the NAO had come to believe that, "only around 10 – 25 per cent of reactions experienced by patients were reported,"[34] though "a recent study has shown that the reporting rate may rise to around 50 per cent for serious reactions to new medicines".[35] These NAO estimates far exceeded those used by the MCA/CSM,[36] but even they seemed far too high.

The Yellow Card system was founded post-thalidomide. Since 1964, doctors have been encouraged to send in reports of suspected ADRs and, "The Scheme continues to be of the utmost importance for monitoring drug safety" (CSM 2003). Nevertheless most doctors ignored the Yellow Card scheme and ADR reporting rates stayed

---

33 The NAO took little account of safety problems with drugs still sold. The regulatory tendency was to add restrictions and warnings to the label; drugs came off the market only as a last resort.

34 The British Medical Association's *BMA News* (8 February 2003, 6) translated this upside-down: "A Medicines Control Agency inquiry into the yellow card scheme revealed one in four adverse drug reactions was not being reported by health professionals."

35 This estimate cited a study whose authors had emphasised: "Our results should not be extrapolated to calculate incidence rates of adverse drug reactions in the community from spontaneous reports" (Heeley et al. 2001).

36 "It is estimated that only 5-10% of suspected ADRs are reported" (MCA 1999), and "less than 10% of all serious and 2-4% of non-serious adverse reactions are reported" (Pirmohamed et al. 1998).

low. When the MCA inherited the system from the Department of Health (1989), the input was 19,246 Yellow Cards per year – compared with 19,505 in 2001.

The core numbers of Yellow Card reports had stayed constant, though the MCA/CSM had tried to extend the Scheme by permitting pharmacists and nurses to report as well. The NAO also noted with approval that the MCA intended "to roll out patient reporting" in February 2003. Events proved that the MCA/CSM had something much more modest in mind.[37]

The available evidence suggested that the mythical average doctor reported something closer to around one per cent of the ADRs there actually were. General Practitioners sent in just under half of all Yellow Cards (9,232 reports from GPs in 2001) – equivalent to about one-third of a Yellow Card per doctor per year. If the NAO had extrapolated conservatively from the best available ballpark estimates,[38] they might have expected the average doctor to see about 50 significant ADRs each year.

Hospital doctors sent in Yellow Cards at less than half that rate, but saw many more ADRs. The closest to an official (CSM) estimate suggested that ADRs accounted for about 5% of all hospital admissions, and affected 10-20% of hospitalised patients (Pirmohamed et al. 1998). At that time, there were about six million hospital admissions per year.

However, it made no sense to try to produce any average estimate of the level of ADR under-reporting. Nothing pointed to any average. Different drugs had different effects on different people, different ADRs were harder or easier to detect, and different doctors saw and reported different things in different ways. The SSRIs were far from average: Paroxetine was one of 15,000 medicines (Munro 2003) but, even after ten years on the market, it accounted for about one in 40 of all Yellow Cards sent in.

So what was the 'real' incidence of paroxetine withdrawal reactions? In this case, it depended on which company's clinical trials were to be believed. The pre-marketing dossier, based on SmithKline Beecham-sponsored clinical trials, mostly conducted in the 1980s, found withdrawal reactions were rare and generally mild.

---

37 Under obvious pressure to do something, the MCA proposed a modest pilot scheme to encourage patients (in a limited area) to telephone their reports to a nurse on a helpline at *NHS Direct.* Even after publication of the National Audit Office report and the advertised "roll out" date (February 2003), the MCA website suggested little appetite for patient reports: "Why can't patients report? We do not accept reports directly from patients, as we consider that medical interpretation of the suspected reaction is vital. We advise patients who suspect they have had an adverse reaction to their medicine to discuss this with their doctor or pharmacist. The doctor or pharmacist may then report this via the Yellow Card Scheme, if they consider it to be appropriate" (MCA/CSM website, April 2003).

38 In one single practice study, general practitioners estimated 1.7% of their consultations over a six month period was a manifestation of an ADR (Millar 2002). The same estimated figure (1.7%) was reported also by Lumley et al. 1986.

Later, in the mid-1990s, a series of Eli Lilly-sponsored trials on paroxetine concluded quite the opposite (Rosenbaum et al. 1998; Michelson et al. 2000; Judge et al. 2002).

This underlines the point that actually changing the text of a warning in the label is a legally complicated and delicate process. Having originally approved the original text, on the basis of the sponsor company's 'scientific' assessment, the regulators are in a difficult position thereafter. If they later wanted to change the label, the regulators needed 'scientific' grounds for doing so – and risked legal challenges without it. Either way, on both sides of the Atlantic, paroxetine regulators and users were far apart.

The distance between them is roughly quantifiable: the regulators, bound by 'scientific' standards, looked to act only when things seemed upwards of 95% certain ($p < 0.05$). Common sense, and indeed the law, rely more on the balance of probabilities: if a serious risk seems more likely (51%) than not (49%), why not try to reduce it while waiting for evidence to come in?

Self regulation?

The Pharmas routinely pushed to the limits and frequently exceeded them, especially when promoting their products. This was clear from experience with DTCA, both in the US and in New Zealand. Until the shift to deregulation, the FDA filed violation notices for one in four DTC-advertised products (Aitken & Holt 2000), and non-compliance in New Zealand was higher still.[39]

The Pharmas resisted regulation: in line with their preference for free market conditions they proposed self-regulation instead. All over the world, bar the US, the Pharmas insisted they could be trusted to observe their own Codes of Marketing Practice – different ones in different countries, but all in line with the code of their international trade body, the IFPMA.[40]

---

39 In 1998, the New Zealand Department of Health ordered an enquiry into DTCA, when surveys suggested that two-thirds of DTC advertisements did not comply with the industry's voluntary code of practice. A probationary period ensued, and a more recent survey (1999/2000) reported improvement: only one in three DTC advertisements failed to comply. This led to proposals from the industry (adopted in November 2000) for pre-vetting of advertisements at the companies' expense. Following a more recent review, the New Zealand Department of Health recommended "that legislation regulating DTCA should be strengthened to ensure advertisements provide balanced information to consumers" (New Zealand Department of Health: Direct-to-consumer advertising rules will become stricter, Press release, 14 August 2001). Another official enquiry began in 2003, prompted by a report from Toop and colleagues (2003).

40 The International Federation of Pharmaceutical Manufacturers Associations (IFPMA) "is convinced that, so far as marketing activities are concerned, self discipline is the process which best serves the public interest".

These codes had in common some gushing dedication to the highest standards of truth, accuracy and fairness, plus a commitment to uphold them "in the spirit" as well as to the letter. The IFPMA Code first appeared in 1981, as a rapid response to what the industry perceived as a threat by the World Health Organization to introduce or steer towards some sort of supranational regulation.[41] The preamble to the first edition of the IFPMA code set the tone for years to come:

> "The pharmaceutical industry, conscious of its special position, arising from its involvement in public health, and justifiably eager to fulfil its obligations in a free and fully responsible manner undertakes: ... to base the claims for substances on valid scientific evidence, thus determining their therapeutic indications and conditions of use; to provide scientific information with objectivity and good taste with scrupulous regard for truth, and with clear statements with respect to indications, contraindications, tolerance and toxicity; to use complete candour in dealings with public health officials, health care professionals and the public."

Similar expressions of spirit are still to be found in parts of the IFPMA Code, as in many national voluntary codes – with the exception of the US. Through the IFPMA and otherwise, the Pharmas pressed for self-regulation everywhere but in the US. The US Pharmas first introduced a voluntary code in 2002. By then, the British (ABPI) Code had been operating for nearly 50 years.

> *Social Audit* tested the ABPI Code on paroxetine three times (*ADWEB* 2000-2003). The system seemed well organised but the process felt almost impenetrable, requiring much input for little gain. In this case, the self-regulatory system seemed of little consequence in any overall scheme, though the complaints process did throw up useful bits of information from time to time.[42]

Eventually, the Pharmaceutical Research and Manufacturers of America (PhRMA) reacted to the widespread criticism of the US industry. In summer 2002, PhRMA introduced for the first time a voluntary code of practice on Interactions with

---

41 Under intense pressure from the US government, the WHO backed right away from any thought of external regulation. Instead it suggested guidelines of its own. The IFPMA participated in this process and agreed with the results: "The Federation recognises the value of the definition by the World Health Organization in 1998 of Ethical criteria for medicinal drug promotion. The present version of the IFPMA Code is consonant with these criteria, to the extent that they are applicable to our constituents". The WHO criteria applied to "all informational and persuasive activities ... the effect of which is to induce the prescription, supply, purchase and/or use of medicinal drugs". The criteria suggested that: "... All promotion-making claims concerning medicinal drugs should be reliable, accurate, truthful, informative, balanced, up-to-date, capable of substantiation and in good taste. They should not contain misleading or unverifiable statements or omissions likely to induce medically unjustifiable drug use or to give rise to undue risks ..."

Healthcare Professionals. "We decided that if we didn't take the lead, Congress would do it for us," said the man from Eli Lilly who chaired the PhRMA Legal Section" (Peletier 2002).

The industry's new standards were much the same as those proposed by the American Medical Association in 1990 and by the IFPMA in 1981. Matters relating to

---

42 The three complaints arose in connection with statements made by two (different) senior company people – a doctor interviewed on TV in the US, and GSK's "Director, UK Corporate Media". Both had publicly claimed that the symptoms of paroxetine discontinuation were rare and mild.

The ABPI's "Prescription Medicines Code of Practice Authority" dismissed the first complaint, but then upheld it on appeal. The GSK doctor had claimed that discontinuation syndrome affected only two in every 1,000 patients, "when discontinued appropriately", with symptoms mild and short-lived. GSK defended this saying that they had examined their clinical trials database and found that only seven patients out of 8,143 had experienced withdrawal problems. GSK also emphasised how few ADRs there were in relation to the vast amounts prescribed. Neither estimate made sense, and GlaxoSmithKline decided not to attend the appeal. (Very few of these trials involved drug withdrawal, or any attempt to measure what happened when paroxetine was withdrawn. Most patients would have stayed on their drugs, for ethical reasons alone. GSK was specifically asked to provide evidence of trials that were designed to assess withdrawal effects, but declined to do so [*ADWEB* 18 January 2002]).

The second complaint focused on media briefings along the following lines: "There's no reliable scientific evidence to show they (SSRIs) cause withdrawal symptoms or dependency." ... "There have been one or two reports of discontinuation symptoms with abrupt cessation..." The industry's Code of Practice people again dismissed the complaint, but reversed it on appeal.

On appeal, GlaxoSmithKline admitted that their "Director, UK Corporate Media" would have been in breach of the Code, if he had actually said that, but argued he had not. GSK then produced the briefing document that he should have used. This was a confidential *Reactive Key Messages and Issues Document* (December 2001). It advised press officers to tell the media that Seroxat was not addictive and that:

> "Stopping any antidepressant can result in some patients experiencing discontinuation symptoms ... In most cases these symptoms are mild to moderate in nature and self-limiting."
>
> "... the likelihood of discontinuation symptoms is minimised by gradually tapering the daily dose."
>
> "Discontinuation symptoms are completely different to addiction or dependence."
>
> "There has been no reliable scientific evidence from either preclinical studies, long term clinical trials or clinical experience, to suggest that 'Seroxat' is addictive, shows dependence or is a drug of abuse."
>
> "The MCA (Medicine Control Agency) and CPMP (European regulators) have concluded that SSRIs do not cause dependency/addiction."

The Code of Practice panel declined even to consider whether these claims were unacceptable, until a third formal complaint was made. When it was, they upheld some technical breach of the ABPI Code, but declined *Social Audit's* invitation to rule that GSK had breached "Clause 2" – "Activities or materials associated with promotion must never be such as to bring discredit upon, or reduce confidence in, the pharmaceutical industry."

interpretation, training and communication, monitoring, auditing and compliance were left to companies themselves: "Each member company is strongly encouraged to adopt procedures to assure adherence to this Code". The US Pharmas showed no signs of feeling threatened by their proposed new Code; they emphasised that everything was under control:

> "Gino Santini, president of US operations ... said complying with the PhRMA Code has meant only 'marginal changes' in Lilly's marketing." (Swiatek 2002)
>
> "a spokesman for Wyeth Pharmaceuticals said the Collegeville-based company supports the new code, which mirrors its own internal initiatives on the topic." (George 2002)
>
> "Quite frankly, complying with the PhRMA code is not going to require any changes on our part – Merck & Co." (Seglin 2002)

Unlike most other industry-sponsored codes, the PhRMA Code was mainly about the conduct of sales representatives. The US Pharmas have yet to develop standards for the content of advertising and related promotion, whether directed at doctors or at the people they treat.

9
Scientifically tested and approved

Precious little of what passed for medical science seemed to amount to honest seeking after truth. In this case, as in others, the science was mainly directed at pointing to marginal and notional drug advantages and to papering over the cracks. This chapter reviews some of the techniques used in designing and interpreting clinical trials, to produce the desired results; it also looks at clinical trial standards from the standpoint of patients' safety. The analysis proposes that scientific fundamentalism and triumphalism have obscured the importance of vital human factors relating to placebo effects. The scientific community lost sight of their importance not only in the treatment of depression, but also in relation to the conduct of medical science.

Three months before the National Audit Office (NAO) investigation was published, Dr. Keith Jones suddenly left the Medicines Control Agency (MCA). The absence of any tribute to the person who had run the Agency for the previous decade was conspicuous, but the MCA just posted a two-line notice on its website saying Jones had gone. His successor would take over 15 months later, at the beginning of 2004.[1]

At the time, the MCA denied there was any mystery and said Jones' departure had long been planned. No advertisement for his successor then appeared, but the NAO didn't comment on that either. The NAO noted only that the MCA had a new chairman, and was about to get a new name. From April 2003, the MCA became the *Medicines and Healthcare products Regulatory Agency*. The "p" was silent; the acronym was MHRA.

The new chair of the MCA/MHRA was Professor Alasdair Breckenridge, a long-time member of the Committee on the Safety of Medicines (CSM) and its chairman from 2000 to 2003. Breckenridge had been head of the department of Pharmacology and Therapeutics at Liverpool University. Like many other strong departments, the department depended on Pharma funding. It hosted a Glaxo chair of clinical pharmacology,[2] and Breckenridge had long consulted for SmithKline Beecham (SKB), before he took over the CSM chair.

---

1 Professor Kent Woods was appointed Chief Executive of the MHRA in August 2003, to take up the appointment from 1 January 2004.

This closeness between the regulators, the scientific community and the second biggest Pharma in the world had become unavoidable. The new acting head of the MCA/MHRA was Dr. Gordon Munro, who had been with SKB for over 20 years. Another top man, Dr. Ian Hudson, was in charge of licensing new drugs and dossier evaluation. He also came from SKB, where he'd been responsible for the safety of paroxetine.

Within the UK regulatory system, close contact with companies was considered unexceptional and generally desirable – so long as everyone disclosed possible conflicts of interests and withdrew from discussion if they arose. The MCA/MHRA denied that this ever caused problems even with its *Independent Review Panel for Advertising*, eight of whose ten members had personal interests in GSK.[3]

Beyond requesting disclosure of competing interests, the Committee on Safety of Medicines had strict rules on debarment. When particular drugs were discussed, the CSM chair took a view: members with direct or personal interests in the drug were usually asked to leave the room. Otherwise they might be allowed to stay and listen, speaking only if the chairman asked them to do so.

This procedure was strict but the specifics were secret, until the Ombudsman's ruling in 2000. This arose because the MCA had gone to great lengths (*ADWEB* 1998-2000) to avoid explaining what happened when the CSM discussed the key study that underpinned the claim on the label, "Long-term treatment with Seroxat has shown that efficacy is maintained for periods of at least one year."

This was the study that withdrew patients abruptly from paroxetine and then inferred drug efficacy if the depression returned. The study was done jointly by a doctor from SKB and a psychiatrist, Dr. Stuart Montgomery, the main expert on the CSM (1987-1992). Four Selective Serotonin Reuptake Inhibitors (SSRIs) were licensed in those years and Montgomery had personal links to three of the Pharmas that made them.

When the MCA did finally disclose what had happened in those meetings, the record showed that procedures had been scrupulously observed: over the years, Montgomery had often left the room or had spoken only when asked. The general idea was that regulatory integrity was assured provided there was no present evidence of undue commercial influence in moments of decision-making.

By these standards, the system apparently failed only once in many years. In 2002, the MCA/CSM organised an *ad hoc* expert group to look into the safety of SSRIs. The regulators were by then under some pressure. Dr. David Healy's analyses pointed to more and more worrying evidence of the risks of suicidality, and more and more patients were publicly complaining about dependence.

2 This was the seventh university chair endowed by Glaxo in the UK (*SCRIP* No 1840, 23 July 1993).

3 MCA (Dr. June Raine), letter to Social Audit, 4 March 2003.

The first *Panorama* programme, *Secrets of Seroxat*, had intensified the pressure; it precipitated a flood of claims and complaints: they led to questions in Parliament, and the upshot was that a Health Minister promptly announced that the MCA/CSM was mounting an "Intensive Review". The bureaucrats had no doubt prompted this reassuring answer, but it meant that the MCA/CSM *ad hoc* expert group suddenly became much more important that it was ever intended to be. At this point, questions arose about who the experts were.

The Chairman of the "Intensive Review" was Dr. Angus Mackay of the CSM. He was one of the signatories of the MCA/CSM paper (Price et al. 1996) that had concluded that "overall, symptoms due to stopping an SSRI are rare" etc. That paper was based on the NERO defence (no evidence of risk equals evidence of no risk) – an absurd interpretation of inadequate data – but the MCA/CSM had repeatedly refused to modify or withdraw it (*ADWEB* 1998-2002).

There were four other CSM members on the Intensive Review. One was Dr. M. Donaghy, a small shareholder in GlaxoSmithKline. Another was Professor David Nutt. He had personal interests (including a small shareholding) in GlaxoSmithKline and ties with several other SSRI Pharmas. Nutt had also been the main guest speaker engaged by SmithKline Beecham when they launched Seroxat for shyness, i.e. "social anxiety disorder" or "social phobia".

> "According to the professor (and SmithKline Beecham), between two and five per cent of the British population suffer from social anxiety disorder at some time in their lives. Women are more likely to have it than men. It usually strikes before the age of 20. Children have it, but most grow out of it. Sufferers tend to be single, under-educated and under-achieving, and also to depend on alcohol and drugs. They also have much higher suicide rates, partly because of 'co-morbidity', the tendency to develop other conditions – depression, alcoholism – after social phobia has set in."
>
> "It's a common, lifelong, disabling, under-recognised and under-treated illness" said Professor Nutt. The words on the screen said that it led to 'avoidance of social/performance situations' or enduring them with great distress. The 'feared situations' included dating, attending weddings, public-speaking, taking an exam, trying clothes on in a shop, calling someone you did not know on the telephone, writing a cheque, typing when someone was looking over your shoulder (a box, among others, that I'd most certainly tick), and eating in public. The professor said the socially phobic tended to avoid soup and peas in restaurants – giveaways for shaky hands – and go instead for easily-managed forms of pasta." (Ian Jack, *The Independent* 10th October 1998)

At the first meeting of the Intensive Review team, both Nutt and Donaghy disclosed interests and left the room when paroxetine was discussed. This deprived the review of much of the CSM's expertise, but also gave the executive (MHRA) more of a free hand. However, an invited expert, Dr. David Baldwin, stayed on. The minutes recorded that he disclosed "personal non-specific interests" in Lundbeck (citalopram) – but not that he was on an advisory board for Wyeth (venlafaxine) and on a study group for Bristol Myers Squibb (nefazodone). Nor was it recorded that Baldwin was involved with a paroxetine study group and had been co-presenter with Professor Nutt to help SKB launch Seroxat for shyness. On that occasion, Dr. Baldwin had said how safe the drug was. Baldwin said he thought, "Seroxat is one of the safest drugs ever made."

Once these potential conflicts became known – and the subject of another (abortive[4]) referral to the Ombudsman – the MCA/CSM caved in. On day three of the Iraq War (2003), they quietly let slip: "We have now decided to dissolve the original Group and appoint a new Expert Group to conduct the review". Political sensitivities caused the Intensive Review to fall apart. The MCA/CSM had assembled what they regarded as a first class team of scientists. Baldwin had been nominated by another CSM member who couldn't attend, but everyone knew everyone and no one's integrity, reputation and expertise was ever in doubt. The problem was not that Dr. Baldwin had close contacts with the Pharmas, but that he'd not disclosed them. It meant the equivalent of a mistrial.

This episode also revealed the CSM/MCA's perspective on how regulation should be. Decisions about safety should be left to doctors and scientists, without user representation.[5] This also backfired and helped to kill the Intensive Review. It probably wasn't that the MCA/CSM came to their senses. The order would have come from the Department of Health: politicians were more exposed to charges of elitism and sleaze.

In this respect, the British model of drug regulation both tended to the US norm, and also lagged behind it. Consumer representation in the US Food and Drug Administration (FDA) process is guaranteed and Federal regulations generally prohibited the FDA from using experts with financial conflicts of interest. However, the FDA had waived that requirement over 800 times between 1998 and 2000, and over half of the experts on FDA Advisory Panels had financial ties with the companies most affected by the decisions taken (Cauchon 2000).

---

4 The Ombudsman declined to investigate mainly on the grounds that the complainant (CM) had not suffered "some personal injustice". That decision was unsuccessfully appealed (September 2003).

5 The MCA refused Social Audit (CM) permission to appear before the Intensive Review on such grounds. The reason given was that he was "not a scientist".

Reliability of evidence from drug trials

It seems improbable that the CSM ever discussed the Montgomery/Dunbar trial at the time paroxetine was approved. The regulators would have seen no need to do so: years later, they still believed that withdrawal symptoms were rare and usually mild. It would not have occurred to them that withdrawal-induced depression might have confounded the analysis on which their lead expert had relied.

As the regulators saw it, the Montgomery/Dunbar trial had been conducted "scientifically" – even though the trial design discounted the possibility of paroxetine withdrawal symptoms. When *Social Audit* pressed the chairman of the CSM on this, he chided: "The study was a randomised, double-blind, controlled study which provides good evidence for the efficacy of paroxetine in preventing relapse and recurrence of depression over the (one year) period of the study" (Rawlins 1998).

The inference would be that the authorities deemed clinical trials to be "scientific", so long as they obeyed certain rules. This was a bit like assuming that schoolboys were pure in heart, if their caps were straight and their shirts tucked in. In this case, no problem was perceived: as the regulators saw it, the car was in good working order; never mind if it was belting up the wrong road.

Clinical trials could, in other words, accord with scientific standards and still mislead and go wrong. There were, and are, countless ways of pushing the trial design in the direction of desired results, without troubling the regulators. So long as incorrect procedures had not been followed, the FDA tended to accept the results of clinical trials to the nearest decimal point, just as the MCA accepted their broad conclusions.

One way and another, it was relatively easy to follow a range of not-incorrect procedures and still produce the desired result. The Lilly-sponsored study reported by Rosenbaum et al. (1998) gives an outstanding illustration of the options. It is a classic for any student of clinical trial design.

> With a view to demonstrating the withdrawal problems with paroxetine and sertraline, the trial protocol incorporated a rigorous, belt-and-braces approach to establishing the levels of possible ADRs. The investigators recorded adverse effects in two quite different (both perfectly acceptable) ways, and so produced two quite different sets of results.
>
> First, the investigators used the classic, open-ended approach – asking patients, in general terms, how the treatment was suiting them. If a patient complained, the clinician might then record a suspected ADR, perhaps to be classified under some bland term with diffuse meaning. This method of eliciting ADR information predictably led to modest levels of reporting. These were the symptoms of abrupt paoxetine withdrawal that Rosenbaum et al. recorded, using an open-ended approach:
>
>> Dizziness (29%), nausea (29), trouble sleeping (19), headache (17), nervousness (16), fatigue (11), diarrhea (11)

However, as part of the same trial, these investigators also employed a much more searching method. They used batteries of measures, like the HAM-D checklist, to measure mood changes during withdrawal. They also developed a checklist of 43 reported withdrawal symptoms, and asked patients to respond to each one. Using this method, the same patients – after the same drug experience – recorded these symptoms (%) of paroxetine withdrawal:

> Dizziness (50%), worsened mood (45), confusion (42), nausea (40), crying (40), trouble sleeping (39); dreaming (37), irritability (35), nervousness (34), headache (34), fatigue (32), agitation (31), anger (29), emotional lability (26), amnesia (24), sweating (24), diarrhea (24), unsteady gait (23), muscle aches (23), panic (21), depersonalisation (21) shaking (21), chills (18), sore eyes (15); muscle tension (11)

There were many ways of designing and conducting clinical trials to drive to the desired results. How were patients and investigators selected? What measurements were taken, how and when? What drugs were used for comparison and at what dosages? Which statistical methods were used? Where, when and how were the data published, if at all? These and many other factors could radically affect test results and how their significance was perceived (Moore 1995).

From the 1990s, the commercialisation of drug testing rapidly picked up pace. Previously, most studies and trials had been done in teaching hospitals, under the supervision of a notionally independent academic team. Then came a dramatic increase of contract research organisations (CROs), hired by the Pharmas to run clinical trials and do other work. Everything became more streamlined, efficient and money-driven, increasingly on the Pharmas' terms. Academic centres responded to the huge loss of business[6] by trying to provide more favourable environments for the Pharmas, competing as never before.

The dossier accounted for only a fraction of the clinical trials that were done. Most trials were to support the marketing, so their numbers increased, and that meant that patients and test subjects were in short supply. There were several consequences: more trials were done overseas, more clinicians got larger fees for recruiting patients, and patients came under more pressure to get involved. This extended to general practice and in Britain led to some significant abuse (Inman 1999).

---

6 In 1991, 80% of industry money for clinical trials went to academic medical centres; by 1998 that figure had dropped to 40% (Bodenheimer 2000). Worldwide, CROs had estimated revenues of US$7 billion in 2001 (Relman & Angell 2002).

The ostensible reason for most general practice trials was "Post-Marketing Surveillance". In Britain, this noble purpose had been written into guidelines developed by the triumvirate of industry-regulators-professionals, in the late 1980s. The idea was that companies should organise large-scale trials when new drugs were first used, to add to the limited understanding of safety from the dossier. In practice, most such trials contributed little or nothing to the understanding of safety, and it was hard to imagine they were intended to do so.

> Breckenridge and Rawlins were among the authors of a review of 31 such sponsored studies: 22 were uncontrolled and 26 failed to recruit enough patients – the main reason why 11 were abandoned. One study had identified an important new hazard, but overall, they made "a limited contribution ... principally because of weak study design and difficulties in recruitment." (Waller et al. 1992)
>
> Another audit of 100 trial protocols reported more of the same: "a significant incidence of inconclusive results". This was the conclusion of the research ethics committee of the Royal College of General Practitioners. They also made the key point that, if research wasn't scientific, it wasn't ethical. On that basis, they identified "substantial ethical concerns." (Wise & Drury 1996)

The true purpose of most general practice trials was to "familiarise" doctors with products, in the hope that patients were switched to the test drug and then stayed on it for years. But what of the quality of mainstream studies and trials, those conducted by specialists in dedicated clinical settings? To summarise: most of what purported to be "science" was no such thing. On a strict interpretation, one could not honestly say that most published scientific papers met the standards required in European Union laws for drug advertising:

> "No person shall issue an advertisement relating to a relevant medicinal product unless that advertisement encourages the rational use of that product by presenting it objectively and without exaggerating its properties."

The dividing line between worthy science and product promotion had largely disappeared. Just as regulators could believe that product advertising promoted rational drug use, so the research community was increasingly compromised by the demand for good news.

The problem was also partly to do with impossible volumes of information, and the heady speed at which messages came and went. The Internet increased this pressure, as did the crisis in drug innovation: as the quality of innovation declined, so volumes of information increased. The overall quality also declined. Most of the estimated 20,000 biomedical journals were dependent on Pharma funding and many members of editorial advisory boards were much in their thrall. Not many of these journals critically reviewed what they published, and the few editors that really did were clearly dismayed.[7] These prime movers were concerned even about the quality of the papers submitted to them. If much of the best was poor, it held out little hope for the rest of them:

> The best of the papers submitted to *The Lancet* ("candidates for publication") were referred for statistical review. Only half were deemed acceptable or acceptable after revision. "Descriptions of methods and of results were found inadequate in about half of the papers; about one-quarter of papers had inadequate abstracts and conclusions. Major errors of inference ... went hand in hand with major criticisms of analysis or design." (Gore et al. 1992)

> Dr. Richard Smith, editor of the *British Medical Journal*, told the 1998 annual meeting of the Royal College of Psychiatrists, he estimated that only 5% of published articles reached minimum standards of scientific soundness and clinical relevance: "In most journals it's less than 1 per cent. Many trials are often too small to be relevant and many of the studies that are published are the positive ones – there is a lot of negative evidence that never sees the light of day." (Boseley 1998)

> Essentially the same was reported by the former editor of the *New England Journal of Medicine* (Angell 2000): "We reject over 90% of the papers submitted to us, primarily because the research is of poor quality. The design or methodology of the study may be inadequate to address the hypothesis, the analysis of the data may be inappropriate, the conclusions may not be supported by the data or the data may support alternative conclusions, and so forth. The possible flaws, many of them fatal, are virtually endless."

By this time, one could safely generalise: sponsored and independent studies of the same drug tended to produce more and less favourable results, respectively. This trend was detectable in papers published in the top medical journals too (Bodenheimer 2000, Kjaergard & Als-Nielsen 2002).

Clinical research practice

Over the years, a variety of protocols had been developed for the proper organisation of clinical trials – the standards of implementation rather than the study design. The International Conference on Harmonisation (ICH) had consolidated these into guidelines, destined to pass into global law in 2004. On paper, the ICH guidelines on

---

7 Through the International Committee of Medical Journal Editors, the leading journals developed a series of statements and standards on editorial policy issues ranging from conflict of interest to editorial freedom, confidentiality, and advertising policy (Davidoff 2000, 2001; Jefferson et al. 2002).

Good Clinical Practice tightened things up: in themselves, the requirements were important and worthwhile. But what mattered was standards of implementation.

The Pharmas had adopted the ICH standards for Good Clinical Practice years before they became law, but in a manner that sidestepped the need for public accountability. The Pharmas undertook to be "GCP compliant" and to have formal audits done on trials submitted for regulatory approval. However, the regulators got to see only the audit certificate – a one-page statement that simply certified that a GCP audit had been done. The regulators rarely if ever saw the actual results.

These audits for Good Clinical Practice (GCP) compliance were mostly done by specialised contract research organisations (CROs). The audit process revolved around a huge 1,500-item checklist, all the requirements for safe and proper procedure in clinical research. On each point, the auditor recorded a pass or fail, with notes to explain. This core information was tailor-made for a database, but destined never to be disclosed.

One fine exception proved that rule. It originated with the publication of a guest editorial in a far-away professional journal, *Clinical Research Focus* (November 1998). The author, Wendy Bohaychuk PhD (microbiology), was co-Director of an independent CRO that specialised in training and auditing for compliance with GCP. Her assessments were based on ten years experience with over 800 GCP audits,[8] involving over 200 companies in over 25 countries, but mainly the UK. She and her colleagues had computerised all their core results and they added up to this:

> "Our database of GCP compliance assessment basically shows that new GCP guidelines and regulations have not yet improved the situation for patients over the last few years and frankly, after 10 years of detailed auditing, I would never go into a clinical study myself and I would certainly try to discourage anyone in my family from doing so." (Bohaychuk 1998)

Unusual factors help to explain this exceptional assessment. These heartfelt remarks were based on the content of perhaps the best GCP compliance database outside of the FDA, and the database itself was the product of a long-term commitment by a small, close team of family and professional friends. The team revolved around Wendy Bohaychuk and her professional and life partner, Dr. Graham Ball. They had become disillusioned at the lack of progress and were dismayed about the general lack of concern. They had analysed their data and tried to get it discussed and acted on. When that failed, they resolved to publish their findings (Bohaychuk & Ball 1999). They strictly mentioned no names, but focused on the main problems and the urgent need to address them.

---

8 Including audits of investigator sites, clinical reports, clinical laboratories and Standard Operating Procedures.

Overall, no company they had audited had achieved compliance of 80% or more. The range was from 43% to 79%, with an average compliance level of 64% in the UK, as for all other countries combined. These were some of the main problem areas described:

> "Ethics committees[9] were not informed of all serious safety events occurring in the study or elsewhere during the study." (81% of audits)
>
> "There was significant under-reporting of safety information arising during the study." (31%)
>
> "General practitioners were not informed that their patients were entered into clinical studies before the study began." (71%)
>
> "Study subject was not clearly informed of instructions for using the medicine/device." (43%)
>
> "There was inadequate (or incorrect) supporting evidence that suitable patients were entered into the study." (29%)
>
> "Informed consent was obtained from study subjects after the start of the study or after the start of any study procedures." (37%)
>
> "The consent documents submitted to the ethics committee/IRB differed from the documents actually used at the study site." (26%)
>
> "There were unexplained or unacceptable discrepancies in study medication accountability." (36%)

Beyond the obvious inference – much scope for improving patient safety – these data paradoxically also gave some evidence that GCP was taken seriously. This highly professional audit team had been much in demand for many years. After disclosure, demand for their services naturally fell.

From 2004, specific provisions in the ICH Guidelines on GCP ensured at least that governments would never reveal such data in future. From then on, all the main

---

9 Ethics Committees (UK) are Institutional Review Boards (US) and should play an important part in protecting the interests of people who become "subjects" in trials. Their main job is to scrutinise and approve clinical trial protocols. In the UK (and presumably in many other countries) the overall quality of Ethics Committees is not high, and some seem shambolic. For chapter and verse, refer to the Bulletin of Medical Ethics (R.H. Nicholson (ed.). In the US, Institutional Review Boards tend to be better organised (and have greater legal liabilities) and some of the biggest are run on a commercial basis. About half of all members of IRBs have served as pharmaceutical industry consultants; conflict of interest issues arise (Campbell et al. 2003; Boyd et al. 2003; OIG 2000).

global drug regulators became legally obliged *not* to monitor how the Pharmas complied with good clinical practice requirements.[10] The safety of patients in clinical trials therefore very much depends on the sponsors. The lack of enforcement is underlined by the absence of any legal requirement on auditors to notify the regulators even of any major safety violation.

The subsequent lack of demand for the services of Drs. Wendy Bohaychuk and Graham Ball might have been crippling, but was not.[11] They might have fared much worse, but for their compelling evidence, and because disclosure was evidently in the public interest as no companies were named.

Whistleblowers – conscientious objectors at work – typically ran great risks. As a rule, the pressures on individuals and their dependents were intense, always bordering on the intolerable. Company employees were particularly exposed and fear (Gonçalves 2000) was never far away:

> Dr. Koos Stiekema joined the Dutch-based Pharma, Organon, in 1982; he was a medical research manager when he left in 1999. He left under a dark cloud, following a dispute over the design of a clinical trial of a new anticoagulant drug. Stiekema was concerned about risks to patients involved in the trial, fearing that some would be exposed to ineffectively low doses of the study drug; the company was otherwise advised that the trial design was safe. After Organon ended Stiekema's employment, he wrote outlining his concerns to the three ethics committees that were overseeing the study and this led to a three-month delay. Two years later a Dutch court accepted Organon's claim that Stiekema had breached confidentiality undertakings in his employment contract and awarded the company € 900,000 to compensate for the "considerable financial disadvantage" caused by the delay (Sheldon 2002). Over a year later, that decision was reversed on Appeal, by an Amsterdam court. At the time of writing, Organon is considering a further appeal to the Dutch Supreme Court. (Sheldon 2003)

Similar pressures increasingly impinged on the academic community and they were hard to resist. A national survey of the top 108 US academic institutions found they "routinely engage in industry-sponsored research that fails to adhere to ICMJE

10 International Conference on Harmonization GOOD CLINICAL PRACTICE: CONSOLIDATED GUIDELINE (1997) 5.19.3 (e) *Auditing Procedures:* "To preserve the independence and value of the audit function, the regulatory authority(ies) should not routinely request the audit reports.

Regulatory authority(ies) may seek access to an audit report on a case by case basis when evidence of serious GCP non-compliance exists, or in the course of legal proceedings. When required by applicable law or regulation, the sponsor should provide an audit certificate."

11 The dramatic lack of demand was not unexpected and effectively planned for. Wendy Bohaychuk continues to write fearlessly; she edits *The Quality Assurance Journal* – CM.

guidelines regarding trial design, access to data and publication rights" (Shulman et al. 2002).

These were the guidelines of the International Committee of Medical Journal Editors. One of its prime movers commented: "Any study that has strong pharmaceutical backing is highly likely to be defective ... You get the data the drug company wants you to have".[12] Commercial pressures had led to restrictions on academic freedom that were, "draconian for self-respecting scientists" (Davidoff et al. 2001).

Even in the most sensitive areas of clinical practice, the influence of the Pharmas was pervasive. It affected everything from the review of ethical standards in clinical trials, to treatment guidelines, to the drawing up of the definitions in DSM-IV (APA 1994). A survey of the authors of the top clinical guidelines used in the US and Europe, found over half had close relationships with companies whose products were involved (Choudry et al. 2002).[13]

Even in published reports of clinical trials, there was always uncertainty about the dividing line between personal privacy and public interest. Full disclosure of possible conflicts of interest by authors was the exception not the rule (Krimsky 1999, 2001). Indeed, such disclosures could take up large amounts of journal space.

> Dr. Martin B. Keller was one of the prime movers in the making of DSM-IV (1994). Head of the psychiatry department at Brown University, he was a leading expert on long-term psychiatric illness and drug treatment for it. He was prominent in global psychiatry and the recipient of numerous awards; he also had close connections with five major medical journals.[14] According to *The Boston Globe*, more than half of Keller's earnings of US$842,000 at Brown had come from the pharmaceutical industry, notably from the manufacturers of SSRIs. He had failed to disclose the extent of these financial ties either to medical journals or to the American Psychiatric Association, which sponsored the meetings at which Keller presented his findings. (Bass 1999)

---

12 This was Dr. Drummond Rennie, deputy editor of the *Journal of the American Medical Association* and professor of medicine at the Institute of Health Policy Studies at University of California, San Francisco (quoted in UPI Science News: "Research contracts violate guidelines", 23 October 2002).

13 That survey was based on replies received from the authors themselves, and the sample comprised only half of those contacted.

14 Keller (2001) was Vice-Chairperson of the Mood Disorders Work Group for DSM-IV. He was also on the International Advisory Board of the World Psychiatric Association, and a member of the Executive Committee of the Scientific Advisory Board of the National Depressive and Manic Depressive Association (NDMDA 1997). He was co-editor, with Dr. Stuart Montgomery of the *International Journal of Clinical Psychopharmacology*, and on the editorial boards of *Journal of Clinical Psychiatry*, *Journal of Affective Disorders*, *Depression and Anxiety*, and the *World Journal of Biological Psychiatry*.

The following year the *New England Journal of Medicine* published a sponsored study on nefazodone (Serzone/Dutonin): Keller (2000) was the principal author, but 28 other, mainly heavyweight authors were involved. Even the short summaries of their combined declarations of interest filled two full pages of journal text. Keller's set the tone.

"Dr. Keller has served as a consultant to or received honorariums from Pfizer, Bristol-Myers Squibb, Forest Laboratories/Parke-Davis, Wyeth-Ayerst, Merck, Janssen, Eli Lilly, Organon, and Pharmacia-Upjohn. He has received research grants from Wyeth-Ayerst, SmithKline Beecham, Upjohn, Pfizer, Bristol-Myers Squibb, Merck, Forest Laboratories, Zeneca, and Organon. He has served on the advisory board of Wyeth-Ayerst, Pfizer, Bristol-Myers Squibb, Eli Lilly, Forest Laboratories/Parke-Davis, Organon, SmithKline Beecham, Merck, Janssen, Mitsubishi Pharmaceuticals, Zeneca, Scirex, and Otsuka."

Scientific Integrity

Close contact with the Pharmas worked both to good and bad effect, but as financial pressures and dependencies grew, so did the risks. Across the whole of medicine, it became clear that personal and institutional financial interests not only brought benefits, but also threatened the integrity of science and the fabric of health research.

Enforcement-wise, the focus was on prosecuting the tiny minority of doctors and researchers who flagrantly went astray.[15] Partly this was because of the difficulties involved in defining what exactly "research integrity" was – and how to get it. The "overarching conclusion" of a long study by the US Institute of Medicine was that "no established measures for assessing integrity in the research environment exist." The IOM (2002) was therefore unable to suggest how to promote integrity in research: they proposed lamely that education might help (or not) and that, "institutional self-assessment is one promising approach."

The high profile cases that did come to light proposed a clear dividing line between fraud or not, typical or not, and bad or not. The British Pharmas, for example, thought that fraud was "of great concern" but that, "fewer than one per cent of trials are thought to have a fraudulent element". The Association of the British Pharmaceutical Industry (ABPI) spokesman told Consumers Association: "Frankly, I would be astonished if any scientist would skew his results because he got money from a certain source" (Meek 2001). The implication was that nearly all was well.

15 In 2002, the US Office of Research Integrity dealt with 191 "allegations or queries;" they closed 30 investigations, with "misconduct findings" against 13 individuals.

The UK Pharmas had by this time become centrally involved in the prosecution of outright fraud, typically perpetrated by lone practitioners. The purge began after Dr. Frank Wells (see Chapter Three) left as the ABPI Medical Director to found a specialised enforcement agency, MedicoLegal Investigations:

> "In July 1996 Frank Wells a doctor and Peter Jay, a former detective, took up the challenge to reduce fraud and misconduct in clinical research. It had to be tackled such was the extent of the problem. In the absence of an official body to deal with and having the necessary expertise at their fingertips they embarked upon the challenge that many thought was too risky. They were deemed too vulnerable. MedicoLegal Investigations (MLI) was born regardless. In 1998, the investigation team expanded following the arrival of Jonathan Jay, formerly a sergeant in the Army Special Investigation Branch." (MLI 2003)

Since then, the agency (MLI) had expanded, "with the full weight of the ABPI" behind it. Having investigated over 80 studies, the organisers reported in 2002 that, "other opportunities now present themselves to expand the company". These included training programmes for the ethics committees that screen clinical trials, "providing the ideal platform to promote the best interests of the industry".

Regardless of the importance of its work, the way in which MLI operated fuelled the perception that lack of research integrity was essentially to do with the odd rotten apple in the barrel. This model of investigation was also appealing because institutional embarrassment was minimised: the MLI agency offered "a confidential service for the pharmaceutical industry and health sectors".

Meanwhile, there was little evidence that the Pharmas had done much to control fraud in their midst. A steady flow of unsavoury headlines underlined the point, but perhaps the best evidence came from the "European Economic Crime Survey" by PricewaterhouseCoopers (PWC) (2002). Levels of fraud were relatively high and detection rates low. This was a culture of wide-open blind eyes.

> PWC interviewed senior representatives of 76 pharmaceutical companies as part of a survey involving 3,400 companies across Europe. Levels of fraud were higher in the pharmaceutical sector than elsewhere and also 50% higher in Pharmas than in smaller pharmaceutical companies. Risk factors for Pharmas included "pressure to meet targets (including, for example, sales targets and the progress of clinical trials)." Breach of trust was the second most reported fraud (35%), "including such areas as outside conflicts of interest, manipulation of R&D results, grey/parallel trading, counterfeit products and breaches of EU competition guidelines. Pharmaceutical companies also suffered from over 40% more cases of corruption than other industry sectors, including such areas as supplier collusion, bribery and price fixing."

> Management intervention played a part in uncovering about half of all fraud, but the other half came to light by chance: "The role of 'chance' in the discovery of fraud raises the question of how much fraud remains undiscovered. Whilst impossible to quantify with any accuracy, experts agree that the value is substantial."
>
> Informants and tip-offs played a minor part in detection: "This confirms our view that while many people will be aware that a fraud is taking place, very few will be prepared to report it, either anonymously or otherwise." Finally, many companies never reported economic crimes: "a corporate culture where fraud is not reported leads companies to be more open to future abuses."

The major threat to scientific integrity thus seemed mainly to do with commonplace self-interest and soft greed. Rogue doctors and researchers created problems enough, but the real threat was widespread acceptance of more or less casual malpractice, rather than lone practitioners involved in blatant fraud. The real problem was obscured by the tendency to favour the utmost discretion, with strict adherence to approved process and ways of thought.

The resulting lack of academic freedom helped to isolate and oppress the handful of whistleblowers with the courage to speak out when things did seem to go wrong. They were generally discredited and often accused of having political or other agendas of their own. Their treatment was overwhelmingly unfair.

Dr. David Healy endured such treatment for years – too much to convey more than the gist of it.[16] Healy's research and clinical experience, plus an assiduous analysis of data, had convinced him of the capacity of Prozac and other SSRIs to induce suicidality in some patients. He had expressed such views in peer-reviewed journals and many scientific meetings, since 1991. He had "regularly offered to debate the issues in a public forum with anyone the company cares to put up to defend their position". It never happened.

Healy's evidence became increasingly stronger, as did his reputation on two fronts: he was a leading historian of psychopharmacology. He had published three extensive and valuable volumes of interviews with the founding fathers of psychiatric drug treatment. Healy had also acted as an expert witness for the plaintiffs in several lawsuits involving SSRI trials. This was critical: it gave him privileged access to company data.

---

16 This account relies on the extensive documentation available at www.pharmapolitics.com also bmj.com – and on Healy's correspondence with the MCA/MHRA and CSM at socialaudit.org.uk. See also the analysis by Sarah Boseley (2001) in *The Guardian:* what happened and quite why, and how, "is a story with Le Carré reverberations". See also: Healy 2003.

In March 2000, Healy set out his views again in an article in the *Hastings Center Reports.* Soon after, he learned that "Lilly withdrew their funding from the Center, citing this specific issue as the reason for doing so." In the summer of that year, he presented more evidence, from a study of sertraline he had conducted, that shed further light on the risk of SSRI-induced suicidality.

Healy presented this evidence at three scientific meetings in Europe; at one of these he had "a very scary meeting" with Charles Nemeroff: he "told me my career would be destroyed if I kept on showing results like the ones I'd just shown" (CBC 2001). Professor Nemeroff was another of the 28 co-authors of the nefazodone paper in the *New England Journal of Medicine (NEJM)* (Keller 2001).[17] He had been described in a psychiatric journal as the "Boss of bosses," perhaps "the most powerful man in psychiatry" and "among the most coveted advisers to the pharmaceutical industry" in the US.

In August 2000, Healy was offered a professorship at the Centre for Addiction and Mental Health (CAMH) at the University of Toronto. Over the years, CAMH had received more than US$1.5 million from Eli Lilly, among many other donors. Before taking up his new post, Healy gave a lecture at the University, to celebrate the Psychiatry Department's 75th anniversary. Professor Nemeroff was a speaker too. Within days of giving this lecture, Healy was advised by his CAMH hosts that the job offer was rescinded because, there was "not a good fit" between him and CAMH. Thereafter:

> "Dr Healy found that his views were not being challenged in the lecture theatre or the seminar room – they were being undermined in private conversations. Somebody rang senior figures at Cornell, where he was due to speak just after Toronto, suggesting that he was manic depressive and even violent." (Boseley 2001)

Withdrawal of the job offer sparked publicity and this led to public vilification. James Coyne, professor of psychology at the University of Pennsylvania, briefed the *Boston Globe* that Healy "has almost no published research" and also wrote to the *British Medical Journal*: "Is Healy's Work Scientific or Ethical?" (6 July 2001). The Royal College of Psychiatrists was implicated in "an extraordinary personal attack on the integrity and professionalism of Dr Healy" as well (Meek 2002).

All this was happening around the time Healy appeared as the main witness in a tragic and exceptional US civil action – in which, two days after starting paroxetine, a

---

17 Dr. Nemeroff has been a consultant to or received honorariums from Abbott, AstraZeneca, Bristol–Myers Squibb, Forest Laboratories, Janssen, Eli Lilly, Merck, Mitsubishi, Neurocrine Biosciences, Organon, Otsuka, Pfizer, Pharmacia–Upjohn, Sanofi, SmithKline Beecham, Solvay, and Wyeth–Ayerst. He has received research support from Abbott, AstraZeneca, Bristol–Myers Squibb, Forest Laboratories, Janssen, Eli Lilly, Organon, Pfizer, Pharmacia–Upjohn, SmithKline Beecham, Solvay, and Wyeth–Ayerst.

60-year old man had shot his wife, daughter and granddaughter before killing himself. It was a high profile case and GlaxoSmithKline lost (Boseley 2001; *Panorama* 2002).

In the meantime, Healy himself had taken legal action against the University of Toronto, strongly supported by the Canadian Association of University Teachers (CAUT):

> "For them, there was a troubling resonance with the case of Nancy Olivieri, the Toronto-based researcher who incurred the wrath of a pharmaceutical company when she told the world of the results of a clinical trial which showed, she believed, that a drug for thalassaemia would harm, rather than help, sick children. The Hospital for Sick Children, where she worked, part of the University of Toronto, tried to fire her when she refused to cooperate with an investigating committee whose members, she said, had too many links to drug companies." (Boseley 2002)

Healy's legal action was supported also by a petition for academic freedom, signed by a long list of distinguished scientists from all over the world. In April 2002, a settlement was announced: "a complete vindication for Dr Healy", said the president of CAUT. The University said that, "it underscores its support for free expression of critical views and acknowledges Dr Healy's scholarship by confirming it will be appointing him as a visiting professor in the faculty of medicine".

Placebo factors and beyond

It will be clear that the perceived therapeutic value of a drug is determined by factors that go far beyond the process of scientific appraisal and evaluation. In a crisis, the drug itself is considered "responsible", yet the problems described in this case-history are clearly the product of a complex of non-pharmacological factors, whatever else. All sorts of human beliefs, motivations and styles of organisation make medicines work as they seem to do. These factors are typically invisible, go largely unrecognised and have no other name. They go largely incognito: hence the term.

Incognito factors and effects are the drivers and vectors of the Conspiracy of Goodwill; they play a critical part in determining whether, how and to what effect medicines are used. The fact that they have no collective name underlines that their impact is generally unrecognised and therefore poorly understood. Probably the main reason is that the word "placebo" has come to stand for *all* the non-drug factors that affect treatment outcomes. It does not seem an appropriate word: it does not take account of many non-pharmacological factors on treatment outcomes and is a word with unsavoury connotations. Perhaps the word "placebo" should be abandoned, and "incognito" used instead?

Placebo effects stand for all the human capacities that make medicines seem to work, but with the focus overwhelmingly on the individual patient's response.[18] The word "placebo" comes from the Latin: "I will please." It implies a relationship between powerful and pleasing doctor, dependent patient and empty drug.

This is an encumbrance on meaning, because it proposes that the capacity for health resides in the doctor rather than in the patient. It also locates all healing power in the pill, distracting from the idea of pill as sacrament, with placebo factors linked to the aura around it. The implication is that, beyond the doctor-patient relationship, non-drug factors hardly count. This is also misleading: when Pharmas fund conferences, promote experts and sponsor so much, something analogous to placebo effects are surely at work. Everything the Pharmas do to inspire confidence in their products produces such effects; even the trinkets that drug reps supply to doctors give evidence of ritual pleasing at work.

The irony is that it took until the second half of the 20th century to recognise and label the placebo phenomenon – from which point its reputation went into terminal decline. Instead of investigating the power and nature of this vital human capacity, the conspirators of goodwill subtracted from its reputation. The whole concept of the placebo effect as a therapeutic advantage was overtaken by the introduction of anti-infective and other valuable drugs. Their potency and importance was clear – they could save and improve lives far better than any placebo – and the reputation of placebos was left in tatters as a result. As numerous clinical trials proved countless medicines to be more active than placebo, so came a shift in meaning.[19] The classic placebo changed from being an ineffective nostrum, to the "sham" treatment or "dummy" pill used in a clinical trial to provide a baseline measure of drug effectiveness.[20]

---

18 Until well into the 20th century, the benefits patients felt from medical treatment would have been mainly due to a placebo response, and often in spite of the drug effect. Placebo factors made medicines seem to work long before the advent of effective drugs – because bodies tend to heal themselves and because confidence and faith in treatment positively causes it to work. "The history of medicine is the history of the placebo effect" (Benson 1996), and yet the word "placebo" didn't exist. The word "placebo" entered the medical vocabulary only after Medicine came of age. There was no reference to it in the great 1911 edition of *Encyclopedia Britannica.* The first, tentative definitions date from the mid-20th century – the great turning point, when largely ineffective drug treatments gave way to many that worked. Until the founding of organised, evidence-based medicine, placebo effects were a complete mystery, as much of Medicine was too. Secrecy was the main guarantor of what medicine had to offer: it sustained the apartheid between users and providers that began to crumble only in the last quarter of the 20th century, when the branding of medicines began.

19 Once a drug is proven even slightly better than placebo, legally it becomes "effective" – so much so that doctors consider it "unethical" to prescribe the "ineffective" placebo thereafter. The array of products available by the close of the 21st century meant there was always something better than placebo; in time it became virtually unthinkable to prescribe anything else.

By the 21st century, the word, "placebo", had become almost synonymous with lack of effectiveness, unethical standards of treatment, the deception of patients and devaluation of their need and distress. Companies emphasised that their drugs were much better than placebos and doctors wanted nothing less – and no-one wanted to pay high prices for treatment that amounted to "nothing". This case history also explains why patients might look askance at placebos. With depression explained as a "disease" – and widely believed to be caused by low levels of brain serotonin – the demeaning implication of being identified as a "placebo responder" would be that one wasn't really depressed at all.

The point that may be missed is that countless clinical trials of active drugs have also consistently demonstrated the effectiveness of non-pharmacological treatment in numerous organic diseases, including severe pain and mental distress. Across the board, about one in three people respond as well to placebo as to an active drug, and with antidepressants often more – but with all the attention focused on active drugs, interest waned in the clinical relevance of placebo effects. The mindset that a placebo meant "nothing" may well be reflected in the tendency to set drug dosages too high.

Denigration of the word "placebo" helped to force an unreal distinction between benefit and risk, and what worked or didn't – and the difference between them is still often characterised as the difference between drug and non-drug treatment, and between medical intervention or not. The same attitude has underlined the orthodox thinking that homeopathic and alternative medicine had little more to offer than a placebo. It misses the point that placebo effects can be extremely powerful and effective – also that none of the drugs in this case history proved much more effective than that.

The wider point is that the perceived and felt effectiveness of a medicine is not just to do with the relationship between patient and doctor, or user and drug. The influence of reward, punishment, suggestion and faith are also major factors in drug reputation, as are the dependencies of individuals on the power of organisations. Timing alone is also a key factor in appreciating the relationship between benefit and risk.[21]

In the last analysis, the SSRI crisis was not essentially to do with rogue molecules. The shape of the crisis was much influenced by the relationships that developed between the professional, business and governmental organisations involved – and between individuals and organisations. How else would collaborations of essentially decent, honest, intelligent people end up in such a mess?

---

20 Placebos may be regarded as "a continuum ranging from the tangible to the intangible" and include, "scars, pills, tablets, injections, appliances, touch, words, gestures, local ambience, social interventions" (de Saintonge & Herxheimer 1994).

Organisms in organisations

Organisations both lead and contain personal expression. Individual commitment to corporate imperatives is sustained by reward and punishment systems to promote high levels of compliance. Keen identification with corporate values promotes profit and gain – professional advancement, prominence and enrichment, scientific endeavour and therapeutic satisfaction. Belonging to an organisation means being in company, and the opportunity to see purpose, to be engaged and employed.

At the same time, individual members of organisations tend to have responsibilities defined for them and to know their place. The compartmentalisation of work and the fragmentation of responsibilities within organisations further reduce the incentive for individual employees to step out of line. The division of duties inevitably tends to fragment and dilute personal responsibilities – typically to the extent that proxies (e.g. publicity agents, press officers) are charged with responsibilities they cannot possibly assume, even if they readily do. Thus problems may arise even when everyone is doing their job and deemed to be doing it well.

Beneath the surface, conflict between personal values and corporate objectives may be a commonplace, but outright dissent is rare. Organisational integrity depends on strength and unity of commitment and on the ability to manage information to promote corporate objectives. Conformity and compliance are the norm; conscientious dissent becomes harder and harder all the time.

> Compliance?
> Stanley Milgram conducted a classic series of experiments on "obedience to authority" at Yale University in 1961-1962; his findings have been replicated often since. Milgram found that two-thirds of his subjects – ordinary residents of New

---

21 The present is never the right time to be raising questions about the present: it is that much harder to see straight when the evidence is incomplete and still pouring in, and it threatens established views. There is no time to take stock when racing into the future – so new technologies tend to descend much faster than our collective ability either to understand and manage them, or to trust each other to do so. Present overload and the prospect of dazzling futures always threaten to put medicine far beyond the discipline of public control.

With drugs, it may take years to assess the value of "new" and "now". How long depends on many factors – especially whether news is welcome or not. If not, it may easily take a generation for understandings, attitudes and practice to change. The drug, doxorubicin, provides a neat example of this. Doxorubicin is a drug for advanced breast cancer; it was introduced in the early 1970s and is still widely used as the comparator drug in clinical trials of newer drugs. Analysis of the most reliable trials involving doxorubicin show that its measured effectiveness diminished by 10% every five years, between 1975 and 1999. "Wish bias" favours new treatments over old and is marked when measurement is not "blind". In this case, the person measuring the tumour size before and after treatment usually knew which drug patients had received (Fossati et al. 2002).

Haven, Connecticut – willingly gave electric shocks of up to 450 volts to a protesting victim, when a scientific authority directed them to do so, though the victim did nothing to deserve it. Often the test subjects believed the "victim" had died. In fact, the victims were actors who cried in pain but did not actually receive shocks – but this was revealed to subjects only at the end of the experiment. During these experiments, "with numbing regularity good people were seen to knuckle under the demands of authority and perform actions that were callous and severe. Men who are in everyday life responsible and decent were seduced by the trappings of authority, by the control of their perceptions, and by the uncritical acceptance of the experimenter's definition of the situation, into performing harsh acts ... A substantial proportion of people do what they are told, irrespective of the content of the act and without limitations of conscience, so long as they perceive that the command comes from a legitimate authority." (Milgram 1974)

Conformity?
In the 1950s and 1960s, Solomon Asch conducted a series of classic classroom experiments on social conformity and stress. He drew a series of three lines of different lengths on the blackboard, adding a fourth line and asking students which line the last was equal to. Though the answer was obvious, Asch instructed everyone in the class to say that the line of middle length was the longest; he then brought in a naïve student who thought he/she was participating in a study of visual acuity. After several trials in which everyone gave the right answer to establish trust, the class began to answer that the medium-length line was the longest, and most of the time the naïve student (always the last to answer) agreed with the group. Only a minority of the naïve subjects said that his or her classmates were wrong. (Asch 1963)

These examples serve as reminders of the intense pressures individuals may feel as members of organisations of all kinds. In a world in which the fate of a company hangs on the reputation of a small handful of drugs, sensitivities become extreme. Hence the rigorous emphasis on the need to communicate approved understandings and to stifle unauthorised dissent. Much of this is done invisibly, and perhaps unconsciously, but the methods used are effective, well established and widely applied.

Against that background, this case history takes on new meanings. Global market development has seen pharmaceutical medicine increasingly develop as a system, with power concentrated in fewer and fewer organisations with mainly political and economic objectives. The resulting dependencies did not only concern user and drug. Compulsory consumption and subordination of individual will and conscience may also be considered as adverse reactions to power.

10

Iatrogenesis

Adverse drug reactions (ADRs) exemplify direct "iatrogenesis" – harm from medical intervention – but what does this story reflect of what Ivan Illich called "social" and "cultural" iatrogenesis – implying loss of personal autonomy, reduced confidence in health and diminished opportunity for making sense of illness and disease? Their impact has barely been explored – the supposition being that ADR reporting systems reveal all the major risks. However, a unique analysis of health professionals' reports about paroxetine reveals the operation of the UK Yellow Card system to be "chaotic and misconceived". In this case, the combination of low levels and standards of reporting, flawed data processing, uncritical interpretation and lack of follow-up had a devastating effect on perceptions and understandings of benefit and risk.

Well before the Pharmas came to dominate medicine, Ivan Illich (1977) took a scythe to the widely unchallenged assumption that meaning well meant doing good. The first line of his classic, *Limits to Medicine – Medical Nemesis: the Expropriation of Health*, set the tone: "The medical establishment has become a major threat to health."

Illich coined the term, "iatrogenesis",[1] to identify doctors as architects of the problem. He proposed a model of medicine in which lack of professional self-control caused epidemic disability. To blame the drug industry for prescribed-drug addiction was, he thought, "as irrelevant as blaming the Mafia for the use of illicit drugs"...

> "The current pattern of over-prescribing of drugs – be they effective remedy or anodyne; prescription item or part of everyday diet; free, for sale, or stolen – can be explained only as the result of a belief that has so far developed in every culture where the market for consumer goods has reached a critical volume. This pattern is consistent with the ideology of any society oriented towards open-ended enrichment, regardless whether its industrial product is meant for distribution by the presumption of planners or by the forces of the market. In such a society, people come to believe that in health care, as in all other fields of endeavour, technology can be used to change the human condition according to almost any design."

---

1 "*Iatrogenesis*", the name for this new epidemic, comes from *Iatros*, the Greek word for "physician", and *genesis*, meaning "origin".

At the time, the medical establishment took a dim view of what Illich had to say. The response was slight and rather mean: "The silence in the medical world has been deafening" (Horrobin 1978). The editorial in the *British Medical Journal (BMJ* 1974) was huffy and aloof: "doctors must be one of the most self-critical professions, constantly examining and challenging traditional beliefs".

But time passed and things moved on: 25 years later, the editor of the *BMJ* reread and reviewed it again. He had first read *Medical Nemesis* as a medical student; now he found, "The power of the book is undiminished, and its prescience seems remarkable. What was radical in 1974 is in some sense mainstream in 2002" (Smith 2002).

Illich redefined the idea of "iatrogenesis" and the thinking that went with it. He introduced two main ideas: that it was in the nature of medical practice to produce ill-health, and that the damage done went much deeper than "clinical iatrogenesis" – the direct harm caused by treatment and medical intervention.

Illich was also concerned about the "social iatrogenesis" that resulted from the medicalisation of life. This promoted "cultural iatrogenesis", which implied general lack of confidence and loss of autonomy in achieving health and making sense of illness and death. In microcosm, this case history illustrates some of these themes, but challenges others. Illich was quite specific in accusing the medical profession; he largely discounted the influence of trade-related factors or external regulation. He argued, for example, that the level of drug consumption "seems to have little to do with commercial promotion" but was mainly linked to the numbers of doctors in practice.[2]

The progress of this case history suggests that some unacceptable professional tendencies remain constants. But since Illich wrote, clinicians have been increasingly relieved of any monopoly of sickness-producing behaviour. By the time the SSRIs arrived, doctors had lost some independence and largely abdicated their rights to "clinical freedom".[3] Collectively, the doctors may have failed as gatekeepers, but their responsibility was clearly diminished under the influence of the Pharmas, a

---

2 Drug consumption "correlates mostly with the number of doctors, even in socialist countries where the education of physicians is not influenced by drug industry publicity and where corporate drug-pushing is limited."

3 Clinical freedom was the term used to define the traditional rights of prescribers to prescribe as they chose, not as government or others might dictate. "Clinical freedom is dead, and no-one need regrets its passing ... Clinical freedom died accidentally, crushed between the rising cost of new forms of investigation and treatment and the financial limits inevitable in an economy that cannot expand indefinitely. Clinical freedom should, however, have been strangled long ago, for at best it was a cloak for ignorance and at worst an excuse for quackery. Clinical freedom was a myth that prevented true advance. We must welcome its demise, and seize the opportunities now laid out before us" (Hampton 1983).

flood of regulatory and professional guidelines, and financial and organisational constraints, as well.

In time, the label "iatrogenic" became more and more of a misnomer. As the Pharmas and regulators gained power, the problem wasn't so much created by doctors, as unknowingly or sometimes reluctantly helped along by them. This case history suggests that problems arise not because doctors don't know enough, but when they behave as if they do.

Illich looked to "the public" and "society" for solutions, but they never came – perhaps one reason being that his ruthless logic seemed detached from so much personal experience. Everyone knows that doctors and medicines really can be marvellous – and surely your doctor bears no resemblance to any character in this story. Vicarious experience made its mark as well: a steady diet of evidence-based soap endlessly demonstrates tireless professional endeavour and the benefits of dramatic intervention.

Medicine and medicines have developed so much as a part of a world of optimistic misunderstanding that what are initially perceived as heresies take time to sink in. For all the gloss and dross, enough of the miracles are real and true – more than enough to inspire hope and adulation on a grand scale. Hence the general tendency to hugely over-estimate drug effectiveness and to assume that Medicine means health – and to want to discount the disadvantages and risks.

Individually, we so depend on medicines, we are all drawn into this grand, universal delusion,[4] a Conspiracy of Goodwill. We all want good medicines that will spare and save us; doctors and drug companies want this too. Everyone wants drugs that are effective, affordable and safe. Partnership in this conspiracy is naturally strong: matters of personal, professional, commercial and political life and death are involved.

We know medicines can work wonders and hope and pray they will. We want and need to believe this so much, we systematically pretend they do.

Clinical iatrogenesis

Illich died in 2002. He lived just long enough to see the first credible, but preliminary, estimates of the harm caused directly by medical intervention in US hospitals:

---

4 Under the *DSM-IV* classification, "The essential feature of Delusional Disorder is the presence of one or more non-bizarre delusions that persist for at least one month. A diagnosis of Delusional Disorder is not given if the individual has ever had a symptom presentation that met Criterion A for Schizophrenia (Criterion B) ... Apart from the direct impact of the delusions, psychosocial functioning is not markedly impaired, and behaviour is neither obviously odd nor bizarre (Criterion C) ..." (APA 1994).

America led the rest of the world once again.[5] It was the first country by years to begin to sweep away a complete history of denial, and to try to assess the dimensions of the drug injury problem. The evidence revealed the problem to be huge. Even in a fair sample of world-class hospitals, iatrogenesis ranked as a leading cause of death:

> "... at least 44,000 Americans die each year as a result of medical errors ... the number may be as high as 98,000 ... deaths due to medical errors exceed the number attributable to the 8th leading cause of death ... Medication errors alone, occurring either in or out of the hospital, are estimated to account for over 7,000 deaths annually. Medication-related errors occur frequently in hospitals and although not all result in actual harm, those that do, are costly ... If these findings are generalizable, the increased hospital costs alone of preventable adverse drug events affecting inpatients are about $2 billion for the nation as a whole. These figures offer only a very modest estimate of the magnitude of the problem since hospital patients represent only a small proportion of the total population at risk, and direct hospital costs are only a fraction of total costs." (Institute of Medicine 2000)

No problem of this kind had been quantified at the time Illich wrote, and the figures that seem realistic today might have seemed unbelievable then. Dr. Lewis Thomas is a good source on this. In his review of *Limits of Medicine*, Thomas (1976) suggested the reality of drug injury to be "a much milder set of problems than the picture of devastation called up by Illich's prose". So things were generally perceived.

The estimates of the iatrogenic burden that began to appear in the US at the very end of the 20th century related only to hospital treatment. Estimates varied, but perhaps 10% of hospitalised patients would experience an ADR, about half classified as avoidable, with upwards of 10% proving serious or worse.

There was much less evidence about ADRs outside the hospital environment. Few estimates yet exist of the extent of the problem in the community, or in populations at higher risk (e.g. children, people in nursing homes).[6] Only ballpark estimates exist, but ADRs seem to account for about 5% of all hospital admissions (suggesting an order of 250,000 hospitalisations in the UK each year), and present in about 2% of all general practice consultations. As this case history shows, many problems go unrecognised beyond the consulting room, as well.

The UK Yellow Card scheme was never intended to measure the overall extent and impact of adverse drug effects. The purpose of the scheme was to get qualitative data – clues and signals about possible problems that needed following up. It was set

---

5 "American doctors have a particular facility for admitting past mistakes and jumping on new bandwagons" (Illich 1977).

6 It has been estimated that over 350,000 ADRs occur in US nursing homes each year (Gurwitz et al. 2000). Over two million *serious* ADRs are believed to occur in the US each year (CDER 2003).

up as an early warning system and to establish the confidence of the community in "the safety of medicines". The Yellow Card system was the product of an age in which the prevailing wisdom was that medicinal drugs were, as a rule, remarkably safe – even if there was some low risk of painful exceptions.

The Yellow Card scheme that emerged came to be recognised as world class. In Britain it was the mainstay of "post-marketing surveillance", the system for checking drug safety in use. The Committee on the Safety of Medicines/Medicines Control Agency (CSM/MCA 2003) promoted the Yellow Card scheme to patients in terms that suggested it was pretty streamlined and watertight.[7] The CSM/MCA's Guidance Notes (2003) said the scheme operated, "in order to ensure that new side effects are detected," and problems were played down: "It is accepted that not all adverse reactions are reported," but the scheme was "under continual review in order to increase its effectiveness."

The reality was that most doctors – perhaps four out of five – never sent in Yellow Cards.[8] And maybe one-third of the Yellow Cards that doctors sent in were unusable

---

7 *"How are medicines monitored in order to ensure that new side effects are detected?*
"The main way in which we monitor medicines is to collect reports of possible or suspected side effects ('adverse reactions') from doctors, dentists, pharmacists, coroners and nurses, as well as from pharmaceutical companies. The reports are made by completing a 'Yellow Card' form which asks for details about the suspected adverse reactions; this is known as the Yellow Card Scheme.

"We collect the Yellow Cards and enter them onto our Adverse Drug Reactions On-line Information Tracking (ADROIT) system. This system is a specialised database which allows us to process and analyse the reports rapidly. Since the Scheme was set up in 1964, we have received over 400,000 Yellow Cards. We evaluate the reports on a weekly basis in order to identify previously unidentified potential hazards, and new information on recognised side effects. We also evaluate information from additional sources such as the world-wide medical literature, and data from a number of world-wide databases.

"When we identify a new possible side effect or learn more about a recognised one, we carefully consider this in the context of the overall side effect profile for the medicine. We also consider this in comparison with the side effects of other medicines which can be used to treat the same condition, and compare the risks with the benefits of the medicine as described above. If necessary we may take action to ensure that the medicine is used in a way which minimises risk, and maximises benefits to the patient. We might include details of a new side effect in the product information, reduce the dose to be used, or give out warnings about groups of patients who should not be given the medicine. In rare circumstances, we may need to withdraw a medicine from the market, when we believe that the risks of a medicine are greater than its potential benefits" (MHRA website 2003).

8 A comprehensive survey (Griffin 1984) of the first 20 years of operation found that only 16% of doctors employed in the UK's National Health Service (NHS) had ever sent in a Yellow Card, and that 7.4% of all doctors sent in 80% of all reports. A more limited survey of reporting over a 21-month period in the Merseyside region found that one in eight doctors who were eligible to report had actually sent in Yellow Cards (Morrison-Griffiths et al. 2003).

– not "judged appropriate according to criteria established by the regulatory authority".[9]

Beyond this, not much was known. Since the beginning of the Yellow Card scheme in 1964, reports of suspected ADRs had been treated as secret, and this had prevented any independent analysis or review.

Misplaced emphasis on numbers of ADRS

The sensitivity and traditional confidentiality of data partly explain why regulators everywhere always pointed to the *numbers* of reports they receive, by way of demonstrating that the system worked and that drugs were reasonably safe. Year on year, the CSM's annual reports have stuck to this theme.[10]

By translating everything into numbers, the MCA/CSM deflected enquiries about individual drugs. Why were they not concerned about the record number of paroxetine withdrawal reactions? It was mainly because they compared the number of Yellow Cards with the numbers of prescriptions issued. Far from ever suggesting that the number of Yellow Cards received was only a fraction of those due, the MCA/CSM took scrupulous care to alert non-scientists to the limitless risks of exag-

---

9 This figure was mentioned in passing in a paper letter in the *Lancet* from, among others, Dr. Alasdair Breckenridge, the new head of the Medicines and Healthcare products Regulatory Agency (MHRA) The authors gave no indication they thought this remarkable, though the Yellow Card scheme had by then been running for almost 40 years. The paper was about the opening up of the Yellow Card scheme to nurses – armed with an information pack and given one hour of training. The point the paper was making was that nurses were fit reporters of ADRs. More nurses (77%) sent in reports "judged appropriate according to regulatory authority criteria" than did doctors (69%) (Morrison-Griffiths et al. 2003).

10 "There has been a decrease in the number of reports received this year in comparison with previous years. The Committee will be examining ways of encouraging reporting" (1994). "The recent decrease in reporting has been of considerable concern to the Committee. It has reviewed, carefully, possible reasons for the decline and has introduced (with the Medicines Control Agency) a series of measures designed to reverse the trend" (1995). "The Committee is concerned that the numbers of reports of suspected drug reactions have fallen over the past four years and is taking steps during 1997 to attempt to reverse this trend (1996). No comment on the numbers: the CSM received the lowest number of Yellow Cards in a decade (1997). "The Committee was pleased to note the increased number of reports" (1998 and 1999). "The Committee is encouraged to note that ... reporting of ADRs continued the upward trend of the previous two years ..." (2000). "The committee is encouraged to note that despite an overall decrease in the number of ADR reports received in 2001, there was an increase in the number of reports received from hospital & community pharmacists (4.7%) and hospital doctors (6.7%). Due to the drop in the volume of ADRs received in 2001, there has been a decrease of 17% on all serious reports received compared to last year. However, the percentage of serious reports as a total of all reports received has increased from 54 to 57%" (2001).

geration. *"It is important to note that the suspected reactions are not necessarily caused by the drug".*

There were always extenuating circumstances, confounding factors and ready explanations.

Were the MCA/CSM concerned that there were many more reports of paroxetine withdrawal than for all benzodiazepines? They said not: "a quantitative comparison would be inappropriate in view of different market, lives, usage, publicity and other factors that influence the number of spontaneous reports received" (Price 1997).

At this point another Glaxo SmithKline (GSK) antidepressant drug (bupropion) makes a cameo entrance – and in two different guises. In the US, it is best known as Wellbutrin – not an SSRI, though in many ways similar, including some risk of withdrawal symptoms and suicidal ideation. In Britain, the same drug is licensed only as Zyban, an aid to quit smoking.

Originally headlined a "'miracle' smoking cure" (Veash 1999), Zyban attracted more critical headlines within a few of months of its UK launch. It created a new record – accounting for one in three Yellow Cards sent in between January and April 2001. They included 57 suspected fatalities among other serious reactions.

The regulators responded with an Important Safety Message, in the name of Professor Alasdair Breckenridge, then chairman of the CSM (2001). His statement illustrated how far, *in extremis*, the number games could go: "the considerable public interest has stimulated reporting of adverse reactions" ... "the contribution of Zyban to these fatal cases is unproven" ... "the reports received are in line with the known safety profile of Zyban ..."

The CSM statement also emphasised that the proportion of fatal reports with Zyban was "much lower" than for all other medicines – less than 1% for Zyban, compared with 2% for all other drugs. No reference was made to the fact that Zyban had proved only slightly more effective than nicotine patches as an aid to smoking cessation:

"Preliminary results suggest that bupropion is possibly more effective than a nicotine skin patch, but this needs confirmation ... At present there is no clear evidence to favour bupropion over NRT (nicotine replacement therapy)." (*D&TB* 2000)

The best evidence suggested that smokers who used nrt had around a 1 in 6 chance of giving up for a whole year, compared with a 1 in 5 chance with bupropion. This implied a possible additional benefit for 34 people out of every 1,000 people – meaning that. 966 people would be exposed to the risks of Zyban for no extra benefit. The way in which the MCA/CSM reconciled benefit and risk on this occasion illustrated the "safety of medicines" mindset. If the focus had been on the safety of users, or of treatment, then Zyban might have come off the market like a shot. It seems safe to assume that, if the safety profile of nicotine patches had remotely resembled that of bupropion, they would have been taken off the market fast. In fact, patches proved safe enough to be sold off prescription. Ironically, that made Zyban the main treatment prescribed, so GSK's "disease awareness" campaigning naturally directed people to their doctors.

In general, the numbers of suspected ADR reports bear little more relation to reality than football results have to what happened in the games. As the *Panorama* emails had shown, many clues lie in the descriptions in the individual reports – or emerge just from listening. The Dutch Pharmacovigilance Foundation had done just that – taking reports from users who telephoned. The wheat-to-chaff ratio was less favourable overall, but the investigators still found that patients identified nine previously unidentified suspected adverse reactions to paroxetine as often as health professionals, and generally sooner (Egberts et al. 1996).

The limitations of numerical data explain *Social Audit's* request to the MCA/MHRA to release a batch of anonymised Yellow Cards (ASPPs – anonymised single patient printouts) for paroxetine (see Chapter Five). To their everlasting credit, the regulators agreed: they supplied anonymised Yellow Card data for "suicide and parasuicide" (92 reports); "injury and poisoning" (93); "withdrawal reactions" (1,370) and "dependence" (33). The analysis was written up and later reported in the *International Journal of Risk & Safety in Medicine* (Medawar & Herxheimer 2003/4).

Analysis of paroxetine Yellow Cards

No regulatory agency anywhere had ever published a thorough analysis of the quality of suspected ADR reports received. The usefulness of Yellow Cards (and equivalents elsewhere) had often been described in signalling problems with specific drugs. But no overview of quality had ever been seen. This was the only analysis of its kind.

How complete was the information these (anonymised) Yellow Cards contained? Did their professionalism leave users upstaged? Were they a source of good drug intelligence? Overall, what did Yellow Cards seem to contribute to drug safety, taking into account the key role they play in post-marketing surveillance?

The short answer is complicated, because the ASPPs before us were an amalgam of two things: the information sent in, and the processed data. If there was a short answer, Andrew Herxheimer provided it. He said it quite early on: "Here is a fascinating slice of data, but what you actually see is a kaleidoscope – every time you shake it you see completely different patterns. It all feels as if it is packed with meaning, but it is an illusion. It's all done with mirrors".

His point can be illustrated by comparing how users and professionals reported the characteristic eye and visual problems linked to the electric shock sensations in the head, during paroxetine withdrawal.

User reports:
"The electric explosions in my head were triggered off by the movements from left to right of my eyes"; "An 'electrical zapping' in my head when I move my eyes quickly or move my head from side to side"; "my eyes zap as I move my head", "my eyes felt jumpy when I looked from side to side"; "impulses when I move my head/eyes"; "brain shocks each time I turn, or even just move my eyes are just too much to bear"; "funny feeling when I move my eyes in my chest like electric (very hard to explain)"; "eye movement was out of the question if I wanted to remain standing and if I move my head or my eyes quickly I get a strange feeling in my head as if there's an electric current being discharged into my brain."

Yellow Card reports:
"abnormal eye movements" (5/1370 reports); "abnormal eye sensations" (3); "abnormal vision" (3); "accommodation abnormal" (12); "flashing vision" (8); "vision blurred" (24); "visual acuity reduced" (3); "visual disturbance NOS" [not otherwise specified] (25). Direct references to electric shock sensations were treated as exceptions to the general rule – to record faithfully the terms the reporter actually used. References to withdrawal-related electric shock sensations were coded to a "preferred term" – *paraesthesia* (181/1370 reports), unless miscoded as a blast from the mains electricity supply. (6 reports)

The overall analysis showed that most Yellow Cards (ASPPs) lacked important information. Three reports out of four said nothing about the patient's past medical history, and one in four recorded the "Outcome" of the reported reaction as "Unknown". There was no evidence of regulatory follow-up of any reports of suicidal behaviour and injury/poisoning.[11] Descriptions and comments were often non-existent and typically brief, sometimes alarmingly so.

These were the *full text* comments in about 10% of the Yellow Cards reporting suicidal behaviour. Their brevity seemed breathtaking. They demanded follow-up, but there seemed to be none:

"Suicide by cutting his throat." (Hospital)

"Only mild depression. Suicide 10 days later ... Patient was fit and well, had no suicidal thoughts." (GP)

"Pt shot himself a few days after starting medication." (GP)

---

11 The ASPPs for "withdrawal reactions" showed that the CSM/MHRA had made contact with reporters to find out more. This follow-up would have been done in connection with the review by Price et al. (1996) and in the unpublished review following publication of *The Antidepressant Web* (1998).

"Felt depression got worse – made her feel suicidal." (GP)

"Seroxat started at 10 mg daily. Dose increased to 20 mg after 2 weeks. Pt committed suicide after 4th day on the increased dose. Pt did not seem suicidal when prescribed Seroxat." (GP via company)

"Deliberate self harming behaviour became much worse after starting Seroxat. She only started cutting herself after starting Seroxat." (Hospital)

"Extremely agitated, violent reaction. Attempted suicide recovering 23/01/2001." (Community pharmacist)

"Pt received Seroxat for approximately one month. On an unspecified date pt experienced visual hallucinations and suicidal thoughts. On a date not specified the patient committed suicide by hanging. Blood levels of Seroxat were 3 to 4 times the therapeutic norm. A large quantity of alcohol was found in the patient's blood." (Hospital via company)

"Felt suicidal-thoughts (never before).Other odd religious thoughts – unusual for patient (atheist) – psychotic reaction." (GP)

"On reducing treatment very slowly from 20 mg to 10 mg to 10 mg alternate days, severe recurrence of depression and suicidal. Started first day of reduction and persisted until off treatment for 1 month. Now feels 100%." (GP)

UK health professionals send in 80% of all Yellow Cards, directly to the MCA/CSM. Companies submit, on average, only 17% of all Yellow Cards[12] – compared with about 90% of all reports in the US.[13] No audit of the relative strengths and weaknesses of company and professional reporting has ever been done.

These paroxetine Yellow Cards were therefore highly untypical. Compared with the average of 17%, company reports accounted for 70% of the ASPPs for injury/poisoning; 37% of those relating to suicidal behaviour, and 33% of those for withdrawal reactions. This was significant because companies tended to describe risk in terms that softened meaning and understanding – and because the MCA/MHRA professional staff who processed the actual Yellow Card into an ASPP worked to a strict rule, to use the reporter's exact terms when transcribing.

---

12 Sources: CSM annual reports 1994 to 1998. Data for 1999 to 2002 supplied by the MHRA to Social Audit, by letter, 1 July 2003.

13 Both US and EU law require companies to report all serious and unexpected ADRs to the regulators. In the US, Pharma companies send in around 90% of the ADR reports that reach the FDA. About 60% of the ADR reports from companies originate from health professionals, and about 40% come from consumers (CDER 1997, 2002).

Choice of terminology played a decisive part in obscuring what was going on. From the mid-1990s, the term, "discontinuation" measurably started to creep in. Terminology alone also accounted for the difference between reports coded as "dependence" and those coded as "withdrawal reaction". With a few exceptions (involving outright abuse), they described exactly the same thing.

The most striking example of terminological inexactitude involved use of the terms, "Non-accidental overdose" (NAO) or "Overdose not otherwise specified" (O/D NOS), both euphemisms for suicidal behaviour. Most of the Yellow Cards that used such terms were company reports: 91% of the ASPPs classified as "Non-accidental overdose" (NAO), and 57% of reports classified as "Overdose NOS".

The use of obfuscating terminology, plus lack of information and follow-up, meant these reports were classified as if they had nothing to do with suicidality. Some were so classified when the text suggested otherwise. *Full text* examples as follows:

> "Patient (sex unknown) took an overdose of 'Seroxat', approximately 60 tablets were taken and the Patient became extremely sedated. Outcome unknown." (Classified as NAO and 'Sedation' – Hospital via company)
>
> "Died from an overdose of Seroxat and Manerix. Took 30 tablets of both. Developed a tachyarrhythmia which progressed to ventricular fibrillation. Blood level of paroxetine was 1.3mg/dl. moclobemide was 19.3 mg/dl about 2 hrs post-ingestion." (NAO – Hospital via company)
>
> "Patient (male) had no previous psychiatric history. His history of depression dated back to 10/1997 and that was the first depressive illness he had experienced. No previous suicide attempts and no other psychiatric disorder. Outcome: Fatal – association direct or indirect. Other drugs: Co-Codamol, Zopiclone. Hepatic level of paroxetine 212 mg/kg. There was no evidence of any other drug." (NAO – Hospital via company)
>
> Female patient "Took overdose of paroxetine. Blood levels 1.25 mg/l at post mortem. Also filled bathroom with burning paper; carbon monoxide level 41% on admission. ... Cause of death smoke inhalation & paroxetine poisoning." Outcome: Fatal – association direct or indirect. (NAO – Hospital via ABPI)
>
> Sex unspecified: "Fatal – association direct or indirect ... Intentional. Death due to AE."[14] – (O/D NOS – GP via company)
>
> "Female [experienced] Agitation, Euphoria, Hyperkinetic syndrome, Concentration impairment. Outcome: Recovered." (O/D NOS – GP via company)

---

14 Presumably, AE means adverse event.

> Male patient "attempted suicide, overdose. 13/07/02 – violence assault of others. Withdrawal effects of 'electric shock'. Onset days: 184, 238. Other reactions: aggression. Outcome: Recovered." (O/D NOS – GP)

Very few Yellow Cards explained the significance of ADRS in people's lives. Use of medical terminology meant that ASPPS used fewer words than user reports, but often at the expense of detail and meaning. The focus on medical rather than human factors was poignantly illustrated in several reports that gave compelling evidence of the skill and dedication of the medical team, in explaining the procedures for saving a life after an overdose – but gave virtually no indication of how the patient came to be there in the first place.[15]

Yellow Cards on suicidal behaviour

The 1,370 Yellow Cards that described "Withdrawal Reactions" added little to the intelligence from user reports. The descriptions typically listed dominant symptoms, but gave little detail. Our analysis therefore focused mainly on suicidal behaviour and cases of injury/poisoning.

For years, there had been suspicions of some linkage between these effects and the onset of drug treatment, but the *Panorama* user reports had also suggested an association with dosage changes and during severe withdrawal. The 91 Yellow Cards for suicidal behaviour were analysed with this in mind.

At first sight, there seemed to be no obvious relationship between cause and effect. Two-thirds of the Yellow Cards didn't record the critically important coded term, "Onset Time" – to establish how long after taking the drug the adverse reaction set in. In the whole sample, 17 reports (19%) described suicidal behaviour within the first week after starting treatment.

However, nine more reports appeared miscoded. The Yellow Cards did not state "Onset Days", when the text clearly did (e.g. "Within one hour of ingestion." "one day after starting;" "After the second dose"). The text in three other reports hinted at

15 For example: "... Nystagmus developed & progressed to a full oculogyric crisis. Procyclidine given IM & repeated after 20 mins with no effect. Condition deteriorated. Glasgow coma scale decreased from 15 to 7 & became increasingly tremulous until all muscle groups involved. Generalised twitching of all limbs & especially of face & jaw. Both pupils dilated to 7 mm diameter & were equal & reactive to light. All reflexes were extremely brisk & plantar reflexes were extensor. BP increased to 160/100 & heart rate to 200 bpm. Profuse sweating remained & axillary temperature was 37.6. Transferred to resuscitation room & 100% oxygen given ..."

early onset, but did not specify a time. ("After starting Seroxat;" "Suicidal thoughts since being on Seroxat" and a reference to "New symptoms on treatment").

In 11 more Yellow Cards, the text but not the coded information, indicated linkage between thoughts and acts of violence or self-harm and dose increase. For example:

> The ASPP recorded "Onset Time" as 18 days, but "Dose increased from 10 to 20 mg daily after 2 weeks on treatment. On the fourth day of starting the 20 mg dose patient committed suicide by hanging himself."
>
> The ASPP recorded "Onset Time" as 16 days, but "Patient committed suicide after having increased dose from 20 to 30 mg."
>
> "Onset time" not stated but: "Patient was fine on 20 mg paroxetine. Suicidal ideation on starting 30 mg which settled on stopping this dose."

In another 16 Yellow Cards, suicidal ideation was linked to severe drug withdrawal: eight reports specified gradual withdrawal; four mentioned abrupt withdrawal; and three did not specify. This challenged the widely promoted view that withdrawal problems could be avoided by dose tapering. Again, the coded "Onset Time" did not always correspond to the actual sequence of events. For example, one Yellow Card recorded "Onset Time" as 181 days, but the text indicated that the patient hanged himself four days after abrupt drug withdrawal.

In short, at least half of the Yellow Cards for suicidal behaviour seemed to be linked to changes in drug concentration in the body – during the first week of treatment, or with dose increase or severe symptoms on drug withdrawal. This apparently strong linkage had not previously been reported and was not reflected in either warnings or dosage advice.

A further six Yellow Cards indicated onset of problems within one month, and ten more were in some way suggestive of causation; all begged follow-up, again there appeared to be none. These explicitly linked paroxetine to abnormal and/or uncharacteristic behaviour; some also hinted at problems linked to a change in the level or timing of dose. The following are *extracts* from the full text:

> "We have evidence that suspect drug drove patient to suicide." (GP)
>
> "He clearly stated that he had not thought about suicide until taking Seroxat but that he subsequently felt driven to end his life." (GP)
>
> "At onset of treatment Patient was not suicidal, the disorientation & fear were new symptoms on treatment. Previously well." (GP)
>
> "Threw herself under a train. No past medical history of suicide thoughts or attempts." (GP)

> "Patient reported 'don't care about life' and suicidal thoughts since being on Seroxat. Almost attempted suicide twice." (GP)

Of the remaining reports, 15 (16%) contained wholly insufficient information and 5 (5%) identified complicating factors that made a causal connection seem unlikely. The table summarises the picture overall.

Classification after reanalysis of 91 reports

Onset within 1 – 2 days after starting paroxetine:

- 10 reports with onset time coded
- 4 reports with onset time not coded

Onset 3 – 7 days after starting paroxetine:

- 6 reports with onset time coded
- 2 reports with onset time not coded

Onset 8 – 30 days after starting paroxetine:

- 5 reports with onset time coded
- 4 reports with onset time not coded
- 11 reports linking suicidal behaviour to dose increase
- 16 reports linking suicidal behaviour to withdrawal
- 3 reports with onset time recorded as > 30 days
- 10 reports give no indication of onset time but comments indicate suspected drug causation
- 15 reports give no indication of onset time and otherwise insufficient information
- 5 reports indicate causation unlikely

These findings went some way to explaining how the MCA/CSM – after conducting at least six reviews (1990-2002) into problems of suicidal behaviour and dependence with SSRIs – consistently found little cause for concern. The reality was that generally low standards of reporting, miscoding and flawed analyses of Yellow Cards had led to substantial under-estimation of the risks, impeding recognition of the apparently close relationship between suicidal behaviour and changes in drug concentration.

Such problems in this case were compounded by the MCA/CSM's refusal to accept reports from patients, as the regulators in 23 other countries appear to do (Lindqvist 2003). This reduced the intelligence: patients, in their own words, communicated essential information which professional reporters could never be expected to provide. Here, patients (or relatives) provided reports that were often much better at explaining the nature, significance and consequences of adverse drug effects.

The way in which Yellow Cards were processed added to the fragmentation of the human condition into symptoms. The labels attached made sense as professional shorthand, but not as reckonings of personal experience. Patient reports converted the more technical terms that professionals used into understanding. Individually, patient reports were often deficient, they might exaggerate or get it wrong – but collectively they reflect good common sense. Patient reports, in this case, elucidated the real dimensions of an adverse drug reaction – what withdrawal reactions, weight gain, suicidal behaviour, or loss of libido actually meant, in the context of personal and social life. This aspect of iatrogenesis remains largely unexplored.

Patients' reports also reveal how much people can't or won't communicate with doctors, and how often people feel their doctors will not listen. Lack of consultation time and resources clearly constrain the doctor-patient relationship, but so does professional insistence that the doctor knows best. In this case, many didn't, and left patients feeling bullied and stuck. Thus some doctors may never get to know the kinds of things that patients might be scared to talk about – e.g. the effects of paroxetine on driving, or the feeling they were going mad. The underlying fear of loss of driving licence or liberty might feel too much.

The processing of Yellow Cards, and lack of follow-up, thus contributed to a critical and calamitous oversight. If the available data had been made public as they came to light, much tragedy might have been avoided.

The wider point is that clinical iatrogenesis remains largely a mystery, and that "pharmacovigilance" and "post-marketing surveillance" fall far short of explaining it.

Medicalisation

The key ideas behind "social" and "cultural" iatrogenesis were individual and collective loss of autonomy, independence and confidence in health. The process of medicalisation promoted unhealthy dependence on intervention and support systems, and the inability to cope with illness and death as integral parts of life (Illich 1977).

The underlying risks of medicalisation were apparent even before the marketing revolution and the pressures of globalisation. Lewis Thomas (1979) vividly described not only what would happen to the spirit of health, but also how it might bankrupt any community. Thomas was writing here only about the US: problems would be so much the greater, both for poorer countries struggling to get "health for all" systems off the ground, and for richer nations beset by the cost of maintaining them.

> "The trouble is, we are being taken in by the propaganda, and it is bad not only for the spirit of society; it will make any health-care system, no matter how large and efficient, unworkable. If people are educated to believe they are fundamentally fragile, always on the verge of mortal disease, perpetually in need of health-care professionals at every side, always dependent on an imagined discipline of 'preventive' medicine, there can be no limit to the numbers of doctors' offices, clinics, and hospitals required to meet the demand. ... We are, in real life, a reasonably healthy

> people. Far from being ineptly put together, we are amazingly tough, durable organisms, full of health, ready for most contingencies. The new danger to our well-being, if we continue to listen to all the talk, is in becoming a nation of healthy hypochondriacs, living gingerly, worrying ourselves half to death."

Progress in medicine uncovers more and more aspects of human vulnerability and states of ill-health, yet the more medicine can promise, the less we seem to be able to do for each other and ourselves. In the US and other richer countries, objective evidence of significant improvements in collective health seems to be matched by declining satisfaction with personal health. A staple diet of "disease awareness" has tended to create both "health anxiety" and unsustainable demand:

> "Although our society's fascination with health has had many substantial benefits, it has at the same time eroded the sense of well-being. Paying increased attention to one's body and one's health care tends to make one assess them more negatively, with greater feelings of ill-health. Several investigations have shown that bodily awareness, self-consciousness, and introspection are associated with a tendency to amplify somatic symptoms and to report being troubled by more symptoms. Studies in conceptual and experimental psychology suggest that, in general, the more aware people are of their characteristics and attributes, the more negatively they assess them. This appears to be particularly true for physical attributes, bodily sensations, and perceptions of health." (Barsky 1988)

The US market today exemplifies what is fast becoming a global trend: the air is thick with the promise of medicine and talk of better prospects for health. Endlessly, people are confronted with news of risk and illness to remind them how healthy they need to be. Each day brings a new health agenda and more health messages, all with the promise and temptations of chronic joy. Whatever the benefits, the risk is that people come to believe that human health is the product of assiduous risk aversion and medical intervention, day after day.

The justification for this torrent of health messages is hardly questioned; it is taken almost for granted that such information is needed and wanted, that it promotes personal responsibility, health awareness, empowerment and choice. But how can a body of understanding grow on a diet saturated with messages about the need for health? Will people really learn how to "Stay Safe, Stay Happy", by taking in the advice behind the headlines. Only the other day (28 May 2001), these were top website stories on ABC-TV.

> "Why should you avoid eating tuna and other foods with strong odors outdoors? What are the most intense hours of sunlight – and sunburn? What should you do if a wasp approaches? Find out in our summer safety tips. And check out the series: 'The Dangers of Summer' ... Beware:

- There's a tetanus vaccine shortage – and that's a reason to be more careful in your garden or when doing water sports this summer ...
- Pool-Borne Bacteria on Rise – Federal health officials are launching a 'healthy swimming' awareness campaign. Find out what you can do to avoid getting sick.
- Fireworks safety tip: Here's how to make sure the rocket's red glare stays under control in your backyard.
- The number of cell phones keeps rising, as does the number of brain tumors. But is there a connection between the two?
- Migraine headaches cause severe pain and tremendous disability, and yet less than half of all people who suffer from these disabling headaches are receiving appropriate treatment.
- Your Cash Could Make You Sick – Dollar bills have so much bacteria, they may infect you or others ..."

Alongside such tips for health and happiness are the nagging threats. Countless health "news releases" reveal sickening truths to add to the burden of hope. Rapid access to new medicines is the solution: so they say on the newswires, day after day after day:

> "40 million men in the U.S suffer from low testosterone, But Most Don't Know it" ... "over 17 million people in the U.S. suffer from overactive bladder" ... "Over 40 millions Americans suffer with debilitating sleep disorders, and surveys show an additional sixty million people experience sleep difficulties" ... "Four out of ten (42 per cent) adults say they experience pain daily, according to a Gallup survey" ... "More than 4 million children over the age of five wake up each morning in wet beds" ... "more than 41 million women in the United States have unwanted facial hair" ... "20 million people will have full-blown posttraumatic stress disorder (PTSD) ... "an estimated 24 million Americans suffer with varicose veins" ... Osteoporosis "is a major public health threat for more than 28 million Americans" ... and clinical obesity becomes ever closer to the norm.

The US leads the world in "disease awareness" and concern about unmet medical need. Americans revere 170 official "health observances", including 74 "awareness months" and 64 "awareness weeks", each year. But what is the effect on the health of the community, when everyone is constantly alerted to this threat or that affliction and urged to screen body and mind for every sign of disease?

The risk is that this intense emphasis on self and health prompts many people to feel ill and turn to medicine in vain – and they are all around and their numbers are increasing. On the average British day, 70-80% of people have a health complaint, and "medically unexplained symptoms" account for one in five new episodes of illness presenting in primary care. UK studies have suggested that no firm diagnosis can be made in 20-60% of patients attending general practice (Chaput de Saintonge & Herxheimer 1994, Thomas 1994, *D&TB* 2001).

The drugs in this case history serve to meet this demand, whatever else – which is not to discount the importance of effective treatment for depression. The World Health Organization (2000) has estimated that, by 2020, depression will be the second leading cause of death and disability worldwide. The underlying point, inadvertently made, is that antidepressants cannot be anything like as effective as claimed.

But how would it be if antidepressants or tranquillisers really were as effective as everyone might want? Then there would be no reason or excuse for stress and depression, and society would tolerate it less. Then there would be no need to bother about the causes, or to wonder about the lifestyles that fuel demand for drugs.

To the extent they work, drugs like Valium or Prozac quietly but emphatically encourage the community to adapt to anxiety and depression – and to tolerate ways of life that make us ill. Chemical interventions that may sometime seem miraculous to the individual may also be disastrous for the community, promoting tolerance to lifestyles ever more stressful, depressing and bleak.

11

The story so far

The Working Group on Selective Serotonin Reuptake Inhibitors (SSRIs) was due to report in early 2004, but already it seems certain that the review will miss the wider point – the need for new management, a coherent drug safety policy and standards of public accountability as never before. The SSRI story is specifically about drugs that work on the mind, but it illustrates what seems to be happening with medicines of many kinds. Market-driven medicine seems now to have surpassed the point of diminishing health returns. If health is the desired outcome, can it really make sense to invest in drug innovation and consumption on the Pharmas' terms? There can be no end of better alternatives – none more radical than the notion that medicine produces health only when conducted within a framework of honest science and decent human and democratic values. For everyone's sake, this must be a global goal.

The UK's Committee on Safety in Medicines (CSM) "Intensive Review" of the SSRIS was abandoned in March 2003. The closest thing to an explanation was in a Parliamentary Question[1] that gave little away:

> Mr. Dhanda: To ask the Secretary of State for Health ... what action he is taking to ensure that the review of selective serotonin reuptake inhibitor class antidepressants being conducted by the Committee of Safety of Medicines is fully independent.
>
> Ms Blears: "... Members of the Medicines Act advisory committees, such as the CSM, are required to follow a code of practice relating to declarations of interests in the pharmaceutical industry. The code is applied where members attend meetings of expert working groups and this was the case on 21 November 2002. A new CSM expert group is being appointed to conduct further *review of SSRIs and appropriate membership is being considered in the light of issues raised at the meeting and the further work these will require, as well as further legal advice on interests in the particular circumstances of this class.*"

1 *Hansard* 3 April 2003 : Column 847w.

Parliamentary intervention seemed to make little difference to the main course of events this case history describes. The procedures available to Members of Parliament (MPs) for calling government to account are weak and ineffectual (John 2003); lack of resources and access to information rule out preventive parliamentary medicine. Individual parliamentarians play their part mainly by informing government of constituents' concerns.

The first *Panorama* programme, "Secrets of Seroxat", prompted many complaints from constituents to MPs. These were passed on as questions to Ministers and that translated as pressure on the regulatory machine. That is how things happened in the UK – quite different from the US: the average MP has minimal research support, nothing to compare with the staff of a member of Congress.

Procedure in the House of Lords distinguished the UK from all other democracies. Until 2000, the House of Lords was dominated by inherited nobility and one political party. Patronage lives on but nowadays most Lords are appointed only for their lifetime: they continue to represent partisan and other special interests rather than constituents, and the obsequies remain largely intact. The following exchange[2] was prompted by the second *Panorama* programme, "E-mails from the Edge". The questioner was a professor of fertility studies.

> Lord Winston: "My Lords, I declare an interest as the director of research and development at Hammersmith Hospitals NHS Trust. Does the Minister not agree that Seroxat and the class of drugs that deal with serotonin in the brain are the most effective anti-depressants that we currently know? Seroxat has been in use for more than 12 years and is available in more than 100 countries where none of the side effects mentioned has been highlighted. The 'Panorama' programme has not always been noted for its accuracy in other areas. It would be premature to condemn what is an extremely good drug. The side effects reported are those commonly reported in recovering depressive patients who are not taking the drug."

> Baroness Andrews (for the government): "My Lords, I can hardly improve on that description. Seroxat is an effective treatment for depression and anxiety disorders. Four million prescriptions are made every year in this country alone. We have a wealth of evidence from Europe and the United States that it is a safe and very effective drug. Nevertheless, we want to respond to the concerns raised in the 'Panorama' programme. We do not want people suddenly to stop taking their medication. That is why the Committee on Safety of Medicines has set up an expert working group to see how it can address some of the issues as appropriately as possible."

---

2 *Hansard (Lords)* 15 May 2003 : Column 371.

One week later, the Department of Health announced the start of the new inquiry.[3] The terms of the press statement underlined the domination of the bureaucracy: "the MHRA has set up an expert group of the CSM ...". The statement quoted Professor Alasdair Breckenridge, the new chairman of the Medicines and Healthcare products Agency (MHRA), at length. There was no reference to Professor Gordon Duff, his successor as chair of the CSM.

No-one from the old "Intensive Review" was on the new "Working Group", and this time the team included two lay members. The greater emphasis on independence was underlined by the appointment of Richard Brook, head of the leading grass-roots network of mental health service users, MIND.[4] The inaugural press release signalled this shift as well: "patient reports are going to form an important part in the assessment of the safety of SSRIs", Breckenridge said.

At its meeting on 29 May, the CSM was told they could expect to receive the report of the working group in September 2003. This was not to be. The pace picked up and the plot thickened from this point on.

SSRIs and children

The lead story on the City & Finance pages of the *Daily Mail* (9 June) was based on leaked information; it announced, "Glaxo faces Seroxat storm". The story revealed that, in a "very, very unusual" move, the MHRA was proposing a Good Clinical Practice (CGP) audit of all Seroxat files. The possibility of criminal prosecution was mentioned.

The following day, the Department of Health held a press conference[5] to announce that Seroxat "must not be used for treatment of children with depression". The urgency was underlined by the Chief Medical Officer cascading this news to prescribers the same day. The press briefing gave no hint of regulatory action directed at GlaxoSmithKline (GSK) though the MHRA didn't deny the possibility, when pressed.[6]

---

3 Department of Health press release 2003/0214, 23 May 2003.

4 MIND, the National Association for Mental Health, has a strong tradition of independence (funded more by government, not companies), plus an impressive track record in this field. MIND worked in close cooperation with *Panorama* on the Seroxat issue – and had also played a major part in revealing the benzodiazepine problem, again in association with the BBC (Lacey & Woodward 1985).

5 This was another meeting from which *Social Audit* was debarred – this time on the grounds that CM was not a journalist. The correspondence that ensued with the Department of Health press office established that the DoH demanded "bona fides" and "credentials". When asked what bona fides and credentials the press office required, they were unable to produce any specification. *Social* Audit need not apply. See *ADWEB* June/July 2003.

Few details emerged, but it appeared that, on 21 May, GSK had sent the MHRA its Clinical Summary of the results of clinical trials – with a view to getting Seroxat licensed for children.[7] It is safe to assume that GSK's Clinical Summary claimed that paroxetine was effective and safe enough but, for whatever reason, the MHRA decided to examine the full documentation from the trials. Dr. Healy's submissions and the revelations by *Panorama* would have had a lot to do with this – but whatever the prompt, the regulators would have examined the raw data that supported the Clinical Summary, only if strong suspicions had been aroused.

The MHRA went on to examine some part of the contents of, apparently, 184 boxes of raw data, for nine trials involving about 1,100 teen and pre-teen children. The MHRA found no evidence of paroxetine efficacy in depression, but a two-fold increase in risk of what *The Lancet* described as "emotional lability". This was the euphemism a US Food and Drug Administration (FDA) reviewer had complained of four years earlier (see Chapter 8) – but the term had stuck, and *The Lancet* let it by:

> "The frequency of emotional lability (crying, mood changes, attempts at self-harm, suicide and attempts) was 3.2% in those taking paroxetine, compared with 1.5 in those on placebo."

These developments led the CSM Working Group and the MHRA to look at other trials, in adults as well as children and for other SSRIs. This meant the Working Group needed much longer for its enquiries than previously imagined. They had opened a can of worms, and their findings would reverberate worldwide, especially in the US.

Little was known about the effects of SSRIs in children, in spite of extensive and increasing use, mainly in the US. Paediatric drug testing was not required for drug licensing, and few companies found it worthwhile – other than to gain patent life extensions (Lurie 2002). The FDA had licensed Prozac for childhood depression in 2003 (and Lilly was even then testing it for pre-menstrual symptoms in schoolgirls).[8] However, SSRIs were overwhelmingly prescribed for children on an "off-label" basis, a

---

6 "The Agency is 'urgently investigating whether there are grounds for thinking the new data could have been provided sooner'" (*Lancet*, editorial 14 June 2003). "But June Raine, director of the MHRA's post-licensing division said the results of Seroxat tests on under-18s had 'raised serious regulatory issues' about SSRIs that the working group had to explore" (*Financial Times* 11 June 2003).

7 GSK was trying to extend the indications for Seroxat, to include paediatric obsessive compulsive disorder, social anxiety disorder and major depressive disorder within the meaning of DSM-IV.

8 A Canadian newspaper, *The Hamilton Spectator*, reported how a Lilly-funded expert on PMS, Dr. Meir Steiner, surveyed girls at a local high school, aiming to recruit at least 30 between the ages of 12 and 17. The survey consent form did not mention this was part of a sponsored drug trial, because girls with appropriate symptoms wouldn't actually enter the trial until going for the consultation offered (Walters 2002).

non-officially-approved use, for which the prescriber takes the main responsibility. On this basis, many hundreds of thousands of prescriptions for SSRIs were written in the US, each year.[9]

This exposed a loophole in drug control, one that still applies to all drugs, especially in the US. It might be remedied if companies were required to submit evidence of safety and efficacy, as if for marketing approval, when off-label prescribing for children reached significant levels.[10] No such requirement exists.

Meanwhile, the SSRI Pharmas had been actively testing their drugs in children for some years. By 1998, SmithKline Beecham (SKB) had trial results from two big studies on 550 children. Neither had found paroxetine was more effective than placebo, and the risk of adverse effects was found to be "the same as for adults". In other words, at least five years before the regulators addressed the problems in children, SKB had reason to believe that paroxetine offered no measurable benefit in depressed children, but did carry significant risks. An internal SKB memorandum (1998) discussed what the company should do; it did not dwell on the ethical implications.

This memo defined the "target" objective – "to effectively manage the dissemination of these data in order to minimise any potential negative commercial impact". And because SKB considered "there are no safety issues in adolescents", they decided that, "it would be commercially unacceptable to include a statement that efficacy had not been demonstrated, as this would undermine the profile of paroxetine".

Four years later, the first *Panorama* programme turned the spotlight from efficacy to safety – questioning some worrying results from a recent study, the largest sponsored trial of Seroxat in children there had been (Keller et al. 2001). The GSK spokesman by-passed the matter of efficacy, comparing side effects to those on placebo and the other test drug:

---

9 In the US, the top ten drugs for children – but unapproved for such use – were prescribed more than five million times in 1994. They included Prozac (349,000 prescriptions) and Zoloft (248,000) above Ritalin (226,000). SSRI use in children increased substantially between 1995 – 1999 (Shatin & Drinkard 2002). Prozac was approved for depression in children aged eight or older, but antidepressants were prescribed to pre-school US children (aged two to four) at an estimated frequency of 3.2/1000 (Zito et al. 2000). That compares with a rate of 4.4/1000 in The Netherlands, for all users aged under 20 (Schirm et al. 2001).

10 The original rationale for permitting "off-label use" (an example of "clinical freedom" for better and worse) was to provide for treatment in exceptional cases, when other treatment options had failed. No doubt there were many off-label SSRI prescriptions for children that were thoroughly well justified – but common sense might suggest that the likelihood of this diminished when large markets grew. Throughout the 1990s, the FDA knew that hundreds of thousands of children were taking SSRIs, and that there was barely evidence of safety and effectiveness in children. That would give all the more reason for Americans to wonder what an independent scrutiny of ADR reports might reveal. How would the FDA system compare with the UK's Yellow Card scheme? See *ADWEB*, from 2004.

SHELLEY JOFRE, *Panorama* reporter: "There were five children out of ninety-three children on Seroxat who had suicidal thoughts and gestures. Another five out of that ninety-three had serious psychiatric side effects. Don't you think parents would be worried about that if their child was to be given this drug?"

Dr ALASTAIR BENBOW, Head of European Clinical Psychiatry, GlaxoSmithKline: "I think what parents would be more worried about is the risk that their children have of committing suicide and other symptoms of severe depression if no treatment was available. I think parents would want treatments to be properly evaluated during clinical trials before their children are given any medicine."

JOFRE: "But the evidence here suggests that their children might be at more risk of suicide if they go on Seroxat."

BENBOW: "No, the evidence is not there, there is no statistical difference between the groups. The reality of the situation is that in this trial, Seroxat was generally well tolerated by this difficult to treat population."

By the summer of 2003, the CSM/MHRA Working Group had more on its plate. Within a few weeks of each other, Wyeth circulated a "Dear Doctor" letter in the US, to warn of an increased risk of hostility and suicidality in children on venlafaxine (Effexor/Efexor), while Pfizer started broadcasting the benefits of Zoloft (sertraline, Lustral). Neither drug was licensed for childhood or adolescent depression, but Pfizer was hoping to increase its market share, as younger patients were switched from the other brands. Pfizer was putting out the results of a faintly positive trial, and the mainstream media was lapping it up.

A search on Google, in September 2003 (Zoloft + approved + children + 2003) produced 16,200 citations – variations on the top headline theme, "Study: Antidepressant Zoloft Safe For Kids". Under the headline in the *Philadelphia Inquirer* (Associated Press) report was also this memorable claim: "In a breakthrough, the drug outperformed placebos. Other drugs didn't in previous research."

At the end of this ten-week multi-center study (involving 189 children and adolescents on active drug; 187 on placebo), 69% of children on sertraline showed improvement, compared with 59% on placebo. "There were four adverse events that occurred in at least 5% of sertraline-treated patients and with an incidence of at least twice that in placebo patients: diarrhea, vomiting, anorexia, and agitation. Seventeen sertraline-treated patients (9%) discontinued the study because of adverse events ... Seven sertraline-treated patients and six placebo patients had adverse events that met the established criteria for a 'serious' adverse event, including suicide attempt (2 sertraline and 2 placebo), suicidal ideation (3 sertraline), and aggressive reaction (1 sertraline), as well as medical hospitalizations (1 sertraline and

> 4 placebo)." The investigators concluded: "The results of this pooled analysis demonstrate that sertraline is an effective and tolerated short-term treatment for children and adolescents with Major Depressive Disorder." (Wagner et al. 2003)
>
> The lead author of this study was also one of the investigators in GSK's studies of paroxetine in children. They had concluded that paroxetine was effective and well tolerated shortly before the UK regulators decided otherwise. (Boseley 2003)

Two weeks before Christmas 2003, the CSM/MHRA Working Group completed its review of SSRIs for depression in under 18-year-olds. But for Prozac, they banned ('contraindicated') the lot: they were not effective but they could cause suicidal behaviour and other serious effects.

The Working Group had made an exception for Prozac on the basis of two trials, involving 315 under 18-year-olds. This evidence suggested a lower level of risk with Prozac, though not much benefit. Reading between the lines, only about one child in ten might be helped by Prozac: the benefits for them were presumed to outweigh the lack of benefit or risks for the other nine. The closest the CSM/MHRA came to admitting this was in a technical note belatedly posted to the MHRA website – rather than in the advice rushed to doctors. The note said that the Working Group had found, "both trials demonstrated short-term efficacy of fluoxetine although the size of the effect is modest (similar to that in adults)".

That was not what was said in the formal advice that the CSM/MHRA had rushed to doctors, to communicate the regulatory view of the Working Group's findings: "Data from clinical trials have demonstrated that fluoxetine (Prozac) is beneficial in the treatment of depressive illness and these benefits outweigh the risks of treatment. This does not mean that fluoxetine will work for everyone or that it is not associated with any side effects." Probably not many doctors realised the underlying significance of this: whatever else, it meant that the CSM/MHRA was not going to challenge the US FDA, which had licensed Prozac for children aged 7 years and above, only a few months earlier.

On behalf of the Working Group, the CSM/MHRA also rushed doctors a leaflet to pass on to their patients – to explain, *"Why is Prozac OK?"* This added more layers of gloss, in suggesting that most patients would benefit from the experience: "The group of experts has looked at the research with Prozac and decided that on balance it does more good than harm in most of the under 18s." Well-intentioned deceit is a classic feature of the Conspiracy of Goodwill. This was considered 'good advice' because it reassured patients and didn't embarrass prescribers, but it was patently untrue.

For all this, the safety of SSRIs in under 18-year olds was an aspect of the SSRI crisis that the CSM/MHRA Working Group had neither expected nor intended to investigate. Thus, the Working Group took over six months even to begin the task it was meant to address: the risks of suicidal behaviour, dependence and other adverse effects in the vast majority of users – everyone from young adults to the elderly. The reasons for individual susceptibility were assumed to be age-related, but wholly unknown.

Still at the end of 2003, the CSM/MHRA Working Group and the SSRI Pharmas both emphasised that there was no evidence of a causal connection between SSRIS and suicidal behaviour in adults. The element of risk was put aside. By the end of 2003, there was no sign that user reports and evidence from Yellow Cards had had any impact, and the CSM/MHRA had still not responded to the detailed critique that Dr. David Healy had put to the Intensive Review, at the end of 2002.

Seroxat label transformation

On 25 June 2003, the Seroxat label was changed. This was not only to contraindicate use in children, but also to remove the claim that it was not addictive. The new UK label quietly announced a 50-fold increase in the previous "two per 1,000" estimate of withdrawal symptoms, that GlaxoSmithKline[11] and the regulators had relied on only a few months before.

Actually, there was a 125-fold increase. GlaxoSmithKline's new estimate was that one-in-four users were likely to get withdrawal reactions, even after gradual drug withdrawal. However, GSK then got the numbers down by "correcting for placebo". With full regulatory approval, GSK subtracted from the true figure, the exceptionally high count of "withdrawal reactions" among patients on placebo. The new UK label said this:

> "In recent clinical trials which used a taper phase to discontinue treatment with paroxetine ... approximately 25% of patients on paroxetine and approximately 15% of patients on placebo experienced such symptoms. That is, approximately 10% of patients in the paroxetine group experienced symptoms potentially attributable to the withdrawal of therapy when corrected for placebo."

Why would the regulators have approved such an interpretation? In this case, they had a clear interest in keeping the numbers down: higher figures would have made their earlier estimate (Price et al. 1996) seem more of a sham. Presumably, neither GSK nor or the CSM/MHRA actually believed that stopping a placebo was as tough as paroxetine withdrawal. They merely invite you to mislead yourself by comparing the numbers, as if there was some equivalence in *severity* of symptoms between the two.

---

11 The credibility of the 2 per 1,000 estimate of withdrawal symptoms was basic to GSK defence in complaints referred to the industry's self-regulatory system, the Prescription Medicines Code of Practice Authority (PMCPOA). See Chapter 7.

Over the previous decade, GSK/MHRA/CSM had been unable to detect anything more than occasional withdrawal reactions after abruptly stopping the active drug – yet now they proposed a 15% incidence of placebo-induced withdrawal reactions that were indistinguishable from paroxetine withdrawal. Minimal common sense – if not regulatory "science" – suggests that the frequency of "mild", "moderate" or "severe" withdrawal reactions would not be the same on active drug and placebo.[12]

Unsuitable for publication

Meanwhile, the analysis of paroxetine Yellow Cards (Medawar & Herxheimer 2003) suggested that prescribers and users did need to consider the possible importance of adjusting SSRI dosage slowly, both up and down. And because the full paper in *International Journal of Risk & Safety in Medicine* wouldn't be published until the end of 2003, we decided to try to get a short summary published, fast. This was also partly an attempt to pressure the CSM/MHRA Working Group to acknowledge some element of risk.

A summary of the Yellow Card paper was therefore submitted for publication to the *British Medical Journal*, and also sent as evidence to the CSM working group. The *BMJ* agreed to consider fast-track publication,[13] and circulated the summary to four external reviewers.[14] However, the final decision on publication fell to the editorial team: they unanimously rejected the paper, but invited resubmission as a shorter (1,000-word) article for the *BMJ's* "Education and Debate" feature.[15] An abbreviated

---

12 This practice is widespread: it applies to other adverse reactions and for other kinds of drugs: it has been traditional to present ADR data in this way (Medawar 1997).

13 When the *BMJ* pulls out all stops, it can publish a peer-reviewed paper in two to three weeks. The whole process is state-of-the-art, with everything done over the Internet: submission of paper, consideration by editorial staff, circulation to reviewers and submission of their comments and recommendations, re-consideration by editorial staff and authors, and then rejection or modification of the paper before publication. The *BMJ* is also one of very few medical journals committed to open peer-review, allowing authors to see which reviewers said what. Most journals have no system of peer-review and those that do rarely reveal the names of reviewers. The traditional system of peer-review has attracted criticism as "something rotten at the core of science" (Horrobin 2001). The *BMJ* leads also, in requiring reviewers as well as authors to disclose any possible conflicts of interest.

14 Three had some direct interest in the issue; they included a CSM member, a former member of the Intensive Review, and the head of one of the main regional centres of the Yellow Card scheme. The latter found it hard to credit any point the paper made. Two of the four thought it important to publish, and the other reviewer found some merit in the paper. All reviewers recommended changes of emphasis and tone, and wanted more information and discussion; they listed proposals which, if properly addressed, might have doubled the (strictly limited) length.

paper was prepared; this was rejected too. An invitation to submit a more journalistic, background piece was not pursued.[16]

The *BMJ* rejection came on 22 July, the same day Herxheimer & Medawar gave evidence to the CSM Working Group. Our presentation tripped lightly past the introduction in the written submission,[17] and discussion turned to the main points in the summary Yellow Card paper.[18]

The Working Group seemed to take seriously our concerns about dosage, but raised queries about the apparent association between dosage increase and suicidal behaviour. How could one be sure, in these cases, that the doctor hadn't raised the dose because the user had become more depressed? One couldn't, because the CSM/MCA/MHRA had never followed them up. The Working Group responded, saying perhaps there should be further investigation, but it decided no warnings should be issued in the meantime. The quest for scientific exactitude again tied regulatory hands. The authorities have yet to develop ways of communicating the uncertainties of risk.

---

15 "We think your paper reads more as a polemic than a research paper, and we do not think the methodology and data are robust enough to substantiate the conclusions. However, we are interested in the subject and think the piece would be suitable for the Education and Debate section of the *BMJ*, in the form of an essay with some data. We would like you to focus on the process itself, how the reports were analysed, and what you would recommend in terms of the way forward in future. We suggest you refer to the data that has been published elsewhere, but we strongly advise against overanalysis and overinterpretation of your own data."

16 "Education and Debate pieces read more like essays, and do not contain analyses of this kind. What we are looking for is more of a journalistic style article which includes: background information about the situation and why it came to light, how you became involved, how you set about analysing the data (but NOT the analysis itself which is referenced elsewhere), what you have learned from the experience, your recommendations for the future based on your experience. We would seek to publish a suitably revised article quickly but I need to stress that the current article is still a long way from being suitable for publication."

17 "The terms of reference of the SSRI Working Group duck the most important issues: could this crisis have been avoided, and what might now be done to avoid similar problems in future?

For the record, our view is that the regulators themselves played a major part in creating the problems now being addressed. We believe that nothing short of a thorough overhaul of the drug safety monitoring system is essential and that comparable problems will arise in future unless and until that is done.

The present crisis has been looming for years (Teicher et al. 1992; Healy 2003; Medawar 1994, 1997). We believe the regulatory response was inadequate for three main and related reasons: over-reliance on misleading definitions and on data represented as 'scientific' and reliable, at times to the point of defying logic and common sense; a chronic tendency to marginalise, dismiss or ignore critical comment; and inadequate, sometimes incompetent analyses of the available data."

18 A slightly edited version of the paper was later posted on *ADWEB*, but otherwise not published.

Yellow Card prohibition?

Meanwhile, there were dramatic developments on another front. Back in June, *Social Audit* had asked the MHRA for access to the anonymised Yellow Cards (ASPPs) for all the other SSRIs, to see if they showed the same as paroxetine. As nothing seemed to be moving, in our written submission to the Working Group, we asked them to endorse this request.

The point was never discussed. On 21 July, the day before we gave oral evidence, the Department of Health announced an official enquiry, the first of its kind in 40 years. The Minister was pleased to announce an independent review of theYellow Card scheme, by Dr. Jeremy Metters, former deputy Chief Medical Officer at the Department of Health (DoH). He was asked to report to Professor Breckenridge by the end of 2003.

Dr. Metters' terms of reference[19] effectively limited his review to just one question: who should *not* be allowed access to the data? There were all the hallmarks of a rushed decision. There was no evidence the CSM (co-sponsors of the Yellow Card scheme) had ever been consulted, and neither they nor the MHRA even announced the review.[20]

The DoH press office had bent over backwards to attract little attention, and with much success. The way it announced the Yellow Card review stirred neither *The Lancet* nor the *British Medical Journal* enough to report it. The few papers and journals that did carry the story hardly departed from the press release, give or take some spin: "Researchers may soon see yellow card data" was the unexplained headline in a note in the *Pharmaceutical Journal* (26 July).

At this point, Andrew Herxheimer briefed the *BMJ*, then they weighed in.[21] On the same day (9 August), an update on the *Social Audit* website looked on the bright side:

> "... the Metters review provides an opportunity to recommend more openness – to the extent of putting all such anonymised ADR data on the Internet ... the emerg-

---

19 "To identify and describe the range of issues which should be considered when considering access to data generated by the Yellow Card scheme including ethical, operational, financial and statutory (including open Government/FOI); to identify relevant stakeholders to the scheme and to define how such interests arise; to consider in what circumstances access to the data generated by the scheme could be said to be in the public interest and the extent to which this falls within existing legal provisions; to make proposals for guiding principles and a mechanism for handling such requests; to make recommendations for action."

20 The review was not mentioned on the website of the CSM, nor in the "What's New?" section on the MHRA website (Sample "What's New?" item: "The details of parallel import licences granted in July 2003). The announcement of the Yellow Card review was buried in a press statement, belatedly posted to the aforementioned corner of www.mhra.gov.uk.

ing scandal and tragedy of the SSRIs would not have happened if the chapter and verse of professional experience with SSRIs had been up on the Internet – along with the countless reports from users, posted over the years."

"It could go either way, but I'll hazard an optimistic guess. Notwithstanding the deployment of the DoH/MHRA news management cavalry, the political fallout from the SSRI affair will make it almost impossible to put the lid on such an important source of drug safety information. This is an incentive for Dr. Metters to recommend changes that would make the Yellow Card system truly the best in the world, and by far."

In November 2003, Herxheimer and Medawar had a meeting with Dr. Metters, plus two members of a belatedly appointed advisory panel. Denying knowledge of any attempt to suppress Yellow Card data, Dr. Metters led an interesting and apparently quite productive discussion on a range of issues, almost all of which departed from his terms of reference. Later enquiries to the MHRA, produced this worryingly reassuring response:

"Please don't be concerned at the wide ranging discussions we had. It is very important to take this opportunity to consider all aspects of the Yellow Card scheme, however far removed they may seem from the precise terms of reference of the independent Review. It is vital that the role of the scheme in protecting public health is not threatened by any new proposals, and if possible it should be enhanced." (MHRA 2003)

The tone of this email signalled some thaw. By this time, the gravity of the situation was sinking in on both sides of the fence. *Social Audit* had come closer to believing that the Yellow Card review might conceivably lead to improvements, and that CSM Working Group on SSRIs had picked up the scent – and it was clear that both enquiries had difficult issues to confront. At the same time, perhaps the authorities began to see they could use support in finding solutions. Hostilities nervously declined.

In its own time, and strictly by instalments, the MHRA did send *Social Audit* the further data requested on the other SSRIs. The first thing to arrive was the simple tabulation from the Yellow Card database of the top 20 drugs (of all kinds) suspected of causing suicidal behaviour.

---

21 "Calls for a major review of the United Kingdom's 'yellow card' system for monitoring drug safety were headed off by a government announcement that an inquiry into the system was under way ... taking the wind out of the experts' sails ... a Department of Health press spokesman said, they had had a number of requests for such data and 'No one request has driven this review'."

The big five SSRIs featured prominently; all were ranked in the top ten in each of five categories: accomplished suicide, attempted suicide, suicidal ideation, non-accidental overdose and overdose NOS. In each of these categories, paroxetine was in the top three, with fluoxetine and venlafaxine never far away. Andrew Herxheimer then compiled a table that seemed to reveal another remarkable thing. Yellow Card reports about "suicidal ideation" were a commonplace for SSRIs and related drugs[22] – but unheard of, either with tricyclic antidepressants or antipsychotics. Here was another piece of the jigsaw, but where did it fit in? At the time of writing, no-one knows.

Towards 2004

As 2003 drew to a close, it felt like a decent moment to step back from the SSRI story, to pause for breath, take stock and see what the Working Group and *Panorama* would make of it. By this time, *Panorama* was contemplating a third programme about Seroxat – three in a row would be some sort of record – with more focus proposed this time on the quality of drug regulation.

From the other side of the fence, expectations of the CSM Working Group were very low. There was a mountain of data to take on board, giants to confront, reputations to protect, national interests to take into account, and delicate, sensitive issues to explore. However much some individuals might want to grapple with the issues, it was hard to imagine that the official process would not defeat them.

> "Something of the problem was evident from the MIND press release, published on the same day (September 19) as the new DoH/MHRA warning about the risks of venlafaxine for under 18-year olds. The director of MIND, Richard Brook – a member of the CSM Working Group – was quoted in the press release in no uncertain terms: MIND had the 'deepest concerns about the way psychiatric drugs are regulated in the UK. We want to see urgent action to question how drugs are regulated and licenced and how clinical trials are carried out and reported as part of this process'."

Whatever the Working Group comes up with, and however much its members want to get at the truth, it seems bound to fall short of what needs to be done. Dependence and suicidality were only two of the problems with SSRIs.[23] Many users had

---

22 Venlafaxine, bupropion, mirtazepine and nefazodone.

23 Bristol-Myers Squibb withdrew nefazodone (Dutonin, Serzone) from the European market in January 2003, because of serious liver toxicity problems. The Food and Drug Administration (FDA) allowed it to remain on the US market, with added warnings, in spite of this. See Health Research Group petition (Barbehenn 2003).

other problems, sometimes severe – especially mood changes, loss of libido and weight gain – and the neurological implications and clinical significance of the "electric head" phenomenon had never been explained.[24] Moreover, concerns about the risks of long-term use had barely been investigated, and long-term drug effectiveness was in question too. The risk of drug sensitisation needed investigation (Fava et al. 2003), as did the evidence of drug tolerance ("poop out") during treatment – and the tendency to increase dosage (Goldberg & Kocsis 1996) or use "therapy augmentation" to counteract it.[25] In addition, basic problems to do with drug dosage and concentrations remained unaddressed, and little was known about tuning dosage to genetically determined differences and individual needs. Even so, there were proposals to make SSRIs available off prescription.[26]

For all such uncertainties, towards the end of 2003, one could imagine the beginning of some end to the SSRI story, and even some aftermath. As this narrative draws to a close it seems as if, on the Richter or Beaufort scales of drug crisis, the SSRIs rank somewhere between 7 and 11, where thalidomide ranks 10.[27] The thalidomide crisis will always be unique because of the innocence of the victims and the sudden, shocking evidence of harm. But thalidomide happened because there was no independent control of drug safety – whereas the SSRI crisis had grown under the *aegis* of an elaborate and expensive global system of drug control.

It was no part of the Working Group's remit to examine whether or how the system failed, and the firm intention not to examine the causes of the SSRI crisis was underlined by the role of Professor Breckenridge, Chairman of the MHRA. Ironically, because his personal integrity was never in doubt, no-one seemed to notice the political sensitivities involved.

---

24 "We do not have evidence of long term neurological or clinical implications of the electric shock sensations that are experienced on withdrawal of SSRIs. The present expert working group on SSRIs includes neurological expertise and ... the wording in the SPC and PIL is currently under review". Letter from Dr. J.M. Raine, Director, MCA Post Licensing Division, to Social Audit, 7 January 2003.

25 "Therapy augmentation" is a ritual in psychiatric drug prescribing, used to prop-up the effects of the main drug as they wear off. The objective is not to increase the main drug dosage, but to achieve the same effect by adding another, "booster" drug to the regimen. The extent of this practice is unknown, and it goes largely unaudited, but a significant literature exists on the subject and a range of auxiliary drugs has been tried alongside SSRIs.

26 "Psychotropic medications ... vary widely in their safety. Some of the most widely prescribed, however, are some of the safest. It has often been said that SSRIs are remarkably safe medications with side-effect profiles as benign as most over-the-counter medications and very wide therapeutic indexes. Overdoses of many current over-the-counter medications are far more dangerous. Could they be sold over the counter?" (Thomas A. M. Kramer, MD, Associate Professor of Psychiatry, University of Chicago, Posted 13 November 2003 to http://www.medscape.com/viewarticle/ 463920). *Medscape General Medicine* 5(4) 2003.

27 C. Medawar, No Bridge Too Far, *MIND OUT*, September 2003.

The CSM Working Group on the safety of SSRIs, and the DoH review of access to Yellow Card data, were running in parallel – with the findings of both due to arrive on Professor Breckenridge's desk early in 2004. A key issue would be how Breckenridge responded and how others regarded his involvement in the problems to be revealed.

The CSM/MHRA Working Group report seemed bound to acknowledge many problems and that much had gone wrong, and that might put Breckenridge in a difficult position. He was a central figure in the development of this crisis. He had close links with the manufacturers of Seroxat and they went back a long way: he had quit as a member of the SmithKline Beecham Advisory Board in 1999 to become Chairman of the Committee on Safety of Medicines (to April 2003). Between 1997 and 1999, he had also chaired the CSM's Sub-committee on Pharmacovigilance; it was directly responsible for the Yellow Card scheme, and had led the 1998 review in response to "The Antidepressant Web". At the time, Breckenridge disclosed the possible conflicts, but his colleagues put the issue aside.

> "Professor Breckenridge declared a personal non-specific interest in SmithKline Beecham. The Committee decided this paper was a general discussion about the class of SSRIs and not a discussion about the individual drugs. Therefore Professor Breckenridge should continue to chair this item." (CSM/SCOP minutes, 24 February 1998)

As a reflection on the individual, that seemed entirely appropriate, but to take regulatory action on such a basis did not. It overlooked the need to be seen to be independent; it took little account of commercial realities; and it disregarded the MCA/CSM's previous finding, that paroxetine was by far the most troublesome of the SSRIs (Price et al. 1996).

And the climate would have changed by the time Breckenridge re-visited the problem, in early 2004. As the first chairman of the MHRA, he had become more exposed as a high-profile regulatory figurehead. The problem had moved on too: complainants now formed a critical mass, huge legal liabilities loomed,[28] questions of propriety were in the air, and there seemed to be compelling evidence of avoidable harm.

Is it conceivable that the US Congress and the UK and European and other parliaments will just let this all pass by? Will they allow public servants and institutions

---

28 By mid-2003, The leading UK legal action – endlessly frustrated by lack of Legal Aid and government non-cooperation – was on behalf of 6,500 claimants, members of the Seroxat Action Group. The action was led by Mark Harvey of Hugh James Solicitors, Cardiff (www.hjfs.co.uk).

The number of prospective claimants in the US litigation was unknown: actions proceeded at state level and were typically run on a test case basis, in the names of a relatively small, representative sample of claimants. See: http://www.baumhedlundlaw. com/Paxil/paxilupdate.htm2

with vested interests to investigate all their own mistakes? How long can it be before there is an honest, open, thorough, independent investigation into this critical state of affairs? That remains to be seen; the story will continue on *ADWEB*: www.socialaudit.org.uk

Discussion

Doing more with less

This case history focused on drugs for mental distress, notably SSRIs, but it explains something of the style and impact of other drugs as well. Though pharmacologically distinctive, the SSRIs have much in common with other leading drug brands. All these products go through the same mill. At any one point in time, they are tested, approved, recommended, marketed, regulated, prescribed, promoted and consumed in much the same way.

The SSRI story reveals something of a system and culture at work. The culture is modelled on a system dominated and increasingly driven by the Pharmas and their dynamic allies in the Conspiracy of Goodwill. In a word, this system is "tainted": there are not only countless reasons to celebrate what medicine has achieved and what it stands for, but also countless reasons not to.

How much more tainted will medicine become, and how damaging would that be in a turbulent world, ever more dependent on both licit and illicit drug solutions?[29] The need for a systematic review of the relationship between medicine and health seems all the more urgent, with medicine increasingly driven by global trade imperatives and at the start of an age of designing life itself.

---

29 This case history rather exaggerated the point, but the relationship between licit and illicit drug use seems nothing like as clear-cut as the law would suggest. From alcohol onwards, almost all these drugs made the transition from over-enthusiastic prescribing to drugs of abuse. Each time, the assumption was made that new was better than old and, over the years, the nub of the debate did not change. This was the key question, time and again: where was the dividing line between consuming drugs to dispel dysphoria or to promote euthymia or euphoria? (Dysphoria: "Inappropriate affect, usually used in association with anxiety, restlessness, depression"; Euphoria: "A sense of extreme elation generally accompanied by optimism and a deep sense of well-being and heightened activity"; Euthymia: "Tranquillity, a pleasant related state" (*Penguin Dictionary of Psychology* 1985). One may wonder about the extent to which the explosive increase in illicit drug use and alcohol consumption in the last quarter of the 20th century may have been influenced by legitimate, subtle and relentless advancement of the idea that drugs solved the problems of life. The growth of that idea suggests possibilities for drug education focused on simple pharmacological issues, to provide the basis of what everyone needs to know about the actions and effects of drugs of all kinds.

Medicine now has the whole human genome to explore, but still operates as an "open loop" system – a primitive and inadequate system, in engineering terms. The lack of a "control loop", connecting output to input, signals major structural weakness. In this case, gross errors resulted from not listening to patients and not properly investigating professional adverse drug reaction reports.[30] This waste of intelligence, coupled with endemic secrecy and pervasive and intrusive marketing, led to systematic misunderstanding and misrepresentation of benefit and risk.

In this case history, commercial and official secrecy proved a major and enduring vector of ill-health. Secrets hid the truth and made public accountability impossible; it corrupted understanding about what medicines could and couldn't do. This secrecy was self-reinforcing. It promoted "ignorance of ignorance" – widespread misunderstanding about how much ignorance there was. Nothing much will change, until this vicious circle is broken: it would mean investigating and treating secrecy as a disease of power and a disfigurement of medical science.[31]

Truth emerges when nothing is hidden. In this case history, it always emerged too late, and never in sufficient concentrations to ensure that the same mistakes weren't repeated, time and again. That tradition continues: the great bulk of the hard data remains hidden, and most of what is published is positioned to sway. The SSRI years liberated the tendency to bombard the community with images of benefit, while always softening the picture of risk. The crisis that emerged captured exactly the difference between the words of patients who speak their minds and the formal terminologies that blunted meanings and minced words.

The 1990s saw "depression" formally redefined as a serotonin-deficiency disease and the scourge of millions – a convenient, seductive, and deeply simplistic view. The term, drug "dependence" was redefined, to propose that loss of personal autonomy could never arise in a therapeutic setting, but only when the behaviour of patients signalled abuse. The ubiquitous term, "discontinuation symptoms" – *newspeak* for withdrawal symptoms – implied that antidepressants carried no risk of dependence.[32] Wishful thinking proposed "discontinuation symptoms" as evidence of the effectiveness of vital remedies, important for reducing maybe life-threatening

---

30 CM writes: As this book approaches publishing deadlines, I regret there has not yet been space and time to fully comprehend the model interpretation of paroxetine ADRs proposed by Graham Aldred. He is a retired engineer who believes (as Healy, I and others do) that he lost his wife, Rhona, to Seroxat. Graham Aldred's great loss prompted him to develop a logic-based model that challenged to its foundations the assumptions underlying the operation and interpretation of the Yellow Card scheme. This too is for 2004, and beyond.

31 A disease? "An alteration in the state of the body or of some of its organs, interrupting or disturbing the performance of the vital functions, and causing or threatening pain and weakness; malady; affection; illness; sickness; disorder; – applied figuratively to the mind, to the moral character and habits, to institutions" (*Webster's Revised Unabridged Dictionary* 1996, 1998). The reference to secrecy as a disfigurement of science comes from Medawar P.B. (1979).

risks. Users clearly described the incapacitating effects of electric shock sensations in the head and problems with eyes, but these were translated into terms like "dizziness" and "paraesthesia" and their significance ignored. The regulators were largely complicit in all this: they themselves described uninvestigated reports of apparent suicide as "non-accidental overdose". The regulators claimed science was on their side, yet they lived with terms like, "emotional lability" that failed to distinguish even between a drug-induced suicide and an outburst of tears.

If there is a silver lining to this emerging crisis, it is that users' experiences with drugs cannot credibly be ignored, ever again. In this case, users collectively provided evidence that proved more reliable than the data from numerous published clinical trials. Evidence of this was notable in GlaxoSmithKline's upward revision of the incidence of paroxetine withdrawal reactions – from 0.2% to 25% between 2002 and 2003. Margins of optimism of the same order applied to "scientifically determined" and officially approved dosages. They were set at levels that exposed many users to higher drugs doses than they needed and therefore to increased risks.[33]

Sometimes, the better course may be exactly the opposite of what one is inclined (and/or led) to think or do. The slavish emphasis on drug innovation is a case in point. It chronically distracts from the need to do more and better with what there already is. This case history underlined that point: from a health standpoint, desisting and intervening less would have achieved far more than the added value of drug innovation. This lesson has yet to be learned:

> "We do have some science in the practice of medicine, but not anything like enough. And although we have achieved, through the application of science, a degree of mastery over many infectious diseases formerly responsible for great numbers of premature deaths, the introduction of science into medicine did not really begin with the management of infection. Long before that event, some time in the middle of the nineteenth century, medicine showed its first signs of scientific insight by undergoing quite a different sort of professional transformation. It stopped doing some things." (Thomas 1979)

Mass marketing, global standardisation and the pressures of life itself tend to blind us to the possibility that small can be beautiful and that less may mean more. More information doesn't necessarily mean greater understanding and it tends to bury quality.

---

32 GlaxoSmithKline (Benbow A., CBC-TV, October 2003) appeared to stop using the term "discontinuation" in late 2003, referring to "Symptoms on Stopping" instead.

33 What dosing strategy might make sense, when it is clear that maybe one in ten users is unusually sensitive to a drug's effects – but without knowing who they were? One solution might be to require manufacturers to supply all such drugs in a dosage form corresponding to the minimum effective dosage for 10% of prospective users. Then doctors wouldn't need to prescribe full-strength drugs to all-comers, where a safer "test dose" might well work well.

Having more drugs, faster, may not do much for health, any more than higher doses do – and beyond limits, disease awareness may not help at all. The failure to take stock of such things now threatens to turn pharmaceutical medicine into something of a polluting enterprise, deeply damaging to the atmosphere of health. This may seem far-fetched, but then so does global warming to the driver of your average car.

First principles of reform

The nub of the antidepressant crisis is not that the SSRIs could do so much harm but how they were allowed to, especially when the precedents seemed so plain. If and when this crisis is ever properly investigated, it will raise questions about what medicine is and should be. This case history showed up alarming flaws in the evaluation, regulation and use of medicines, so basic and embedded as to suggest some deepening rift between the forces that drive medicine and health.

From a democratic perspective, the spirit of medicine seems sick. Some two and a half thousand years ago, even before the founding of some of the dominant religions of today, Hippocrates envisioned the embryo of Western medicine as both a scientific and democratic enterprise. He saw it as a system of honest enquiry, respectful of nature and patients alike. The objective was to learn how to alleviate human suffering and above all to do no harm.

Hippocrates exemplified the point of medicine. He gets only a passing mention in this story, but his standing as a figurehead compares to that of a prophet. He was a physician, surgeon and teacher, the founder of a school of medicine and the author of many of its writings.[34] In the words of one modern medical encyclopedia, Hippocrates gave medicine its soul: "The content of the(se) books, the wealth of original observation, the unerring sense of what is relevant, would set them among the great works of genius. What makes them unique is the spirit in which they are written. They establish for all time how medicine ought to be practised and what doctors should try to be" (Wingate 1996).

It seems to speak for the resilience of the human body, and the proper place of medicine, that our forebears knew that the natural human lifespan was around 70 years.[35] The great leap towards three score years and ten was not mainly due to advances in medical treatment.[36] This widely held view has resulted "from failure to distinguish clearly between the activities of the doctor and the outcome for the patient, a common error in the interpretation of medical history" (McKeown 1988). Until the mid-20th century, the advancement of health resulted mainly from adequate nutrition, clean water and shelter – the outcome of social and political reform rather than medical intervention.

In developed countries, between 1870 and 1970, life expectancy at birth rose from around 40 to 70 years. This norm applied in countries with very different health systems: life expectancy at birth in the United States, Great Britain and the USSR in 1967, for example was 70.5, 71.6 and 70 years respectively. In the US, life expectancy is now of the order of 10% higher, notwithstanding a ten-fold increase in spending on healthcare and drugs, and a doubling in the number of doctors.[37]

---

34 Hippocrates defined medicine as an art and a calling. He denounced exploitation and superstition, distinguishing doctors from priests and sorcerers – as human observers, counsellors and servants of the sick. The need for accountability was fundamental to the practice of medicine Hippocrates had in mind. It extended to the doctor-patient relationship. Hippocrates pronounced that a doctor had failed if he could not explain, even to the "illiterate vulgar". "Whoever treats of this art should treat of things which are familiar to common people. For of nothing else will such a one have to inquire or treat, but of the diseases under which the common people have laboured – which diseases, and the causes of their origin and departure, illiterate persons cannot easily find out for themselves. But it is still easy for them to understand these things when discovered and expounded by others, for it is nothing more than that everyone is put in mind of what has occurred to himself. But whoever does not reach the capacity of the illiterate vulgar and fails to make them listen to him, misses his mark" (Wingate 1996).

Medicine lost sight of Hippocratic ideals, as tidal waves of religion brought new and backward-looking ideas. The leaders of the new orders appropriated and systematically perverted medicine, creating vast amounts of ill-health as they did so. Underlying their beliefs was the idea that the human body was the property of a divine being, and that it was up to his most important representatives on earth to decide how to treat it. For centuries thereafter, these no doubt well-meaning mal-practitioners developed to extremes the practice of blaming patients. Mental illness was interpreted as possession by the devil and treatment was severe and cruel as a result. Routine torture and explicit punishment stopped years ago, though neglect and ill-treatment of mental patients is still commonplace in many countries (O. Thorold, Personal communication [CM], 2000-2003) and the tendency to hold patients responsible for treatment failures still seems strong.

35 "The days of our age are threescore years and ten; and though men be so strong that they come to fourscore years: yet is their strength then but labour and sorrow; so soon passeth it away, and we are gone" (Psalm 90, The Bible).

36 "In general, medical measures (both chemotherapeutic and prophylactic) appear to have contributed little to the overall decline in mortality in the United States since about 1900 – having in many cases been introduced several decades after a marked decline had already set in and mostly having no detectable influence. More specifically, with reference to those five conditions (influenza, pneumonia, diphtheria, whooping cough, and poliomyelitis) for which the decline in mortality appears substantial after the point of intervention – and on the unlikely assumption that all of this decline is attributable to the intervention – it is estimated that at most 3.5% of the total decline in mortality since 1900 could be described to medical measures introduced for the diseases considered here" (McKinley & McKinley 1977).

37 Source: US life expectancy at birth (both sexes, all races); Data based on the National Vital Statistics System, from Table 28, Health, United States, 2000, page 160. Data on number of doctors from Table 103, Health, United States, 2000, p.307. US health expenditure data compiled by OECD, from Table 114, Health, United States, 2000, page 321. Expenditure on pharmaceutical goods from OECD Health Data 2001. R&D investment data from Pharmaceutical Research and Manufacturers of America, Backgrounder, January 1998, accessed September 2001 at www.phrma.org/publications/backgrounders/development/spending.phtml

The huge investment in medicine made in the second half of the 20th century led to great improvements in standards of treatment and levels of understanding, but with relatively smaller gains in general levels of health. Meanwhile, the cost of Medicine and medicines became increasingly unaffordable, raising public outcry in the richest and poorest countries alike.

Year	*US life expectancy at birth (years)*	*US health spend (as % of GDP)*	*US health spend (US$ per capita)*	*US pharma companies' research spend (US$ bn)*	*US spend on pharmaceuticals etc (US$ bn)*	*Number of active doctors of medicine (thousands)*
1970	70.8	7.1	341	1.0	42.3	311
1980	73.7	8.9	1,052	2.0	95.7	415
1990	75.4	12.2	2,689	8.4	247.4	547
1997	76.5	13.4	3,912	18.6	375.5	665

For all the astonishing progress made, the grip of market values and the dominant US influence in the global development of Pharmaceutical Medicine, now presents even developed countries with major problems. Overall health expenditure in the US costs twice as much per head as the average for the 15 member countries of the European Union. The US model would be unaffordable and unsuitable in any country committed to community-based health.

Measured in terms of quality of care, the US may be unbeatable. But in terms of investment and basic health output, the US appears to offer outstandingly poor health value for money. The following table, based on World Health Organization (WHO) data,[38] compares the health spend in different countries, all with higher than US levels of "health attainment".

---

38 Source: Statistical Annex, Tables 5, 8, *The World Health Report 2000,* (Geneva, World Health Organization, May 2000), pp. 176-182, 192-195. Omitted: Malta (70.5 years – US$755/head), Andorra (72.3 – US$1,216), San Marino (72.3 – US$1,301), Monaco (72.4 – US$1,799). These WHO data refer to Disability Adjusted Life Expectancy (DALE). "To calculate DALE, the years of ill-health are weighted according to severity and subtracted from the expected overall life expectancy to give the equivalent years of healthy life." Thus "DALE summarises the expected number of years to be lived (for babies born in 1999) in what might be termed the equivalent of 'full health'."

Country	*Total health expenditure in international dollars/head*	*Disability-adjusted life-expectancy (overall years)*
Greece	964	72.5
United Kingdom	1,193	71.7
Spain	1,211	72.8
Israel	1,402	70.4
Finland	1,539	70.5
Australia	1,601	73.2
Norway	1,708	71.7
Belgium	1,738	71.6
Iceland	1,757	70.8
Japan	1,759	74.5
Italy	1,824	72.7
Canada	1,836	72.0
Netherlands	1,911	72.0
Sweden	1,943	73.0
Luxembourg	1,985	71.1
France	2,125	73.1
Germany	2,365	70.4
Switzerland	2,644	72.5
US	3,724	70.0

These data suggest a trend of ever-greater investment producing strong financial returns and diminishing health outputs. This underlines a tough reality: important innovations are hard to procure and correspondingly rare, and becoming prohibitively expensive. The Pharmas' put the average cost of developing each new drug at close to US$1 billion, which means it costs upwards of perhaps US$5 billion to develop one important new drug. This seems a madness, when the whole African drug market was valued at US$5.3 billion in 2002 (Inpharm, July 2003).

It is essential here to distinguish between what it costs the Pharmas to innovate, and what innovation might otherwise cost. Good evidence suggests that truly vital drugs might be developed for a fraction of what it costs the Pharmas to produce them. For example, an analysis of the economics of drug development for tuberculosis funded by the Rockefeller Foundation projected "a total cost of between $115 million and $240 million to discover and develop a new anti-TB drug (including the costs of failure)".[39]

Market-driven models of medicine present huge problems in developing countries, impossible dilemmas too. Poorer countries could meet almost – but not all – basic health needs without new, branded drugs. The great and important exceptions are effective treatments for HIV/AIDS, and notably those developed by GlaxoSmithKline. These are the only branded Essential Drugs, vital for tens of millions of people, and effective medicines for other illnesses are badly needed too. So the value of new drugs may be great: on the other hand, billions spent on marginal advances seems unconscionable, with upwards of 750 million people in need of essential health interventions that would cost less than US$40 per year (WHO 2001).[40]

The cost and complexities of drug innovation have put the Pharmas under great pressure and they naturally turn to marketing and harder selling to fit the gap. Their very size now dictates a dominant trend in new products rather than genuine innovation, to appeal predominantly to chronic users in affluent markets. The Pharmas steer innovation and treatment values towards recognition of such need.

Health for one and all?

The current emphasis on drug innovation seems to link two major world health problems: under-medication and over-medication. Trade imperatives squeeze access to essential medicines; at the same time they focus health priorities on drug solutions for the problems of life.

The current emphasis on drug solutions and innovation seems perverse. It is turning medicine away from the solution of health problems, towards routine life management, social support, diagnostic labeling and medical intervention.[41] With the emphasis overwhelmingly on treatment, user dependencies are increased and investigation of the causes of ill-health is overlooked. What causes so much depres-

---

39 "Without considering the costs of failure (see below), the costs of successfully developing an NCE for TB have been estimated to total approximately $36.8 million to $39.9 million (US costs). This estimated range covers preclinical development ($4.9 million and $5.3 million), pharmaceutical development (at least $5.3 million), and Phases I through III of clinical development ($26.6 million). These efforts are designed to reach regulatory approval. The investment required depends on the extent to which the sponsor of the development effort partners with other organisations ...

"Estimates of the costs of developing an NCE based on this method to include the costs of failure are approximately $76 million to $115 million for preclinical development through Phase III trials and regulatory approval. These estimates do not include the costs of discovery, which are estimated to range from $40 million to $125 million (including the costs of failure). As suggested by the breadth of this range, discovery costs are difficult to estimate. Even so, one can use these rough estimates of discovery and the estimated costs of development calculated for this report to project a total cost of between $115 million and $240 million to discover and develop a new anti-TB drug (including the costs of failure)." Global Alliance for TB Drug Development, *The Economics of TB Drug Development* 2001. http://66.216.124.114/pdf/Economics%20Report%20Full%20(final).pdf

40 A European cow receives US$2 a day – US$730 per year – in agricultural subsidies (Brown 2003). US subsidies per cow unknown.

sion these days: the wrong molecules, or the impossibility of reconciling more and more euphoric expectations with the pressures of global life?

Now we all lead global lives. Individually, we cannot help feeling the effects of war, terrorism, oppression, corruption, greed, instability, poverty, misery, stress, unhappiness and ill-health. They have become an inescapable part of our own lives; they come closer and closer to home.

We allow ourselves to be counted increasingly as winners or losers; and money rules more and more. Collectively, we still nourish the illusion that mass marketing brings out the rugged individuality in each of us – so there can be no limits to dissatisfaction with personal health. But superlative health makes no sense as a health objective for any community: when there are no health losers, everyone wins. Meanwhile, the clamour for health feels sickening and it makes no sense either. Just the length of waiting lists confirms this: the more everyone else makes demands on health services, the less there will always be for you.

The moral of this story is that medicine can produce health only when conducted within a framework of honest science and decent democratic values. The remedy can only be to inject Medicine with a heroic dose of common and democratic sense. The test of this accomplishment will have much to do with the future of the Pharmas in their present shape.

What will happen to the Pharmas of today? On present form, probably most will be absorbed into mega-Pharmas and they will gravitate to the US. The survivors will increasingly evolve not as centers of drug innovation, but as investment institutions and drug marketing organisations. The Pharmas already finance most clinical research and communication and, so long as they survive, they will increasingly do so. Will the Pharmas survive? To the extent that they are well protected, probably yes. Are they impregnable? No. The Pharmas seem quite vulnerable, to the extent they have enjoyed great privileges and protections, buying favours instead of addressing the many problems they create. They have become far too large for their own good, or ours. They are also extremely sensitive to political conditions: in a global climate, the risks increase that they will be perceived as instruments of market forces, not

---

41 "Something strange is happening in American medicine. No longer is it being used merely to cure illness. Medicine is now being used in the pursuit of happiness. In America, we take Viagra at bedtime and Ritalin before work. We inject Botox into our wrinkled brows and rub Rogaine on our balding heads. We swallow Paxil for shyness, Prozac for grief, and Buspar for anxiety. For stage fright we use beta blockers; for excessive blushing and sweating, we get endoscopic surgery. We ask surgeons to trim down our noses, suck fat from our thighs, transform us from men to women, even amputate our healthy arms and legs in the pursuit of what some people believe to be their true selves. Twenty years ago, most doctors said no. Now many have changed their minds" (Elliot 2003).

only a blessing but also a curse on health. The Pharmas' impaired inability to understand or acknowledge such problems could prove self-destructive in the extreme.

The rest goes almost without saying. Wonderful drugs are wonderful – but worthless without access in the face of dire health need. The same goes for medical science – glorious at best, but debased by secrecy and spin. It is time to close the open loop in Medicine and to respond to real need as never before.

True, your health reflects your uniqueness as an individual – as does your ability to negotiate life, and your body's response to specific drugs. On the other hand, what you experience of the quality of medicine and medicines is overwhelmingly decided by institutional and community standards and behaviour, and by other factors beyond your immediate control.

Personal health is overwhelmingly predicted by the health and well-being of others – by their example, attitudes, traditions and behaviour. Your health and well-being depend ultimately on community: just as you benefit if other people don't sneeze or smoke, so you gain if they are well looked after, reasonably well contented and aren't oppressed, intoxicated, distressed or consume to extremes. Increasingly in future, we are all in this together: no one escapes when other people feel ill or are impoverished, desperate, miserable or insecure.

Are medicines out of control? The question reflects concerns about endemic and pathogenic institutional secrecy; rampant conflicts of interest; systematic manipulation of 'scientific' evidence and perversion of understanding; the marginalisation of dissenting, inconvenient and unwanted views; official indifference to essential and valuable evidence from patients; the rising dominance of trade imperatives and the sickening promotion of disease awareness; the emphasis on pharmaceutical innovation as the source of health solutions; the size and cost of the Pharmas in relation to their health value; the inadequacy of self-regulation and lack of democratic accountability – and the consequences of all this for health for one and all. These and related issues will be further explored on www.socialaudit.org.uk

References

ABC-TV "Primetime" program: Influencing doctors – How pharmaceutical companies use enticement to 'educate' physicians, 21 February 2002.

ABPI – Association of the British Pharmaceutical Industry, Code of Practice for the Pharmaceutical Industry, 1st edition, 1958–2003.

— *Compendium of Data Sheets and Summaries of Product Characteristics* 1974-2000, London: Datapharm publications.

ABPI spokesman, Richard Lay, quoted in Meek C., Fraud & misconduct in medical research, *Health Which?* December 2001, 21-24.

— Press Release: European proposals on medicines information for public flawed, says ABPI, 25 June 2002.

— Press Release, Audit report on regulatory authority welcomed by industry, 16 January 2003.

— Press release, Guidance on disease awareness campaigns, 24 April 2003.

— Mission statement, www.abpi.org.uk 2003.

Abraham J., Sheppard J., *The Therapeutic Nightmare: the battle over the world's most controversial sleeping pill*, London: Earthscan, 1999.

Agelink M.W., Zitselsberger A., Kleiser E., Withdrawal symptoms after discontinuation of Venlafaxine (letter), *Am. J. Psychiatry*, 154, **10**, October 1997, 1473-1474.

Aitken M., Holt F., A prescription for direct drug marketing, *The McKinsey Quarterly*, 22 March 2000, 82.

"Alaniz13" – Message board response, posted 10:16 PST, 24 February 2002 in response to ABC-TV "Primetime" program, 2002.

Alexander E.J., Withdrawal effects of sodium amytal, *Dis. Nerv. Sys*, 1951, **12**, 77-82.

AMA – American Medical Association, Health literacy: Report of the Council on Scientific Affairs, *JAMA*, 1999, **281**, 552-557.

American Psychiatric Association, *Diagnostic and Statistical Manual of Mental Disorders*, 3rd edition, Washington DC: APA, 1980.

— Task Force on Benzodiazepine Dependency. *Benzodiazepine Dependence, Toxicity, and Abuse.* Washington DC: APA, 1990.

— *Diagnostic and Statistical Manual of Mental Disorders*, 4th edition, Washington DC: APA, 1994.

— (Online public information), *Electroconvulsive Therapy (ECT)*, published April 1997 at http://www.psych.org/public-info/ECT~1.HTM

Amsden G.W., Georgian F., Orthostatic hypotension induced by sertraline withdrawal, *Pharmacotherapy*, 1996, **16**, 4, 684-686.

Anderson I.M., Tomenson, B.M., Treatment discontinuation with selective serotonin reuptake inhibitors compared with tricyclic anti-depressants: a meta-analysis. *Brit Med J* 1995; **310**, 3 June: 1433-8.

Angell M., Is academic medicine for sale? *N Engl J Med* 2000, 18 May; 342: 1516-1518.

— Conversation: Open science or junk science, *The American Prospect,* 2000 June 5, **14**, 11.
Angell M., Relman A. S., Prescription for profit, *Washington Post,* 20 June 2001, Page A27.
Anstie F.E, Physiological and therapeutical action of alcohol, *Lancet,* 23 September 1865, 343.
Antonuccio D.O., Danton W.G., DeNelsky G.Y., Greenberg R.P., Gordon J.S., Raising questions about antidepressants, *Psychotherapy and Psychosomatics* 1999, 68: 1, 3-14.
Appleton W.S., *Prozac and the new antidepressants,* New York: Plum, 1997.
D'Arcy P. F., Epidemiological aspects of iatrogenic disease, in D'Arcy P.F. & Griffin J.P. (eds), *Iatrogenic Diseases* (3rd Ed), Oxford: OUP, 1986), 29-58.
Arlington S., *Pharma 2005: The challenges, presentation to the American Society for Clinical Pharmacology and Therapeutics,* PriceWaterhouseCoopers, 2001.
Arno P., Davis M., Paying twice for the same drugs, *Washington Post,* 27 March 2002, A21.
Arya D.K., Withdrawal after discontinuation of paroxetine (letter), *Aust NZ J Psychiatry,* October 1996, **30** (5), 702.
Åsberg M., Schalling D., Traskman-Bendz L., Wagner A., Psychobiology of suicide, impulsivity, and related phenomena, in Melzer H.Y. (ed.), *Psychopharmacology: the third generation of progress,* New York: Raven Press, 1987, 655-668.
Ashton H., Dangers and medico-legal aspects of benzodiazepines, *J. Med. Defence Union,* Summer 1987, 6-8.
Asch S., Effects of Group Pressure Upon the Modification and Distortion of Judgments. In Harold S. Guetzkow (ed.), *Groups, Leadership and Men.* New York: Russell and Russell, 1963, pp. 177-190.
Ashton H., Young A.H., Ferrier N., Psychopharmacology revisited, (comment on Healy and Tranter, 1999) *J Psychopharmacol.*, 1999, **13** (3), 296-298.
Asscher W.A., Strategy of risk-benefit analysis, in D'Arcy P.F., Griffin J.P. (eds) 1986, 108-116.
— Statement made at a meeting organised by the Campaign for Freedom of Information (Committee room 6, House of Commons) 29 April 1993.
Atlanta Journal-Constitution: Editorial: Drugmakers' cash packs wallop, 14 October 2002, cited at www.bamcoalition.org/News/HW/10.14.02.htm
Ayd F.J., *Recognising the Depressed Patient, with Essentials of Management and Treatment,* New York, Grune, 1961.
— The discovery of antidepressants, interview with D. Healy in *The Psychopharmacologists,* London: Chapman & Hall (Altman), 1996, 179.
— *Lexicon for Psychiatry, Neurology and Neuroscience,* Williams & Wilkins, Baltimore, 1996(b).
Baer L., Ricciardi J., Keuthen N., Pettit A.R., Buttolph M.L., Otto M., Minichiello W., Jenike M.A., Discontinuing obsessive-compulsive disorder medication with behavior therapy (letter), *Am. J. Psychiatry,* December 1994, **151** (12), 1842.
Baglole J., FDA effort to halt drugs from Canada stirs uproar, *Wall Street Journal,* 13 March 2003.
Bain & Co., Has the pharmaceutical blockbuster model gone bust? Reposted in *Business Wire* (New York), 8 December 2003.
Bakker A., Severe withdrawal symptoms with fever upon stopping paroxetine (letter, in Dutch), *Ned Tijdschr Geneeskd,* 28 August 1999, **143** (35), 1795, discussion 1795-6.

Baldessarini R.J., Drugs and the treatment of psychiatric disorders, in Goodman L.S., Gilman A. (eds), *The Pharmacological Basis of Therapeutics* (6th Edition). New York: Macmillan, 1980, 435.

— Viguera A.C., Tondo L., Discontinuing psychotropic agents, (comment on Healy and Tranter, 1999) *J Psychopharmacol.*, 1999, **13** (3), 292-293.

— Viguera A.C., Relapse of depressive symptoms after discontinuing sertraline (letter, plus response), *JAMA*, July 28 1999, **282** (4), 323-324.

Ban T.A., They used to call it psychiatry, interview with D. Healy in *The Psychopharmacologists*, London: Chapman & Hall (Altman), 1996, 589.

Bangemann H. (European Commissioner: chair), Second Round Table, *Completing the Single Pharmaceutical Market*, Frankfurt, 8 December 1997.

Barbui C., Hotopf M., Forty years of antidepressant drug trials (review article), *Acta Psychiatr.* Scand, 2001, 104, 92-95.

Bardelay D., email to Ewen M., 8 April 2002.

Barr L.C., Goodman W.K., Price L.H., Physical symptoms associated with paroxetine discontinuation (letter). *Am J Psychiatry* 1994 Feb, **151** (2), 289.

Barsky A.J., The paradox of Health, *N Engl J Med.* 1988 Feb 18; **318** (7): 414-8.

Bass A., Drug companies enrich Brown Professor, *The Boston Globe*, 4 October 1999, A1.

Beaumont G., The place of clomipramine in psychopharmcology, interview with D. Healy in *The Psychopharmacologists*, London: Chapman & Hall (Altman), 1996, 327.

Beasley C.M.. Dornseif B.E., Bosomworth J.C., Sayler M.E., Rampey A.H., Heiligstein J.H. et al., Fluoxetine and suicide: a meta-analysis of controlled trials of treatment for depression, *Brit. Med. J*, 1991, **303**, 685-692.

Beasley C.M., Suicidality with fluoxetine, *CNS Drugs* 1998, **9**, 513-514.

Belkin L., Prime time pushers, *Mother Jones* , March/April 2001.

Belloeuf L., Le Jeunne C., Hugues F.C., Paroxetine withdrawal syndrome [Article in French], *Ann Med Interne (Paris)* 2000 Apr; 151 Suppl. A: A52-3.

Benazzi F., Venlafaxine withdrawal symptoms, *Can. J. Psychiatry*, September 1996, **41**, 487.

— SSRI discontinuation syndrome related to fluvoxamine, *J Psychiatry & Neuroscience*, 1998, 23, (2), 94.

— Nefazodone withdrawal symptoms, *Can. J. Psychiatry*, March 1998, **43**: 2, 194-195. – SSRI discontinuation syndrome treated with fluoxetine [letter], *Int J Geriatr Psychiatry* 1998 June, 13: 6, 421-2.

— Sertraline discontinuation syndrome presenting with severe depression and compulsions, *Biol. Psychiatry*, 1998, **43**, 929-930.

Bennett J.R. (Chairman, Campaign on the restriction and use of the barbiturates), Barbiturate Abuse, circular letter to doctors, May 1976.

Benson H., *Timeless Healing: The Power and Biology of Belief*, Simon and Schuster, 1996.

Berbehenn E., Lurie P., Stolley P., Wolfe S.M., Petition to the FDA to Ban the Antidepressant Drug Nefazodone (SERZONE), Health Research Group publication #1657, 6 March 2003.

Berlin C.S., Fluoxetine withdrawal symptoms. *J Clin Psychiatry* 1996 Feb, **57** (2), 93-4.

Berridge V., Professionalisation and narcotics: the medical and pharmaceutical professions and British narcotic use, 1868-1926. *Psychological Medicine*, 1978, **8**, 361-372.

Bhuamik S., Wildgust H.J., Treatment outcomes including withdrawal phenomena with fluoxetine and paroxetine in patients with learning disabilities suffering from affective disorders (letter), *Human Psychopharmacology*, 1996, **11**, 337-338.

Black D.W., Wesner R., Gabel J., The abrupt discontinuation of fluvoxamine in patients with panic disorder. *J Clin Psychiatry* 1993 Apr, **54** (4), 146-9.

Black K., Shea C., Dursun S., Kutcher S., Selective serotonin reuptake inhibitor discontinuation syndrome: proposed diagnostic criteria, *J Psychiatry Neuroscience*, 2000, **25** (3), 255-261.

Blacker R., Clare A., Depressive disorder in primary care, *Br. J. Psychiatry*, 1987, 150, 737-751.

Blackwell B., Simon J.S., Antidepressant Drugs, in M.N.G. Dukes (ed.), *Meyler's Side Effects of Drugs*, 11th ed., Amsterdam, Elsevier, 1988, 27-76.

Blair T., Speech on open government, Campaign for Freedom of Information's annual Awards ceremony, 25 March 1996.

— Foreword: PICTF, 2001.

Blau N., Time to let the patient speak, *BMJ* 1989 Jan 7; **298** (6665): 39.

Bloch M., Stager S.V., Braun A.R, Rubinow D.R, Severe psychiatric symptoms associated with paroxetine withdrawal. *Lancet* 1995 Jul 1, **346** (8966), 57.

Blomgren S.L., Krebs W., Wilson M., Ascroft R., Fava R.M., Rosenbaum J., SSRI Dose Interruption Study: Interim Data, *American Psychiatric Association, 150th-Annual-Meeting*, San-Diego, 1997.

BMJ (Anon), Today's drugs – Drugs of Addiction 2, *Brit. Med. J.*, 31 October 1964, 1119-1120.

— (Anon), Benzodiazepine addicts to sue, *Brit. Med. J.*, 26 January 1991, **302**, 2000.

BNF – Joint Formulary Committee, *British National Formulary*, London British Medical Association, Royal Pharmaceutical Society of Great Britain, published twice yearly.

Bodenheimer T. Uneasy alliance: clinical investigators and the pharmaceutical industry. *N Engl J Med* 2000; **342**:1539-1544.

— *Conflict of Interest in Clinical Drug Trials: A Risk Factor for Scientific Misconduct* (Department of Health and Human Services, Office for Human Research Protections, August 15, 2000), available at http://ohrp.osophs.dhhs.gov/coi/bodenheimer.htm

Bogetto F., Bellino S., Revello R.B., Patria L., Discontinuation syndrome in dysthymic patients with SSRIs: a clinical investigation, *CNS Drugs*, 2002, **16**, 4, 273-283.

Bohaychuck W., Ball G., *Conducting GCP Compliant Clinical Research* (Chichester and New York: Wiley, 1999).

Boseley S., Medical studies 'rubbish', *The Guardian*, 24 June 1998, 5.

— Drug firm asks public to insist NHS buys its product, *The Guardian*, 29 September 1999.

— Murder, suicide. A bitter aftertaste for the 'wonder' depression drug, *The Guardian*, 11 June 2001.

— Bitter pill, *The Guardian*, 21 May, 2002.

— Drug firm issues addiction warning, *The Guardian*, 23 January 2002, 5.

— Scientist in rethink over drug link to suicide, *The Guardian*, 1 October 2003.

Bowe C., US drug regulator slams European pricing, *Financial Times*, 25 September 2003.

Boyd E.A., Cho M.K., Bero L., Financial conflict-of-interest-policies in clinical research: Issues for clinical investigators, *Academic Medicine*, 2003, **78**, 769-774.

Boyd I.W., Venlafaxine withdrawal reactions, *Med. J. Aust.*, 1998, July 20, **169** (2), 91-92.

Bracewell M., Escape capsule, *The Observer* (Life section), 7 November 1993, 30-31.

Brandt W. (Chairman) et al., *North South: A Programme for Survival* (London: Pan, 1981).

Brecher E.M., *Licit and Illicit Drugs*, Mount Vernon, NY: Consumers Union, 1973.

Breggin P.R., A case of fluoxetine-induced stimulant side-effects with suicidal ideation associated with a possible withdrawal reaction ("crashing"), *Int. J. Risk & Safety in Medicine*, 1992, **3**, 325-328.

Breggin P.R., Breggin G.R., *Talking back to Prozac*, New York: St. Martin's, 1994.

P. Brown, Drug regulation – a life sentence on the industry? *Scrip Magazine*, Sept 1996, 23-24.

Brunel P., Vial T., Roche I., Bertolotti E., Evreux J.C., Follow-up of 151 pregnant women exposed to antidepressant treatment (excluding MAOIs) during organogenesis (translation of title in French), *Therapie*, March-April 1994, **49** (2), 117-122.

Brunet P. (Head of Pharmaceuticals Unit, DG Enterprise), letter to Bas van der Heide, (Coordinator, Health Action International), 4 July 2000.

— Letter to *Social Audit*, 20 February 2002.

— Letter to *Social Audit*, 2 April 2002.

Bülow-Olsen A. (Chair, Danish Migraine Association), personal communication (CM), November 2000.

Brown G. (UK Chancellor of the Exchequer), Drugs are just the start, *The Guardian*, 28 August 2003, 25.

Brown P., Drug regulation – a life sentence on the industry? *Scrip Magazine*, Sept 1996, 23-24.

Bryois C., Rubin C., Zbinden J.D., Baumann P., [Withdrawal syndrome caused by selective serotonin reuptake inhibitors: apropos of a case]. In German. *Schweiz Rundsch Med Prax*, 4 March 1998, **87**:10, 345-348.

Byck R., Drugs and the treatment of psychiatric disorders, in L.S. Goodman, A. Gilman (eds), *The Pharmacological Basis of Therapeutics* (5th Edition). New York: Macmillan, 1975, 187.

Byrne S.E., Rothschild A.J., Loss of antidepressant efficacy during maintenance therapy: possible mechanisms and treatments. *J. Clin. Psychiatry* 1998, **59**, 279-288.

Cabinet Office, *Code of Practice on Access to Government Information* (2nd Edition), and *Guidance Notes* (2nd Edition); London, 1997. See: Department for Constitutional Affairs website, http://www.dca.gov.uk/foi/codpracgi.htm

Campbell E.G., Weissman J.S., Clarrige B., Yucel R., Causino N., Blumenthal D., Characteristics of medical school faculty members serving on institutional review boards: Results of a national survey, *Academic Medicine*, 2003, **78**, 831-836.

Campomori A., Brambilla P., Barbui C., Safety of Selective Serotonin Re-uptake Inhibitors, Unpublished review, 1999.

Carpenter G., (citing Kass T.), Campaigning for awareness, *Pharmafocus*, 2 June 2003.

Carrazana E.J., Rivas-Vazquez R.A., Rey J.A., Rey G.J., SSRI discontinuation and buspirone, *Am J Psychiatry*, June 2001, 158 (6), 966-967

Castagnoli W.G, The coming showdown on DTC, *Medical Marketing and Media* magazine, September 1998.

Castañeda R., Levy R., Westreich L.M., et al., Drug craving and other negative reactions after abrupt substitution of nefazodone for other serotonergic agents. *J Clin Psychiatry* 1996 Oct, **57** (10), 485-6.

Cauchon D., FDA advisers tied to industry, *USA Today*, 24 September, 2000.

CBC – Canadian Broadcasting Corporation, News and Current Affairs interview transcript, 12 June 2001.

CBS-TV Network sales, A study of attitudes, concerns and information needs for prescription drugs and related illness, (New York, CBS, June 1984).

Cetera P., Pharmaceutical Marketing: this means war. *Pharmaceutical Executive*, July 1992, 50-58.

CDC – Centers for Disease Control and Prevention (US Department of Health and Human Services), Prevalence of healthy lifestyle characteristics – Michigan, 1998 and 2000, *Morbidity and Mortality Weekly Report*, 2001; 50, 758-761.

CDER (Center for Drug Evaluation & Research, FDA), Approval package, Paxil CR (paroxetine hydrochloride), 16 February 1999.

— Annual Adverse Drug Experience Report, 30 October 1997.

— Office of Drug Safety Annual report, FY 2001, 2002.

— Preventable Adverse Drug Reactions: A Focus on Drug Interactions (2002).

Chambers C.D., Johnson K.A., Dick L.M., Felix R.J., Jones K.L., Birth outcomes in pregnant women taking fluoxetine, *New Eng J Medicine*, 3 October 1996, 335, **14**, 1010-1015.

CFOI – Campaign for Freedom of Information. See www.cfoi.org.uk

Chang K., Tobacco industry fought drugs' marketing, *New York Times*, 14 August 2002.

Chaput de Saintonge D.M., Herxheimer A., Harnessing placebo effects in health care, *Lancet.* 1994 Oct 8; 344(8928): 995-8.

Charatan F., US drug companies help pay for Bush inauguration, *Brit Med J*, 2001; 322: 192.

Chouinard G., Saxena B., Bélanger M-C., Ravindran A., Bakish D., Beauclair L., Morris P., Vasavan Nair N.P., Manchanda R., Reesal R., Remick R., O'Neill M.C., A Canadian multicenter, double-blind study of paroxetine and fluoxetine in major depressive disorder, *J. Affective Disorders*, **54**, 1999, 39-48.

Clark K., Parliamentary debate: Opren, *Hansard*, 27 January 1983, cols 1106-1130.

Clift A.D., Factors leading to dependence on hypnotic drugs, *Brit Med J*, 1972, **3**, 614-617.

Cohen J.S., Overdose – The case against the drug companies, New York: Jeremy P. Tarcher/Putnam, 2001.

Cole J.O., Therapeutic efficacy of antidepressant drugs, A review. *JAMA*. 1964 Nov 2, **190** (5), 124-131.

— Evaluation of psychotropic drugs, interview in D. Healy, *The Psychopharmacologists*, London: Chapman & Hall (Altman), 1996.

Committee on the Review of Medicines, Systematic Review of the Benzodiazepines. *Br Med J*. 29 March 1980, 910-912.

Conan Doyle A., The Science of Deduction in *The Sign of Four (*First published in Nov. 1887 as the main part of Beeton's Christmas Annual. The first book edition by Ward, Lock & Co. in July 1888. The first American edition was published by J. B. Lippincott Co. in 1890. Full text is available on many websites, notably: http://homepages.ius.edu/JRBURGES/Sherlock_The%20Sign_Of_Four.html

Congress Watch: *America's other drug problem – A briefing book on the Rx Drug debate.* (Washington DC: Public Citizen, 2002).

Consumers Union: Backgrounder: *The Pharmaceutical Industry and Consumers – Key Factors Affecting Affordability of Prescription Drugs* (Washington DC; Consumers Union, February 2003).

Cooper G.L., The safety of fluoxetine – an update, *Br J Psychiatry*, 1988, **153** (suppl 3), 77-86.

Coppen A., Biological psychiatry in Britain, interview in D. Healy, *The Psychopharmacologists*, London: Chapman & Hall (Altman), 1996, 279, 265-286.

Cornwell J., *The Power to Harm – mind, medicine and murder on trial*, London: Viking, 1996.

Costei A.M., Kozer E., Ho T., Ito S. Koren G., Perinatal outcome following third trimester exposure to Paroxetine, *Arch Pediatr Adolesc Med.* 2002; 116:1129-1132.

Coupland N.J., Bell C.J., Serotonin reuptake inhibitor withdrawal, *J. Clin. Psychopharmacol.*, 1996, **16**, 3, 356-362.

Cowley G., Springen K., Leonard E.A., Robbins K., Gordon J., The promise of Prozac, *Newsweek,* 26 March 1990, 42-45.

Croasdale M., CME providers gear up to comply with PhRMA code, *AMNews* (American Medical Association) 7 October 2002.

Cross J., Lee H., Westelinck A., Nelson J., Grudzinskas C., Peck C., Postmarketing drug dosage changes of 499 FDA-approved new molecular entities, 1980-1999, *Pharmacoepidemiology and Drug Safety,* 2002 September, 11 (6), 439-446.

Crossman R.H.S., Parliamentary debate on Thalidomide, 8 May 1963.

Cunningham L.A. for the Venlafaxine XR 208 Study Group, Once-daily venlafaxine Extended Release (XR) and venlafaxine Immediate Release (IR) in outpatients with major depression, *Ann Clin Psychiatry*, 1997, **9**, 3, 157-164.

CSM – Committee on Safety of Medicines, Annual Reports, London: Medicines Commission/Department of Health, 1987-1992.

Committee on Safety of Medicines, Medicines Control Agency, Benzodiazepines, dependence and withdrawal symptoms, *Current Problems in Pharmacovigilance*, No 21. London: CSM/MCA, January 1988, 1-2.

– Minutes of CSM meeting of 26 March 1998, item 7.3.3

— Fluvoxamine (Faverin): Adverse reaction profile. *Current Problems in Pharmacovigilance*, No 22, May 1988, 1-2.

— Dystonia and withdrawal symptoms with paroxetine (Seroxat). *Current Problems in Pharmacovigilance* 1993, February, **19**, 1.

— Views on the Yellow Card scheme, July 1995, 21, 8.

— Adverse Drug Reactions Online Information Tracking (ADROIT) Drug Analysis Prints, 1997–2002.

— Medicines Control Agency, Suspected adverse drug reaction (ADR) reporting and the Yellow Card scheme: Guidance Notes, October 2002.

Cushny A.R, *A Textbook of Pharmacology and Therapeutics*, 10th edition, London: Churchill, 1928.

Dahl M.L., Olhager E., Ahlner J., Paroxetine withdrawal syndrome in a neonate (letter), *Br J Psychiatry*, 1997, Oct, **171**, 391-2.

Dallal A., Chouinard G., Withdrawal and rebound symptoms associated with abrupt discontinuation of venlafaxine (letter), *J Clin Psychopharmacol*, 1998, August, **18**:4, 343-344.

D'Arcy P.F., Griffin J.P. (eds), *Iatrogenic Diseases* (3rd edition), Oxford, OUP, 1986.

Davidoff F., News from the International Committee of Medical Journal Editors, *Ann Intern Med.* 2000;133: 229-231.

— Sponsorship, authorship, and accountability, *Lancet*, 15 September 2001, 358, 854-856.

Debattista C., Schatzberg A.F., Physical symptoms associated with paroxetine withdrawal (letter). *Am J Psychiatry* 1995 Aug, **152** (8), 1235-4.

De Buck R., Clinical experience with lorazepam in the treatment of neurotic patients; *Curr Med Res Opin*, 1973, **1**, 5, 291-295.

Delgado P.L., Price L.H., Heniger G.R., Charney D.S., Neurochemistry, in Paykel E.S. (ed.), *Handbook of Affective Disorders*, 2nd Edition, London: Churchill Livingstone, 1992.

Demyttenaere K., Haddad P., Compliance with antidepressant therapy and antidepressant discontinuation symptoms, *Acta Psychiatr Scand* 2000, **101** (Suppl 403), 50-56. ('Proceedings of a consensus meeting ... sponsored by Eli Lilly & Company').

Department of Health (Statistics Division, Branch SD1E). *Prescription Cost Analysis* England 1996. London: Department of Health, 1989 – 2003.

Department of Health, Death rates for suicide and undetermined injury chart, viewed in July 1997 at: http:www.open.gov.uk/doh/NHS96_96/chart04.htm

De Quincey T., *Confessions of an opium eater*, (1821), London: Walter Scott, 1886.

Detmer D.E., Singleton P.D., Macleod A., Wait S., Taylor M., Ridgwell J., The Informed Patient: Study Report, Cambridge, Judge Institute of Management, March 2003.

Devanand D.P., Kim M.K., Nobler M.S, Fluoxetine discontinuation in elderly dysthymic patients, *Am. J. Geriatric Psychiatry*, Winter 1997, **5** (1), 83-87.

De Wilde J., Spiers R., Mertens C., Bartholomé F., Schotte G., Leyman S., A double-blind, comparative, multicentre study comparing paroxetine with fluoxetine in depressed patients. *Acta Psychiatr Scand*, 1993, **87**, 141-145.

Diler R.S., Tamam L., Avci A., Withdrawal symptoms associated with paroxetine discontinuation in a nine-year-old boy, *J Clin Psychopharmacol* 2000 Oct; **20** (5): 586-7.

Dilsaver S. C., Greden J.F., Antidepressant withdrawal phenomena, *Biological Psychiatry*, 1984, 19, 2, 237-256.

Dilsaver S.C., Antidepressant withdrawal syndromes: phenomenology and pathophysiology, *Acta Psychiatr. Scand.*, 1989, **79**, 113-117.

— Withdrawal phenomena associated with antidepressant and antipsychotic agents, *Drug Safety*, 1994, **10** (2), 103-114.

— See also: M. Lejoyeux

DOH – Department of Health, *Science and Innovation Strategy*, September 2001.

Dominguez R.A., Goodnick P.J., Adverse events after the abrupt discontinuation of paroxetine. *Pharmacotherapy*, 1995 Nov-Dec, **15** (6), 778-80.

Donoghue J.M., Tylee A., The treatment of depression: Prescribing patterns of antidepressants in primary care in the UK. *Brit J Psychiatry* 1996, **168**, 164-168.

Donoghue J., Haddad P., Pharmacists lack knowledge of antidepressant discontinuation symptoms [letter], *J Clin Psychiatry* 1999 Feb, **60:2**, 124-5.

Donovan S., Clayton A., Beeharry M., Jones S., Kirk C., Waters K., Gardner D., Faulding J., Madeley R., Deliberate self-harm and antidepressant drugs, investigation of a possible link, *Br. J Psychiatry*, 2000, **177**, 551-556.

Doyle C., The cloud over 'bottled sunshine', *Daily Telegraph*, 1 March 1994, 17.

Drill V.A. (ed.), *Pharmacology in Medicine*, 2nd edition, New York: McGraw Hill, 1958.

DSRU (Anon), Fluoxetine, PEM Report No. 5, Southampton, Drug Safety Research Unit, 1993.

DTB (Anon), Some problems with benzodiazepines, *Drug & Therapeutics Bulletin*, 1985, 25 March, **26**, 11-12.

— Problems when withdrawing antidepressives, 1986, 21 April, **24**, 29-30.

— Fluvoxamine (Faverin): Another antidepressive drug, 1988, **26**, 11-12.

— Bupropion to aid smoking cessation, 2000 October, **38** (10), 73-75.

— Fluoxetine, suicide and aggression. 1992, 20 Jan, **30** (2), 5-6.

— Withdrawing patients from antidepressants, July 1999, **37** (7), 49-52.

— Bupropion to aid smoking cessation, 2000 October, **38** (10), 73-75. See also the attached, *Treatment Notes*, Medicines to help you stop smoking, Consumers' Association, December 2000.

— What to do about medically unexplained symptoms, January 2001, 39(1), 5-8.

Dukes M.N.G, The Van der Kroef Syndrome, Side Effects of Drugs Essay 1990 (Amsterdam: Elsevier, 1990).

Duphar Laboratories Ltd. (now Solvay Healthcare), Faverin (fluvoxamine) advertisement, *GP*, 1987, Aug 21, 9.

Edwards G.A., Hodgson R. et al., Nomenclature and classification of drug- and alcohol-related problems: a WHO memorandum, *Bulletin of the WHO*, 1981, **59**, 2, 1981: 225-242.

Egberts T.C.G., Smulders M., de Koning F.H.P., Meyboom R.H.B., Leufkens H.G.M., Can adverse reactions be detected earlier? A comparison of reports by patients and professionals, *Brit Med J.*, 1996,**313**, 530-531.

Einarson A., Selby P., Koren G., Abrupt discontinuation of psychotropic drugs in pregnancy: fear of teratogenic risk and impact of counselling, *J. Psychiatry Neurosci* 2001 January, **26** (1), 44-48.

Einbinder E., Fluoxetine withdrawal? *Am J Psychiatry* 1995 Aug, **152** (8), 1235.

Elfenbein D. (ed.), *Living with Prozac and Other Selective Serotonin Reuptake Inhibitors*, San Francisco: Harper Collins, 1995.

Elgie R., Direct to Consumer Advertising – A matter for debate, *Clinical Journal*, European Union of General Practitioners, 2002, 60-61.

Ellen E.F., Visits from pharmaceutical reps, *Psychiatric Times*, January 2001, 18(1).

C. Elliott, Pursued by happiness and beaten senseless: Prozac and the American Dream, *Hastings Center Report*, 2000, **30** No 2, 7-12.

Elling M.E., Fogle H.J. et al., Making more of pharma's sales force. *The McKinsey Quarterly*, No. 3, 2002.

Elliott C., Is ugliness a disease? *Guardian, 26* August 2003.

Ellis S.J., Matthews C., Weatherby S.J.M., Informed consent is flawed, *Lancet*, 2001 January 13, **357**, 149-150.

Ellison J.M., SSRI withdrawal buzz (letter), *J Clin Psychiatry*, 1994, **55**, 544-545.

EMEA – European Medicines Evaluation Agency, Public Statement on Selective Serotonin Uptake Inhibitors (SSRIs) and Dependency/Withdrawal Reactions, Position paper, EMEA/CPMP/2775/99, London, April 2000.

EMEA, CPMP Position Paper on Possible Pre-Clinical Studies to Investigate Addiction and Dependence/Withdrawal Related to the Use of SSRIs. London: CPMP/2278/00, December 2000.

EMEA, Summary report of the heads of agencies ad hoc working group: Establishing a European risk management strategy, http://heads.medagencies.org/summary.pdf January 2003.

Entsuah A.R., Rudolph R.L., Hackett D., Miska S., Efficacy of venlafaxine and placebo during long-term treatment of depression: a pooled analysis of relapse rates, *International Clinical Psychopharmacology*, 1996, **11**, 137-145.

Epelde F., Pla R., Aguilar M., Crisis comicial tras supresion brusca del tratamiento con fluoxetine; Letter: in Spanish, re: Seizures crisis following sudden withdrawal of fluoxetine, *Med Clin (Barc)* 1999 Oct 16; 113(12): 479.

Era News, EC to reconsider advertising rules, November 1998.

European Parliament, *Analysis of Issues and Trends in the EU Pharmaceuticals Sector*, Environment, Public Health and Consumer Protection Series E-1, External Study (Belcher P.J., Chambers B.R. (eds), The European Parliament, Directorate General for Research, March 1994.

Evans J.G., Jarvis E.H., Nitrazepam and the elderly, *Brit Med J*, 1972 November 25, 487.

Fagan M., Withdrawal syndrome after the use of serotonin reuptake inhibitors (in Norwegian] *Tidsskr Nor Laegeforen.* 2000 Mar 20; **120** (8): 913-4.

Farah A., Lauer T.E., Possible venlafaxine withdrawal syndrome. *Am J Psychiatry* 1996 Apr, **153** (4), 576.

Fava G.A., Do antidepressant and antianxiety drugs increase chronicity in affective disorders? *Psychother Psychosom*, 1994, **61**, 125-131.

— Holding On: Depression, sensitisation by antidepressant drugs, and the Prodigal Experts, Ibid, 1995, 64, 57-61.

Fava G.A., Grandi S., Withdrawal syndromes after paroxetine and sertraline discontinuation (letter). *J Clin Psychopharmacol* 1995 Oct, **15** (5), 374-5.

Fava G.A., Tomba E., The use of antidepressant drugs: some reasons for concern, *Int J of Risk and Safety in Medicine*, 1998, **11**, 271-274.

Fava G.A., Can long-term treatment with antidepressant drugs worsen the course of depression? *Clin Psychiatry*, 2003 February, **64**, 2, 123-133.

Fava M., Rappe S.M., Pava J.A. et al., Relapse in patients on long-term fluoxetine treatment: response to increased fluoxetine dose, *J. Clin. Psychiatry*, 1995, **56**, 52-55.

— with Mulroy R., Alpert J., Nierenberg A.A., Rosenbaum J.F., Emergence of adverse effects following discontinuation of treatment with extended-release venlafaxine, *Am J Psychiatry*, December 1997, **154** (12), 1760-1762.

Favaro A., Friederici S., Santonastaso P., Predictors of sertraline discontinuation syndrome in anorexia nervosa, *J Clin Psychopharmacol*, 21(5), 2001 October, 533-535.

FDA, *Fluoxetine hydrochloride, Summary Basis of Approval*, NDA 18-936, Rockville Md., US Food & Drug Administration, 3 October 1988.

— Letter to Eli Lilly & Co, 16 November 2000. See http://www.fda.gov/cder/warn/nov2000/dd9523.pdf

— *MedWatch Form 3500*, See: http://www.fda.gov/medwatch/report/consumer/instruct.htm – June 2003

Fernando A.T., Schwader P., A case of citalopram withdrawal, *J. Clin Psychopharmacol*, 2000 October, **20** (5), 581-582.

Ferrier I.N., Treatment of major depression: Is improvement enough? *J. Clin. Psychiatry*, 1999, **60**, Suppl. 6, 10-14.

Ferriman A., Pep-up drug deaths. *The Observer*, 5 June 1988.

Fieve R.R., *Prozac*, London: Thorsons, 1994.

Flanagin A., Carey L.A., et al., Prevalence of articles with honorary authors and ghost authors in peer-reviewed medical journals, *JAMA*, 1998 July 15, **280** (3), 222-224.

Fossati R., Confalonieri C., Apolone G., Cavuto S., Garattini S., Does a drug do better when it is new? *Ann Oncol.* 2002 Mar; 13 (3): 470-473.

Freeman H.L., Listening to Prozac (letter), *Nature* 1994 May 19, **369**, 178.

Freudenheim M., Psychiatric drugs are now promoted directly to patients, *The New York Times*, 17 February 1998, A1-D3.

Friedman E.H., Neurobiology of behavioural changes after prenatal exposure to paroxetine (Paxil), *Am J Obstet Gynecol* 2000 August, **183** (2), 518-519.

Frost L., Lal S., Shock-like sensations after discontinuation of selective serotonin reuptake inhibitors (letter). *Am J Psychiatry* 1995 May, **152** (5), 810.

Fullerton A.G., Boardman R.H., Side effects of Tofranil, *Lancet*, 6 June 1959, 1209.

Galbally R., (Chair) (2000): *Review of Drugs, Poisons and Controlled Substances Legislation*, draft final report. See http://www.health.gov.au/tga/docs/html/revdp.htm.

Gambardella A., Orsenigo L., Pammolli F., Global competitiveness in pharmaceuticals, A European perspective, Report prepared for the Directorate-General Enterprise of the European Commission (2000), available at http://pharmacos.eudra.org/F3/g10/p3.htm

GAO – General Accounting Office, Report to the Chairman, Subcommittee on Human Resources and Intergovernmental Relations, Committee on Government Operations, House of Representatives, *FDA Drug Review – Postapproval drug risks 1976-95*, Report No GAO/PEMD-90-15, Washington DC: GAO, 1990.

Garattini S., The role of independent science in psychopharmacology, interview with Healy D. in *The Psychopharmacologists*, London: Chapman & Hall (Altman), 1996, 142.

George J., Big Pharma kills doc giveaways, *Philadelphia Business Journal*, 28 June 2002.

Gerola O. et al., Antidepressant therapy in pregnancy: a review from the literature and report of a suspected paroxetine withdrawal syndrome in a newborn. *Rivista Italiana di Pediatria*, 1999, **25**, 216-218.

Gerth G., Stohlberg S.G., Medicine merchants: Birth of a blockbuster, *New York Times*, 23 April 2000.

— Drug industry has ties to groups with many different voices, *New York Times*, 5 Oct 2000.

Giakas W.J., Davis J.M., Intractable withdrawal from venlafaxine treated with fluoxetine, *Psychiatric Annals*, February 1997, **27** (2), 85-86 and 92.

Glass A., European Commission may reform drug advertising legislation, *Lancet*, **358**, 28 July 2001, 306.

Glenmullen J., *Prozac Backlash* – overcoming the dangers of Prozac, Zoloft, Paxil, and other antidepressants with safe, effective alternatives, (New York: Simon & Schuster, 2000).

Gluck M.E., *Federal policies affecting the cost and availability of new pharmaceuticals*, The Henry J. Kaiser Family Foundation, July 2002, p. 35.

Goldbery J.F., Kocsis J.H., Relapse during SSRI treatment for depression, *Medscape Psychiatry & Mental Health Journal*, 1996, 1, 5. www.medscape.com/viewarticle/431525

Goldberg R., Cloning Kessler – a bad choice for the FDA, *National Review Online*. 11 January 2002.

Goldberg R.J., Diagnostic dilemmas presented by patients with anxiety and depression. *Am J Medicine*, 1995 Mar. **98**, 278-284.

Goldstein T.R., Frye M.A., Denikoff K.D., Smith-Jackson E., Leverich G.S., Bryan A.L., Ali S.O., Post R. M., Antidepressants and discontinuation-related mania: critical prospective observation and theoretical implications in bipolar disorder, *J. Clin Psychiatry*, August 1999, **60** (8), 563-567.

Goodman L.S., Gilman A. (eds), *The Pharmacological Basis of Therapeutics*, New York: Macmillan, 1941.

Gore S.M., Jones G., Thompson S.G., The *Lancet's* statistical review process: areas for improvement by authors, *Lancet*, July 11 1992, **340**, 100-102.

Gram L.F., (in Danish) Seponeringssymtomer ved anvelndelse af selektive serotoningen-optagelseshæmmere (SSRI), *Ugeskr Læger*, 1998, 7 Dec, **160** (50), 7291-7293.

Grant R., The Prozac generation, *The Independent on Sunday*, 30 Jan 1994, 12-16.

Green B., Persistent adverse neurological effects following SSRI discontinuation, Psychiatry On-Line, accessed January 2000 on http://www.priory.com/psych/panes.htm

Greenberg R.P., Greenberg D., Bornstein R.F., Fisher S., A meta-analysis of antidepressant outcome under "blinder" conditions, *J. Consulting & Clinical Psychology*, 1992, **60** (5), 664-669.

Greenberg R.P., Fisher S., Examining antidepressant effectiveness: findings, ambiguities and some vexing puzzles, in R.P. Greenberg & S. Fisher (eds), *The Limits of Biological Treatments for Psychological Distress – Comparisons with Psychotherapy and Placebo*, [Hillsdale, New Jersey: Lawrence Erlbaum Associates, 1989], 1-37.

Griffin J.P., Is better feedback a major stimulus to spontaneous adverse reaction monitoring? *Lancet*, 1984, November 10, 1098

Groppe M., Lilly beefs up lobbying staff to flex political muscle, *Indianapolis Star*, 21 July 2002.

Gurwitz J.H., Field T.S., Avorn J., et al., Incidence and preventability of adverse drug events in nursing homes, *Am J Med, 2000*, **109** (2), 87-94.

Haddad H. cited in McGregor G., Ban on Ads to Stay: McLellan, *The Ottawa Citizen*, 23 March 2002.

Haddad P., Lejoyeux M., Young A., Antidepressant discontinuation reactions are preventable and simple to treat, *Brit Med J*, 11 April 1998, **316**, 1105-1106.

Haddad P., Anderson I., Antidepressants aren't addictive: clinicians have depended on them for years, (comment on Healy and Tranter, 1999) *J Psychopharmacol.*, 1999, **13** (3), 291-298.

Haddad P., Do antidepressants have any potential to cause addiction? *J. Psychopharmacol.*, 1999, **13** (3), 300-307.

Haddad P., Qureshi M., Misdiagnosis of antidepressant discontinuation symptoms, *Acta Psychiatr Scand* 2000 Dec, **102** (6), 466-468.

Haddad P., Antidepressant discontinuation syndromes, *Drug Safety*, 2001, **24** (3), 183-197.

Haddad P., The SSRI discontinuation syndrome, *J. Psychopharmacology*, 1998, **12** (3), 305-313.

Hale A.S., Anxiety, *Brit. Med. J.*, 1997, 28 June, **314**, 1886-1889.

Halle H., Del Medico V.J., Dilsaver S.C., Symptoms of major depression: acute effect of withdrawing antidepressants, *Acta Psychiatr. Scand.*, 1991, **83**, 238-239.

Hallstrom C., Benzodiazepine dependence: who is responsible? *J. Forensic Psychiatry*, 1991, **2** (1), 5-7.

Hamburger T., Drug industry moves to boost image before vote, *Wall Street Journal*, 16 September 2002, A6.

Hamilton, M., Development of a rating scale for primary depressive illness. *Brit J Soc Clin Psychol* 1967, **6**, 278-296.

Hamner M. & Huber M.: Discontinuation of antidepressant medications prior to ECT, *Convulsive Ther*, 1996, **12**, 125-126.

Hampton J.R., Clinical freedom, *Brit Med J*, 1983 October 29, **287**, 1237-1238.

Hare E.H., Dominian J., Sharpe L., Phenelzine and dexamphetamine in depressive illness, *Brit. Med. J.*, 6 Jan, 1992, 9-12.

Hare D., 'My vote? I would like to punish Blair', *Daily Telegraph*, 17 May 2001.

Harris G., Drug firms stymied in the lab, become marketing machines, *Wall Street Journal,* 6 July 2000.

Harry T.V.A., (Wyeth UK), Oxazepam (Serenid D) dependence, *Brit. J. Psychiatry,* 1972, **121**, 235-236.

Hawley C.J., James D.V., Birkett P.L., Baldwin D.S., M.J. de-Ruiter, R.G. Priest, Suicidal ideation as a presenting complaint. Associated diagnoses and characteristics in a casualty population, *Br J Psychiatry* 1991 Aug, **159**, 232-8.

Hawkins B., Paxil is forever, *City Pages,* 23, 1141, 16 October 2002.

Healy D., The structure of psychopharmacological revolutions. *Psychiatr. Dev.* 1987. **5**, 349-376.

— The psychopharmacological era: notes towards a history. *J Psychopharmacol* 1990, **4** (3), 152-167.

— The marketing of 5-Hydroxytryptamine: Depression or anxiety? *Br J Psychiatry* 1991, **158**, 737-742.

— *The Psychopharmacologists,* London: Chapman & Hall (Altman), 1996.

— *The Antidepressant Era,* Cambridge, Mass., Harvard University Press, 1998.

— *The Psychopharmacologists* II, London: Chapman & Hall (Altman), 1998.

— Commentary on Moncrieff J. et al., Meta-analysis of trials comparing antidepressants with active placebos, *Brit J Psychiatry,* 1998, **172**, 232-234.

— with Tranter R.: Pharmacological stress diathesis syndromes, *J Psychopharmacol.,* 1999, **13** (3), 287-290. And: In the shadow of the benzodiazepines (Responses to commentaries on the above paper), ibid, p. 299.

— Good science or good business? *Hastings Center Report,* 2000, **30** No 2, 19-22.

— *The Psychopharmacologists* III, London: Arnold (with OUP), 2000.

— Lines of evidence on the risks of suicide with selective serotonin reuptake inhibitors, *Psychotherapy and Psychosomatics,* 2003; **72**, 71-79.

— *Let them eat Prozac,* Toronto: Lorimer, 2003.

Heeley E., Riley J., Layton D., Wilton L.V., Shakir S.A.W., Prescription-event monitoring and reporting of adverse drug reactions, *Lancet,* 1 December 2001, **358**, 1872-1873.

Heerdin E.R., Urquhart J., Hubert G., Leufkens H.G., Changes in prescribed drug doses after market introduction, *Pharmacoepidemiol Drug Saf.* 2002 Sep; **11** (6):447-53.

Helling-Borda M., Memories of the First Expert Committee Meeting and celebrating 25 years later, *Essential Drugs Monitor,* 2003, **32**, 14-15.

Hicks C., The truth about Nature's Prozac, *Independent,* 8 July 1997, tabloid section, 9.

Herxheimer A., How much drug in the tablet? *Lancet,* 1991, Feb 9, **337**, 346-348.

Hindmarch I., Kimber S., Cockle S.M., Abrupt and brief discontinuation of antidepressant treatment: effects on cognitive function and psychomotor performance, *Int Clin Psychopharmacol* 2000 Nov; **15** (6): 305-18.

Hirose S., Restlessness related to SSRI withdrawal, *Psychiatry and Clinical Neurosciences,* 2001, **55**, 79-80.

Hirschfeld R.M.A., Keller M.B., Panico S., et al., The National Depressive and Manic-Depressive Association Consensus Statement on the Undertreatment of Depression. *JAMA,* 1997, **277** (4), 333-340.

Hollister L. E., Motzenbecker F.P., Degan R.O., Withdrawal reactions from chlordiazepoxide ('Librium'), *Psychopharmacologia,* 1961, **2**, 63-68.

— et al., Diazepam in newly admitted schizophrenics, *Dis Nerv Sys,* 1963 December, 746-750.

— Clinical use of psychotherapeutic drugs, *Drugs,* 1972, **4**, 321-360.

— The prudent use of anti-anxiety drugs, *Rational Drug Therapy*, 1972 March, **6** (3), 1-6.

— (Chairman, proceedings of a roundtable discussion on diazepam held in Chicago, 20 May, 1976), Valium: a discussion of current issues. *Psychosomatics* 1977, **18** (1), 44-58.

— 'Pharmacological stress diathesis syndromes': commentary, (on Healy and Tranter, 1999) *J Psychopharmacol.* 1999, **13** (3), 293-294.

Horrobin D.F., *Medical Hubris: A reply to Ivan Illich*, London: Churchill Livingstone, 1978.

— Innovation in the pharmaceutical industry, *J. Roy. Soc. Med*, July 2000, 93, 341-345.

— Something rotten at the core of science? *Biomednet* (bmn.com), February 2001.

Horton R., Lotronex and the FDA: a fatal erosion of integrity, *Lancet*, 19 May 2001, 1544-5.

Huffstutler S.Y., Management of antidepressant withdrawal reactions, *J Am Acad Nurse Pract*, 1998, April, **10:4**, 161-165.

Hunt M.I., *Prescription Drug Costs: Federal Regulation of the Industry*, Report for the Blue Cross and Blue Shield Association, September 2000.

Hunt L., Mind drug 'no miracle', *Independent on Sunday*, 31 October 1993, 2.

Hunt P., McKillop T. (co-chairs), Pharmaceutical Industry Competitiveness Task Force, Final report, March 2001. Available at http://www.doh.gov.uk/pictf/index.htm

Hunter R.A., The abuse of barbiturates and other sedative drugs with special reference to psychiatric patients, *British J Addiction*, 1957, **53**, 2, 93-100.

Hyman S.E., Nestler E.J., Initiation and adaptation: A paradigm for understanding psychotropic drug action. *Am J Psychiatry* 1996 Feb, **153** (2), 151-162.

Ibister G.K., Dawson A., Whyte I.M., Prior F.H., Clancy C., Smith A.J., Neonatal paroxetine withdrawal syndrome or actually serotonin syndrome? *Arch Dis Child Fetal Ed*, 2001, Sept, **85** (2), F147-148.

Illich I., *Limits to Medicine – Medical Nemesis: the Expropriation of Health*, (London: Marion Boyars, 1976 (originally published in *Ideas in Progress*, January 1975).

Inman W.H.W., Detection and investigation of drug safety problems, in Gent & Shigamatsu (eds), *Epidemiological issues in reported drug-induced illnesses*. Hamilton, Ontario: McMaster University Library Press, 1976.

— Kubota K., Pearce G., Wilton L., PEM Report Number 6. Paroxetine, *Pharmacoepidemiology and Drug Safety*, 1993, **2**, 393-422.

— *Don't tell the patient*, Los Angeles and Hampshire: Highland Park, 1999.

Inpharm: http://www.inpharm.com/External/InpH/1,2272,5-204-0-0-inp_free_front-0-A,00.html accessed February 2003.

Inpharm.com, Africa Pharmaceutical Sector Development, 11 July 2003, Source: World Pharmaceutical Markets.

IOM – Institute of Medicine: *Sleeping Pills, Insomnia and Medical Practice*, (Washington DC: National Academies Press, 1979).

— *Integrity in Scientific Research: Creating an environment that promotes responsible conduct*, 2002.

Isbell H., Altschul S., et al., Chronic barbiturate intoxication – An experimental study, *Arch. Neurology & Psychiatry*, 1950 July, **64**, 1, 1-28.

Jackson C.A., Pitkin K., Kington R., (1998), 'Evidence-based decision-making for community health programs.' http://www.rand.org/publications/MR/MR933/MR933.pdf/.

Jacob J., Welcoming or wary? Drug reps increasing, *AMNews*, American Medical Association, 16 April 2001.

Jacobs D., Cohen D., What is really known about psychological alterations produced by psychiatric drugs? *Int. J. Risk & Safety in Medicine*, 1999, **12**, 37-47.

James O., Camden C., Power of the psychodrug, *Guardian* (Magazine section), 23 November 1993, 14-15.
Jefferson T., Wager E., Davidoff F., Effects of editorial peer review: a systematic review. *JAMA.* 2002 Jun 5;287(21):2784-6. Review. Also: Measuring the quality of editorial peer review, 2786-90.
Jeffries M., The mark of Zorro, *Pharmaceutical Marketing,* May 2000, 4-5.
Jick S.S., Dean A.D., Jick H., Antidepressants and suicide. *Brit Med J* 1995, **310**, 215-8.
John K., Democracy, accountability, and international health: Westminster from a medical perspective, *Lancet,* 2003 September 6, **362**, 826-827.
Johnson H., Bouman W.P., Lawton J., Withdrawal reaction associated with venlafaxine, *Brit. Med. J.*, 19 September 1998, **317**, 787.
Jones E., *Sigmund Freud: Life and Work,* Vol 1, London: Hogarth Press, 1953.
Jones G., Mann R., Better reporting of adverse drug reactions, *Brit Med J,* 4 April 1987, 901-902.
Judge R., Parry M.G., Quail D., Jacobson J.G., Discontinuation symptoms: comparison of brief interruption in fluoxetine and paroxetine treatment, *Int. Clin. Psychopharmacol,* 2002, **17**, 217-225.
Kaiser Family Foundation study cited in Agovino T., Drug companies revise guidelines for marketing drugs to doctors, Associated Press, 19 April 2002.
Kales A., Bixler E.O., Tjiauw-Lin Tan, Scharf M.B., Kales J.D., Chronic hypnotic drug use – ineffectiveness, drug-withdrawal insomnia and dependence, *JAMA*, 1974 February 4, **227** (5), 513-517.
— Manfredi R.L. et al., Rebound insomnia following only brief and intermittent use of rapidly eliminated benzodiazepines, *Clin Pharm Ther,* 1991, **49**, 468-476.
Kallet A., Schlink F.J., *100,000,000 Guinea Pigs,* Dangers in everyday food, drugs and cosmetics, (New York, Vanguard, 1932).
Karp D.A., *Speaking of Sadness* New York City and Oxford, UK: Oxford University Press, 1996.
Kasantikul D., Reversible delirium after discontinuation of fluoxetine. *J Med Assoc Thai,* 1995 Jan, **78** (1), 53-54.
Kaufman M., Since Bush's inauguration, partisan politics and industry demands have delayed appointment, *Washington Post,* 15 July 2002.
Keller M.B., in discussion of the natural history and heterogeneity of depressive disorders: Implications for rational antidepressant therapy, *J Clin Psychiatry* 1994 Sept., **55**, 9 (suppl A), 32-33.
Keller M.B., Hanks D.L., Anxiety symptom relief in depression treatment outcomes, *J. Clin. Psychiatry,* 1995, **56** Suppl. 6, 30-36.
Keller M.B., McCullough J.P., Klein D.N., Arnow B., Dunner D.L., Gelenberg A.J., Markowitz J.C., Nemeroff C.B., Russell J.M., Thase M.E., Trivedi M.H., Zajecka J., A comparison of nefazodone, the cognitive behavioral-analysis system of psychotherapy, and their combination for the treatment of chronic depression. *N Engl J Med.* 2000 May 18; **342** (20): 1462-70.
Keller M.B., Ryan N.D., Strober M., Klein R.G., et al., Efficacy of paroxetine in the treatment of adolescent major depression: A randomized controlled trial. *J Am Acad Child Adolesc Psychiatry* 2001; **40** (7): 762-72.
Kennedy P., Has the US lost its way? *Observer,* 3 March 2002.
Kent L.S.W., Laidlaw J.D.D., Suspected congenital sertraline dependence *Brit J Psychiatry* 1995 Sep, **167** (3), 412-3.

Kerr M.P., Antidepressant prescribing: a comparison between general practitioners and psychiatrists. *Brit J Gen Pract* 1994, **44**, 275-276.

Keuthen N.J., Cyr P., Ricciardi J.A., et al., Medication withdrawal symptoms in obsessive-compulsive disorder patients treated with paroxetine. *J Clin Psychopharmacol* 1994 Jun, **14** (3), 206-7.

Kirsch I., Sapirstein G., Listening to Prozac but Hearing Placebo; A Meta-Analysis of Antidepressant Medication, *Prevention & Treatment*, Vol 1, Article 0002a, posted June 26, 1998 at http://journals.apa.org/prevention/volume1/pre0010002a.html

Kirsch I., Moore T.J., Scoboria A., Nicholls S.S., The Emperor's new drugs: an analysis of antidepressant medication data submitted to the U.S. Food and Drug Administration, *Prevention & Treatment*, Volume 5, Article 23, Posted 15 July 2002, at http://journals.apa.org/prevention/volume5/pre0050023a.html

Kirsch M., Hard habit to break, *The Observer Magazine*, 3 February 2002, 46.

Kissinger H., Opening address to the World Food Conference, UN Food & Agriculture Organization, Rome, November 1974.

Kjaergard L.L., Als-Nielsen B., Association between competing interests and authors' conclusions: epidemiological study of randomised trials published in the *BMJ*, *Brit Med J*, 3 August 2002 **325**, 249-252.

Kline N.S., The practical management of depression. *JAMA*, 1964 Nov 23, **190** (8), 122-130.

Koerner B.I., Disorders made to order, *Mother Jones*, 1 August 2002.

Koopowitz L.F., Berk M., Paroxetine induced withdrawal effects, *Human Psychopharmacol.*, 1995, **10**, 147-148.

Kotlyar M., Golding M., Brewer E.R., Carson S.W., Possible Nefazodone withdrawal syndrome (letter), *Am J. Psychiatry*, July 1999, **156** (7), 1117.

Kramer J.C., Klein D.F., Fink M., Withdrawal symptoms following discontinuation of imipramine therapy, *Am. J Psychiatry*, 1961, 118, 549-550.

Kramer P.D., *Listening to Prozac.* New York: Viking, 1993.

— The valorization of sadness: Alienation and the melancholic temperament, *Hastings Center Report*, 2000, **30** No 2, 13-18.

Kreider M.S., Bushnell W.D., Oakes R. et al., A double-blind randomised study to provide safety information on switching fluoxetine-treated patients to paroxetine without an intervening washout period, *J. Clin Psychiatry*, 1995, **56**, 142-145.

Krimsky S., Conflict of interest and cost-effectiveness analysis, *JAMA*, 1999 October 20, **282**, 15, 1474-1475.

— Conflict of interest policies in science and medical journals: Editorial Practices and Author Disclosures, *Science and Engineering Ethics*, 2001, **7**, 205-218.

Lacey R., Woodward S., That's Life! survey on tranquillisers, London, British Broadcasting Corporation in association with MIND (National Association of Mental Health), 1985.

Lader M., Benzodiazepine withdrawal states. In M.R. Trimble (ed.), *Benzodiazepines Divided* (Chichester: John Wiley & Son, 1983).

— Benzodiazepine dependence syndromes and syndromes of withdrawal. In Hallstrom C. (ed.), *Benzodiazepine Dependence* (Oxford University Press, 1993).

— Withdrawal from antidepressants (Unpublished Opinion), November 1997.

Lancet, Editorial, 11 February 1865, 153-154.

— Editorial, 1 January 1870, 15.

— Editorial, 1889, ii, 1047.

— Editorial, 1954, ii, 75.

— Annotation, 21 May 1955, 1065.

— Editorial: Just how tainted has medicine become? 2002 April 6, 359, 9313, 1167.

Landry P., Roy L., Withdrawal hypomania associated with paroxetine, *J. Clin. Psychopharmacol*, 17, 1, February 1997, 60-61

Lane R.M., Withdrawal symptoms after discontinuation of selective serotonin reuptake inhibitors, *J. Serotonin Res.*, 1996, 3, 75-83.

La Revue Prescrire, A look back at 2000: overabundance and deregulation. *Prescrire International* 2001, **10**: 52-4.

Larkin M., Whose article is it anyway? *Lancet*, 2002, **354**, 9173, 136.

Lasser K.E., Allen P.D., Woolhandler S.J., Himmelstein D.U., Wolfe S.M., Bor D.H., Timing of new black box warnings and withdrawals for prescription medications. *JAMA*, 2002 May 1; 287(17): 2215-2220. See also Wolfe S.M., Drugs banned since the time of the JAMA study, at http://www.citizen.org/publications/print_release.cfm?ID=7171

Lauber C., Nefazodone withdrawal symptoms, *Can J Psychiatry*, April 1999, **44** (3), 285-286.

Lazarou J., Pomeranz B.H., Corey P.N., Incidence of adverse drug reactions in hospitalized patients – A meta-analysis of prospective studies, *JAMA*, 1998;279: 1200-1205.

Lazowick A.L., Levin G.M., Potential withdrawal syndrome associated with SSRI discontinuation. *Ann Pharmacother* 1995 Dec, **29** (12), 1284-85.

Lehmann H., Psychopharmacotherapy, interview with D. Healy in *The Psychopharmacologists*, London: Chapman & Hall (Altman), 1996, 178-179, 182, 185.

Leiter F.L., Nierenberg S.A., Sanders K.M., Stern T.A., Discontinuation reactions following sertraline. *Biol Psychiatry* 1995 Nov 15, **38** (10), 694-5.

Lejoyeux M., Ades J., Mourad I., Solomon J., Dilsaver S., Antidepressant withdrawal syndrome – recognition, prevention and management, *CNS Drugs*, 1996, April; **5**, 4, 278-292.

Lewis A. J., *J. Ment. Sci*, 1934, **80**, 277.

Leyburn P., A critical look at antidepressant drug trials. *Lancet* 1967 25 Nov, 1135-1138.

Eli Lilly & Co (Dista Products), First line for all nine ... symptoms of depression, *J. Clin. Psychopharmacol.*, 1993, 13, 5, advertisement facing p. 303.

Lindqvist M., *Seeing and Observing in International Pharmacovigilance*, Uppsala, Sweden: Uppsala Monitoring Centre, 2003.

Lonngren T. (Director, EMEA) quoted in Anon, Dry pipelines undermining EMEA, *Pharmafocus*, 30 December 2002.

Louie A.K., Lewis T.B., Lannon R.A., Use of low dose fluoxetine in major depression and panic disorder, *J Clin. Psychiatry* 1993, Nov, **54** (11), 435-438.

Louie A.K., Lannon R.A., Ajari L.J., Withdrawal reaction after sertraline discontinuation (letter). *Am J Psychiatry* 1994 Mar, **151** (3), 450-1.

Louie A.K., Lannon R.A., Kirsch M.A., Lewis T.B., Venlafaxine withdrawal reactions (letter). *Am J Psychiatry* 1996 Dec, **153** (12), 1652.

Lu L., Su W.J., Yue W., Ge X., Su F., Attenuation of morphine dependence and withdrawal in rats by venlafaxine, a serotonin and noradrenaline reuptake inhibitor. *Life Sci*, 2001 May, **69**, 1, 37-46.

Luckhaus C., Jacob C., Venlafaxine withdrawal syndrome not prevented by maprotiline, but resolved by sertraline (letter), *Int J Neuropsychopharmacology*, 2001, **4**, 43-44.

Luckhaus C., Müller W.E., (in German) Withdrawal symptoms after prolonged intake of specific serotonin reuptake inhibitors, *Psychopharmacotherapie*, 2000, 7, 57-62.

Lumley C.E., Walker S.R., Hall G.C., Staunton N., Grob P.R., The under-reporting of adverse drug reactions seen in General Practice, *Pharmaceutical Medicine,* 1986, 1, 205-212.

Lurie P, Statement of Peter Lurie, M.D., MPH before National Academy of Sciences' Committee on Clinical Research Involving Children (HRG publication No. 1668). Washington DC: Health Research Group, 2002.

Lynch T., *Beyond Prozac: Healing Mental Suffering Without Drugs,* Dublin, Marino Books, 2001.

Lynn M., *The Billion Dollar Battle – Merck v Glaxo,* Heinemann, London, 1991, 195.

Macbeth R., Rajagopalan M., Venlafaxine withdrawal syndrome, *Aust NZ J Med,* 1998, **28**, 218.

Macdonald L., Discontinuation symptoms and SSRIS, *CMAJ,* 1998, Oct 6, **159**(7), 846-847, and (in French) 850-852.

Mackay F.J., Dunn N.R., Wilton L.V., Pearce G.L., Freemantle S.N., Mann R.D., A comparison of fluvoxamine, fluoxetine, sertraline and paroxetine examined by observational cohort studies, *Pharmacoepidemiology and Drug Safety,* 1997, **6**, 235-246.

Mahendran R., Chan A., Selective Serotonin Reuptake Inhibitor discontinuation symptoms, *Ann. Acad. Med. Singapore,* 1999, July, **28**, 596-599.

Maixner S.M., Greden J.F., Extended antidepressant maintenance and discontinuation syndromes. *Depress Anxiety* 1998, **8**, Suppl 1, 43-53.

Maletzky B.M., Klotter J., Addiction to Diazepam, *Int. J of the Addictions,* 1976, **11** (1), 95-115.

Malitz S., Kanzler M., Are antidepressants better than placebo? *Am. J. Psychiatry,* 1971, **127**, 1605.

Mallya G., White K., Gunderson C., Is there a serotonergic withdrawal syndrome? *Biol Psychiatry* 1993 Jun 1-15, **33** (11-12), 851-2.

Manolis D.C., The perils of Prozac. *Minnesota Medicine* 1995 Jan, **78**, 19-23.

Mareth T.R., Brown T.M., SSRI withdrawal (letter). *J Clin Psychiatry* 1996 Jul, **57** (7), 310.

Marinker M. in Parish P.A., Williams W.M., Elmes P.C. (eds), The Medical Use of Psychotropic Drugs, a report of a symposium sponsored by the Department of Health and Social Security, held at University College, Swansea, 1-2 July 1972.

Markowitz J.S., Selective serotonin reuptake inhibitor discontinuation with ECT and withdrawal symptoms (letter), *J ECT*, 1998, March, **14:1**, 55.

— Nefazodone withdrawal symptoms, *Can J Psychiatry,* April 1999, **44** (3), 286-287. Letter, Comment on Benazzi F., March 1998.

Marks J., *The Benzodiazepines – Use, Overuse, Misuse, Abuse.* Lancaster UK: MTP Press, 1978.

— The benzodiazepines – for good or evil. *Neuropsychobiology* 1983, **10**, 115-126.

Mathew T. (Chair, ADRAC), SSRIS and withdrawal syndrome, *Australian Adverse Drug Reactions Bulletin,* **15**, 1, November 1996, 2.

Mathew T., SSRIS and neonatal disorders: Withdrawal reactions, Breast milk transfer, *AADRB*, **16**, 4, November 1997, 14.

Mathews A.W., FDA chief targets Europe's controls on drug price, *Wall Street Journal,* 25 September 2003.

Maudsley H, *The Pathology of Mind,* London: Macmillan, 1895.

MCA – Medicines Control Agency, Quinquennial review and prior options study, May 1999.

McBride M. (Honorary Secretary of Council, Royal College of General Practitioners), Unpublished correspondence, 18 May 1992.

McCallum R.D., Kell G.C., Phelps A., Deposition, 4 September 2002, in Re Paxil litigation, CV-01-07937 MRP (CWx)

McKeown T., Lowe C.R., *An Introduction to Social Medicine*, Oxford, Blackwell, 1974.

— *The Role of Medicine: Dream, Mirage, or Nemesis?* Princeton, NJ, Princeton University Press: 1979.

— *The origins of human disease*, Oxford, Blackwell, 1988.

McNair D.M., Anti-anxiety drugs and human performance, *Arch Gen Psychiatry*, 1983 November, **29**, 611-617.

Medawar C., See also www.socialaudit.org.uk (1998-2003)

— *Power and Dependence: Social Audit on the safety of medicines*. London: Social Audit, 1992. (*P&D* is the prime source for Chapters one and two in this book)

— Through the doors of deception? *Nature*, 24 March 1994, **368**, 369-370.

— Secrecy and medicines. *Int J Risk & Safety in Medicine* 1996, **9** 133-141.

— The Antidepressant Web – Marketing depression and making medicines work, *Int. J. Risk & Safety in Medicine*, 10, 1997, 75-126.

— Herxheimer A., Bell A., Jofre S., Paroxetine, *Panorama* and user reporting of ADRs: consumer intelligence matters in clinical practice and post-marketing drug surveillance, *Int. J. Risk & Safety in Medicine* 2002; **15**, 161-169.

— Herxheimer A., Risk of suicidality and dependence with Paroxetine: Comparing Yellow Card reports of suspected adverse drug reactions with reports from users, *Int. J. Risk & Safety in Medicine*, 2003, **16**, 3-17.

Medawar J., Pyke D., *Hitler's Gift – Scientists who fled Nazi Germany*, (London: Richard Cohen, 2000)

Medawar P.B., *Advice to a Young Scientist*, (New York: Harper Row, 1979).

Médecins Sans Frontières: see MSF.

Medical Letter (Anon), Librium, 13 May 1960, 2, 10, 37-38.

— Drugs for psychiatric disorders, *Med. Lett.*, 11 April 1997, **39**, 998, 33-40.

Meek C., Fraud & misconduct in medical research, *Health Which?* December 2001, 21-24.

— Questioning antidepressants, *Health Which?* February 2002, 22-25.

Melrose D., *Bitter Pills*, medicines and the third world poor, Oxford: OXFAM, 1982.

Menecier P., Menecier-Ossia L., Bern P., Fluoxetine dependence and tolerance. Apropos of a case (English abstract, French text), *Encephale*, 1997, Sept-Oct, **23(5)**, 400-401.

Merry J., Biochemistry and drug treatment of depression, *Lancet*, May 27 1972, 1175-1176.

Mhanna M.J., Bennet J.B., Izatt S.D., Potential fluoxetine chloride (Prozac) toxicity in a newborn, *Pediatrics*, 1997, **100**, 158-159.

Michaels A., Pfizer R&D unable to sustain group growth rate, *Financial Times*, 12 September 2001, 30.

Michelson D., Fava M., Amsterdam J., Apter J., Londborg P., Tamura R., Tepner R.G., Interruption of selective serotonin reuptake inhibitor treatment, *Br J Psychiatry*. 2000 Apr; **176**:363-8.

MHRA – Medicines and Healthcare products Regulatory Agency – email to Social Audit, 12 November 2003.

Milgram S., *Obedience to authority; an experimental view*. New York: Harper & Row, 1974.

Millar J.S., Consultations owing to adverse drug reactions in a single practice, *Br J Gen Practice*, 2001, **51**, 130-131.

Miller M. C., Symptoms that start when an antidepressant stops, *Harvard Mental Health Letter*, February 2001, 6-7.
Mintzes B., *Blurring the Boundaries* – new trends in drug promotion, Amsterdam: Health Action International, 1998.
MLI – MedicoLegal Investigations: http://www.medicolegal-investigations.com/about1.htm (accessed November 2003).
Mohan C.G., Moore J.J., Fluoxetine toxicity in a preterm infant, *J Perinatol* 2000 Oct-Nov, **20** (7), 445-446.
Moncrieff J., Wessely S., Hardy R., Meta-analysis of trials comparing antidepressants with active placebos, *Brit J Psychiatry*, 1998, 172, 227-231. with Commentary (D. Healy) pp. 232-234.
Moncrieff J., Review of randomised controlled trials of antidepressants using active placebos [Protocol]. In P. Bech, R. Churchill, D. Gill, P. Hazell, M. Oakley-Browne, M. Trivedi, S. Wesseley (eds), Depression, Anxiety and Neurosis Module of the Cochrane Database of Systematic Reviews, [updated 1 September 1997]. Available in The Cochrane Library [database on disk and CD-ROM]. The Cochrane Collaboration; Issue 4. Oxford: Update Software; 1997. Quarterly.
— Are antidepressants overrated? A review of methodological problems in antidepressant trials, *J Nervous & Mental Disease*, 2001, 189(5), 288-295.
— *Is psychiatry for sale?* an examination of the influence of the pharmaceutical industry on academic and practical psychiatry, Maudsley discussion paper No. 13, London: Institute of Psychiatry, 2003.
Montgomery S.A., Lambert M.T., Pitfalls in assessing efficacy and side-effects of antidepressants, *Int. J. Clin. Pharm. Res*, 1989, 9 (2), 95-100.
— Green M., Baldwin D., Montgomery D., Prophylactic treatment of depression: a public health issue, *Neuropsychobiol.*, 1989, **22**, 214-219.
— The efficacy of fluoxetine as an antidepressant in the short and long term, *Int. J. Clin. Psychopharmacol.*, 1989 Jan., **4**, Suppl. 1, 113-119.
— Long-term treatment with SSRIs, *Clin. Neuropharmacol*, 1992, **15**, Suppl 1 Part A, 450A-451A.
— Introduction (Antidepressants: perspectives in primary and secondary health care) *Postgrad Med J* 1994, 70 Suppl 2, S1.
— Dunbar G., Paroxetine is better than placebo in relapse prevention and the prophylaxis of recurrent depression, *Int. J. Clin. Psychopharmacol.*, 1993, **8**, 189-195.
— Roberts A., Patel A.G., Placebo-controlled efficacy on antidepressants in continuation treatment, *Int. J. Clin. Psychopharmacol.*, 1994 Jan., **9**, Suppl. 1, 49-53.
— Antidepressants in long-term treatment, *Annu. Rev. Med.*, 1994, **45**, 447-457.
— Long-term treatment of depression, *Brit. J. Psychiatry* 1994, **165**, Suppl. 26, 31-36.
— Efficacy in long-term treatment of depression, *J. Clin. Psychiatry*, 1996, 57, Suppl. 2, 24-30.
Moore T.J., *Deadly Medicine*, New York: Simon & Schuster, 1995.
— Hidden dangers of antidepressants, *The Washingtonian*, December 1997, 68-71 and 140-145.
— It's what's in your head, *The Washingtonian*, October 1999, 45-48.
MORI Public Opinion Polls: Attitudes towards Depression: Research study conducted for the 'Defeat Depression' Campaign. London: Royal College of Psychiatrists, Royal College of General Practitioners, January 1992.

Morrison-Griffiths S., Walley T.J., Park B.K., Breckenridge A.M., Pirmohamed M., Reporting of adverse drug reactions by nurses, *Lancet,* 2003, April 19, **361**, 1347-1348.

Mourad I., Lejoyeux M., Ades J., Evaluation prospective du sevrage des antidepresseurs, L'Encephale, 1998, 24, 215-222.

Mowatt G., Shirran L., et al., Prevalence of honorary and ghost authorship in Cochrane reviews. *JAMA* 2002 Jun 5; **287** (21):2769-71.

Moynihan R., Celebrity selling, *Brit Med J,* 2002 June 1, **324**, 1342 and *Brit Med J,* 2002 August 3, **325**, 286.

Mrela C.K., Mortality Topic 1, Arizona Center for Health Statistics, seen at http://www.hs.state.az.us/plan/suicid95/topic1.htm on 7/7/97.

MSF – Médecins Sans Frontières: *Fatal Imbalance The Crisis in Research and Development for Drugs for Neglected Diseases,* Brussels: MSF International, 9 October 2001.

Mukamal K J., Conigrave K.M., Mittleman M.A., et al., Roles of drinking pattern and type of alcohol consumed in coronary heart disease in men, *N Eng J Med,* 2003, January 9, **348** (2), 109-118.

Munro G., Evidence to the Parliamentary Public Accounts Committee Enquiry: Safety, quality, efficacy: regulating medicines in the UK, HC 505, 5 March 2003, 32.

Nakielny J., The fluoxetine and suicide controversy. A review of the evidence. *CNS Drugs* 1994, **2**, 252-253.

NAO – National Audit Office: *Safety, quality, efficacy: regulating medicines in the UK,* Report by the Comptroller and Auditor General, HC 255, Session 2002-2003, 16 January, 2003 (London: The Stationery Office, 2003).

Nathan R.G., Kinney J.L., Long-term dependence on antidepressants, *Am J Psychiatry,* April 1985, **142** (4), 524.

National Institute of Mental Health Consensus Study, *Electroconvulsive Therapy,* excerpt published April 1997 at http://www.schizophrenia.com/ami/meds/ect.html

NDMDA –The National Depressive and Manic-Depressive Association Consensus Statement on the Under-treatment of Depression, *JAMA,* 1997, **277**, 333-340.

Nemeroff C.B., DeVane C.L., Pollock B.G., Newer antidepressants and the cytochrome P450 system, *Am J Psychiatry,* 1996 March, **153**, 3, 311-320.

N Eng J Med – New England Journal of Medicine (Anon), Drug abuse control amendments of 1965, *N. Eng J Med,* 1965 25 November, **273**, 22, 1222-1223.

New York Times (Editorial), Ending a patent scam, 22 October 2002.

NIHCM, *Prescription Drugs and Intellectual Property Protection – Finding the Right Balance between Access and Innovation,* Issue Brief, (Washington DC: National Institute for Health Care Management and Educational Foundation, August 2000).

— *Prescription Drugs and Mass Media Advertising, 2000,* a research report by The National Institute for Health Care Management Research and Educational Foundation, 20 November 2001.

Nijhuis I.J., Kok-Van Rooij G.W., Bosschaart A.N., Withdrawal reactions of a premature neonate after maternal paroxetine (letter), *Arch Dis Child Fetal Neonatal Ed* 2001 January, **84** (1): F77-78.

Noonan D., Cowley G., Prozac vs. placebo, *Newsweek,* 15 July 2002, 48-49.

Nordeng H., Lindemann R., Perminov K.V., Reikvam A., Neonatal withdrawal syndrome after *in utero* exposure to selective serotonin reuptake inhibitors, *Acta Paediatr,* 2001, 90, 288-291.

Norton C., Spare your blushes: doctors create pill to stop shyness, *The Sunday Times* (London), 4 October 1998.

Nuland S.B., The pill of pills, *New York Review of Books*, 9 June 1994, 4-6.
Nuss S., Kinkaid C.R., Serotonin discontinuation syndrome: does it really exist? *W V Med J.* 2000 Mar-Apr; **96** (2): 405-7.
Nutt D.J., Addiction: brain mechanisms and their treatment implications. *Lancet* 1996; **346**, 31-36.
J. O'Dwyer's Newsletter, Internet ed. http://www.odwyerpr.com – 10 July 2002, p 1
Oca M.J. et al., Association of maternal sertraline (zoloft) therapy and transient neonatal nystagmus, *J. Perinat*, 1999, **19**, 6, 460-461.
Oehrberg S., Christiansen P.E., Behnke K., Borup A.L., Severin B., Soegaard J., Calberg H., Judge R., Ohrstrom J.K., Manniche P.M., Paroxetine in the treatment of panic disorder. A randomised, double-blind, placebo-controlled study, *Brit. J. Psychiatry*, 1995, **167**, 374-379.
OHE – Office of Health Economics, *Medicines which affect the mind* (London: OHE, 1975).
OIG – Office of the Inspector General, US Department of Health and Human Services.
Olver J.S., Burrows G.D., Norman T.R., Discontinuation syndromes with SSRIS. Are there clinically relevant differences? *CNS Drugs*, 1999, **12**, 171-177.
Office of the Inspector General, US Department of Health and Human Services: *FDA's Review Process for New Drug Applications, A Management Review*, OEI-01-0100590, March 2003.
Opler L.A., Bialkowski C., *Prozac and Other Psychiatric Drugs*, New York: Pocket Books, 1996.
Oswald I., Drugs and sleep, *Pharmacological Reviews*, 1968, **20** (4), 273-303.
— Lewis S.A., Dunleavy D.L.F. et al., Drugs of dependence though not of abuse: fenfluramine and imipramine. *Brit. Med. J.*, 1971, 10 July, 70-73.
Pacheco L., Malo P., Aragues E., Etxebeste M., More cases of paroxetine withdrawal syndrome, *Brit J Psychiatry*, Sept 1996, **169** (3), 384.
Palmer J.L., Postoperative delirium indicating an adverse drug interaction involving the SSRI, paroxetine, *J. Psychopharmacol* 2000 June, **14** (2), 186-188.
Pare C.M.B., Treatment of depression, *Lancet*, 1 May 1965, 923-925.
Parker G., Blennerhassett J., Withdrawal reactions associated with venlafaxine. *Aust N Z J Psychiatry* 1998 April, **32**:2, 291-4.
Parish P.A., Williams W.M., Elmes P.C. (eds), The Medical Use of Psychotropic Drugs, report of a symposium held at University College, Swansea, 1–2 July, 1972. Parry V., The art of branding a condition, *Medical Marketing & Media*, May 2003, 43-49.
Parssinen T.M., Kerner K., Development of the disease model on drug addiction in Britain, 1870-1926, *Medical History*, 1980, **24**, 275-296.
Patris M., Bouchard J-M., Bougerol T., Charbonnier J-F., Chevalier J-F., Clerc G., Cyran C., van Amerongen P., Lemming O., Hopfner Petersen H.E., Citalopram versus fluoxetine: a double-blind, controlled, multicentre, phase III trial in patients with unipolar major depression treated in general practice, *Int. Clin. Psychpharmacol* (1996), 11, 129-136.
Paykel E.S., Priest R.G., Recognition and management of depression in general practice: consensus statement, *Br. Med. J.*, 14 November 1992, **305**, 1198-1202.
PDUFA – Prescription Drug User Fee Act – FDA and public stakeholders public meeting, Washington DC, DHHS (PHS, FDA), 15 September 2000.
Peeters F.P.M.L., Zandbergen J., Violent withdrawal symptoms with fever while tapering off paroxetine (In Dutch, with English abstract); *Ned. Tijdschr. Geneeskd*, 1999, 3 July, 143 (27).

Pekkanen J., *The American Connection*, Chicago, Follett Publishing, 1973.

Peletier S., Pharma feels the heat, *Association Meetings*, 1 August 2002.

Petersen M., Madison Avenue plays growing role in drug research, *New York Times*, 22 November 2002.

Petursson H., Lader M.H., Withdrawal from long-term benzodiazepine treatment, *Br Med J* 1981, **28**, 643-645.

Pfizer Forum, 1998. See www.pfizerforum.com/authors/elgiebio.shtml

Phillips S.D., A possible paroxetine withdrawal syndrome. *Am J Psychiatry* 1995, **152** (4), 645-6.

Physicians' Desk Reference, 50th edition, Montvale, NJ: Medical Economics Co, 1996.

Piasecki M.P., Antonuccio D.O., Steinagel G.M., Kohlenberg B.S., Kapadar K., Penetrating the blind in a study of an SSRI, *J. Behav Ther and Exper Psychiatry*, 2002, 33, 67-71.

Pichot P., The discovery of chlorpromazine and the place of psychopharmacology in the history of psychiatry, interview with D. Healy in *The Psychopharmacologists*, London: Chapman & Hall (Altman), 1996, 14.

PICTF – Pharmaceutical Industry Competitiveness Task Force, first report, UK Department of Health, March 2001.

Pincus H.A., Tanielian T.L., Marcus S.C., Olfson M., Zarin D.A., Thompson J., Zito J.M., Prescribing trends in psychotropic medications, *JAMA*, 18 February 1998, **279** (7), 526-531.

Pinzani V., Ginies E., Robert L., Peyriere H., Abbar M., Blayac J.P., Syndrome de sevrage de la venlafaxine: a propos de six cas et review de la literature, *Rev. Med. Interne*, 2000, **21**, 282-294.

Pippard J., Audit of electroconvulsive treatment in two NHS regions, *Brit. J. Psychiatry*, 1992, **160**, 621-637.

Pirmohamed M., Breckenridge A.M., Kitteringham N.R., Park B.K., Adverse drug reactions, *Brit Med J*, 25 April 1998, **316**, 1295-1298.

Plewes J.M., Koke S.C., Sayler M.E., Adverse events and treatment discontinuations in fluoxetine clinical trials: an updated meta-analysis. *European Neuropsychopharmacology*, 7, S169, 1997.

Pollock B.G.: Discontinuation symptoms and SSRIs (letter), *J Clin Psychiatry*, 1998, Oct, **59**: 10, 535-537.

Pomerantz J.M., A case of inappropriate use of patient pharmacy data, *Drug Benefit Trends*, 2000, **12** (1), 2, 6.

Porter A.M.W., Depressive illness in a general practice. A demographic study and a controlled trial of imipramine, *Brit. Med. J.*, 28 March 1970, 773-778.

Preskorn S.H., Update on antidepressant therapy, *J Clin Psychiatry* 1994 Sept., **55**, 9 (suppl A), 3-5.

— in discussion of the natural history and heterogeneity of depressive disorders: Implications for rational antidepressant therapy, *J Clin Psychiatry* 1994 Sept., **55**, 9 (suppl A), 32-33.

Price J.S., Waller P.C., Wood S.M. (Medicines Control Agency), Mackay A.V.P. (Committee on Safety of Medicines), Comparison of the post-marketing safety profiles of fluoxetine, fluvoxamine, paroxetine and sertraline using spontaneous adverse drug reaction reporting, *Pharmacoepidemiol. & Drug Safety*, 4, Suppl. 1, S62 (Abstract from the 11th International Conference on Pharmacoepidemiology, Montreal, Canada, 27-30 August, 1995).

— A comparison of the post-marketing safety of four selective serotonin reuptake inhibitors including the investigation of symptoms occurring on withdrawal, *Br. J. Clin. Pharmacol.*, 1996, 42, 757-763.

Price J.S., (Medicines Control Agency), Letter to Social Audit, 15 September 1997.

Priest R.G., It's only a cry for help, *World Medicine*, 15 August 1979, 27-30.

— Improving the Management and Knowledge of Depression. *Brit J Psychiatry* 1994, **164**, 285-287.

— Recent clinical development with reversible and selective amine oxidase inhibitors: A valuable addition to the armamentarium, Chairman's Introduction. *J Clin Psychopharmacol* 1995, **15** (4 suppl. 2), 1S-3S.

Vize C., Roberts A., Roberts M., Tylee A., Lay people's attitudes to treatment of depression: results of opinion poll for Defeat Depression Campaign just before its launch, *Brit. Med. J.*, 5 October 1996, 313, 858-859.

Prosser H., Almond S., Whalley T., Influences on GPs' decision to prescribe new drugs – the importance of who says what, *Family Practice*, 2003, **20**, 1, 61-68.

Public Citizen, *Rx R&D Myths*: the Case against the Drug Industry's R&D "Scare Card", (Washington DC), 23 July 2001.

Pyke R.E., Paroxetine withdrawal syndrome. *Am J Psychiatry* 1995 Jan, **152** (1),149-150.

Quintiles Press Release, July 9 2001, Rx's and RSVP's: Pharmaceutical companies holding more physician events and meetings, seen 15 October 2002 at www.quintiles.com/product and services/informatics/scot levin/ press release/2001 archives.

Raach J.H., book review of Ayd F.J., *Recognising the depressed patient, JAMA,* 21 Oct 1961, **178** (3), 357.

Raby W.N., Treatment of venlafaxine discontinuation symptoms with odansetron (letter), *J Clin Psychiatry*, 1998, Nov, **59**(**11**), 621-622.

Rajagopalan M., Little J., Discontinuation symptoms with nefazodone, *Aust & NZ J. Psychiatry*, 1999, **33**, 594-597.

Rapport D.J., Calabrese J.R., Tolerance to fluoxetine. *J Clin Psychopharmacol* 1993 Oct, **13** (5), 361.

Rauch S.L., O'Sullivan R.L., Jenike M.A., Open treatment of obsessive-compulsive disorder with venlafaxine: a series of ten cases, *J. Clin Psychopharmacol.*, Feb 1996, 16 (1), 81-84.

Rawlins, M.D., letter to *Social Audit*, 14 July 1987.

Rawlins M.D. (Chair, Committee on Safety of Medicines, 1993-2000), letter to Social Audit, 8 May 1998.

RCP/RCGP – Royal College of Psychiatrists, Royal College of General Practitioners, Defeat Depression Campaign press release: MORI poll reveals public confusion about antidepressants and tranquillisers: "Antidepressants not addictive", says Defeat Depression Campaign. London: RCP & RCGP, 1992.

RCP – Royal College of Psychiatrists, Twenty-Third Annual Report, London: RCP, 1996.

— Press pack for Defeat Depression Action Week, 3-11 March 1994.

Redwood H., *The Pharmaceutical Industry – Trends, Problems and Achievements* (Felixstowe, Suffolk: Oldwicks Press, 1997).

— Pharmapolitics 2000 – Key issues for the industry, Richmond, Surrey, *SCRIP* Reports, 1997).

Reeves R.R., Pinkofsky H.R., Lhermitte's Sign in paroxetine withdrawal, *J. Clin. Psychopharmacol*, **16**, 5, October 1996, 411-412.

Reimherr F.W., Amsterdam J.D., Quitkin F.M., Rosenbaum J.F., Fava M., Zajecka J., Beasley C.M., Michelson D., Roback P., Sundell K., Optimal length of continuation therapy in depression: A prospective assessment during long-term fluoxetine treatment: *Am J Psychiatry*, 1998, September, **155**, 9, 1247-1253.

Relman A.S., Angell M., America's other drug problem, *The New Republic*, 16 December 2002, 27-41.

Reus V.I., Management of Treatment-Resistant Unipolar and Chronically Depressed Patients, in M. Hornig-Rohan, J.D. Amsterdam J.D. (eds), Treatment-Resistant Depression, The Psychiatric Clinics of North America, June 1996, 19 (2), 201-213.

Reynolds J.E.F. (ed.), *Martindale The Extra Pharmacopoeia*, 31st Ed., London: Royal Pharmaceutical Society, 1996, 299.

Rickels K., Downing R., Schweitzer E., Hassman H., *Archives of General Psychiatry*, 1993, **50**, 884-895.

Rimer S., With millions taking Prozac, a legal drug culture arises, *New York Times*, 13 December 1993, A1-B8.

Roberts I., Li Wan Po A., Chalmers I., Intellectual property, drug licensing, freedom of information and public health, *Lancet* 1998, **352**, 726-729.

Roberts D.T., Taylor W.D., Boyle J., British Association of Dermatologists, Guidelines for treatment of onychomycosis, *Br J Dermatol.* 2003 Mar; **148** (3): 402-10.

Rochon P.A., Berger P.B., Gordon M., The evolution of clinical trials: inclusion and representation, *CMAJ*, 1998, **159**, 1373-1374.

— C. Rojas-Fernandez, J. Gordon: Selective serotonin reuptake inhibitor discontinuation syndrome: putative mechanisms and prevention strategies (letter), *Can J Psychiatry*, 1998, June, **43**(5), 523-524.

Rosenbaum J., Risk of Adverse Events and Depressive Symptom Breakthrough Following Brief Interruption of SSRI therapy, pp 555-557. In Thompson C, chairperson, Discontinuation of Antidepressant Therapy: Emerging Complications and Their Relevance (ACADEMIC HIGHLIGHTS), *J. Clin Psychiatry*, 1998, **59**, 541-548.

Rosenbaum J.F., Fava M., Hoog S.L., Ascroft R.C., Krebs W.B., Selective Serotonin Reuptake Inhibitor discontinuation syndrome: A randomised clinical trial, *Biol Psychiatry*, 1998, **44**, 77-87.

Rosenblat J.E., Toxicology and drug interactions: two more cases of fluoxetine withdrawal (and SSRI withdrawal symptoms online), *Currents in Affective Illness*, 1994, **13**, 11, 15-17.

Rosenstock H.A., Sertraline withdrawal in two brothers: a case report. *Int Clin Psychopharmacol* 1996 Mar, **11** (1), 58-9.

Ross W., It's no FDA but it works, *Medical Marketing and Media*, August 2000.

Rothman D., That Prozac moment, *The Guardian* (Review), 4 February 1994, 2-4.

Roy A., Virkkunen M., Linnoila M., Serotonin in Suicide, Violence, and Alcoholism, in Coccaro E.F., Murphy D.L. (eds), *Serotonin in Major Psychiatric Disorders*, Washington DC, American Psychiatric Press, 1990, 187-208.

Rudolph R.L., Fabre L.F., Feighner J.P. et al., A randomised placebo-controlled dose-response trial of venlafaxine hydrochloride in the treatment of major depression, *J. Clin Psychiatry*, 1998, **59**, 116-122.

Sackville T. (UK Minister of State for Health), Medicines Information Bill, *Hansard*, Standing Committee C, 24 February 1993, 48.

Sager, A., Socolar D., Drug Industry Marketing Staff Soar While Research Staff Stagnates, Health Reform Program, Health Services Department, Boston University School of Public Health, Brief dated 6 December 2001. http://dcc2.bumc.bu.edu/hs/ushealthreform.htm

Sainsbury Lord (Chairman), Report of the Committee of Enquiry into the Relationship of the Pharmaceutical Industry with the National Health Service, 1965-1967. Cmnd. 3410, London: HMSO, 1967.

Sargant W. (discussant in conference proceedings), Depression, *Lancet*, 3 October 1959, 509-511.

— Drugs in the treatment of depression, *Brit Med. J.*, 28 January 1961, 225-227.

— Discussant in Parrish et al., (eds), 1972.

— Dally P., Treatment of anxiety states by antidepressant drugs, *Brit. Med. J.*, 6 Jan, 1962, 6-9.

Sartorius N., Depressive Illness as a Worldwide Problem, in P. Kielholz (ed.), Bern: Hans Huber, 1974.

— Depressive disorders – a major public health problem, in Ayd F. (ed.), *Mood Disorders: The World's Major Public Health Problem*, Baltimore: Ayd Medical Communications, 1978.

Schatzberg M., Haddad P., Kaplan E.M., Lejoyeux M., Rosenbaum J.F., Young A.H., Zajecka J., Antidepressant Discontinuation Syndrome: update on serotonin reuptake inhibitors, *J Clin Psychiatry*, 1997, **58** (suppl 7), 1-4.

Schirm E., Tobi H., Zito J.M., de Jong-van den Berg L.T., Psychotropic medication in children: a study from the Netherlands, *Pediatrics*, 2001 Aug, **108** (2), E25.

Schofield I., Committees, careers and corruption, *Scrip Magazine*, November 1993, 41-44.

Sclar D.A., Robinson L.M., Skaer T.L., Galin R.S., Trends in the prescribing of antidepressant pharmacotherapy: office-based visits, 1990-1995. *Clin Ther* 1998 Jul-Aug **20:4** 871-84; 870.

Scottowe I., Drugs in the treatment of depression, *Lancet*, 1955 May 8, 1129.

SCRIP – (Anon), Norway rejects fluoxetine on appeal, *SCRIP* No 1618, 22 May 1991, 26.

— (Anon), Lilly attacks Prozac hype, *SCRIP* No 1913, 12 April 1994, 11.

— (Anon), US DTC campaigns – Caverject, Effexor, *SCRIP* No 2208, 21 February 1997, 14.

— (Anon) Update for EU advertising rules, *SCRIP* No 2378, 14 October 1998.

— (Anon) European Commission *SCRIP* No 2712, 16 January 2002, p. 3.

Seglin J.L., Just saying No to gifts from drug makers, *New York Times*, 18 August 2002.

Sempere E., Martinez I., Martinez-Mir I., Rey A., Withdrawal syndrome and citalopram (letter, in Spanish) *Med Clin (Barc)* 2000 March 11, **114** (9): 359.

Senn S., Are placebo run ins justified? *Brit. Med. J.*, 19 April 1997, **314**, 1191-1193.

Sharkey S. Morphinomania, *Nineteenth Century*, 1887, **22**, 335-342.

Sharma V., Loss of response to antidepressants and subsequent refractoriness: diagnostic issues in a retrospective case series, *J Affective Disorders*, 2001, **64**, 99-106.

Shatin D., Drinkard C.R., Ambulatory use of psychotropics by employer-insured children and adolescents in a national managed care organization, *Ambul Pediatr*, 2002, Mar-Apr; **2** (2), 111-119.

Shelton D.L., Mistaking medicine, *AMNews*, 21 September 1998.

Sheldon T., How whistleblowing cost one doctor £550,000, *Brit Med J*, **324**, 25 May 2002, 1240.

— Drug company employee who queried trial wins appeal, *Brit Med J*, **327**, 9 August 2003, 307.

Shoenberger D., Discontinuing paroxetine: a personal account, *Psychother Psychosom*, 2002, **71**, 237-238.

Shopsin B., Cassano G.B., Conti L., An Overview of New 'Second Generation' Antidepressant Compounds: Research and Treatment Implications, in Enna S.J., Malick J.B. & Richelson E. (eds), *Antidepressants: Neurochemical, Behavioural, and Clinical Perspectives* [New York, Raven Press, 1981], 219 – 251.

Shorter E., *A History of Psychiatry – From the Era of the Asylum to the Age of Prozac.* Toronto, John Wiley & Son, 1997.

Shriver A.E., Sachs G.S. et al., Mania and hypomania following antidepressant discontinuation, in New Research Program and Abstracts, Abstract NR 161: 111, American Psychiatric Association, 151st Annual Meeting, Toronto, June 1998.

Sierra Santos L., Raigal Marin Y., Ortega Carcia A., Berriochoa Martinez de Pison C., Aparicio Jabalquinto G., Venlafaxina y sindrome de discontinuacion, *Atencion Primaria,* December 1999, 24 (10), 115-116.

Sigelman D.W., Dangerous medicine, *The American Prospect,* 23 September 2002, **13**, 17.

Silverstein K., Prozac.org, *Mother Jones,* December 1999.

Silvestri R., Pace-Schott E.F., Gersh T., Stickgold R., Salzman C., Hobson J.A., Effects of fluvoxamine and paroxetine on sleep structure in normal subjects: a home-based Nightcap evaluation during drug administration and withdrawal, *J Clin Psychiatry,* 2001 Aug, **62**, 8, 642-652.

Sims A.C.P. (President, Royal College of Psychiatrists), Unpublished correspondence, 6 February 1992.

Sindrup S.H., Brosen K., Gram L.F., Pharmacokinetics of the selective serotonin reuptake inhibitor of paroxetine: nonlinearity and relation to the sparteine oxidation polymorphism. *Clin. Pharmacol. Ther.*, 1992, **5**, 3, 288-295.

Skottowe I., Drugs in the treatment of depression, *Lancet* 1955, May 8, 1129.

Smith A., Traganza E., Harrison G., Studies on the effectiveness of antidepressant drugs. *Psychopharmacology Bulletin,* (Special issue), March 1969, 1-53.

Smith R., Review: *Limits to medicine. medical nemesis: the expropriation of health* (Ivan Illich), *Brit Med J,* 2002 April 13, **324**, 923.

Song F., Freemantle N., Sheldon T.A., et al., Selective serotonin reuptake inhibitors: meta-analysis of efficacy and acceptability. *Brit Med J* 1993, **306**, 683-7.

Spencer M.J., Fluoxetine hydrochloride (Prozac) toxicity in a neonate. *Pediatrics* 1993 Nov, **92** (5), 721-2.

Spijker J., de Graaf R., Bijl R.V., Duration of major depressive episodes in the general population: results from the Netherlands mental health survey and incidence study (NEMESIS), *Br. J. Psychiatry,* 2002, **181**, 208-212.

Stahl M.M.S., Lindquist M., Pettersson M., Edwards I.R., Sanderson J.H., Taylor N.F., Withdrawal reactions with selective serotonin reuptake inhibitors (SSRIs) as reported to the WHO system, *Eur. J. Clin. Pharmacol.*, 1997; **53** (3-4): 163-9.

Stein M.B., Chartier M.J., Hazen A.L., Kroft C.D.L., Chale R.A., Coté D., Walker J.R., Paroxetine in the treatment of generalised social phobia: open-label treatment and double-blind placebo-controlled discontinuation, *J. Clin Psychopharmacol,* **16** (3), June 1996, 218-222.

Stevens J., Hypnotics – A GP's view, *Prescribers Journal,* October 1973, **13** (5), 102.

Stewart J.W., Quitkin F.M., McGrath P.J., Amsterdam J., Fava M., Fawcett J., Reimherr F., Rosenbaum J., Beasley C., Roback P., Use of pattern analysis to predict differential relapse of remitted patients with major depression during 1 year of treatment with fluoxetine or placebo: *Arch Gen Psychiatry*, 1998, September, **55**, 334-443.

Stiskal J.A., Kulin N., Koren G., T. Ho, S. Ito, Neonatal paroxetine withdrawal syndrome (short report of four cases), *Arch Dis Child Fetal Neonatal Ed*, 2001, **84**, F134-F135. See comment (and author's response) by Ibister et al in *Arch Dis Child Fetal Ed*, 2001, Sept, 85(2), F147-148.

Stoukides J.A., Stoukides C.A., Extrapyramidal symptoms upon discontinuation of fluoxetine, *Am. J. Psychiatry*, 1991 September, **148**, 9, 1263.

Strickland G.M., Hough D.W., Unilateral facial numbness and visual blurring associated with paroxetine discontinuation (letter), *J Clin Psychopharmacol* 2000 April, **20** (2), 271-272.

Suppes T., Baldessarini R.J., Motohashi N., Tondo L., Viguera A.C., Special treatment issues: maintaining and discontinuing psychotropic medications. *Mod Probl Pharmacopsychiatry* 1997, **25**, 235-254.

Swiatek J., New rules limit drug reps, *Indianapolis Star*, 16 October 2002.

Szabadi E., Fluvoxamine withdrawal syndrome. *Brit J Psychiatry* 1992 Feb, **160**, 283-284.

Tamam A., Ozpoyraz N., Selective serotonin reuptake *Adv Ther*, 2002 Jan-Feb, **19**, 1, 17-26.

Taylor D., Truth withdrawal, *Open Mind* (National Association for Mental Health), September/October 1999, 16.

Teicher M.H., Glod C.A., Cole J.O., Antidepressant drugs and the emergence of suicidal tendencies, *Drug Safety*, 1993, 8, 3, 186-212.

Temple R. (FDA), Deposition, 4 September 2002, in Re Paxil litigation, CV-01-07937 MRP (CWx).

Terao T., Misdiagnosis of antidepressant discontinuation symptoms, *Acta Psychiatr Scand*, 2001 104(1), 77-78.

Thase M.E. (for the Venlafaxine XR209 Study Group), Efficacy and tolerability of once-daily Venlafaxine Extended Release (XR) in outpatients with major depression, *J Clin Psychiatry*, September 1997, **58** (9), 393-398.

Therrien F., Markowitz J.S., Selective serotonin reuptake inhibitors and withdrawal symptoms: a review of the literature, *Human Psychopharmacology*, 1997, **12**, 309-323.

Thomas K.B., The placebo in general practice. *Lancet*.1994 Oct 15; **344**, 1066-7.

Thomas L., The health-care system, in *The Medusa and the Snail – more notes of a biology watcher*, New York: Bantam, 1979.

— *Late Night Thoughts on Listening to Mahler's Ninth Symphony*, New York, Viking, 1983.

— *The Youngest Science*, Notes of a Medicine-Watcher, New York, Viking, 1983.

— In Briggs A., Shelley J. (eds), *Science, Medicine and the Community: The Last Hundred Years*, Amsterdam: Excerpta Medica, 1986, 19.

Thompson C., Discontinuation of antidepressant therapy: emerging complications and their relevance. *J Clin Psychiatry* 1998 Oct, **59:10**, 541-8.

Thompson L., Memorandum 7/2/90, *Forsyth v Eli Lilly*, Plaintiff's exhibit 98, 1990-1999, cited in Healy (1999).

Tollefson G.D., Adverse drug reactions/interactions in maintenance therapy. *J Clin Psychiatry* 1993 Aug, **54** (8 Suppl), 48-58.

Toop L., Richards D., Dowell T., Tilyard M., Fraser T., Arroll B, *Direct to Consumer Advertising of Prescription Drugs in New Zealand – For Health Or Profit?* Report to the Minister of Health supporting the case for a ban on DTCA (New Zealand Departments of General Practice, Dunedin, Wellington and Auckland Schools of Medicine, February 2003).

Torrey E.F., *The Mind Game – Witchdoctors and psychiatrists*, New York: Emerson Hall, 1972.

Toufexis A., The personality pill, *Time*, 11 October 1993, 53-54.

Toynbee P., *Radio Times*, 13-19 August, 1995, p 22.

Tracey A.B., *Prozac – Panacea or Pandora?* Salt Lake City, Cassia Publications, 1994.

Tranter R., Healy D., Neuroleptic discontinuation syndromes, *Journal of Psychopharmacology*, 1998, **12** (3), 306-311.

Trenque T., Piednoir D., Frances C., Millart H., Germain M.L., Reports of withdrawal syndrome with the use of SSRIs: a case/non-case study in the French Pharmacovigilance database. *Pharmacoepidemiol Drug Saf*, 2002 Jun, **11**, 4, 281-283.

Tufts Center for the Study of Drug Development pegs cost of a new prescription medicine at $802 million, Press Release dated 30 November 2001.

Turkington C., Kaplan E.F., *Making the Prozac Decision – A Guide to Antidepressants*, Los Angeles: RGA Publishing Group, 1995.

Tyrer P., Rutherford H.D., Hugget T., Benzodiazepine withdrawal symptoms and propanolol. *Lancet*, 7 March 1981, 520-522.

Tyrer P., Stress diathesis and pharmacological dependence, (comment on Healy and Tranter, 1999) *J Psychopharmacol.*, 1999, **13** (3), 294-295.

US Congress: Subcommittee on Oversight and Investigations of the House of Representatives Committee on Energy and Commerce: *Prescription Drug Advertising to Consumers.* Washington: GPO, September (1984).

US FTC: Generic Drug Entry Prior to Patent Expiration, Washington DC: Federal Trade Commission, July 2002.

US Food and Drug Administration, Center for Drug Evaluation and Research: Sample written request for antidepressants (re: requirements for safety, efficacy and other studies relating to treatment of pediatric depression), 10 September 1999. See: http://www.fda.gov/cder/pediatric/antidepressant_wr_template.htm

VandeHei J., Eilperin J., Drug firms gain church group aid, *Washington Post*, 23 July 2003, page A01.

Van Grooheest K., De Graaf L., de Jong-van den Berg L.T.W., Consumer adverse drug reaction reporting: a new step in pharmacovigilance? *Drug Safety*, 2003; **26** (4): 211-217.

Van Noorden M.S., Vergouwen A.C., Koerselman G.F., (In Dutch – Re: delirium in venlafaxine withdrawal), *Ned Tijdschr Geneeskd*, 2002, June 29, **146**, 26, 1236-1237.

Van Praag H., Psychiatry and the march of folly?, interview with D. Healy in *The Psychopharmacologists*, London: Chapman & Hall (Altman), 1996, 367.

Veash N., 'Miracle' smoking cure cuts craving, *The Observer*, 11 July 1999.

Vedantam S., Drug ads hyping drug ads make some uneasy, *Washington Post*, 16 July 2001, A01.

Venning G., Antidepressant drugs have previously been shown to be ineffective in mild depression, *Brit. Med. J.*, 29 January 2000, **320**, 311.

Vergouwen A.C., Kuipers T., Severe withdrawal symptoms with fever upon stopping paroxetine (letter, in Dutch), *Ned Tijdschr Geneeskd*, 28 August 1999, **143** (35), 1794-5, discussion 1795-6.

Viguera A.C., Baldessarini R.J., Friedberg J., Discontinuing antidepressant treatment in major depression, *Harvard Rev Psychiatry*, 1998, 5, 293-306.

Wade G.S., Controlled withdrawal for psychotropic drugs, *Lancet* 2000 May 20, **355** (9217); 1822-1823.

Wagner K.D., Ambrosini P., Rynn M., Wohlberg C., Yang R., Greenbaum M.S., Childress A., Donnelly C., Deas D., for the Sertraline Pediatric Depression Study Group: Efficacy of sertraline in the treatment of children and adolescents with major depressive disorder, *JAMA*, 2003, August 27, **290**, 8, 1033-1041.

Walker-Kinnear M., McNaughton S., Paroxetine discontinuation syndrome in association with sertindole therapy, *Brit J Psychiatry*, April 1997, **170**, 389.

Wall Street Journal (Editorial), Europe's addiction, 2 January 2002.

Waller P.C., Wood S.M., Langman M.J.S., Breckenridge A.M., Rawlins M.D., Review of company post-marketing surveillance studies, *Brit Med J*, 6 June 1992, **304**, 1470-1472.

Waller P.C., Evans S.J.W., A model for the future conduct of pharmacovigilance. *Pharmacoepidemiology and Drug Safety*, 2003: **12**, 17-29.

Walters J., Prozac research targets local girls, *The Hamilton Spectator*, 2 November 2002.

Warner J., Outlook: Glaxo's Garnier struggles under mountain of patent lawsuits, *The Independent*, 24 October 2002.

Washington Post (Editorial) Big drug makers' tactics, 16 September 2002, A18.

Wayne L., Petersen M., A muscular lobby tries to shape the nation's bioterror plan. *New York Times*, 4 November 2001.

Wells F.O., Prescribing barbiturates: drug substitution in general practice, *J. Roy Coll Gen Practit*, 1973, **23**, 164.

Wernicke J.F., Dunlop S.R., Dornseif B.E., Bosomworth J.C., Humbert M., Low-dose fluoxetine therapy for depression, *Psychopharmacology Bulletin*, 1988, **24**: 183-188.

Wheadon D., broadcast statements (on behalf of SmithKline Beecham Pharmaceuticals and GlaxoSmithKline) relating to paroxetine (Paxil®) withdrawal, on the '20-20' programme, *A Painful Withdrawal*, ABC TV, 25 August 2000.

Wingate P., Wingate R., *Medical Encyclopedia*, (4th edition), London: Penguin, 1996.

World Health Organization – Expert Committee on Drugs liable to produce addiction – report of the second session, (Technical Report Series No 21), Geneva: World Health Organization, 1950.

WHO Expert Committee on Drug Dependence. 13th report, TRS No 273. Geneva: World Health Organization, 1964.

Expert Committee, *The Selection of Essential* Drugs TRS 615, Geneva: WHO, 1977

— Expert Committee, *New Approaches to health education in primary health care*, WHO, Geneva, 1983.

— *The International Classification of Diseases, ICD-10, Classification of Mental and Behavioural Disorders, clinical descriptions and diagnostic guidelines.* Geneva: WHO, 1992.

— 28th report, WHO Technical Report Series No 836. Geneva: WHO, 1993.

— *Lexicon of alcohol and drug terms*, Geneva, World Health Organization, 1995. 28.

— (Anon), Selective serotonin re-uptake inhibitors and withdrawal reactions, *WHO Drug Information*, 1998, 12, 3, 136-138.

— Uppsala Monitoring Centre: print out of drugs most reported to cause withdrawal problems indicative of dependence, dated 27 January 2001. (Extract lists drugs for which 100 or more reports have been received).

— Report of the Commission on Macroeconomics and Health, *Macroeconomics and Health: Investing in Health for Economic Development*, 2002.
— WHO Expert Committee on Drug Dependence, 33rd Report (TRS 915), Geneva, 2003.
Wincor M.Z., Withdrawal symptoms associated with abrupt discontinuation of SSRIS, *J Am Pharm Assoc (Wash)*, 1998, July-August, **38(4)**, 500-501.
Wise J., ECT clinics are below standard, *Brit. Med. J.*, 25 January 1997, **314**, 248.
Wise P., Drury M., Pharmaceutical trials in general practice: the first 100 protocols. An audit by the clinical research ethics committee of the Royal College of General Practitioners, *Brit. Med. J.*, 16 November 1996, **313**, 1245-1248.
Wisner K.L., Gelenberg A.J., Leonard H., Zarin D., Frank E., Pharmacologic treatment of depression during pregnancy, *JAMA*, 6 October 1999, **282** (13), 1264-1269.
Wolpert L., *Malignant Sadness – The anatomy of depression*, London: Faber and Faber, 1999.
Wurtzel E., *Prozac Nation: Young and depressed in America*, London: Quartet, 1996.
Yamey G., Drug industry writers propose code of ethical conduct, *Brit Med J*, 2002 April 6, **324**, 808.
Yapp P., Ilett K.F., Kristensen J.H., Hackett L.P., Paech M.J., Drowsiness and poor feeding in breast-fed infant: association with nefazodone and its metabolites, *Ann Pharmacocother* 2000 Nov, **34** (11), 1269-1272.
Young A.H., Currie A., Physicians' knowledge of antidepressant withdrawal effects: a survey, *J Clin Psychiatry*, 1997, 58 (suppl 7), 28-30.
Young A., Haddad P., Discontinuation symptoms and psychotropic drugs (letter): *Lancet*, **355**, 1 April 2000, 1184.
Zajecka J., Tracy K.A., Mitchell S., Discontinuation symptoms after treatment with serotonin reuptake inhibitors: a literature review, *J Clin. Psychiatry*, July 1997, **58**, 7, 291-297.
Zajecka J., Fawcett M.D., Amsterdam J., Quitkin F., Reimherr F., Rosenbaum J., Michelson D., Beasley C., Safety of abrupt discontinuation of fluoxetine: A Randomised, Placebo-Controlled Study, *J. Clin Psychopharmacol.*, 1998, **18**, 3, 193-197.
Zimmerman M., Posternak M.A., Chelminsky I., Symptom severity and exclusion from antidepressant efficacy trials, *J Clin Psychopharmacol*, 2002 Dec, **22**, 6, 610-614.
— Mattia J.I., Posternack M.A., Are subjects in pharmacological treatment trials of depression representative of patients in routine clinical practice?, *Am J Psychiatry*, 2002, March, 159, 3, 469-473.
Zito J.M., Safer D.J., DosReis S., Gardner J.F., Boles M., Lynch F., Trends in the prescribing of psychotropic medications to preschoolers, *JAMA*, 23 February 2000, 283(8), 1025-1030.
Zito J.M., Safer D.J., DosReis S., Gardner J.F., Soeken K., Boles M., Lynch F., Rising prevalence of antidepressants among US youths, *Pediatrics* 2002 May; 109(5):721-7.
Zito J.M., Safer D.J., DosReis S., Gardner J.F., Magder L., Soeken K., Boles M., Lynch F., Riddle M.A., Psychotropic practice patterns for youth: a 10-year perspective, *Arch Pediatr Adolesc Med* 2003 Jan; 157 (1): 17-25.
Zubenko G.S., Cohen B.M., Lipinski J.F., Antidepressant-related akathisia, *J. Clin. Psychopharmacology*, 1987, 7, 254-257.

Glossary

Drug names and identification

Medicines may be described either by the 'generic' name – which identifies the drug itself – and/or with a brand name, which identifies a particular manufacturer's version of the drug. Regulatory requirements mean there should be no significant difference between different manufacturers' versions of the same drug.

Generic drug names are mostly internationally standardised, but occasionally, different countries apply different generic names – e.g. amfebutamone (US) = bupropion (UK); and acetaminophen (US) = paracetamol (UK). However, the identification by brand name can get complicated – e.g. when the manufacturer uses different brand names in different countries, to describe the same drug – or when the same drug is supplied under different brand names, for different applications. For example, Glaxo- SmithKline sells the same drug, paroxetine, as Paxil (US), Seroxat (UK) and Aropax (Aus). In the US, Eli Lilly & Co sells the drug, fluoxetine, both as Prozac (for depression) and as Sarafem (for severe menstrual disorders).

During the period of patent protection, which typically lasts for about ten years after a drug is first introduced, brand names predominate. When a drug comes off patent, allowing other manufacturers to produce the originally patented drug, brand names tend to give way to generic names. The main drugs mentioned in this book are:

alprazolam = Xanax®
amfebutamone = bupropion
amitryptyline = a tricyclic antidepressant
Aropax® = paroxetine
Ativan® = lorazepam
atomoxetine = Strattera®
benoxaprofen = Opren®
bupropion = Zyban®, Wellbutrin®
Celexa® = citalopram
chloral hydrate = a sedative/hypnotic
chlordiazepoxide = Librium®
cimetidine = Tagamet®

Cipralex® = (es)citalopram
Cipramil® = citalopram
Cymbalta® = duloxetine
Dalmane® = flurazepam
diamorphine = Heroin
diazepam = Valium®
duloxetine = Cymbalta®
Dutonin® = nefazodone
Efexor®, Effexor® = venlafaxine
Equanil® = meprobamate
Faverin® = fluvoxamine
fluoxetine = Prozac®, Sarafem®
flurazepam = Dalmane®
fluvoxamine = Luvox®, Faverin®
Halcion® = triazolam
Heroin = diamorphine
imipramine = a tricyclic antidepressant
Lexapro® = (es)citalopram
Librium® = chlordiazepoxide
Lustral® = sertraline
Luvox® = fluvoxamine
meprobamate = Miltown®, Equanil®
Miltown® = meprobamate
Mogadon® = nitrazepam
nefazodone = Serzone®, Dutonin®
nitrazepam = Mogadon®
Opren® = benoxaprofen
oxazepam = Serax®, Serenid-D®
paroxetine = Paxil®, Seroxat®, Aropax®
Paxil® = paroxetine
Prozac® = fluoxetine
ranitidine = Zantac®
Ritalin® = methylphenidate
Sarafem® = fluoxetine
sertraline = Zoloft®, Lustral®
Serzone® = nefazodone
Seroxat® = paroxetine
Serzone® = nefazodone
Tagamet® = cimetidine
temazepam = Restoril®
triazolam = Halcion®

Wellbutrin® = amfebutamone, bupropion
Xanax® = alprazolam
Zantac® = ranitidine
Zoloft® = sertraline
Zyban® = bupropion

Currency equivalents: £, $ and €

Significant fluctuations in the relative value of different currencies over the years meant it would not have been realistic to give dual values (£/US$) in the text. At the time of going to press, US$1 = £0.58 or €0.83; £1 = US$1.72 or €1.42; and €1 = US$1.21 or £0.70.

Institutional identities and acronyms

ABC	American Broadcasting Corporation
ABPI	Association of the British Pharmaceutical Industry
ADR	Adverse Drug Reaction
ADROIT	Adverse Drug Reactions On-line Information Tracking (UK)
ADWEB	The Antidepressant Web
APA	American Psychiatric Association
ASPP	Anonymised Single Patient Print (anonymised ADR report, UK)
BBC	British Broadcasting Corporation
BMJ	British Medical Journal
BNF	British National Formulary
CFOI	Campaign for Freedom of Information (UK)
CPMP	Committee on Proprietary Medicinal Products (EU)
CRM	Committee on Review of Medicines (UK)
CRO	Clinical research organisation
CSM	Committee on Safety of Medicines (UK)
DG Enterprise	Directorate-General Enterprise (EC)
DOH	Department of Health (UK)
DSM	Diagnostic & Statistical Manual
DTB	Drug & Therapeutics Bulletin
DTC	Direct To Consumer
DTCA	Direct To Consumer Advertising
EC	European Commission
ECDD	Expert Committee on Drug Dependence (WHO)
ECT	Electro-convulsive therapy

EEG	electroencephalogram
EFPIA	European Federation of Pharmaceutical Industry Associations
EMEA	European Medicines Evaluation Agency
EU	European Union
FDA	Food & Drug Administration (US)
G10	Group of Ten (EC-founded pharma competitiveness taskforce)
GCP	Good Clinical Practice
GSK	GlaxoSmithKline
HAI (E)	Health Action International (Europe)
HAM-D	Hamilton depression rating scale
HIV	Human Immunodeficiency Virus
ICH	International Conference on Harmonisation (on technical requirements for registration of pharmaceuticals for human use)
ICMJE	International Committee of Medical Journal Editors
IFPMA	International Federation of Pharmaceutical Marketing Associations
IOM	Institute of Medicine (US National Academy of Sciences)
IRB	Institutional Review Board (US); Ethics Committee (UK)
JAMA	Journal of the American Medical Association
MAOI	Monoamine Oxidase Inhibitor
MCA	Medicines Control Agency (UK)
MEP	Member of the European Parliament
MHD	Mental Health Division (WHO)
MHRA	Medicines and Healthcare products Regulatory Agency (UK)
MIND	National Association for Mental Health (UK)
NAMI	National Alliance for the Mentally Ill (US)
NAO	National Audit Office (UK)
NCE	New Chemical Entity
NEJM	New England Journal of Medicine
NERO defence	'no evidence of risk = evidence of no risk'
NHS	National Health Service (UK)
NICE	National Institute for Clinical Excellence (UK)- performance
NIH	National Institutes of Health (US)
NOS	Not otherwise specified
O/D	Drug overdose
PDUFA	Prescription Drug User Fee Act (US)
PhRMA	Pharmaceutical Research and Manufacturers of America (US)
PICTF	Pharmaceutical Industry Competitiveness Taskforce (UK)
R&D	Research and development
RCGP	Royal College of General Practitioners
RCP	(RCPsych) Royal College of Psychiatrists

SKB	SmithKline Beecham (GSK from 2000)
SSRI	Selective Serotonin Reuptake Inhibitor
TABD	Transatlantic Business Dialogue (EU-US)
UK	United Kingdom (England, Scotland, Wales, Northern Ireland)
UMC	Uppsala Monitoring Centre (WHO)
WHO	World Health Organization
WPA	World Psychiatric Association
WTO	World Trade Organization
Yellow Card	UK adverse drug reaction report